The Quintessential Zerka

The Quintessential Zerka documents the origins and development of the theory and practice of psychodrama, sociometry and group psychotherapy through the work and innovation of its co-creator, Zerka Toeman Moreno.

This comprehensive handbook brings together history, philosophy, methodology and application. It shows the pioneering role that Zerka, along with her husband J.L. Moreno, played in the development not only of the methods of psychodrama and sociometry, but of the entire group psychotherapy movement worldwide. It demonstrates the extent to which Zerka's intuitive and intellectual grasp of the work, combined with her superb ability to organize and synthesize, continues to exert an influence on the field. Toni Horvatin and Edward Schreiber have selected articles that span a career of some sixty years, from Zerka's very first publication to recent, previously unpublished, work. Personal anecdotes and poetry from Zerka herself provide a valuable context for each individual article. The selection includes:

- Psychodrama, Its Relation to Stage, Radio and Motion Pictures.
- Psychodramatic Rules, Techniques and Adjunctive Methods.
- Beyond Aristotle, Breuer and Freud: Moreno's Contribution to the Concept of Catharsis.
- Psychodrama, Role Theory and the Concept of the Social Atom.

This book provides a rich source of insight and inspiration for all those interested in the history, development and practice of psychodrama, sociometry and group psychotherapy, whatever their level of experience. It will be of interest to anyone involved in the fields of psychology, counseling, sociology, social work, education, theater, or human relations.

Toni Horvatin is a social worker, counselor, and Playback Theatre practitioner in New York.

Edward Schreiber is Director of the Moreno Institute East in Northampton, Massachusetts and a Trainer, Educator, Practitioner (TEP) of psychodrama.

The Quintessential Zerka

Writings by Zerka Toeman Moreno on Psychodrama, Sociometry and Group Psychotherapy

Edited by Toni Horvatin and Edward Schreiber

Routledge
Taylor & Francis Group
LONDON AND NEW YORK

Published 2006 by Routledge
27 Church Road, Hove, East Sussex BN3 2FA

Simultaneously published in the USA and Canada
by Routledge
711 Third Avenue, New York, NY 10017, USA

First issued in paperback 2015

Routledge is an imprint of the Taylor & Francis Group, an informa business

Typeset in Times by Garfield Morgan, Mumbles, Swansea
Cover design by Hybert Design
Cover photo: Zerka Moreno by Marcia Karp

British Library Cataloguing in Publication Data
A catalogue record for this book is available from the British Library

Library of Congress Cataloging-in-Publication Data
Moreno, Zerka T. (Zerka Toeman)
The quintessential Zerka : writings by Zerka Toeman Moreno on psychodrama, sociometry, and group psychotherapy / compiled and edited by Toni Horvatin and Edward Schreiber.
p. cm.
Includes bibliographical references and index.
ISBN-10: 1-58391-728-4 (hbk)
ISBN-13: 978-1-58391-728-2
1. Moreno, Zerka T. (Zerka Toeman) 2. Psychodrama. 3. Sociometry. 4. Group psychotherapy. I. Horvatin, Toni. II. Schreiber, Edward. III. Title.
RC489.P7M67 2006
616.89'1523–dc22

2006007582

ISBN 13: 978-1-138-87186-1 (pbk)
ISBN 13: 978-1-5839-1728-2 (hbk)

*This book is dedicated to
all those around the world who
devote their lives to working in mental
health facilities, hospitals, business administration,
industry, the community, and private practice,
training and educating others in applying
Moreno's ideas in these fields. May
they continue to Pioneer!*

Contents

Foreword

There are moments in every person's life that are profound. My first meeting with J.L. and Zerka Moreno was one of those profound moments. Each fall, the staff and interns of the Psychodrama Department at Saint Elizabeths Hospital, Washington, DC, made a pilgrimage to Beacon, New York, to study at the Moreno Institute. In October 1971 I was a first year intern and was inspired by J.L. Moreno's articles and books. He had become my hero. My expectations were that I would meet a charismatic genius, a compassionate healer, a soulful poet and a wise, humble and joyful man. I had little knowledge and few expectations of Zerka. When we first met what I found in him was the frail and elderly man he had become. Zerka, however, was a delightful surprise. She was vibrant and present with all the qualities I had hoped to find in Moreno. That winter and throughout the following years, I returned on my own to experience Zerka as a trainer, director and double. In my professional development at Saint Elizabeths Hospital from staff member to chief of the Psychodrama Department, to director of clinical therapies, Jim Enneis, also at Saint Elizabeths, was my intellectual father, and Zerka was my emotional mother.

Our travels to the Moreno Institute continued until it was sold in 1982. Over the years Zerka asked me, and I enthusiastically agreed, to collaborate on several projects. When she again became President of the American Society of Group Psychotherapy and Psychodrama (after Moreno's death), she asked me to serve as her Vice President. Our most important collaboration was serving as co-chairs of fundraising for the endowment of the J.L. Moreno Collection at the Francis A. Countway Library of Medicine of Boston and Harvard Universities.

Today the art, science and craft of the professional practice of psychodrama are flourishing worldwide. There are more certified psychodramatists and more published books than at any other time in history. Psychodrama in all its many forms is used not only in mental health and psychotherapy, but also in education, training, criminal justice, business, government, religion and the arts. My 34 years of experience at Saint Elizabeths, in private practice, and in leadership positions in the American Society of Group

Psychotherapy and Psychodrama and The American Board of Examiners in Psychodrama, Sociometry and Group Psychotherapy have convinced me that without the steadfast support and constant vigilance of Zerka Moreno, psychodrama would be a lost art.

When Celine Zerka Toeman met J.L. Moreno in the summer of 1941 it was the beginning of the most successful partnership in the history of psychiatry. She was a 24-year-old recent *émigrée* from England who had traveled to Beacon Sanitarium in hopes of finding a treatment that would restore her sister, whom she had rescued from Nazi Europe, to sanity. By each one's account, theirs was a historic meeting. After a period of traveling to Beacon for weekend trainings, Zerka began working as Moreno's secretary, translating his German-English into fluent English. She brought order to the chaos of his writing by providing a discipline and organization that had been severely lacking. Her role evolved from secretary to editor and she began to challenge him to deepen and ground his visionary ideas in practical applications that could be communicated clearly to others. She began to attend clinical sessions and accompanied him during his trainings. She specialized in the double function, and became his preferred auxiliary ego in psychodrama demonstrations.

After their marriage, J.L. was still the clear leader in the field, and Zerka was always at his side. She soothed his ruffled feathers and provided the social grace that mended his tumultuous relationships with others. She cultivated and maintained her own independent friendships with many of the great leaders in the field of group psychotherapy. In 1941–42, she was one of the founders of the American Society of Group Psychotherapy and Psychodrama, the first organization in the United States devoted to the professional practice of group psychotherapy. Over time her knowledge, skills and abilities increased and she became more of an equal partner in their professional realms.

By the early 1950s, Zerka became J.L.'s full partner, and they collaborated as authors, teachers and clinicians. He chose her to become editor of the *Journal of Group Psychotherapy, Sociometry and Psychodrama*. She edited *Psychodrama Volume I*, and *Who Shall Survive?*, second edition. One has only to compare the original edition of *Who Shall Survive?* written by J.L. in 1934 with the second edition published in 1953 to become aware of her substantive contributions during these early years. She also co-authored the two subsequent volumes of *Psychodrama* and wrote her own articles, many of which are contained in this book, which further illuminated Moreno's ideas and incorporated her own enhancements to the theory and practice.

J.L. and Zerka were in the forefront of promoting the group psychotherapy movement worldwide. In 1951 they first organized an International Committee on Group Psychotherapy. Several subsequent international congresses resulted in the formation of the International Council on Group

Psychotherapy. In 1973 that became the International Association of Group Psychotherapy.

In the years preceding his death, as J.L.'s health gradually deteriorated, Zerka appeared to be his partner, but it was she who was the clinical director, director of training, chief executive officer and chief financial officer for the Moreno Institute and its many forms (sanitarium, training institute, and publishing house). Prior to Zerka's contributions, J.L. had taught students through a variety of "spontaneous" clinical sessions and armchair conversations on a wide range of topics. She developed a curriculum, student outcomes, and standards for certification.

After Moreno's death, Zerka emerged from his shadow to gain her own place in the pantheon of pioneers in psychodrama, sociometry and group psychotherapy. She continued to write, fleshing out his ideas and staking out new ideas of her own that complemented and augmented the body of work. She became the President of the American Society of Group Psychotherapy and Psychodrama once again, to help its transition during the post-Moreno years. Zerka was one of the founders of the American Board of Examiners in Psychodrama, Sociometry and Group Psychotherapy, which established nationwide standards for the certification of practitioners and trainers.

From the 1940s to the present, Zerka has traveled across North America and throughout the world teaching and training generations of students in psychodrama, sociometry and group psychotherapy. This 60-year span is a singular achievement in the field.

J.L. was visionary and cosmic while Zerka was attentive. His intellect was like quicksilver, bouncing from one intellectual endeavor to the next; hers was grounded, steadfast and rigorous. He provided the seminal intellect of the movement; she provided its heart and soul. There were also many similarities between them. They both had emigrated from Europe to America in search of freedom, opportunity and a better life. They both championed the isolated and rejected. His causes were prostitutes in Europe and prisoners and delinquents in the United States. Hers were gay, lesbian, bisexual and transgendered persons, and later those living with HIV and AIDS. In the early 1980s, during the height of the AIDS hysteria, I recall how she calmly took the hand of a person ravaged by AIDS, and informed the group that AIDS was a virus, and that you could not get a virus by holding someone's hand or touching them. She further challenged the group by stating that what this man needed, and what we all need, is love.

What was extraordinary about the partnership of Zerka and J.L. was not just what it produced professionally, but rather that their personal, intellectual and emotional relationship more than endured; it thrived. They wrote poetry, traveled, and enjoyed attending theater and movies. Each was a voracious reader and worker. Family was important to them. Regina, Moreno's daughter from his first marriage, came to live with them in 1950 at age 11. She grew up in Beacon and went on to raise her own family as well as to have a successful career as a teacher in early childhood education. In 1952 the Morenos' son Jonathan was born. Jonathan D. Moreno, PhD is now Kornfeld Professor of Biomedical Ethics and Director of the Center for Biomedical Ethics at the University of Virginia. Jonathan and his wife Lesley, an attorney in Washington, DC, are parents of Jarrett and Jillian, two grandchildren who are the light and joy of Zerka's life.

Over the years, Zerka has endured physical disability, pain, and life-threatening illnesses. From hearing loss in her right ear, to sarcoma that took her right arm and shoulder, to a recent hip replacement that required five surgeries and caused excruciating and prolonged pain, her courage and buoyancy have been an inspiration. At 88, Zerka's physical body may be challenged, but her intellect, heart and spirit remain alive and vital. She no longer travels around the world teaching and training; groups of students from Europe, Australia, South America and Asia now come to study with her.

Besides teaching and professional writing, Zerka spends time organizing and writing her memoirs. It is my hope that one day the autobiography of Zerka Moreno will be published and will serve as the companion to this volume. As J.L. Moreno said, "More important than evolution of the creation is the evolution of the creator." How a young woman fleeing from Nazi-threatened Europe with no formal training or education in psychiatry evolved to be one of the premier teachers and trainers in psychotherapy is a most fascinating story, and one that must be shared.

In the past we have spoken of the work of J.L. Moreno. In the present we speak of the work of Zerka Toeman Moreno. In the future, when we speak of the development of the fields of psychodrama, sociometry and group psychotherapy, as evidenced by the work you are about to read, we will undoubtedly speak of both Morenos.

Dale Richard Buchanan, PhD, TEP
Director Clinical Therapies (Retired)
Saint Elizabeths Hospital
Washington, DC

Preface

This book was born on the original psychodrama stage, some years after the stage was relocated from its home in Beacon, New York to Boughton Place, a community center in nearby Highland. Zerka was conducting monthly trainings there at the time. We would gather on the top level of the circular tiered stage for morning check-in and post-session processing. It was there that Toni heard her fellow students express the desire to read what Zerka had written about psychodrama.

At that time copies of the early journals in which Zerka had published were hard to come by. Toni envisioned a single source, which would combine Zerka's professional writings with brief, more personal commentary that would provide a context. Fellow student Ed heard about the project, and soon our collaboration began.

Life circumstances being what they were for both of us, time passed. Meanwhile, the sessions at Boughton Place became limited to summers, and ultimately Zerka moved to Charlottesville, Virginia. Finally our long warm-up turned into action and we had the good fortune to have our proposal for publication accepted by Routledge.

During the intensive process of reviewing all of Zerka's written work, we were impressed with its timeless significance. Her words are those of a pioneer; one who learned the method from the inside out.

The "quintessential" of the title of this book is meant to express the duality of the practical and ethereal that Zerka has brought to this work. The reader will encounter, for example, in the article entitled "The 'Double Situation' in Psychodrama," her clear and precise description of applying her entirely intuitive "feeling into" the protagonist. From Zerka's own exploration of this process came her teaching that role reversal is the *sine qua non* of psychodrama. Without her, it is doubtful that the role of auxiliary ego as a therapeutic tool would have been as thoroughly developed. For those of us who did not experience the early work at Beacon and who have not applied this method with psychotics, her description and clarification of the function of the auxiliary ego as it was originally developed provide special insight that can be applied to any auxiliary work.

It was during the time that we were studying with her that Zerka was more publicly claiming her rightful place as J.L. Moreno's equal partner in the development, growth and dissemination of psychodrama, sociometry and group psychotherapy in the world. Our intention is that this selection of Zerka's own work will further establish her singular contribution. Without Zerka's tireless efforts and superb organizational skills, as applied to her roles of explorer, birther, historian, reporter, presenter, researcher, colleague, spouse, and mother, among others, the philosophies and methods of J.L. Moreno could easily have remained excellent dreams and brilliant visions without realization. Moreno may have provided the vehicle, but Zerka drew all the road maps.

Zerka has called herself "a participant actor in one of the major revolutions in social science." In "The Seminal Mind of J.L. Moreno" (1967) she says, "Many of Moreno's ideas have reached such a level of universality that they are becoming widely accepted, as if they had always been." We encourage readers to think about a world without group psychotherapy or without the concept of human beings acting as therapeutic agents for each other by their presence in a group. Perhaps then we can come to some appreciation of the significance of the legacy that Zerka carries on to this day. We asked Zerka during the interviews for this book if sometimes, even given Moreno's powerful vision, she felt like she was "wandering in the wilderness" with people just not comprehending what they were trying to do. She replied, "Moreno's vision of what the world could be inspired us. I thought that *others* were wandering in the wilderness."

Work-was-life-was-family to Zerka. In working with her own son Jonathan and doubling him, she traveled as far back to the "First Universe" as any adult possibly could. As you will read in "Psychodrama in a Well-Baby Clinic" (Chapter 2), Zerka was the bridge for new mothers to join with the psyches of their babies. Her writings about raising children the psychodramatic way offer all parents a model from which to build a relationship with their children.

A few comments about the organization of the text: The articles span the period from Zerka's very first publication in 1944 to unpublished material from 2004 that she has chosen to debut here. The chapters group the articles chronologically within a framework of life events: in Chapter 1 (1944–1948) we explore the beginning writings of young Zerka Toeman, who is caught in the passion and excitement of the movement. Chapter 2 (1949–1965) begins with her marriage to J.L. and displays some of Zerka's efforts to document their pioneering work together. Chapter 3, "Transitions," reflects the era of Zerka's gradual assumption of responsibility for all aspects of the Moreno legacy. Chapters 4 and 5 are part of her own rich legacy.

Each chapter begins with one of Zerka's poems taken from her volume *Love Songs to Life* (1993). Each article is presented with its professional citation followed by a section called *Zerka's comments*; a brief observation from Zerka about the context in which the article was written. These comments are the result of many interviews and conversations with Zerka. She reviewed and approved their final form.

Editing has included the following.

- Text has been adjusted to present a uniform citation style that references a comprehensive bibliography at the back of the book. Bibliographies that originally appeared at the end of some articles have been listed in a chapter note (chapter notes are located before the bibliography) and incorporated into the comprehensive bibliography.
- Minor adjustments in grammar or punctuation have been made where to do so would make meaning more clear.
- In the case of several articles, more extensive text revisions have occurred. These are indicated in the relevant chapter notes.

We have chosen to retain certain instances of language or custom in order to keep the text reflective of the era in which it was written. For instance, a number of articles contain the words "Negro" or "colored" where today we would use the terms "Black" or "African American." Also, especially in the early articles, the male pronoun is used exclusively in instances referring to both genders. We recognize that the author's original usage bore no disrespect.

In reviewing the articles with Zerka, we discovered that over the years examples or case studies that were particularly illustrative of a certain point would be repeated in subsequent articles. In compiling this selection, we have extended to Zerka the author's prerogative to make revisions so as to present the most cohesive explanations and best examples of the concepts and methods she was trying to convey. Thus we have created with her a reworking of certain articles in order to achieve the fullest presentation of a case or point. These articles, then, would upon comparison deviate from their original sources. In yet other cases the reader may encounter a duplication of an idea across articles because it was a new presentation of a previous idea and simply bore repeating. By approaching the text in this way, in some cases we are providing a "second edition" of the original article.

We have often heard Zerka expand on a quote of Socrates: "The unexamined life is not worth living, and the unlived life is not worth examining." We hope that readers will appreciate the depth and breadth to which Zerka has examined and lived her life, as here reflected in her professional writing and personal comments. It is our pleasure and privilege to present this work.

Toni Horvatin
Highland, New York

Edward Schreiber
Northampton, Massachusetts

June, 2005

Acknowledgments

There are a number of people to thank for their support, without whom this book could not have been written.

First and foremost, we thank Zerka for her love, her teaching, and her support of this project. She made herself completely available to us for interviews, conversations, review of the manuscript, and final approval.

We also want to appreciate and acknowledge the following.

- Dale Richard Buchanan, whose dedication to the scholarship and teaching of psychodrama, sociometry and group psychotherapy, coupled with his very specific knowledge and appreciation of Zerka's contributions to this field, made him a natural choice to write the foreword to this book. His enthusiasm for doing so inspired us.
- Jonathan D. Moreno for his counsel on preliminary aspects of the book, and for his generous permission to reprint articles that describe in detail his childhood in the world of psychodrama.
- Fred Harris, for being there always, brilliantly and creatively, and for his incisive comments regarding the manuscript.
- Adam Barcroft for his big heart and generosity of spirit and for assuming the role of Associate Director of the Moreno Institute East.
- Tony and Barbara Horvatin, for helping Toni find her way to psychodrama in the first place.
- Barbara Schreiber, for her loving support of Ed and friendship to Toni.

We wish to acknowledge and thank the following people for providing assistance such as helping to shape the vision of this book, coaching, providing access to or copies of the various journal articles, and providing workplace and internship scheduling adjustments: The American Society of Group Psychotherapy and Psychodrama (ASGPP) Publication Committee, especially John Rasberry; SUNY New Paltz Library – especially student Sean Endress; Kate Castell, Mario Cossa, Tian Dayton, Jonathan Fox, Marcia Karp, Louise Lipman, René Marineau, Donnell Miller, Peter Pitzele, Jenny Salimbene, and Rebecca Walters.

We thank the staff at Routledge, Joanne Forshaw, senior editor, and Claire Lipscomb, senior editorial assistant, for their pleasant and professional assistance. We are grateful to Brendan O'Brien and Nicola Ravenscroft for their excellent production assistance.

We thank all of our colleagues and friends in the psychodrama community who have provided encouragement and love.

We remember with gratitude all of the protagonists, auxiliaries, and group members from the beginning who helped Zerka and J.L. to define, refine and practice this method, and we think of those today and in the future who will join us on the psychodrama stage.

Permissions

Permission has been granted by Zerka Toeman Moreno to reprint all articles before 1980 attributed to Beacon House, Inc., and all heretofore unpublished material that is included.

- Articles from the journal *Group Psychotherapy, Psychodrama and Sociometry* after 1980 are used with permission of Heldref Publications.
- Copyright permission for excerpts from *Love Songs to Life* and *Who Shall Survive?* (student edition) is granted by the American Society for Group Psychotherapy and Psychodrama, 301 N. Harrison St, Ste 508, Princeton, NJ 08541.
- "The Saga of Sociometry" contains a questionnaire that appeared in the January 1966 edition of *McCall's* magazine. Permission for its reproduction has been granted by Gruner & Jahr USA.
- "Evolution and Dynamics of the Group Psychotherapy Movement" and "Sociogenesis of Individuals and Groups" from *The International Handbook of Group Psychotherapy* are used with permission of the Philosophical Library, New York, NY.
- "The Seminal Mind of J.L. Moreno" includes a quote from the article "Complementary Psychotherapy" by J.L. Moreno that appeared in the *American Journal of Psychiatry.* It is reprinted with permission from the *American Journal of Psychiatry*, Copyright 1967. American Psychiatric Association.
- "Psychodrama" appeared in *Comprehensive Group Psychotherapy*, Harold I. Kaplan, MD and Benjamin J. Sadock, MD (eds), (2nd edn, 1983). It is used with permission of Lippincott, Williams & Wilkins, Philadelphia, PA.
- "Psychodrama, Role Theory and the Concept of the Social Atom" appears in J. Zeig (ed.) *The Evolution of Psychotherapy*, and is used with permission of Routledge, Taylor & Francis Books, Inc. and Zerka T. Moreno. (Copyright 1987 by The Milton H. Erickson Foundation and reprinted with permission.)

- In the article "Psychodrama, Role Theory and the Concept of the Social Atom," the quote from Theo Compernolle is taken from an article entitled "J.L. Moreno: An Unrecognized Pioneer of Family Therapy," published in *Family Process* and used with permission of Blackwell Publishing, Oxford, UK.
- "Time, Space, Reality and the Family: Psychodrama with a Blended (Reconstituted) Family" appears in the book *Psychodrama: Inspiration and Technique* (Paul Holmes and Marcia Karp, eds) (1991) pp. 53–74, and is used with permission of Routledge, Taylor & Francis, London, and the author, Zerka Moreno.
- The quote from Patrick Conty in "The Many Faces of Drama" is from *Parabola: The Search for Meaning*, Vol. XVII, No. 2 (Summer 1992).
- "The Function of 'Tele' in Human Relations," in J. Zeig (ed.) *The Evolution of Psychotherapy: A Meeting of the Minds*, Copyright 2000 by The Milton H. Erickson Foundation, is reprinted with permission.

Chapter 1

Beginnings

1944–1948

O God, what strange powers
are here at work.
You bring together two people,
reared oceans apart
and make them meet
in a moment of their great need.
Both are strong,
both are weak,
supporting and clinging,
happy to find themselves back
in each other.

From *Love Songs to Life*
Zerka T. Moreno

Article 1

Role Analysis and Audience Structure

Toeman, Z. (1944) *Sociometry, A Journal of Inter-Personal Relations* VII, 2: 205–221

Zerka's comments

Wartime was my world at the time this article was written. Although we were pacifists, we knew the war had to be won "or else," and everything was geared toward the war effort. The hospital at Beacon was profoundly affected. The staff was swallowed up. Moreno's secretary, Joe, became a soldier. There was a shortage of nurses and aides, as they went off to the front or to work in factories. We did whatever we could to scrape by. I remember a young woman patient and I shoveling a path in the snow from the road to the house so that Sunday visitors could come up the hill.

These associations with the military, although unfortunate in the global sense, were important for us because psychodrama, sociometry and group psychotherapy became better known. They were using group psychotherapy with soldiers at the time at Saint Elizabeths because they couldn't treat thousands of soldiers individually.[1]

The phenomenon of sheer numbers of military personnel who had mental health needs sent professionals searching for solutions. Still, recognition for group psychotherapy, and for Moreno as its pioneer, was slow. While there was no question as to who developed sociometry, it is quite astonishing today that few group psychotherapists agreed concerning group psychotherapy. One example of how prevalent this position was occurred in 1944 during the Second World War when, dining with a group of military men at the American Psychiatric Association convention in Philadelphia, one captain proclaimed: "I just received a directive from Washington that we must practice group psychotherapy with mentally ill soldiers. What the hell is group psychotherapy? I was never trained in that." Moreno and I looked at each other. He shrugged his shoulders as if to communicate, "It's hopeless to start teaching them here under these conditions. That's just the way it is." But it represented an oversight that in some ways has continued to the present day.

We wanted to help with the mental health of the military personnel. In 1948 we were invited by a professor at the University of Maryland to see "sociograms of life and death." He had been part of a group of psychologists sent to the South Pacific to study morale on two military air carriers. They realized that all their psychological tests yielded only individual profiles. They had nothing that could tell them about groups and give them a definition of high morale. Evidently one of the participants (we never found out who) suggested looking at "Moreno's sociometry." I remember wrapping up eight copies of Who Shall Survive? *and sending them to the War Department in Washington.*

A major from the British War Office Selection Boards came incognito to the New York City Institute to study with Moreno, spending long hours in discussion. The major's report was the basis for subsequent implementation of certain strategies adopted by the military in organizing their troops. J.D. Sutherland and G.A. Fitzpatrick described this work in their paper, "Some Approaches to Group Problems in the British Army" (Sutherland and Fitzpatrick 1945).

During the war we continued to have open sessions in New York City twice a week, and that is where this research was conducted. "Role Analysis and Audience Structure" was inspired by the case of a young woman client whose fiancé was pulled in two directions – between marriage and family and his military career. After the session, J.L. remarked that it was an interesting phenomenon and said to me, "Why don't you do an article on it? Why don't we do some research?" That was the first time he suggested that I write something on my own, although I wasn't surprised that he did. After all, we were building a system. The more we explored and wrote, the better.

Moreno saw young people as who they could become. That is why he encouraged us to write up the experiments, the ideas – everything. There was so much to say, and he couldn't possibly do it all, and moreover he believed in us. I credit Moreno with giving myself to me.

Introduction

The session material for this paper was gathered by the author during 1942, and was announced among the Sociometric Researches in Progress under the title "Composition of a Psychodramatic Audience," *Sociometry*, volume 5, number 2, May 1942, p. xlvii. Director of the psychodramatic sessions was J.L. Moreno, MD. Role analysis of a psychodramatic production was undertaken as well as an analysis of the vote structure of three audiences.

The psychodramatic method has an important contribution to make in the education and training of military personnel. Thousands of men are returning from the fronts affected by mental disorders. These men were at the time of their induction apparently well adjusted and able to maintain themselves at a satisfactory level of performance in civilian life. But the rigidity of military service, apart from the scene of battle, calls for a profound readjustment for the individual. It throws him into unfamiliar situations, the cumulative effects of which frequently lead to a breakdown of his morale. The thesis we wish to present is that psychodramatic procedure can educate him to a better adaptation to military life.

The psychodrama stage presents a unique opportunity for studying the human being in dimensions hitherto chained to verbal expression. The prime importance of the *motor sense* in military training makes psychodrama the treatment par excellence. It enables the director to move with the subject into as close a mirroring of his life situation – without actually infringing upon it – as objectification permits. There are no limits to the possibilities of expression upon the psychodrama stage. It is an exploring into new dimensions of realization, the realization of action, and into new dimensions of analysis, the analysis of action. Here the subject can project his conflicts without barriers. He may choose the auxiliary egos to represent absentee persons related to his problem. He may pick the situation, the time, the place, and the persons with whom to paint the picture of his life. The director is given a comprehensive statement of the syndrome of the subject while he presents his problems and initiates the auxiliary egos into their roles. Diagnosis and guidance can thus go hand in hand. By throwing the subject into action, warming him up to the maximum of spontaneity and analyzing the performance immediately after completion, the subject is given insight into his reactions. Once he has gained a certain amount of objective understanding, a program of re-training can be undertaken.

In action training the psychodrama offers many advantages compared with other methods of personality guidance. It is possible to stimulate the subject into action and to stop him, right there, to point out where his action is inadequate. It is possible to make him start again, to warm him up along a different track, to make him realize that his old warming up process would lead to the same conflicts that brought him to the psychodrama laboratory. He is given records of his past actions, and is able to analyze his present performance on the stage in the light of what he has learned. The subject is given fresh opportunities to warm up into a different spontaneous state that would permit him to live as a more fully integrated, better-adjusted person.

Spontaneity is frequently understood in folklore as anarchistic behavior, "doing whatever one pleases whenever and wherever one pleases," or as impulsive, uncontrollable action leading to emotional and social instability. But according to Moreno spontaneity training opens the way for a flexible and systematic process of learning, providing a more reliable foundation for the absorbing of discipline than authoritarian methods. Anchoring discipline upon obedience does not give it as deep a root as can be provided by the spontaneous matrix of the individual, as the individual can be directed *sua sponte* ("from within the self").

We see an interesting parallel in the conserve–spontaneity conflict in the drama. The dilemma of the actor of the conserved drama is that of the actor-creator. Torn between the conserved role – lines, emotions and gestures long rehearsed – and the desire to create a *new* one, to live a new Hamlet experienced only in this moment, the conserved role becomes meaningless to him. The division within him is a torment. It makes his performance unconvincing. Our culture demands a specific rendering of Hamlet. Yet, does our actor really feel these words rehearsed so thoroughly that he no longer searches for their meaning? Is this then, the great Hamlet he has desired to enact? Or is not there, deep down in him a pain for that other Hamlet who had to die before he was born? This dichotomy may eventually interfere with our actor's performance, and often does, to a degree that makes performance in any conserved role impossible for him.

The spontaneity actor knows no such dilemma. His is the privilege of creating a Hamlet of the moment. True, spontaneity acting needs training; nurturing of the creative elements within the actor. It needs guidance in order that his Hamlet is not only spontaneous, but esthetically acceptable, blending harmoniously with the roles of other actors on the stage. But his training does not consist in learning lines and emotions set down for him. It is a training on the level of the actor's own creativity so that the spontaneity will be ready, stored away for an occasion when it will be called upon to carry him over danger zones. His is not the fear that tomorrow night at the same time these same emotions, the same words, have to be repeated, the same inflection of his voice used, in order to rouse his audience. His is a creation of and for the moment, valueless upon repetition, complete in itself – however imperfect it may be from the point of view of the conserved drama. His values have unified to the point where his creative ego is not at pains to prove itself at the price of the conserved self, *that self which is expected of him.*

Mock warfare as applied to our combatants is a true reproduction of the conserved form of the drama. The men follow a rigorously set pattern. Every step is designed so that not a single man is left without a definite set of instructions. Every moment is timed for the next step, which must be equally well prepared, and the next and the one after that, until the enemy is annihilated or surrenders. No amount of mock-warfare training, however carefully constructed its every detail might be, however frequently a soldier is subjected to it, can prepare him for the unknown, for that moment when he will be at a loss because of some unprepared-for surprise tactic on the part of the enemy, or because his equipment fails him. In the latter case his technical skill will help him, but the emergency may be outside the realm of technical knowledge. It is then that his spontaneity, his initiative, his ingenuity for making decisions on the spur of the moment has to come to the rescue.

There is a source of untrained spontaneity in every individual. Everyone is called upon, unknown times a day, to exert spontaneity in situations for which they know no suitable precedent. Obviously, many things depend upon split-second reaction of the soldier in battle. He has been carefully "drilled." He knows his weapons, what to expect from them and how to use them to his own and his fellow soldier's advantage. But he will face situations that demand immediate action of a kind unrelated to his previous training. There is a great need for some training that bridges the gap in the personality adjustment of the *soldier-actor*. That bridge we believe is to be found in the application of psychodramatic methods.

Presentation of a typical problem

The case presented was chosen from among fifteen others dealing with problems of military trainees, because it revolves around one shared by many of them and is thus of great public interest. The problem defined is: Should a soldier marry while in the armed forces, or should he wait until the end of the war?

The subject, let's call him Jack Roberts, was referred to us by a superior officer. He introduced himself when coming up on the stage. He was 25 years old, a second lieutenant, and came from a small town in Ohio. He was the youngest of three. His parents were alive and well-adjusted. He was college-educated and stated that he had been an average student. The interview with the director disclosed that it was his work situation that was first affected by this problem and that it came to the notice of one of his superiors. Thus, the first scene to be portrayed was the work situation. The subject was prepared by the director. Only crucial parts of the material are herewith presented. Many psychodramatic sessions have been combined into one. Lack of space prevents going into details that the case history revealed previous to the subject's appearance in the theater.

Jack is backstage with the auxiliary ego who will represent his superior officer. Jack is warming up the auxiliary ego to his role.[2]

DIRECTOR: When Jack first started to talk about his problem he was bashful. He said he did not think he would do well on the stage. "I am not an actor." The director explained to him that a psychodramatic subject does not have to be an actor. As long as he is honest and has a problem that is burning within him, he will be able to warm up to an adequate presentation of the conflict. Let us see how Jack's problem came to the attention of an officer, and what his conflict consists of.

Jack returns to the stage with auxiliary ego.

DIRECTOR: Jack, describe the situation. Tell us where the scene took place.
JACK: It was a small room at the camp where I was having basic training; rather bare, simply furnished, posters on the wall.
DIRECTOR: What time of day?
JACK: Early evening.

DIRECTOR: Were you in the room first?
JACK: No, the officer was waiting for me.
DIRECTOR: Then go backstage and let the officer warm up to his role.

Jack goes backstage, auxiliary ego paces the floor, warming up to his role, then sits down. Jack enters, salutes. Officer motions to Jack, telling him to sit down.

Officer looks concerned, frowns.

OFFICER: I sent for you Roberts because as a candidate for O.C.S. we have been carefully watching you. Your record has been good up to the past few weeks. Lately you seem less alert. We need men of action for officers. How do you account for the change in you? You seem to be preoccupied with thoughts that have no bearing on your job.
JACK: I did not realize it was so obvious, sir.

Jack fidgets on his chair.

OFFICER: Are you in trouble of some kind? Is there something wrong at home?
JACK: No sir, not exactly at home.
OFFICER: Whatever it is, we don't want it to interfere with your chance for officer's training. I just wanted to warn you. It's not our job to pry into your private life. But we all make sacrifices these days; you realize that.
JACK: I do, sir.
OFFICER: Think you can work it out so that it won't spoil your chances in the army?
JACK: I think so, sir.
OFFICER: Hm, well see you don't slip up again. We'd like to see you get in and make the grade. We need good men. That's all.
JACK: Thank you sir.

Jack salutes and leaves stage. Auxiliary ego leaves after him. Director motions Jack to come back for an interview with him.

DIRECTOR: That scene took place while you were a private. The officer and probably others saw that something was on your mind that interfered with your army duties. But you are a second lieutenant now. That must have been quite a while ago, since you made the grade at O.C.S. meanwhile.
JACK: Yes, it was.
DIRECTOR: What was troubling you that made you less alert?

Jack looks down.

JACK: Whether I should get married or not. It had come up while I was in camp and I was not able to decide, so I pushed it into the background for a while. But now I have to face it.

DIRECTOR: One of the things we do not do here is give you advice. We merely give you a chance to objectify your conflicts on the stage with the aid of auxiliary egos who will try to represent absentee persons. You yourself have to find a solution, either here or later. Your problem, though it is a private one, contains many general elements. It is therefore of interest how the problem came about and how you solve it. Where is your young lady now?

JACK: Back home with her folks.

DIRECTOR: Inform the auxiliary ego who will portray her role how your girlfriend acts, and what happened when you saw her last. It does not have to be exactly as it happened. Just try and show us the essence of the situation, and perhaps of many other situations you may have been in with her.

An auxiliary ego is selected to represent Diane, Jack's girlfriend. Jack informs her of Diane's behavior. After two minutes they start the scene. Jack describes the situation.

JACK: Diane came down to the training school to discuss the possibilities of our marriage. The discussion took place after supper, while we were taking a walk.

Jack and Diane walk around center level of stage, while enacting this scene.

DIANE: I'm sorry if I upset you by coming here. I only wanted to get things straightened out.

JACK: You know I love you, else I would not have asked you to marry me last summer. I know you would have if I'd put some more pressure on you, but your family did not approve and so I hesitated to force you. I was a private and they felt that the future was too uncertain.

DIANE: It was not easy for me, being between two alternatives. I did not know what to do. But after you left I felt as if I'd let you down. It was not right to have let you go.

JACK: I've written you how I feel now. If I get my commission there's a reasonable job waiting for me. I owe as much to my job as I owe you. If we were to be sent overseas I'd be divided between worrying over your welfare and that of my men.

DIANE: But you said I could help if you were sent overseas, you'd have someone to hold on to, to come back for. Does not that still hold good, even if you are an officer? Besides you don't need to worry about me. I can take care of myself. I'll get a new job and live at home if you should be sent away.

Jack takes Diane's hand and stops walking. Diane halts and looks at Jack.

JACK: It's funny, but being an officer does make a difference. Strange how last summer I tried to convince you that we ought to get married. Now you're trying to convince me. We just don't seem to feel the same way at the same time.
DIANE: That's why I came down, so we could get together on it.
JACK: I don't think I'm ready for it now.

Jack starts walking again and Diane walks along with him. Both look unhappy, Jack especially strained.

JACK: Why don't we wait until I'm through with O.C.S. Let me concentrate on that first. Then we'll make a final decision.

Diane looks depressed.

DIANE: You mean, not mention it any more until you make up your mind?
JACK: I know it's hard, but it's the only way I can see my way clear right now.
DIANE: I guess that's the only thing to do then.

Jack is a little more relaxed when Diane says this.

JACK: Maybe we should have got married last summer after all. I just did not want you to do anything without your family's approval.

Jack and Diane leave stage. Jack comes back to interview with the director.

DIRECTOR: Jack, how often did you postpone marriage?
JACK: Oh, it went backwards and forwards a few times.
DIRECTOR: It seems that every time you wanted to marry she did not want to and when she wanted to you could not make up your mind.
JACK: That's right.
DIRECTOR: Your timing did not click. We often see that. And so you sent Diane home without a decision. She was willing to accept your suggestion to wait until you had finished school.
JACK: That's right. But now I'm through with school and I'm due for a furlough shortly. I've got to come to a decision one way or another.
DIRECTOR: Now that you've got your commission, do you feel that your responsibility towards the army weighs against marriage as heavily as before?
JACK: I feel it's just as important as the responsibility towards a wife and eventually a family.

DIRECTOR: Do you think you would have married Diane if the war had not come along?

JACK: If I felt the way I do now about her, probably.

DIRECTOR: Have you ever wanted to marry anyone before?

JACK: Yes, twice. But nothing came of it. Since then Diane has been number one.

DIRECTOR: How does Diane's family feel about you now that you are a lieutenant?

JACK: Well, judging from Diane's letters they seem to have given in somewhat. I suppose that is because she is more anxious to marry me.

DIRECTOR: Why do you think they were against it?

JACK: They were afraid of the uncertainty of the future and thought Diane was too young to tie herself down at a time like this, mostly because she was so hesitant.

DIRECTOR: Do you think Diane would have committed to marry you in the summer if her family had supported your proposal?

JACK: I believe so. She is very attached to her folks and she is quite young.

DIRECTOR: How do you feel about her folks? Do you think they should have not interfered?

JACK: Oh, I don't blame them. In their place I might have done the same thing. But at the same time, I feel that my hesitance now is due to her indecision, which was caused by their pressure.

DIRECTOR: Suppose you had an opportunity to see into the future, say five years from now. The war is over. What would you like to do and where would you want to be? Don't be hesitant, pick yourself the life you dream of.

JACK: I'd like to live on the West Coast.

DIRECTOR: Married or single?

JACK: Well, by that time I'd probably be married.

DIRECTOR: To Diane?

JACK: That depends on whether she'd wait for me.

DIRECTOR: Cautious young man, aren't you? Suppose she waits?

JACK: Rather Diane than anyone I know.

Jack moves about the stage with easy motion, uses his arms to describe the scene.

JACK: We have two children, a boy and a girl. The boy's the eldest. We live in Los Angeles in a lovely rambling house in the suburbs, very cozy and comfortable. There are six rooms. The furniture is modern. It's a beautiful home and we're very proud of it. My flowers in the front yard are the envy of the neighborhood. Diane grows vegetables in the back, by the kitchen entrance. The children have space to themselves to play in.

DIRECTOR: What is your profession?

JACK: I earn the wherewithal as a junior executive in a transcontinental airline firm.

DIRECTOR: What time of day is it?

JACK: It's evening. The children are in bed.

DIRECTOR: Explain to the auxiliary ego how you visualize the future.

Jack and Diane leave the stage again so that Jack can prepare her for this scene.

DIRECTOR: We saw how Jack warmed up so easily to the idea of being married to Diane, and having two children with her. His image of the future is very clear. Jack showed no hesitance. He knew he wanted Diane, to live on the West Coast and be a junior executive. Some people have a strong image of their future. Others have no vision of the future. They are not able to see ahead. Apparently Jack's desire to be married to Diane has colored all his dramas even though he does not entirely admit it on the interview level. We shall see how he imagines his life with Diane will be.

Jack and Diane return. Jack arranges furniture on the stage.

JACK: This is the living room. Diane and I are having our after-dinner chat. The children are sleeping. Diane is doing some needlework and I'm smoking a pipe.

Jack tells Diane where to sit. He himself sits down with his feet upon another chair. He looks very comfortable. Diane pretends to be concentrating upon some needlework.

JACK: You look very nice tonight, dear.

DIANE: Thank you. You look a little tired. Had a busy day at the office?

Jack lights pipe and smokes.

JACK: Rather. We're opening many new airline connections. How were the children?

DIANE: Oh, they're all right. Junior needs some new clothes. He is outgrowing all his things. He's getting to be rather a wise guy. Maybe you should take him in hand. Mary is easy to manage. Nothing special happened today.

JACK: Yes, they are getting big. Makes one feel old. Had a letter from mother today.

DIANE: Is she feeling better?

JACK: Well, she never complains. You know how she is. But Kenneth added a few lines. He wrote that the doctor suggests a change of climate for her, like coming out here.
DIANE: Well, why does not she come? We'd love to have her.

Jack looks searchingly at Diane, then speaks haltingly.

JACK: How would you feel about mother living with us, for good? I have not wanted to ask you before. Old people can be difficult and it would mean an additional burden for you. But she has not been well and needs someone to look after her. I hesitated to bring it up because it means that the children have to move into one room so that mother could have one for herself.
DIANE: But of course she can. We'll make her as comfortable as possible. She's very welcome. You should have not worried about that. We'll simply make room for her. When can she come?

Jack looks relieved, relaxes deeper into his chair.

JACK: It's swell of you to take it like that. I did not know how you'd feel about it and I'd be so relieved to know she's well taken care of.
DIANE: You have been worrying about that, I know.
JACK: It will mean your being tied down to the house more than before.
DIANE: With children one is tied down to the house anyway. You did not say when she'll come.
JACK: If Kenneth can bring her, as soon as I've written for her to come; perhaps sometime next week. If he can't get away I'll have to go and bring her. She's too old to come by herself and too ailing.
DIANE: Any time she comes, she's welcome.
JACK: Mrs. Roberts, I think you're a very nice girl.

Jack smiles and goes over to Diane, patting her on the back.

DIANE: Thank you, Mr. Roberts; you're rather nice yourself.

Jack and Diane leave the stage. Jack comes back for interview with the director.

DIRECTOR: How did the auxiliary ego act as Diane?
JACK: She did a fine job. Before, in the first scene with her I felt at times as if Diane and I were really back there thrashing it out.
DIRECTOR: Does Miss B. look like Diane?
JACK: No, she does not.

DIRECTOR: As long as the auxiliary ego is able to reproduce the atmosphere of the absentee person, the stimulus is sufficient for the subject to warm up to his role. Did you present her with the problem to be portrayed in this last scene before you came out with it on the stage?

JACK: No. I just thought that would be a good thing to bring up. Dad has not been too well. Maybe I worried about what was to become of Mum if she was left alone. I felt it best not to inform Miss B., to see how she'd react.

DIRECTOR: A sort of proxy test of Diane?

JACK: You could call it that.

DIRECTOR: She certainly came through.

JACK: She did indeed.

DIRECTOR: Is that the way you expect Diane to act in such a situation?

JACK: Pretty much like that. I guess I'm prejudiced in her favor.

DIRECTOR: When do you expect to see Diane?

JACK: In a few weeks.

DIRECTOR: We'd appreciate it very much if you would let us know how things work out with Diane. Will you do that?

JACK: I certainly shall. I want to say that I appreciate this opportunity to work things out.

DIRECTOR: Do you feel any easier about it now?

JACK: Not yet, but at least I've had a chance to feel what it might be like to be married.

DIRECTOR: Do you think you're still too close to it to say whether your working it out here has clarified things for you?

JACK: Yes, I think so.

DIRECTOR: We appreciate your honesty, and think you did a fine job here on the stage. In essence, Jack, there is no reason why an officer should not be a good family man as well as a good officer. The two are not incompatible. In the situation of the husband you would be the supporter. Later you would be the father. On the other hand, you will be the leader and authority to your men in the army; a sort of military father. It is possible to gain from one kind of role some experience for the other.

JACK: You mean that by being an officer I may learn about being a husband, and vice versa? But would not the authority I express in one role conflict with the other to some extent?

DIRECTOR: Not if you don't mix up your roles. Roles are, after all, only suitable within the proper frame.

JACK: That's true.

DIRECTOR: The issue in this case is a clear-cut one: Should Jack get married now or should he wait until he comes back from the army and can devote himself to family life? No one can tell him what to do. He must make his own decisions, but he will find that having had a chance to

> place himself and his conflicts in an objective setting will enable him to come to a solution more rapidly and concretely than would otherwise be possible

The final outcome of this session was that Jack wired his girlfriend to be ready for his homecoming and to prepare for the wedding in a few weeks. He has reported to us from time to time. It is noteworthy that he has risen in rank since his marriage, is well adjusted in his married life and has apparently gained self-confidence for his military responsibilities.

Analysis[3]

Methods of role analysis

We consider: (a) how the expectancy of acting in a role in the future affects a subject and each member of the audience; (b) role deficiency of a subject; (c) adequacy and superiority in a role on the stage and in actuality; and (d) whether a role is dominant or secondary to the subject and each member of the audience, on the stage and in actuality.

Expectancy of acting in a certain role may produce a fear of entering situations in which that role comes to expression. In another case, the expectancy of a role may have the opposite effect. Getting a chance at expressing this role may increase courage, self-confidence and satisfaction in the role. In one soldier, marriage expectancy or fulfillment may produce increased role superiority as a fighting man; in another it may reduce his efficiency as a soldier. The role of the soldier may be dominant to a subject at this time. Two years hence the role of the husband may become dominant. In some cases, role deficiency as a husband may influence a man to such a degree that, if this deficiency is not recognized, marriage may become a factor which in turn may reduce his credibility as a fighter. In such a case, if his role deficiency as a husband is recognized before marriage, a decision not to marry or to postpone marriage may increase his value as a soldier. We have found that role-training helps to reduce role deficiencies. In times of war, role-training in military camps and schools might of necessity have to be limited to the soldier role, although it should be realized that the various representative roles in which a subject has to perform are dynamically interrelated and interdependent.

Scoring role dominance, role adequacy and role deficiency of single subjects and audiences[4]

Four methods of scoring have been used by the author as the basis for analysis of role and audience reactions. One method was to have the audience score silently while the proceedings on the stage were in progress.

The second was to have the vote taken immediately after the stage action was completed. In the first method the advantage is that the audience scores its instantaneous reactions, but cannot see the total picture. In the second the total impression is taken into consideration.

It is possible to use a combination of the two methods, which affords a re-evaluation of reactions. Aimed at getting two types of reactions to the action portrayed on the stage, two types of questions were formulated. The first was designed to determine the reaction to the roles portrayed on the stage, the second to determine the role structure of the audience itself. The first question was, "If you were in the place of the subject in the situation of the soldier (lover, husband, son, father, etc.) would you act the same way? Answer yes or no." The second question was, "Do you think that a soldier, a lover, a husband, a son, an officer, etc. should act the way the subject did? Answer yes or no." The same questions were asked applying to the auxiliary egos on the stage with the subject.

A third method for analyzing audience reactions is a further refinement of the first method, and may be called an interview- or *audio-analyzer*. Every member of the audience is asked to write down on paper his reactions to the situation in development on the stage. For instance, the basic questions to which members of the audience respond are: (1) Have you ever been in a similar situation yourself? (2) Did the presentation elate or upset you and why? (3) Is it because of your success or failure in that situation? (4) Did it remind you of something personal that you dislike having portrayed? (5) Did you object to it because the subject on the stage acted in a role with respect to which you have some group membership? Give your reasons for objecting or approving (such as, for example, being a Jew you would rather not see a Jew persecuted on the stage, or being a Negro you would rather not see a Negro lynched, or being a soldier you do not approve of a soldier getting married and making both himself and his wife unhappy in the parting). (6) If you have been in such a situation as the subject was here, have you been able to solve it satisfactorily? (7) If not, do you think that the presentation on the stage was helpful in suggesting possible alternatives to you? (8) Add your own notes that you feel are pertinent in your reactions to the processes on the stage.

Such written audience reactions should always be followed up by short individual interviews and open discussion immediately after the session, to which audiences warm up with great spontaneity.

A fourth method used is the so-called *role analyzer*. Members of the audience are asked to enact their own version of the roles portrayed on the stage by subjects and auxiliary egos. Every version of role-taking is classified into categories – A, B, C, D, etc. – and the balance of the audience is asked to identify themselves with one or another of the categories.

Three different audiences were used in order to determine the extent to which the audience influences role analysis, and in turn the extent to which the role playing on the stage influences audience reactions. The first session took place with an actual subject ("Jack"), in front of an audience largely consisting of soldiers, their wives, prospective wives, and girlfriends, most directly affected by and identified with the proceedings on the stage – the Primary Audience. The second session was presented before a group consisting largely of older people, physicians, teachers, social workers, and so on; objective observers who of the three categories of audience could be called least directly affected by the presentation – Control Audience Number 1. The third session took place before a group made up of adolescents, students and postgraduates, most of them having a future expectancy of such situations – Control Audience Number 2. The two control audiences were unaware of the fact that auxiliary egos were used instead of real subjects. These auxiliary egos reproduced the same situations and conflicts as the original subject had with his auxiliary egos, in an unrehearsed but planned form.

Role analysis

The role analysis is based on the scoring of the subjects by means of question 1 to the audience: "If you were in the place of the subject in the situation of the soldier, the lover, the husband, the son, the father, would you act the same way? Answer yes or no." [Editors' note: in this case, the roles of husband and father would be "future expectance" roles, as the subject is in neither role at the time of the session.]

The Primary Audience scored most positively to the husband role, in essence saying, "If I were in the place of Jack in the situation of the husband, yes, I would act the same way" (future expectance role – 93%). A close second positive response was the soldier (actual role – 92%). This indicates the conflict within Jack: which role should have supremacy? The audience responded the least positively to the subject in the role of the lover, as well as in the lover–pair relation, although the latter score was slightly higher. This indicates that the subject, in interaction with the auxiliary in the lover-situation, did not appear quite as inadequate to the audience, although still on a low level. Perhaps it was felt that the auxiliary contributed a good deal to the total situation. In the husband *interaction* score the subject is rated less than as a husband solely in the role – not in interaction. This again tends to show that the audience felt that the skill of the auxiliary ego in interaction contributed to the subject's warming up to the role of husband as well as he did. This is clearly indicated by the auxiliary ego being given as high a rating in her "wife interaction" role as in her wife role. Her score is consistently higher than that of the subject.

Such analysis points out that training in role taking and role interaction such as the auxiliary ego received, makes for sensitive "tele" awareness which, in turn, stimulates the subject to give of his best in his role. It also indicates that in the testing of pre-marital couples, which is of pertinence in other researches we are making, testing couples on the role level actual at the time of the test, e.g., that of lovers, may cover up many substantial relationships, but via the husband–wife projection, much of the deeper relationship may come to the surface.

As mentioned above, Control Audience 1 was differently constructed than the Primary Audience. Each audience is an individual case, and therefore a different audience gives different votes to the subjects in role-playing. However, according to the role protocols of audience analysis which we have made, the more the plots and roles are representative to the majority of audiences, the more the score of one audience resembles that of another. In Control Audience 1 the role of husband came before the role of soldier. This group, being themselves the least directly affected by the war emergency, responded as civilians, considering a civilian role primarily. However, the son, soldier and father roles followed each other closely, placing them on an almost level plane. The lover role was more prominent than for the first audience.

It is interesting to note that Control Audience 1, being more objective than the primary group, omitted a response many more times than did the first group of respondents. Of the three, this audience voted least in indicating their desire to take the soldier role. This coincides with findings of military authorities who know that older men make less efficient and daring soldiers than young ones. All findings relating to reactions of Control Audience 1 show that the number of neutral members was consistently higher than in the other audiences, indicating their greater remoteness from the problem involved.

The scores for Control Audience 2, with future expectancy of military and lover situation, did not differ greatly from the Primary Audience, except with regard to the soldier role. Positive scores for the son, husband, soldier and father roles were closely contesting, with the son role (the one most likely to be already experienced by this audience) at a slight advantage. Education to a role is shown here to have a deep hold over the imagination of our soldiers in the Primary Audience, for soldiers they were first and foremost. The members of Control Audience 2 had a future expectancy of the soldier, husband and father roles and their conflicting import is here brought to the fore. They are in fact somewhere between the soldier audience and the least affected audience. The overall participation score of this second control audience is closer to that of our Primary Audience, showing their more pressing relation to the problems at hand.

In role scoring of the auxiliary egos, Control Audience 2 participated more fully than even the soldier audience. This points to a more pertinent lover role configuration among them, it being the point upon which they differed most from the primary and first control audience.

Audience analysis

Audience analysis is undertaken to determine the role structure of the audience itself. In this study, it was based on the scoring of the subject (or in the control group, the auxiliary egos portraying the subject) by means of question 2: "Do you think that a soldier, a lover, a son, a father, should act the way the subject did? Answer yes or no." In analyzing the Primary Audience, largely made up of soldiers, we find that they reacted almost unanimously positively to the role of the soldier (99%), with 1% not voting. Every other role was of less importance in this audience, although the husband role ran a close second. This is indicative of the role structure of the audience. Comparing the role analysis (would audience members themselves act the way the subject did?) to the audience analysis (should a soldier, husband, son, etc. act the way the subject did?), the scoring was parallel except that in the latter the son role took precedence over the father role. This is probably due to the fact that, as soldiers were in the majority, they felt that the father role, being a future expectancy for many of them, should not be more important than the son role, which already existed for them before they became soldiers.

It is also noted for the Primary Audience that more votes were cast in the audience analysis than in the role analysis. Possibly it was easier for the audience to vote on the second question because it was generalized. Being indirectly worded, it seemed to carry no personal implications. Using members of the audience as a frame of reference makes the audience itself a subject of analysis, on the basis of their own reactions. These reactions are all the more spontaneous if the audience does not feel that they are "giving themselves away." Such an indirect method enables the director to gain a precise estimate of the role configurations of a given audience, which roles appear indifferent, and which are dominant.

Audience analysis of Control Audience 1 shows that they responded most positively to the roles of husband and son. Control Audience 2 responded equally strongly to the roles of soldier, son, and husband, in that order. This would seem again to reinforce the roles as they existed in the audience at that moment.

Conclusions

The psychodramatic method is a valuable approach to the understanding and solution of psychological and social problems of men and women in the armed forces, or who are about to enter into them. It can be applied to small and large soldier audiences. It permits group treatment of social problems and is able to isolate cases needing individual attention. It is a flexible method and can be used as a preventive measure as well as for rehabilitation programs.

Psychodramatic procedure is presented here in its three major emphases – *the audience portion, the production on the stage, and the reaction of the audience to the production.* Viewed from the historic perspective of two decades of psychodramatic experiment, each of these has made a distinct contribution.

The audience portion in a psychodramatic situation has had group psychotherapy as an offshoot, since it was the analysis of audience combined with sociometric study which stimulated Moreno to coin this term, and to formulate its concept.

The second emphasis is the *production on the stage.* It stimulated a different development that has today become the central theme of the psychological and educational frontiers: training and re-training of individuals, and spontaneity training, especially in the form of role-playing.

The third emphasis in this paper, *the reaction of the audience to productions on the stage*, has been pointed out by Moreno in his pioneering book, *Das Stegreiftheater* (1924). He showed that productions presented to the public – motion pictures, puppet shows, legitimate plays or spontaneous dramas – aroused various degrees of spontaneity in the individuals composing the audience.[5]

Article 2

Psychodramatic Research of Pre-marital Couples

Toeman, Z. (1945) *Sociometry, A Journal of Inter-Personal Relations* VIII, 1: 89

Zerka's comments

The idea for this research came from our experience of couples coming to the open sessions in New York City. It was a litmus test of sorts – if a date found the sessions interesting, the relationship was worth pursuing. If not, it was an indication that they would not be willing to work on the relationship and therefore it would not last. This research was never carried out, but it's a good idea, so I leave it to the next generation of psychodramatists to implement.

1 Partners in twelve pre-marital couples to be interviewed individually.
2 The interview material will be broken up and a system of scoring applied. The score will involve prediction of chance for success.
3 Certain typical situations that occur in all cases will be projected upon the psychodramatic stage by the couples themselves and by auxiliary egos, working out a number of possible variants of these situations.
4 A system of scoring is to be applied to the couples after psychodramatic presentation of their relationship. Here also the score will include prediction of chances for success.
5 The prediction of chances for success to be based on the interview material, compared with the prediction of material gained by the psychodramatic method.
6 The twelve couples will be followed up at regular intervals and the predictions compared to actual developments.
7 The purpose of the study is to determine where prediction made on the basis of interviewing and on the basis of psychodramatic procedures overlap or differ and which of the two methods predicts success or failure more accurately.

Article 3

A Sociodramatic Audience Test

Toeman, Z. (1945) *Sociometry, A Journal of Inter-Personal Relations* VIII, 3–4: 399–409

Zerka's comments

The time during which this article was written was full and exciting. We worked 17–18 hours a day, and it was stimulating all the time. I was open and learning. My small typing table stood at the end of J.L.'s desk, and there was always something to explore, something to discuss, something to write.

The audience tests and personal sharing, such as we mostly do today as the last phase of a psychodrama, developed simultaneously. Once we discovered people were willing to open up sociodramatically, we turned to the personal. At open sessions the psychoanalysts were shocked at the sharing. Of course, at the time this just was not done. Moreno had observed that patients became confused by the interpretations of professionals of varied orientations. When they were dispassionate towards a young woman patient, Moreno got upset and asked one of the psychiatrists, "Do you have children? What is your relationship to your daughter? Here we share our hearts, not our brains." Moreno's vision had a global focus that many people still don't get – psychodrama is shallow if it doesn't include a vision of the person's world.

Moreno meant to emphasize that, while grounded in the clinical setting, psychodrama and group psychotherapy were life-oriented and related to the world outside the hospital. We needed to bring the world onto the stage, just as, when they were ready, we sent the hospital patients into the world – the streets of Beacon – with their aides.

Introduction

In an earlier paper [Article 1] the author pointed out the value of psychodramatic methods for evaluation and adjusting the draftee to the role of the soldier and alleviating strains of the hangovers of roles in civilian life. It is clear that such training need not be limited to training for the military, but that in reverse, it may be employed in the readjustment to civilian life. While considering the problems of the returnee, it is pertinent to consider equally the responsibility of those to whom the men return. Much is heard concerning the rehabilitation of our fighting men but little is done about the rehabilitation of the families they left behind. Their attitudes towards occupation, fraternization, re-education of former enemies, relations with friendly nations, relations to minority groups at home, employment for veterans, to mention but a few larger categories, are of primary importance in a sociodramatic program of rehabilitation.

In psychodrama we deal with collective as well as private ideologies. The method dealing with the former has become known as "Sociodrama." It is, of course, not possible to separate *the* soldier from *a* soldier, *the* son from *a* son. They are the product of influences of both a private and collective nature. However, there are certain aspects of their performance that are shared by all other soldiers, all other sons. It is these collective aspects of their roles with which we deal in sociodrama (Moreno, J.L. 1944b).

We propose to bring forth in this paper some of the highlights of audience tests made at the Psychodramatic Institute in New York and Beacon with the relatives and friends of fighting men.

Categories of standard situations

Three main categories of the standard situations have been used in the past at the Institute. Moreno has called them the *Three Situation Set*: Intimate or Family Situation, Work Situation and Community Situation. The set proved useful in analyzing the range of representative roles in which subjects function. In a recent session Moreno suggested that in dealing with audiences requiring a more refined analysis of role-interaction, the Three Situation Set may be replaced by a *Six Situation Set*: Government–Citizen, Husband–Wife, Parent–Child, Sibling–Sibling, Employer–Employee, Stranger–Native (Moreno, J.L. 1945b).

We will illustrate here how the polarity "role of the stranger–role of the native" can be used in the testing of audiences. In this category may fall many groups, for instance, ethnic minorities, enemies, and refugees, but also in certain situations, our own veterans. Following the pattern of role analysis elsewhere described (Toeman 1944), we used as the subjects of our investigation people who were facing an adjustment problem which they wished to have treated on the stage. Since it is impossible to test every member of the audience, representatives are picked, but such representatives who themselves have a similar problem, to remove the elements of fiction which might otherwise so easily creep into sociodramatic sessions. The problem should always be as concrete as possible, the Negro–White conflict, the GI–the Civilian, etc. using certain typical situations in which this conflict is most clearly demonstrated (Hendry *et al.* 1944). It has become a rule at the Institute to place on the stage three representative samples and to let the audience react to them as soon as the scenes are ended. A greater number of subjects may be used, but experience has shown that in general three are sufficient to allow a cross section analysis of the role structure of the audience. Three subjects chosen at random show, if taken by surprise, widely contrasting enactments of the same situation.

Some of the more popular audience tests are, for example: Three automobile drivers are given the following instructions – You are driving along a parkway. Although the speed limit is 45 miles per hour, you are in a hurry to get somewhere. You may be driving too fast. Go ahead; warm yourself up to driving a car. An auxiliary ego in the role of a state trooper is told to stop them and to give each subject a ticket for speeding. (Subjects are called out one at a time. They do not see anyone else's performance until they have taken their turn.) The results are varied from abject subordination on the part of the testee to bribery of, and lastly, assault on the state trooper. One subject, upon being stopped, threatened to drive fast enough to kill himself. Further inquiry disclosed that he did not know how to drive a car, and this type was entitled "fantasy driver." He behaved in an irrational, fantastic fashion out of proportion to the stimulus offered, much as a mental patient might. Experiments with many fantasy drivers have shown weird reactions, though not all of them so extreme as the above mentioned. An audience vote was taken after three versions had been demonstrated and an analysis of votes made.

Another test dealt with the return of three discharged veterans to their hometown. They were asked how they planned to return, at what time of day or night, and who would be at home to meet them. I recall that in one case a subject returned at night alone, taking his family by surprise. His wife was at home, tinkering with an electric iron that had broken down. She was happy to see him and he immediately made himself useful by repairing her iron. Another returned to his mother and took it easy for at least a month before attempting to look for a job. A third did not go home, but settled down in a big city. He had learnt a new trade in the army and wanted to apply it in civilian life rather than to return to his father's farm, or else to go back to school and to take advantage of the government's program in making up for his lack of education. Again, an audience analysis was made and the votes recorded.

Yet another test was made in which the subjects were all women. The auxiliary ego used in this scene was a serviceman still in uniform. The subjects were "warmed up" to the following theme: You are driving along a lonely highway at night. You are alone and anxious to get home as it is a dark night and quite late. Go ahead. The auxiliary ego (in the soldier's uniform) was instructed to go up to the subject with the request to be given a ride to a point up the road, stating that it was an emergency. On the average, out of a series of three subjects given this test, two did not stop each time to pick up the soldier although he had campaign ribbons and sundry decorations. Reasons given for not doing so were: "Well, I was alone and it was at night." "I'm ashamed to admit it but I'd be afraid to."

"I would if it were day time." "One reads such awful stories in the newspapers. I would only do it if a man were with me." "It was dark and I couldn't tell whether he was a clean-cut man or not." Among the subjects who stopped to give the soldier a lift, one was a "fantasy driver." The second said that she was too old to worry about whether it was safe or not. A third stated that her husband was in the army too, and she'd like to think someone would do the same for him if need be. Again audience reactions were taken, and the testees who did find reasons for giving the soldier a ride did not find as large adherence as those who refused to pick him up.

The following tests were given to nine unselected audiences, using three subjects in all cases. The aim of our investigation was to determine whether this method, used on many audiences, would enable us to find what constitutes: (a) a "typical" audience, (b) a "marginal" audience and (c) a sociopathic or "sociotic" audience. A typical audience (from the point of view of role configuration) was defined as drawing a majority of votes in at least 75% of all potential audiences in the United States, at a time when the test was given. A marginal audience was defined as drawing a minority of votes in 25% or less, of all potential audiences in this country. A sociotic audience, the membership of which are not necessarily mental patients, would show pathological role structure. According to Moreno's definition, while the single individuals may be normal, their *interaction* is abnormal (Moreno, J.L. 1934: 192).

The test situation

Instructions to the subjects

Our subjects were mothers of a son in the service whom they were shortly expecting home. An auxiliary ego represented the son. The situation was: Your son has returned from Germany about a week ago. Before he left for the army he was in love with a girl from your hometown. They planned to be married when he returned from overseas. The girl has come to you today and complained that his affections for her have cooled. She fears that she has lost him. You are deeply disturbed and want to find out what happened to your boy, and why this change has come over him. Act the way you would toward your own son under similar circumstances.

Instructions to the auxiliary ego (not heard by the subjects)

Your function is that of the tester. Your performance has to be the *same* in the case of each subject. Every one of those mothers will probably produce an emotional response to the situation. You, however, must present as much as possible the same in all cases. You are our instrument of measurement (Moreno 1934, 1940, 1943; Moreno & Dunkin 1941). Remember that you have recently come home and are discharged from the army. You were engaged to an American girl before leaving for Germany and you planned to marry her. But, during your stay in Germany you met and fell in love with a German girl whose father had been a member of the Nazi party. You and this girl are devoted to each other and have promised to marry. You have not mentioned it to your family or former fiancée, but you are going to tell your mother now.

Reactions of the subjects

We are merely indicating some crucial moments in the presentation of three of the typical mothers. *Our first mother* reacted as follows, after the boy had stated his plans:

MOTHER: But are you sure you love this girl? Does not the fact that her father was a Nazi make you suspicious of her? Have you given the matter earnest thought?

SON: I have thought it over very carefully, mother. I don't care what her father was. I love her. She is just as sweet and lovable as any other girl and we want to get married. I want to get her over here.

MOTHER: Well, I don't want to stand in the way of your happiness and I'm sure no one else in the family will either if you sincerely believe you're doing the right thing. But how can you be sure? Perhaps she is using you just to get out of the country!

SON: Mother, that is not true. She loved me when I was over there, even before we thought of getting married.

MOTHER: I can't say I'm not disappointed. After all, we've known Ellen since she was a little girl. The families have known one another so long, and you were engaged to her. Who's going to tell her?

SON: I'll have to. I'm sure that Ellen will understand. She wouldn't want me to pretend to her that everything is the same as before.

MOTHER: It's not going to be easy for any of us, but we'll do our best. Of course, you're going to live in a home of your own.

SON: Don't worry. Everything will work out alright.

Mother Number Two presented a more receptive picture.

MOTHER: The important thing is that you love her and that she really loves you.

SON: Oh, but we do love each other. Why pretend?

MOTHER: I feel sorry for Ellen. You'd better tell her. She was very unhappy about you. I can see now why she would be. It's going to be hard for her, living so close by.

SON: I'll tell her, mother. I'm sure she'll understand. You can't fool your own heart.

MOTHER: But what do you plan to do about your girl?

SON: I'm going to have her come here. Then we'll get married.

MOTHER: Well, we shall be very glad to have her. Of course, she'll stay with us.

SON: Thanks, Mom, I knew you'd understand.

MOTHER: It will be lonely for her at times, so far away from her own people. I know that anyone whom you pick for a wife must be a very fine person, no matter what her political connections are. As long as she makes you happy we will all be fond of her, too. We'll try to make her feel at home, you can be sure of that.

Mother Number Three was of a different mind.

MOTHER: But how *can* you fall in love with a girl like that? I don't understand! Her father and his gang have put thousands of our boys to death, and murdered other innocent people. What were you fighting this war for, anyway? How can you call yourself an American and look a girl like that in the face?

SON: But mother, I love her. What difference does it make what her father did, or anyone else, for that matter? She is just like any other sweet, lovable girl and I know she loves me. Don't you think that's important?

MOTHER: Ellen loves you too. Are you thinking about her? How do you suppose she'll feel about this?

SON: I'm sure Ellen will understand. Love is more important than what anyone thinks.

MOTHER: Are you planning to go to Germany and live there?

SON: No, I had thought to bring the girl here, so we could be married at home.

MOTHER: Bring that girl here? Into my house? Never! I will never stand for that, and neither will Dad and your brother. Why, think of it, your brother is going into the army himself this year. How do you think he'd feel? And Ellen living here in town, too. You must be out of your mind. I don't understand you at all. You're not like our boy anymore. The war certainly changed you!

The analysis following the demonstration of the three solutions showed significant differences in the nine audiences. The questions to which audio-egos responded were: With whom of the three mothers did you identify yourself? Why did you pick her? Is it because *you are* in the same situation? Do *you know someone* who is in the same situation? Are any of the other mothers *closer* to your own situation? If so, why did you not choose the one whose problem resembles yours? How did you feel about the son? Do you

Table 3.1[1] Audience analysis – mother role (%)

	Audience								
	I	II	III	IV	V	VI	VII	VIII	IX
Mother 1	11	19	15	31	9	13	23	16	16
Mother 2	29	53	36	22	15	14	49	38	16
Mother 3	55	25	47	41	67	65	24	40	20
No Vote	5	3	2	16	9	8	4	6	48

100 persons in each case, except Audience IX: 25 persons.

think he acted the way a son should have acted towards his mother? Do you think a soldier should do what he did? Would you behave that way if you were in his predicament? How do you feel about his action towards the American girl? If you have such a problem, would seeing these three different versions of behavior enable you to find a solution of your own?

The test was given soon after the war with Germany had come to an end. Table 3.1 was constructed on the basis of answers to the question "With whom of the three mothers did you identify yourself?" It bears out our estimate of what constitutes a "typical" and a "marginal" audience.

All but Audience II and Audience VII gave an overwhelmingly superior vote to the rejecting mother – No. 3. Audience participation was whole-hearted, as can be seen from the relatively few neutral votes. The largest number of neutral votes occurred in Audience IV, 16%, and it is of interest that this is the only case where Mother No. 1 had a larger following in these audiences than Mother No. 2. Mother No. 1, as we recall, was the one whose reaction came closer to that of No. 3: she was not altogether unwilling to accept the German girl, although she foresaw difficulties.

Further questioning of Audience IV revealed that the large number of neutral votes was due to the hesitance voters experienced in casting their vote either totally for or totally against, and this may be why Mother No. 1 came second for the first time. In Audience VI, Mother No. 1 is on almost the same level as Mother No. 2, but Mother No. 3 is still far ahead of both. Our marginal audiences, II and VII, showed a preference for Mother No. 2, the loving type who considered her son's happiness first and his judgment unfailing.

A further study of Table 3.1 shows that Audience VII rated Mothers No. 1 and 3 almost equally, with only a difference of 1 percentage point in favor of the latter. This audience gave a lower score to Mother No. 3 than all the others. Nowhere else did this mother get 24%,[1] the next lowest being in our other marginal audience, No. II, where she received only 25%. It is note-worthy that the contrast between the two extremes, Mother No. 2 and Mother No. 3, is far more explicit, pointing to how high emotions ran, either pro or con. Audience VIII, for example, finds Mother No. 2 only 2 percentage points short of Mother No. 3.

A re-test of this kind at the present time might show a shift in favor of Mother No. 2, now that mothers are no longer bombarded by wartime propaganda. However, at that point the representative of that great national clinical collective, Mother No. 3, was greatly favored. It is of interest that both Ellen and the German girl were symbols. Neither was actually known to the mothers but Ellen was automatically preferred and the German girl rejected, although nothing was brought forward concerning her as an individual that might have placed her in an unfavorable light. It was merely the collective aspect, that of the Nazi affiliation, which was sufficient for her to be pushed aside. Not one of the mothers who rejected her considered the possibility that she might have been in discord with her father's views, or perhaps even of so-called non-Aryan origin. Such findings would indicate that if Mother No. 3 were still at the top of the list at present, the longer the occupation of Germany and Japan lasts, the greater may be the resistance built up by the families of men in the occupation armies to their foreign brides, and the more hostility they would find upon their return home.

In the case of the ninth audience a vote structure resulted which does not resemble that of either the typical or the marginal audiences.[1] Nearly half of the group did not vote. This audience showed some preference for Mother No. 3. The close contest between the three mothers was due to the fact that the problem did not appear as a test to the audience, but as a true case. The reason given for the slight preference for Mother No. 3 was that she was more outspoken. However, the striking thing about this audience is the larger percentage of "No Vote." Upon interview it was found that a number of the spectators belonging to this group felt that "it was not a test, but a real problem." They were convinced that the boy on the stage was not an auxiliary ego, but that he presented his own personal case.

It was further revealed that many had the idea that the presumably Nazi girl was in the audience and that they suspected several girls "from the way they acted." The spectators had many other ideas of a delusionary and illogical nature. An audience of mental patients might show such a structure. However, these were *not* mental patients or disturbed individuals. They were just highly sensitive to the procedure on the stage and to each other (Moreno & Fischel 1942; Moreno & Toeman 1942; Umansky 1944).

We have termed this type of audience a "sociotic" audience and it is felt that, although it may not occur as frequently as the other two, it represents a large faction of the population which must be dealt with. Such an audience may, for instance, be apprehensive to certain films. Careful audience diagnosis is therefore a prerequisite to audience psychotherapy (Moreno 1945c).

We plan a re-test of the *same* audiences for report at a future date. It seems to us that this sociodramatic approach would lend itself to a more intimate public opinion polling of representative samples than do present methods. Expressing an opinion in these sessions is not left unrelated to the voter's own life. His vote is motivated and taken only after he is warmed up to the problem for which he is given a chance to see several alternative solutions. The sociodramatic stimulus in an audience test can be either extemporaneous sociodrama, a rehearsed sociodrama or a specially constructed diagnostic film. Motion pictures have been used at the Institute for audience diagnosis and for therapeutic guidance. In the form of the rehearsed sociodrama and the film, the audience to be tested remains entirely spontaneous. Only the process on the stage or screen is prepared and conserved. Many agencies are using these "conserved" forms of sociodrama today. In time to come it may well be that for use with large numbers of groups the moving picture will supplement the rehearsed sociodrama in the flesh because of its greater ease of reproduction.

Although apparently merely a testing procedure, this sociodramatic approach has cathartic as well as diagnostic value. However, for guidance purposes, in the case of both the rehearsed and film sociodrama, a "director of the audience" must be present to use findings on the spot and turn these findings into therapeutic channels. At times he may have to stop the film in the middle and/or to employ it as a step in the warming up of the audience to a self-presentation. According to Moreno, we cannot hope to use only frozen editions of psychodrama and sociodrama. They should not be regarded as tools that can stand alone, but as adjuncts to actual psychodramatic and sociodramatic sessions.

Conclusions

The sociodramatic audience test is presented as a diagnostic measure for audiences.

To date two sets of standard life situations have been used at the Psychodramatic Institute: the Three Situation Set and the Six Situation Set. The polarity role of the stranger-role of the native was used to test our audiences.

Moreno's audience test is used, exposing nine audiences to the same sociodramatic stimulus. Analysis of the vote is made and categories of subjects are established. Audiences are subjected to the same theme and the same auxiliary egos.

It was found that audiences could be classified as typical, marginal and sociotic, according to the role configurations found within them.

The meaning of symbolic roles and their bearing on individual behavior was discussed.

Sociodramatic methods, spontaneous, rehearsed and in films, could be used as measures of public opinion. It is foreshadowed that sociodramatic films may eventually be used on a large scale. In sociodrama and group psychodrama, it is the audience that is the subject, and therefore conserved forms should be supplementary to sessions in the flesh. An audience director should always be present, especially in the frozen editions of psychodrama and sociodrama, in order to guide the findings on the spot into therapeutic channels.

Article 4

Audience Reactions to Therapeutic Films

Toeman, Z. (1945) *Sociometry, A Journal of Inter-Personal Relations* VIII, 3–4: 493–497

Zerka's comments

We went to the movies a fair amount, and I decided to make some notes when we did. This article was a reaction to the portrayal of therapy in commercial films, which struck me as absurd. Evident to me was the strong influence of an arts culture that granted status to being analyzed. In New York City you weren't considered well-educated if you hadn't spent time "on the couch." I found it all a big bore.

This phenomenon contrasted sharply with Moreno's dream of being able to reach and help many people through this medium. As this article describes, he experimented with the idea in 1932–34 while conducting research with Helen H. Jennings at the Hudson School for Girls.

Introduction

In his new book on psychodrama, in the chapter dealing with therapeutic films,[1] Moreno says:

> In the last few years a number of motion pictures have been planned, as *Lady in the Dark*, *Now Voyager*, *Conflict*, *Love Letters*, *Spellbound*, which represent a dabbling of the motion picture industry with therapeutic (often with straight psychiatric) projects. Due to the fact that the instigators, producers and actors have no psychiatric and psychological training, these films can well be classified as "pseudo" therapeutic. Because of the mass influence which motion pictures exercise they can be called dangerous undertakings, spreading false notions, portraying untrue explanations of causes and distorted cures upon the screen. Upon closer analysis of these films as to their content, the influence of psychoanalytic theory is one of the outstanding features. The import of childhood trauma, of dreams and repressions are some of the most popular hypotheses used for the explanation of psychic conflicts.

> However, there is in these motion picture productions a feature much more involved which is not so obvious: the psychodrama.
>
> The psychoanalytic situation is a patient–physician relation. It is a form of verbal interview. The real stuff of life, the situations and conflicts, when and as they occur, are kept out of it. But the producers of these films do not try to duplicate the psychoanalytic interview as it occurs in fact, which would be rather boring to the public. *They try to produce a "drama," to show that by enacting and re-enacting of scenes a mental catharsis can be produced.* Unconsciously therefore, they have been entering into the domain of the therapeutic drama or, as it is usually called, the psychodrama. When preparing the script, selecting the actors, editing and cutting the film, weighing the effects of the film upon audiences, factors and ideas are introduced by them borrowed from psychodrama, which they make up without sufficient knowledge of its principles of producing therapeutic films and of problems involved in audience catharsis. Unconsciously they are using, during the production, the warming up of actors (always with the idea in view whether the audiences will be similarly warmed up), auxiliary ego methods, and the process of role-playing and role-identification, which have become valuable concepts in the analysis and guidance of audiences.
>
> Such rapid popularization of an idea would be flattering, were it not for the increasing number of psychiatric motion pictures turned loose upon the public by unskilled men, producing undesirable effects. An important medium by which masses of people can be treated simultaneously has come into the hands of laymen who are unwittingly promoting a form of quackery that may become the greatest barrier to the psychodramatic film of the future.
>
> (Moreno, J.L. 1945c)

Moreno's pioneer films *Spontaneity Training*, produced in Hudson, NY in the autumn of 1934, were shown to two types of audiences, one consisting largely of college students, adolescents, mostly female, comparable in age, though not in social and academic background to the subjects in the film, Audience I. The second type of audience consisted mainly of teachers and professional workers, a mature adult audience, Audience II. The difference in reaction to the films was striking and will be discussed later. Sitting in as participant observer the author attempted to collect and analyze these reactions.

Description of the films

The motion pictures are entirely extemporaneous and though they had been made more than eleven years ago, it is pertinent to state that no one experienced them as dated, and that their age did not in any way detract from their impact upon the audience. In order to understand the motives given for the audience reactions, we are describing here the salient points of the films shown. The first film is an introduction to the warming up to and subsequent transfer of simple spontaneity states, as, for instance, a sculptress starting a new creation in clay, a mother visiting her daughter at a boarding school, a girl waiting for someone who does not come, a business executive calling for greater efforts from her staff, a hospital supervisor giving instructions to nurses in an emergency. Criticism and interpretation from the director followed each performance. No scene was repeated.

The second film is a therapeutic film. A young girl from a well-to-do-home, but of emotional instability after having failed in the past in regard to various social demands, learns how to become a waitress. We see her first without training, in the role of a waitress at a restaurant. From the start the subject reveals, besides her deficiencies as a waitress, many personality difficulties which are analyzed and treated, not apart from the vocational task, but in conjunction with it. The film shows her development in the role of a waitress before, during and after the treatment. Fellow students in the film watched her in her first attempt when she got into a heated argument with one of her customers, taking sides for and against. These co-students, chosen because of similar difficulties and interests to sit in on the subject's training, were learning via mirror technique.

Some of the most important features of the films are that they copy in procedure psychodramatic sessions in the flesh. The director interviews the subject and assigns a role for her. The subject warms up to her role by physical starters as arranging the water glasses, setting the table, etc., aided by an auxiliary ego who takes the part of the restaurant hostess. Two other auxiliary egos appear as guests who sit at the trainee's table. Resistances were interpolated by the director, who had instructed one of the auxiliary ego guests to make a complaint in reference to the subject's service. The guest stated that the waitress brought her coffee although she asked for tea. This mild reprimand caused an immediate argument on the part of the subject. Verbatim reports and records of all actions, gestures and carriage were made by a fellow student. Upon completion of the scene every co-student in the film made her comments, criticizing the subject's behavior. The director analyzed the total performance, noting weaknesses to be especially dealt with in further training. The complete records were copied and handed to each of the students, who took them home to study. The next scene shows the subject at home, reading over her report and realizing her error, demonstrating with a friend how she *should* have acted. The last part of the film shows the same girl after several months of spontaneity training, again in a restaurant waiting on customers. She showed poise, composure and ability to handle the implements and her clients with facility.

Training consisted first of a period of learning to handle the dishes and silverware without customers. Later customers entered into the situation: girls well liked by the subject, who offered no interpersonal conflict or criticism to the trainee. During a later phase of training more difficult assignments were given. For example, students to whom the subject was indifferent, and lastly, girls who were rejected in the actual life setting by the subject, were placed opposite her. In this final phase conflict situations were produced which the trainee learned to master. Again, records of every session were made, criticism of the co-students *within* the film carefully noted, and an analysis made by the director.

Reactions, Audience I

Our audience participation ranged from full and partial *role identification* to total rejection of the subject. This adolescent type of audience produced responses that were tinged with a good deal of emotion, as for instance in complete role identification: "That was me. I could just see myself. I always seem to get into trouble with people. I am a salesgirl in a department store but that is the kind of training I need. It would make a world of difference to me." "I never saw anything so simple and yet fantastic in my life, and she learned so quickly." "I thought it was so real. I, too, would have quarreled with the customer." "She did a wonderful job. Imagine standing up in front of your classmates and taking all that criticism from them. She's got courage."

The partial enthusiasts reported: "I might have thought those things, but I would never say them. The customer is always right." "She learned well, but she should not have argued with her guest." "I could never be a waitress, even with training." "I don't think I could have done that well."

Rejections were few in this type of audience, but several critical remarks were made: "She was silly. She looked as if the guest had committed a crime." "All that fuss over a cup of tea." "If I'd been the guest I would have walked out." "It was a good thing she was trained. She'd never have been able to hold a waitress job otherwise."

Reactions, Audience II

This type of audience, that of adults and professional workers, showed little role identification with the subject and verbally produced largely intellectual reactions: "To what extent did the training in this specific situation enable the subject to deal adequately with other life situations, and was training limited to this type of situation only?" "It was something to see her progress; but I would have liked the film to show more of the steps to her training." "Why was treatment and training not directed at her immediate conflicts?" "We can appreciate the fact that co-workers watching her and offering comments would be quite a factor in her ability to take it. I don't believe she would have accepted criticism so well from adults." "Were the girls sitting in on training only taught by indirect, spectator methods, or did they also get a chance to appear as subjects?"

Discussion of audience participation

In audiences of similar construction to whom these films were shown, the participation quotient of Audience type I, ranging from 73% to 89%, was considerably greater than that of type II, which ranged from 31% to 42%. The amount of catharsis received and observable in the first type was thus significantly greater than in the second. The latter showed irritation, rejection, conflicts and endless questioning. It would seem that the amount of catharsis obtained from therapeutic motion films by the audience depends upon: (a) the problem portrayed; (b) the type of actor; (c) the solution to the problem; (d) the type of audience; and (e) the interaction between the members of the audience. Each of these factors contributes to the amount of participation and role identification possible on the part of the spectators.

Conclusion

This sort of inquiry leads us to believe that the limitation of the therapeutic film is that, especially as it is able to stir up audiences, many spectators may leave the theatre with a number of conflicts sensitized and dormant problems reawakened without being able to satisfy and resolve what it has activated. The follow-up, indeed, the completion by an actual psychodramatic session under skilled guidance, appears to be the only alternative to an otherwise risky therapeutic undertaking.

Article 5

Clinical Psychodrama: Auxiliary Ego, Double, and Mirror Techniques

Toeman, Z. (1946) *Sociometry: A Journal of Inter-Personal Relations* IX, 2–3: 178–183

Zerka's comments

During this time at Beacon the air seemed palpable with Moreno's ideas. He was the creator, he expected others to work out the details. It was a role that came naturally to me, because I believed so strongly in his vision. He picked me as double most of the time.

For Moreno doubling was an established form of practice, but new for me. I wrote this article in order to articulate some of the discoveries I was making in action as an auxiliary. It was the first time it had all been so clearly set down. At times I thought "I'll never know enough." However, there really wasn't time to do anything but move forward.

At this point I was not thinking of myself as a psychodrama director. We were dealing with such severe cases that only Moreno directed. It took me a long time to feel myself as a "psychodrama professional." I just wanted to be the best damn auxiliary I could be. This time period was a stimulating adventure. I never knew from day to day what worlds I would be asked to enter.

One instructive doubling experience was with Sylvia, a mute psychotic patient (not her real name). I was told to be the voice she didn't let out. I just did what I felt and a scream arose in me. The patient listened intently. Another patient, who was not at the session and therefore did not see the patient, later reported that he had said to himself upon hearing it, "Oh, Sylvia's screaming" even though he knew she didn't speak.

It should be noted that the use of doubling described in this article was with psychotic patients. These days as director I do not often use a double who stays with the protagonist throughout the drama, because I encourage the "normotic" (that is, "normal neurotic") protagonist to be empowered and responsible to provide their own words and feelings to the greatest extent possible.

Among the factors of consequence in the function of the auxiliary ego are: (a) the relationship to the subject or patient; (b) the relationship to the problem which the patient represents; (c) the relationship to the role which the auxiliary ego is to portray; (d) the warming up process which takes place between the subject and auxiliary ego immediately prior to the action on the stage; and (e) the relationship of the auxiliary ego to the director.

The auxiliary ego, in portraying a role, may go about it as follows: (1) by drawing from his or her own private resources; the ability to do this makes at times a fully untrained person an excellent auxiliary ego within certain limits, for instance, in the role of a father, husband, brother, lover, sister, mother, wife, girl friend, etc., the very fact that he or she is untrained may make the auxiliary ego more spontaneous and less conscious of involvement; (2) a further development of auxiliary ego training results in the learning to adapt his own resources to the subject's expectancies of her brother, husband, child, or whomever the auxiliary ego represents; (3) at a still later stage of training the auxiliary ego may draw into the presentation information obtained about the actual person to be portrayed; this information may have been received either from the subject, or from another person, or directly from the person to be enacted.

The portrayal of the actual person may differ greatly in many respects from the picture the subject has of that person. It can be seen easily that a number of distortions of the role can thus take place: (a) the distortion that comes from the auxiliary ego himself as it is colored by his own experiences; (b) the distortion which the subject suggests to the auxiliary ego because of her subjective experiences in reference to the person to be portrayed by the ego; and (c) the distortion which may come from the actual person. These multiple interactions of distortion or bias require continuous analysis and clarification by the director in order not to hamper the therapeutic process and to constantly "deconserve" the auxiliary ego from clichés and prejudices which otherwise may become confirmed and established during the auxiliary ego's training and performance.

In the double and mirror techniques to which this report will limit itself, the auxiliary ego is closely identified with the patient's problems and, especially in the latter, aware of the social atom of the patient. The double technique has been found extremely valuable in the clarification of the patient's conflicts, both normal and abnormal. For the double ego technique the patient and auxiliary ego are placed on the stage together. In order that the patient (often called "primary ego") accepts the presence of the auxiliary ego on the stage, she is told to consider the ego as her double, the invisible "I," the alter ego with whom she talks at times but who exists only within herself. In the psychodrama this invisible double is projected into space, embodied by an actual person and experienced as outside of the patient. The patient represents the deeper, inner levels of experience while the ego acts as double, copying physical bearing in every way and representing the outer levels. However, in actuality the patient usually begins by first revealing the superficial layers. The auxiliary's task is then, for strategic reasons, the reverse of the director's formal instructions. It is her job to stir up the subject to reach deeper levels of expression by peeling off the outer, socially visible "I" of the subject, and to reach for those experiences and imageries which a person would reveal when talking to herself, alone, in the privacy of her own room.

The task of the auxiliary ego becomes one of producing quick, kaleidoscopic views, "other parts" of the subject's "I." Often therefore, the auxiliary ego represents the subject more fully than the patient realizes and may, at times, become aggressive if the warming up of the patient lags behind. In general, my experience as auxiliary ego in double scenes has been that too much verbal warming up previous to the portrayal disturbs spontaneity and blocks freely flowing action. A sensitive auxiliary ego should not be told everything about the patient or her problem, as this predisposes towards overheating both the subject and the auxiliary ego, while catharsis may take place verbally instead of psychodramatically. Many things are better left unsaid beforehand and brought out in the interaction that follows.

As the auxiliary ego becomes adept at drawing out essentials from the subject, information not gathered in advance and crystallized by the performance itself acts as an inspiration to the ego, a self-propelling force, and increases catharsis for the patient. Usually, before stepping upon the stage we have very little idea of what will actually transpire. It would be unwise for the auxiliary ego to make up her mind that certain aspects *must* be revealed, as this would coerce the subject and would not be therapeutic support. In the main, it is the subject who determines the course of action. The auxiliary ego supports and guides the subject into channels that appear, on the spur of the moment, desirable. Obviously, therefore, predetermined action would prevent spontaneity for the patient, reduce the tele flowing from the patient to the auxiliary, and furthermore throw the ego off the therapeutic track. This double ego technique is carried on in the first person; the two I's interacting as one. The two may disagree violently, the auxiliary ego may challenge the subject, stimulating her to respond more genuinely, or they may agree in every respect. We know from experience that this technique is a potent one in exploring deeper levels and producing catharsis which, however, is often much delayed, showing its effects days and even weeks later.

I recall two specific cases. The first subject was a young woman very much troubled by the fact that, at 28, she was still unmarried. She was attractive, intelligent, and had a number of admirers who were anxious to marry her but towards none of whom she felt an equally strong emotion. After a number of diagnostic scenes were portrayed the director decided that the time had come for reaching beneath the calm surface. I, as the double ego, was instructed to be aggressive in one way or another. The scene was set for late at night in the bedroom of the subject, where she was reviewing the happenings of the day just ended. The patient persisted in evasive talk, which I suddenly interrupted by an outburst of weeping and a cry of "Why do I go on lying to myself! I can lie to others but I can't fool myself." This produced tears in the subject who retorted, "What's the use of crying myself to sleep *again*. I've done that too often." When stepping down she was warmed up to a far greater level of self-presentation than before, and a feeling of relaxation came over her. She stated that I had formulated her situation far more clearly than she had ever done; it seemed almost as if I knew her better than she did. During the performance I was not certain that the patient would actually cry, as this was the first time I had met her. Nevertheless, the feeling came to me that this was the moment to weep or else to give up the action altogether. This particular scene was the real beginning of the therapeutic approach to the patient's problems, which ended in her successful marriage a few months later.

The second scene, which stands out in my mind, is that of a 22-year-old girl who was about to divorce her husband but had not stopped loving him. She came to the Institute for clarification of her conflicts and in the course of portraying her difficulties with her husband displayed much emotion, especially in the scene where she decided to leave him because of his inability to accept her as the only woman in his life. The director then moved into the double technique, and I (as the other part of herself) began to question the purpose of continuing to live, wondering about the possibility of suicide. This may, at face value, seem a dangerous thing to do, but that was what I felt about the subject at that moment, again without having obtained such information from her. It brought the subject to a sudden halt (we had been walking aimlessly around her room) and she broke in "Yes, that's just how I feel, but I know I'd never really do it even though life does not seem worth the trouble right now." This scene was a flashback of an actual one which had taken place a few months before, and upon descending from the stage the subject felt greatly relieved, declaring that this was exactly what had gone through her mind although she had never admitted it before, even to herself.

I want to emphasize that in the double technique the auxiliary ego loses the sense of objectivity and becomes completely enveloped by the subject's problems, feeling her way as if no single direction can be satisfactory, trying this way and that, torturing herself to find a way out. The question has been raised whether this process going both ways from the subject to the ego and from the ego to the subject is not, because of its subjective character, unreliable and invalid. In order to clarify this we have systematically interviewed every subject whose thoughts, feelings or actions I seemed to anticipate in the double situation. Among a group of thirty subjects we found confirmation of the accuracy of these revelations. Often the subjects were amazed to have them come forth without having informed me and admitted that the double came closer to expressing, in a crystallized form, many of their deeper experiences. The question still remained whether the auxiliary ego projects into the subject some of her "own" experiences, experiences sufficiently similar to form a link between them. In order to verify this I began to check myself in the act and found myself frequently choosing and rejecting between my own experiences and experiences that I intuitively felt were those of the subject. It is as if I would have said to myself, "This is not me, that is she." Gradually I learned to choose correctly; that is, my tele experience (interaction feelings) became more accurate the more skill I developed.

In the mirror technique the patient remains in the audience as spectator while the auxiliary ego takes the patient's part, reproducing gestures typical of the patient and creating a series of scenes and situations which the patient will recognize as her own experiences, enabling the patient to "see herself as others see her." This technique is perhaps more difficult, as the patient does not lend support or point the way for the auxiliary ego. It is used (a) with patients who are completely non-cooperative and need to be stirred into action, (b) for the purpose of restoring amnestic experiences to patients, and (c) for patients who have never registered the events taking place around them, that is, not to restore memory but to acquaint them with certain facts and events. The ego then turns into the patient by herself and has to be well acquainted with the patient's social and mental syndromes. In the case of psychotics this becomes a more delicate job, especially with patients who are unable to communicate their experiences. The patient may not know at first that this is she herself being displayed before her eyes. But soon, as she warms up, she becomes interested and may, finally, be stimulated to a self-presentation although having refused to do this for some time.

In the mirror technique as in that of the double the director may indicate the general way in which action should go before the auxiliary ego begins, in order to produce the most potent form of psychodramatic shock in the patient. At times the director has in mind a specific event or image that he wishes to have reproduced and then the auxiliary ego has her task laid out. But often no instruction comes from the director and a more general enactment of the patient's various levels of experience and behavior is required.

The most striking recollection I have concerning this technique is one in which a patient was suffering from pseudo-amnestic breaks in experiences while hospitalized. She stated that she had been brought to the hospital against her will and for no reason since she was not ill. She demanded to be allowed to return home to her husband and children. This was the third episode suffered by the patient within six years and she was completely non-cooperative and without insight at the time the mirror technique was used. She was confused, shallow, full of bizarre ideas, delusional and altogether intractable.

I was picked to represent the patient because of my familiarity with her syndromes and because I had witnessed each of the three attacks. Furthermore, the patient had at one time displayed deep attachment to me, while I had also recently been the object of aggression from the patient. I commenced to warm up to the part of the patient with vigor, throwing and pushing furniture around me, cursing the nurses, the doctors, the hospital, my husband, calling everything and everyone vile names and then, changing abruptly into a dancing stance that I had frequently seen the patient take, peering out of the window of my room, talking about the visions I saw, mostly of deceased relatives and well known figures of remote history.

At this point the nurse who actually took care of the patient (the patient was sitting in the audience with her eyes as if glued to me) was sent upon the stage by the director in order to give me a hypodermic needle containing a sedative. I was immediately stirred into aggressive behavior towards the nurse, threatening to hit her. The nurse went through the act of giving me the injection while trying to soothe me, but when I looked at her I saw a great deal of fear and horror in her eyes. This made me feel wildly triumphant. I thought "Well, I really scared her. I'll show her now. I'll scare them all out of their wits." Thus I revealed to myself how the patient must have felt. I picked up a fairly solid piece of furniture and threw it across the stage, down several levels. It landed below with a crash. The director stopped me and turned to the patient. She was leaning forward with her elbows resting on her knees, completely wrapped up in the performance. Then, somewhat breathlessly she spoke to the director: "Is that the way I behaved? Did I really act like that?"

From this point on the session was turned over to the patient herself who became the subject in her own psychodrama; the first one in a series that hastened her recovery. But one of the most important comments came from the nurse who had participated in the scene: "You really had me scared to death for a moment. I thought you, too, had become mentally ill." How much more then, did this scene mean to the patient who was shocked into some realization of her behavior!

These techniques are interesting from the clinical point of view because of their departure from orthodox therapeutic methods. In these techniques a maximum amount of involvement of the auxiliary ego with the patient is permissible. It should be added that deep action catharsis is gained in the mirror technique, not only by the patient but also by the auxiliary ego who at one time or another has been the recipient of hostility from the patient. Insight into the patient's condition is thereby gained with unusual accuracy and depth.

Article 6

Psychodrama: Its Relation to Stage, Radio and Motion Pictures

Toeman, Z. (1947) *Sociatry, Journal of Group and Intergroup Therapy* I, 1: 119–126

Zerka's comments

Here is an example of how everything in our lives was grist for the mill, because Moreno's vision was so comprehensive. With him one worked all the time because life was constantly presenting itself to us. Everything was about relationships – ours to each other, extending out to our near and far social atoms. Even though we worked hard, Moreno was good about socializing, especially around food.

FIRST DIALOGUE
SETTING: The Theater for Psychodrama, New York City
DRAMATIS PERSONAE: J.L. Moreno and Zerka Toeman

Synopsis: The author plans to bring, at regular intervals, dialogues showing the genesis of psychodrama in contemporary and classic literature, as well as in other forms of art-production.

TOEMAN: I am making the rounds of live and motion picture theaters, broadcasting and television stations, to examine the pseudo-therapeutic devices and detours by which they influence the public mind, and to see what psychodramatic methods can do towards their improvement. Perhaps they can learn from each other. What do you think of it?

MORENO: It is a fine idea. The creative artist of all ages, as the poet, historian, novelist, especially the dramatist, could not help but trespass the esthetic boundaries of his genius and turn into a priest, educator, sociologist, and psychotherapist. He must have had intuitive flashes of situations of therapeutic potentialities which he may have, at times, used to excess, and other times with insufficient vigor.

TOEMAN: This may be the reason for the unevenness of cathartic effects of artistic production.

MORENO: It may be well to differentiate between the "Daimonic" catharsis of the artistic dramatist and the "therapeutic" catharsis of the scientific dramatist.

TOEMAN: In other words, what the artist and dramatist does hit or miss, relying upon his intuition, the psychodramatist does in a systematic way, relying upon a sort of systematized intuition or spontaneity.

MORENO: In order to enlarge our knowledge and to develop a "science" of the drama, which I presume is the aim of your expedition, our first task should be: (1) to identify the *standard techniques* used in the drama of all times but especially in contemporary drama – drama being used here in the broadest sense of the word – which appear to have a therapeutic involvement; (2) to identify techniques that appear with regularity and to tabulate the frequency of their appearance; (3) to reevaluate the effects that each has upon groups exposed to them; (4) to compare them with the standard techniques used in our theatres of psychodrama and to explore their genesis; (5) to suggest how the artistic techniques currently used by artists can be improved; (6) to study the behavior of audiences before, during and after the process of the stage.

TOEMAN: This is approximately what I had in mind. My first step in this quest was to see Shakespeare's *Othello* once more. As you will remember, Othello, a dark-skinned man, presumably part Negro, marries a white woman, kills her out of jealousy at the end and kills himself. It is a standard technique of the drama to tap a solution in a *terminal* form without leaving in the mind of the public the possibility of an alternate solution. In psychodrama there are alternatives of treatment and solution. Here Shakespeare is dictating the solution.

MORENO: He gives it an ultimate form. The suggestive power of Shakespeare's imagination must strike the mind of the public attending very deeply.

TOEMAN: Well, as I was following the plot I wondered whether this effect was the most favorable one for the people who were experiencing the play with me. The playwright, under the cloak of objectivity seems to tell his audience, "That is what happens when a black man marries a white woman. It is bound to happen this way. It ends in tragedy."

MORENO: You mean he does not say explicitly that it *might* happen this way.

TOEMAN: No, he does not. I asked two Negroes who attended the show as to their reactions. One of them said, "Although I was carried away by its poetic beauty and the intensity of emotions involved I was very much angered by the continuous efforts which were made by the white people in the play to break up the marriage because he was black and she was white, and therefore incompatible. In fact, I felt that he was driven into frenzy by them and that the murder was suggested to him. *They* were the murderers, not Othello." The other one stated, "Othello was called a Moor by Shakespeare. What would have happened to him if he would have been a full-blood Negro?" The implication was that they would not have permitted him even the dignity to be a mad murderer; that they would have lynched him immediately. In the play he was given the permission and honor to kill himself. What do you think that Shakespeare would feel if he would live today and witness the effects of his play upon an audience of both white and colored in the United States?

MORENO: I believe he would write the play anew for every new audience before which it played. In other words, he would turn into a psychodramatist, or more precisely into a sociodramatist. He would have on his staff, besides the professional actors who are therapeutically trained, a number of informants on Negro–white relations. By the way, that was quite a provocative remark, that Othello was not the true murderer of Desdemona, he was only the hand; she was killed by her own people. Can you explain this?

TOEMAN: Yes. That brings us to Shakespeare's personal involvement. It is another standard technique of playwrights, in order to propel their play and introduce their pet ideas or values, to use certain characters as their spokesman. This is often done unconsciously by the playwright and hidden by the mask of dramatic objectivity and logic of events. In the case of *Othello* it is particularly Iago who carries not the conflict but Shakespeare's own ideas, methodically, step by step, as a sort of "esthetic auxiliary ego."

MORENO: Do you think that these were Shakespeare's own private feelings in the matter?

TOEMAN: Not necessarily. He may have been a tolerant man, but he tries to explain, to himself and the audience, the chain of causes leading up to such a tragic end, both Desdemona and Othello losing their life.

MORENO: You mean that Iago as "Deus ex Machina" of our cultural value system shapes the plot. He substitutes for the playwright and portrays his ideas. The subjectivistic type of playwright can be contrasted with the objectivistic; one who keeps himself systematically and consciously outside of the play, trying to move his characters in accord with the principles involved in the conflict. As your Negro audience members suggest, the end of *Othello* is a prototype of an *un*therapeutic finale. If the audience is made up of white women, it warns them to keep away from the Negroes. If it is played before Negro audiences it threatens them to stay away from white people; their noblest efforts will end in failure. The great playwright acts as a reactionary force, propagating and promoting racial prejudice. Here the therapist could guide the artist.

TOEMAN: I have noticed, in this respect, an increased influence of psychodramatic techniques upon the dramatic production of contemporaries.

For instance, in Terence Rattigan's *O Mistress Mine* performed by the Lunts, there was some evidence of this phenomenon.

MORENO: Does it have psychodramatic significance?

TOEMAN: Indeed. The story goes like this: a young man, returning from overseas, finds his widowed mother living with another man. He resents his mother's friend and brings about their separation. In the last act a kind of psychodrama takes place.

MORENO: Let's hear about that.

TOEMAN: Well, the mother and son live now alone. The mother's former friend comes to see them. He finds the son concerned about a girl who prefers another boy to him. The older man shows in an improvisation how the son can win the girl's affection. In that improvised scene a restaurant is imagined in which the girl and her other boyfriend are supposedly dining. They do not actually appear on the stage; they're projected by the gestures of the boy's stepfather–producer. The psychodramatic implication here seems to be the following: the stepfather-to-be had a double motive. On the surface he wanted to teach the boy by what strategies the girl could be won. In a deeper sense, however, he wanted, through identification with the son, to force the boy to identify with him in the wooing of his mother.

MORENO: A sort of role reversal! He shrewdly divined that the son would understand him better when undergoing a similar experience and being helped in the solution by him.

TOEMAN: In the improvisation the son wins the girl away from his competitor. With this the projection ends but when immediately afterwards his mother comes into the room, the older man asks her to marry him and all three go into the restaurant to actually get the girl for the son. Because of the psychodramatic interlude the play ends "on the stage" with a catharsis for everyone concerned. How does this strike you?

MORENO: It sounds like a well-known technique in psychodrama – the mirror technique. The stepfather-to-be, by becoming the auxiliary ego of the son, makes the resistant son an auxiliary ego of the father. This way he breaks down the son's protest against him for being in love with his mother and helps the boy to get a substitute for the mother, a girl of his own.

TOEMAN: And that way the son does not mind giving up his mother.

MORENO: The drama itself, if it had been "written" without this interlude, might never have attained the therapeutic catharsis within the play which the son needed in order to permit his future father to make love to his mother.

TOEMAN: In turn, without this mirroring process, the audience would have been deprived of a necessary therapeutic effect.

MORENO: There is another consideration. An audience in our culture may in their "private" minds tolerate a genuine love between two people and resent the son who interferes with their plans. But in their official mind two unmarried people are not supposed to be in love and live together. Some corrective is essential in the dramatic production on the stage to bring it up to the moral standard of the audience. If the production had taken place without the audience, in the anonymity of living itself, it might not have needed this correction. In front of an audience that represents public opinion this interlude is a remedy. It adds to the triple catharsis on the stage, of the father, mother and son, that of the audience. Everybody goes home in a happy mood. Illegitimate love is made legitimate and the son is on the way to conquer his own love.

TOEMAN: Yes, but let us compare the method of the playwright with the methods of the psychodramatist. Let us imagine that the son had been an actual person with this problem. Suppose that – like in the play – two elderly people who are in love and perfectly contented with their situation had consulted you because she has a son by a previous marriage who is disturbed over their relationship. Wouldn't you have handled it differently?

MORENO: In the play the mother is willing to sacrifice her own love for the happiness of the son. She takes her own pill. But in the psychodrama this would already have become part of the treatment, because she might have lost her lover for good by giving him up. On the other hand, she may refuse to give up her lover for her son. Each alternate situation would then be worked out on the stage and the subjects, each of the three in turn, would become the pivot around which the action revolves. Step by step, past relationships and frictions, future projections, besides the present conflicts, would then be re-integrated and analyzed, with possibly an entirely different set of solutions being found by all three.

TOEMAN: There is another play on Broadway concerning which there has been much publicity lately. That is *Christopher Blake* by Moss Hart. It strikes me as being greatly under the influence of psychodramatic principles. In fact, to such a degree that I thought at times that the playwright may have been a guest or subject at our sessions at one time or another. It is first of all a *situational* play. There is *one* situation, a courtroom setting, where two people are appearing before a judge in order to divorce. Their son is to make a choice about which parent to live with. While trying to come to such a decision (the dramatic reality of this part is reduced to a minimum) he has daydreams, mental flights of fancy which are shown to the audience by being enacted.

MORENO: That comes close to one of the basic psychodramatic principles, which is to *let the subject or patient instantly act out on the psychodramatic level the situational reflections which the life setting does not permit him to express*. It is from a therapeutic point of view important for the patient–subject as well as for the audience. That is why the author of *Christopher Blake* allows the boy to dramatize his experience.

TOEMAN: As a patient in a psychodramatic theatre that is exactly what he would be encouraged to do. The trouble is, however, that Christopher's projections showed artificiality at times. They seemed "made to order" rather than created by the anxieties of a real patient. But without these pseudo-psychodramatic interludes the play would be just an old-fashioned, ill-conceived court trial. It is these interludes that give the play its punch.

MORENO: If the author had presented the play in the regular dramaturgic manner the sequence of events would have been within the dimensions of actuality: a court scene, a judge, husband and wife, a son, all kinds of side scenes, building up to the climax, etc.

TOEMAN: Again, if there had been a mental patient in the play it would have been within the realm of actuality to portray some of his delusions and hallucinations on the stage. Or it would have been equally plausible along the classic lines of quasi-psychodramatic involvement, as Shakespeare did in *Hamlet*, to let Hamlet consciously put a play within a play. Hamlet, by projectional methods, showed his royal parents that he knew how cruelly they had conspired the death of his own father. But in *Christopher Blake* the interludes are not "pretended" to be produced by Christopher. They are made by the playwright–producer as an extension of a narrowly bound life situation.

MORENO: Suppose *Christopher Blake* had been a fairy fantasy, outside of actuality. Imagined situations would have been natural within one and the same dramatic continuity. But it is a new principle, used here, to work simultaneously in *two* dimensions; to extend an actual situation because something is happening in the mind of the subject at the time when the actual situation is left out. In other words, to give a psychodramatic portrayal *besides* the portrayal of life-actuality of a particular scene.

TOEMAN: The more normal and regular a certain actual scene is, the more shocking is the effect of a psychodramatic portrayal of it side by side.

MORENO: Similar tendencies have appeared from time to time in dramatic literature, but its conscious and systematic use is largely to be credited to psychodramatic production methods. Don't you recall parallels in our sessions?

TOEMAN: Yes, I do. However, the salient point about psychodrama is that the subject is the producer of both the actual and projected scenes instead of having "an author" set them down for him and imagining that this is the way the subject feels. The psychodramatic actor reflects not only what really happened but also what he experienced and projected into the situation. For instance, do you remember the case of a young man who went AWOL while in the army?

MORENO: Did not he work it out on the psychodrama stage? If my memory does not fail me he was discharged because of the incident that was diagnosed as an amnestic fugue.

TOEMAN: That's right. When he portrayed both the actual and psychodramatic dimension, this byplay took place alongside the "real" scenes. Not only was he producer and subject of both levels of experience, but he was more intense and dynamic in his projections. By contrast, Christopher moved as if in a trance in the projections, pushed by the playwright. It is an "as if" projection.

MORENO: We may put it this way: the play consists actually of two productions. One is that of Christopher living out his torments. The other is that of the playwright that he sandwiches between the actual scenes. Although the author means to imply that they are expressions of experiences going on in Christopher at the time, nevertheless he acts like a god, putting them into the play from above without Christopher's consent, whereas in psychodrama both productions are of one piece, dynamically unfolded by the subject. That may be one of the reasons for the artificiality of the projected parts in *Christopher Blake*.

TOEMAN: As long as the author moves "as Christopher" his language has a certain natural flow but when he assumes the role of god on behalf of Chris he becomes peculiarly unreal. Obviously, in the "as if" the playwright loses the capacity of affective speech and produces a distorted pattern of dialogue.

MORENO: I believe I know the cause of this phenomenon. The playwright felt that projected interludes *must* have a sort of *dream* character and be patterned after the distortions of dreams. That is the true reason why some of his projections are artificial, purposely exaggerated and childish, influenced by experiences a person may have had in the course of being psychoanalyzed, especially his dreams. As a matter of fact this very rarely happens in genuine psychodramatic production where subjects have extremely lucid visions of their experiences. When they project them they bring them into a form that has more the character of a created compact whole than of an unreasonable and unorganized dream. The idea of letting Christopher fall into a trance-like or dream state is at the core of his artificiality. Actually Chris did not fall asleep. He was merely sitting in a court anteroom and thinking. Maybe we should invite the author to come to a few psychodrama sessions *before* he writes his next play.

TOEMAN: Nevertheless, you must admit that the playwright has skillfully interwoven or taken advantage of various psychodramatic techniques in the course of these interludes, bringing actual people (the parents of Chris, for example) into them. That is a "realization technique." Trying to influence his mother's decision against divorce by making her watch him as an actor portraying the woes of a "divorce orphan," that is like a mirror technique. There are "future projections" in which Christopher's parents have landed in the poorhouse while he is in a powerful position as a wealthy ranch owner adopted by South American foster parents.

MORENO: Admittedly these are quasi-psychodramatic techniques. But apart from them the play as a whole is more like a dream than the real thing. There is no adequate motivation given why the two parents should divorce at all. If the author had brought a third person bodily into the conflict, another man or woman, it might have attained a great deal of strength. All the psychodramatic techniques he employs don't help Christopher to make a decision that is in accord with imaginative logic. Just as the divorce remains unmotivated, so does the choice of the father. The author's own biases may have something to do with the formulation of "causes for divorce" and "choice of parent," a result which, because of its ultimate authoritative manner, may have a deeply untherapeutic effect upon audiences. Here we may consider the harm that even a creative playwright may do to audiences when presenting and solving, without the proper intellectual foundation, such intricate problems as matrimonial conflicts.

TOEMAN: How is it, Moreno, that you who know so much about the drama never became a playwright?

MORENO: True enough. This is a personal question. I was many times on the way to become one, but my "Demon" stopped me, whispering, "How can you write a play before having seen one?" And so I went into a theatre. While I was sitting in the auditorium trying to enjoy the drama in which a then-famous actor, well known for his alcoholic habits, was attempting to play a king, my Demon prevented me from enjoying it by whispering, "He is not the king and does not act like one." I made a scene in the theatre, stopped the action on the stage and harangued the actor to play "himself," not to borrow from a king. I was arrested and forced to leave the theatre. From then on I preferred the drama that comes spontaneously and looked for it in the streets, the homes and the places where people themselves live.

Article 7

The "Double Situation" in Psychodrama

Toeman, Z. (1948) *Sociatry, Journal of Group and Intergroup Therapy* I, 4: 436–446

Zerka's comments

Many of the articles I wrote came from J.L.'s suggestions. However, the writing on doubling is much my own. No one up to that time had articulated the ideas and techniques in a clear and systematic way.

During this time we were traveling around the country giving lectures and demonstrations about psychodrama and group psychotherapy. We were especially invited by Veterans Administration hospitals. This was probably due to recognition of Moreno's work with the military during the war. In addition, the VA hospitals were the institutions that had to deal with the large numbers of returning veterans who needed psychiatric care. We were most frequently invited by psychiatrists from the south. Unlike their northeastern counterparts, many of them were not psychoanalytically trained. Therefore they did not have to shed a professional identity and could more easily accept his ideas. They admired Moreno's refusal to accept the norm and called him "the unreconstructed rebel."

These trips were an education for me. As an immigrant I had stayed mostly on the East coast. I was interested to see the varying reactions among the professionals in other parts of the country as to what we were trying to get across. Accepting the practice of group psychotherapy was easier for most than recognizing Moreno's theories. However, there was beginning to be some recognition of the latter by this time as well. Some state hospitals were starting to use group therapy.

Introduction

It has often been pointed out that psychodrama, similar to sociometric procedure, does not discover anything new, but is able, because of the sophistication and flexibility of its methods, to develop an idea further into its most remote and least obvious ramifications. The double appears in the mythology of many cultures and has been described by some of the great writers of ancient and modern literature. In these descriptions the double is a symbolic experience, performing acts of his own, outside of the volition or control of the subject. The hallucinated double of a mental patient comes into the room, sits down, or, as in the well known case of de Maupassant, dictates his work to him. In the psychodrama the double is an objective experience. Both double and subject perform the same act, think and act at times in unison. De Maupassant's double subjugated him to his will and created his work. It was a figment of his own mind and an "involuntary" production he could not share with another person at the time of its occurrence. The psychodramatic double situation is a voluntary production. The subject has either a major share, or at least an equal share in it.

In an earlier paper I described the double technique in psychodrama (Toeman 1946). The production of the subject and auxiliary ego is a common task, witnessed by every member in the audience. It is not merely something that takes place in the mind of a single individual, but a systematic process taking place in an objective setting. In the "imagined" double experience the subject is generally fearful, or at least fear and panic are the outstanding factors in the situation. In the psychodrama double experience fear may enter into the situation when the subject realizes how much the double knows about him, but it is only one of the factors that operate in it and the fear occurs only occasionally. The more the subject warms up to the double situation, the more he loses his fear.

In literature the double is usually depicted either as the person's better self, as in Edgar Allan Poe's "William Wilson," where the double acted as his guardian angel, or as the person's worse self, as in Robert Louis Stevenson's "Strange Case of Dr. Jekyll and Mr. Hyde." De Maupassant recognized his double as an "Intimate Enemy." In psychodrama no moral values are placed on the double. He is neither the better nor the worse part of the self. He is merely there; at times the better, at times the worse part. Nor is there in psychodrama any clear-cut division between the subject and the double. They are fused and separate and fuse again.

One of the most masterful descriptions of the double phenomenon in literature is repeatedly encountered in the works of Dostoievski. However, he too felt the double to be parts of people; the people so divided are as two halves of a third divided personality, halves which, like the doubles, seek themselves and pursue themselves. In psychodrama the purpose of the double is not to claim or prove that the subject is two people. The double may represent many other reflections of the subject, not merely one. In fact, the more doubles the auxiliary ego can produce the more integrating the double experience will be for the subject. The chief purpose of the psychodramatic double is to stimulate, not to pursue, the subject, to help and retrain, not to persecute. Dostoievski injected his double with all the manifestations of the Devil who comes to the subject and declares himself his double, a creation of Man in his own image. To Dostoievski the double is an hallucination. In psychodrama it is a consciously produced and elaborated experience; the very incarnations of the double are put side by side with the subject on the stage, and there he acts out situations as a real person.

We may, therefore, distinguish three types of doubles, (I) the fictitious double constructed by the fertile imagination of a writer, as Dostoievski, etc., (II) the psychotic double which is an hallucination by a mental patient, and (III) the psychodramatic, therapeutic double which is an *experimental device*; by means of dramatic methods he is given three-dimensional reality.

Double technique and double experience in psychodrama

The function of the auxiliary ego in psychodrama has been described elsewhere (Moreno, J.L. 1946c). Usually it relates to representing absentee members of the subject's world. The double technique, however, is a special technique within the auxiliary ego's sphere. A skilled auxiliary will be quick to gather and use information concerning the subject that has been revealed in previous action or in the pre-double situation interview. This information has to be translated into suitable action on the stage and will act as a preliminary starter for the double situation to be enacted. As the double situation is often entered into when the subject warms up too slowly or is unable to get at basic levels of experience, the auxiliary ego has a particularly difficult task. The subject may produce all kinds of resistances. These the auxiliary ego has to make use of and to work through until the deeper levels are reached.

The double situation with Nancy

The following illustrations will serve to explain how the double situation in psychodrama develops.[1] Our first subject, whom we shall call Nancy, was a young married woman who came to us with her husband to obtain some counseling, ostensibly because of problems with her mother-in-law. When we began by psychodramatically exploring the marital relationship, the husband sat on the edge of the stage, watching the scene. We learned how they had met, courted and married and how they lived. We were thus able to assess their total relationship up to the present.

Nancy was tense, unable to warm up freely and, in her anxiety, resisted the development of a session. It became more evident that the mother-in-law problem was only a minor issue. The director decided to use the "double technique." The scene was set late at night. The subject (and I as her double) was preparing to go to bed. Bedtime is a good setting. It is a time for self-reflection and self-revelation, and for reviewing the day's happenings.

Nancy began to reflect upon how she really felt about her marriage, how she often felt alone, and it suddenly became clear that she was three months pregnant. This changed the tone of the situation and I seized upon it at once by including "our baby" into her musings. Nancy tried to escape this by calling out to her husband (who was watching from the group), asking him to come to bed, reminding him to turn out the lights when he did, etc. I continued to try and warm her up by reflecting on whether the baby would be a boy or girl, whether my husband was happy about the event, whether I was glad, whether the marriage was ready for such a complication, etc. Nancy responded to all these remarks in a superficial, unrealistic, slightly manic fashion. She stressed only the "good" things in her life, avoiding all consideration of conflict, difficulties and responsibilities. I began to press closer, questioning "our" maturity for parenthood, worrying about the financial situation since I would no longer be able to work (her husband was getting his Ph.D. and she worked to support them), what the baby would do to me, whether I would be disfigured or incapacitated after the event.

Nancy persisted in her negative warm-up and responded, "What's the use of worrying about such things? We are both so happy that I'm going to have a baby," etc. However, her body no longer conveyed this. Her back had begun to slouch and her face was increasingly furrowed and worried.

The director decided to use the future projection technique at this point, to "rehearse" the future, as it were. He changed the scene: "This is the hospital, the labor pains have begun, the baby is about to be born. Now go ahead, both of you." At this point I felt that Nancy was far more frightened than she had allowed herself to admit. By warming up to Nancy's world I was carried away from myself and I became like Nancy. I could feel like her and with her. Thus I felt that she realized that her production up to now had been unrealistic, but that she was slow to warm up to the double situation. The director moved towards me and prompted me to warm up to the pain, the suffering and so on, but I had already warmed up to my fear of death, death of the baby, my death, who would take care of my husband and "our baby" in that case, that I could but briefly dwell upon the pain as prompted, and began to tremble. I noticed that Nancy, too, was trembling. I said, "I hope everything goes alright" and began to weep. Some audience members told me after the session that Nancy had already started to weep, but I had not noticed it until after I wept myself. I became further involved in her fears when I saw that she too, was weeping. I said: "I hope I won't die." Suddenly Nancy sighed deeply and almost whispered, "No, I don't want to die." Later Nancy asked a friend of hers to convey to me the reasons for her fear. Nancy, a Catholic, had married out of the faith. Many of her problems with her husband arose from this. However, she now admitted that she was afraid of what would happen to her if she should lose her life in childbirth, for she and her child would be without protection in the hereafter in purgatory. As a Jew, I had no knowledge of these religious implications. However, I did catch her fear of death.

This was the moment for me to retract and get back to the positive aspects of the situation, so I said, "Well, I'll probably be alright. People don't die of childbirth these days. This is not the eighteenth century. Doctors know so much about these things today." This reassured Nancy, who said: "He's supposed to be a very good doctor and he told me everything was going just fine." I answered: "Sure, I'm young and healthy, and it will all be over in no time."

After this scene a good deal of reassurance had to be maintained for the subject, so the following scene was a future projection with Nancy and her husband, allowing her complete freedom of expression. She projected the baby as a girl, six months old. Nancy displayed far greater imagination and authority in this scene than heretofore, having been very much dominated by her husband's presence up to this point. The emotional power of doubling had freed her to approach the future with more confidence.

The double situation with Linda

The second case is that of a young woman whom we may call Linda. She had recently divorced her husband and was fearful about her future relationships to men, although she did not realize this. Linda produced first a number of scenes with various men of her acquaintance, warming up only on the superficial, social levels. Then the director suggested a double situation. She tried continuously to slip out of the situation, for instance by saying: "Let's go and tell Mary [roommate] about what happened at school today. She'd laugh at that story with John," or "I forgot to brush my teeth and have to go the bathroom," "I have to empty the ice box" etc., restlessly moving into the background. I, as the double, at first went along with her in space, copying every one of her gestures, but then, when she had accepted me as her double, I began slowly and gently to counter her: "Mary's asleep, I can't wake her now," "Let's empty the ice box first," "I'm too tired to brush my teeth anyway." This brought the subject back to herself and she began to concentrate on preparing her clothes to wear the next day. I again went along with her but began to move back into the proscenium by refusing to make any more decisions. I walked ahead of her to the bed, which was right in front of the audience and the director.

Now Linda followed my actions, rather than setting them herself. Although no coercion was used, she copied my motions, walked behind me. Then she sat down on the bed. So did I. She took off her shoes, and so did I. At this point I felt from Linda's long pauses between acts, slower, pensive moments, and from the way she responded to the total situation that she had reached a level of deeper reflection than heretofore. Therefore, I immediately moved into the fear I had of meeting men, especially those unknown, the fear of people in general, and how hard I always tried to make a good impression on them. Linda agreed at once: "That's what Dick [husband] always used to tell me. I try so hard to overcome my fear that I become overexcited and exhibitionistic. I go out of my way to attract attention and become unnatural." This was the first time she agreed with me. Up to this point she neither denied nor agreed with anything I produced. She merely jumped from one situation to another. Now she began to enlarge upon my production and became enveloped by the process. It had taken a good deal of fencing around the superficial aspects of her life before we could enter into the deeper ones. From this point on Linda warmed up more and more.

It was a fascinating series of stepping-stones in our mutual feeling (tele) process. Once the mutual tele pattern had been sufficiently established for the basic relationship the rest followed easily. In fact, at one point the director asked me to sit down, and Linda said, "Give me back my double!" which he did.

The director asked Linda whether she had lately had a dream. Linda answered: "I often dream." The director instructed us then to fall asleep and to try to dream; he suggested that we see the same things in our dream, and to enact this dream together. We warmed up to sleep and after a little while stepped out of bed. Linda did not speak. I realized that she had not mentioned her parents in the previous scenes at all, but that the dream concerned them, so I took a chance: "It's about Mother and Dad." Linda countered, "Yes, and in our house in Connecticut, our old home. But it's much larger, and it's growing larger all the time." I said, "I'm scared. It's so weird, why should the house grow like this?" Linda: "And what are all these people doing here? I suppose it's one of Mother's socials. I just can't bear them. I'm going to get out of this." Double ego: "I always want to run away and hide when these people swarm around the house. But where can I go without being seen?" Linda: "To my room upstairs, that's where I'll go. Dad, where's Dad? I don't see him. He hates these affairs of Mother's as much as I do, but somehow he gets away with it. I've just got to go upstairs." Double ego: "What will Mother say if she finds out?" Linda: "I don't care, though I guess she'll be mad at me. Oh, where are those stairs? Here they are, and all the time the house is changing. Blue walls? I never saw such a color in this house before!" Double ego: "It's most peculiar. Let's go upstairs."

Upstairs Linda thought she'd better go down again. Linda: "Where are those stairs now? I've got to get down or Mother will scold me. Where are they?" Here she began to run around the stage wildly, looking for the stairs. Her gestures were frantic and her voice rose in pitch. She became far more intensive and dramatic than before. She pointed: "Look! Oh, look!" Double ego: "Where have they gone? Oh, what's happened to them?" Linda: "There they are. They're just a big, black, gaping hole. That's where that woman threw down my shoes. I suppose I'll have to jump down." Double ego: I don't want to jump down there. I'm scared." Linda: "I've got to jump down. I've got to get downstairs. I've got to find my shoes." Both of us jumped down. The director told Linda to replay the last part of the dream alone, the part about the stairs, but she was unable to warm up until the auxiliary ego again took the double role alongside of her. Linda (voice and movements still more frantic than before): "Oh, where are those stairs? Where did they go? How could they disappear like that? How can I get down without them?" Double: "I'll have to find the other stairs, then" (walked around to the other side of the stage, Linda following). Linda: "No, I won't go down there. They're the ones Mother told me she and brother fell down. I don't want to fall down them and hurt myself." Double ego: "But I've got to get down there somehow! How will I get down if I don't use these?" Linda: "I don't want to fall down these steps, I won't go down there. Mother threatened me that I might fall down and harm myself or she might fall down them again and die. She passed out once from falling down them. I can't use these stairs."

Analysis of double technique and double experience

Besides the techniques described in my previous paper, techniques of the pure action type have been found extremely useful with subjects who produce great resistance to start with or a growing resistance in the course of the double situation. The rapport between the subject and the auxiliary ego may be fairly well established on the surface of the verbal associations. Everything seems to run smoothly and the subject appears cooperative. Suddenly the auxiliary ego double feels that the subject tries to bring the double situation to a premature end, that the maximum of production and catharsis has not been reached yet; she realizes that the subject is afraid of what she may reveal if she warms up still further and therefore attempts to interrupt or terminate the double situation. The double ego may, on the verbal level, be soft, gentle, permissive, but produce counter-actions, which are intended to draw the subject back into the situation. For instance, a subject says, "I'm tired now. Let's go to sleep," then she closes her eyes and withdraws from any action; or she may say suggestively to her double, "Let's go into the other room and undress, to get ready for bed" and start to remove herself physically from the scene. Then the double may get into an opposite motion; walk around the subject before she can step off the stage, or get off the bed or chair and break into all kinds of actions that suggest to the subject motorically to stay in the scene and to *continue, to warm up in a different direction.* Just as the resistance of the subject may be silent, so the aggression and persistence of the ego is equally silent, gestural and motorically active.

After this phase is successfully completed, it is interesting to watch a subject when she begins to warm up and accept the double as if she would really be her double. Then the subject stimulates the double to an idea or action, but in reverse, the double stimulates the subject to an idea or action. The closer the double gets to the subject, the more the subject warms up and reveals further experiences. The most intimate personal experiences of the subject are thus highly intensified. It is interesting to note that it is not necessary for the double to be always of the same sex as the subject. Double situations with mixed sexes have been produced effectively and with the subject losing the sense of the presence of a member of the opposite sex and fully accepting the double in terms of a representation of himself or herself.

The illustration of Linda's double production shows the amount of material which can be obtained by the double dream method when the subject is carefully guarding her secrets, anxious not to give herself away. Through the dynamics of the warming up process she was gradually led into her own lifeline and could not resist until the whole episode had been entirely lived out. The latter part of her dream production turned out to be not a dream (as the first part had actually been, and one she had recently dreamt), but an incident which had occurred when her mother had guests in the house, the same house in which Linda had been married but in which her parents no longer lived.

The stimulus that comes to the subject from the body image of the double, when the double lowers his head with the subject, moves his arm with the subject, closes his eyes with the subject, the animal effect of the mere doubling up of the same gestures, purely physical, have a profound effect in producing in the subject the image of a co-existing body and mind. Once this relationship is there, the auxiliary ego can begin to deviate somewhat in action and bodily expression, and stimulate the subject along a different track or set of tracks.

The auxiliary ego started the dream by structuring the situation: "It is strange that I should dream about Mother and Dad." The subject fell in with this and enlarged upon it, producing the house in which she had lived as a child. Her parents had meanwhile moved to a different residence but in the dream Linda was once again a little girl, afraid of meeting her mother's friends at a social gathering. The house looked weird, larger than in reality, and continuously grew until she became so afraid that she had to go upstairs, to her own room, to hide there until the company had left. But when she wanted to return to the stairs again because Mother would be angry, the stairs had disappeared and turned into a gaping black hole into which she finally vanished.

When the latter part of the dream was once again enacted it became evident that these were the stairs down which her mother and brother once fell. Since they were older and more powerful than she, she was afraid to use the stairs for fear of what mother and brother might do to her.

Although the auxiliary ego became far less directive once the subject started her dream, there were a number of times when she was able to stimulate the dreamer by co-experiencing and co-producing, enlarging here and there upon the dream. This is an extremely subtle technique in the double situation and worthy of further study.

The matrix of identity and the double experience

The double experience is probably the foundation of intuitive experiences between lovers, husbands and wives, intimate friends, and may be the basis for what is called "identification" by psychoanalysts. The old Indian *Twa ma si*, "this is me," is another, religious confirmation of the double experience. The role experience of spectator in a theater is a double experience. It is the experience of identity – and not identification, which implies that the self and the mirror are not the same thing, but that the subject imagines that they are the same by adding something to it or subtracting something from it. It is probable that in the double situation one of the oldest experiences of the infant and child is paralleled and that is perhaps the reason for its enormous effectiveness. It is the experience of the child looking into a mirror and seeing another child, a stranger, but someone who looks and acts like himself.

According to spontaneity theory, the first matrix of experience is the matrix of identity. The bodies of several individuals and the shapes of many objects have a share in it. If the double experience would be a transference relationship of the subject towards the double, nothing essential would come of it, except the free association and delusions the subject has in reference to the double. Conversely, if it would be a transference relationship of the double towards the subject, nothing could come of it either, unless the subject would be of such extreme suggestibility that everything produced by the double would be blindly accepted, which has never happened to date. Furthermore, the double experience cannot be explained only by the empathy that the double may have in regard to the subject. Some elements of transference, as well as some elements of empathy, may operate in the relationship, but through empathy or transference alone the double is not able to intuit certain elements which the subject may feel at the time of the double situation.

According to admissions from subjects, what is particularly striking to them is when the auxiliary ego seems to divine something which the subject tries to hide, or of which he was not fully aware; but when struck by this phenomenon of insight which the auxiliary ego seems to have he enlarges on the spot. The auxiliary ego, made bolder by this, retorts with further additions, to which the subject again adds new pieces and this process goes back and forth from subject to ego and ego to subject, until the whole configuration of an experience is lived out. This is not only true on the verbal level, but perhaps still more profoundly on the action level. The double ego, for instance, begins to weep and that is exactly what the subject was on the verge of doing, and now the subject weeps with the ego. Or the ego strikes his head with his fists and the subject goes a step further and jumps down. The subject will say that he wanted to do that; he wanted to hurt himself and die. This two-way feeling out, the auxiliary ego first feeling out the subject, and the subject feeling out the ego, that is, what the ego feels out about himself, produces an interaction on the depth level. It does not deal with projected material but with real events. It is a tele phenomenon. The two doubles are held together by a tele experience; empathy and transference play some part in it but they do not represent the core of the processes of the relationship.

In the double situation what often most propels the subject to a similar experience beneath the surface is the distressed facial expression of the double, gestures he makes; the words he speaks may be immaterial or rather incidental because as the subject warms up to the same or a similar gestural pattern the verbal follows automatically.

An important phase in the double situation is when the double gives herself the fullest possible receptivity by repeating the words of the subject in an auxiliary ego sense, by repeating the feelings the subject has, feelings of mourning, of joy, or resentment, anger or hostility. By giving the subject the experience that the double next to him feels the same feelings, by actually giving him that feeling of identity which we discussed before, the discovery that there is someone in space who is not himself but still entirely like himself, a double who knows everything about him because he *is* himself, who at times reveals certain parts of him which he is not able to reveal himself and so represents an indispensable component of his psyche, the link is established. The double is the beginning of a society. He has always been unconsciously aware that he exists, but it is only in the double situation of the psychodrama that he is brought into the full reality of daylight.

This phase of whole identity is only one of the phases characteristic of the double experience. At times a second phase sets in. The double systematically and consciously elaborates the feelings that the subject has by multiplying their intensity or their quantity. If the subject is somewhat sad, the ego becomes doubly depressed. If the subject is glad about a relation, the ego magnifies it further, far beyond the admission of the subject. This phase of extending the subject's feeling levels has two purposes. On one hand it is meant to bring the subject to agreement with those extensions and to stimulate additional dimensions, on the other hand to provoke him to halt the double's aperçus.

Another phase is one in which the double becomes highly directive and bold in remarks and actions. The subject may show considerable aggression and resentment and produce counter aggression in which the double immediately joins with a permissive and cooperative attitude as if nothing had happened. Still another phase occurs when the double anticipates the subject's actions in the future – what he will do tomorrow.

The deepest and rarest phase in the double experience is when the subject loses the feeling that the double is another, he is like in a "double trance." The threshold[2] between them is gone; he and the double are one. This may well be the basis for the mystic idea of oneness and for the mediumistic experiences described by psychic researchers.

The problem of validation and double "control"

In order to estimate the validity of the double experience the following experimental design was set up: The double situation with Linda was electrically[3] and stenographically recorded, both verbal and action elements. Immediately after the session the double situation with Linda was replayed in the presence of the subject and every item presented to her for evaluation. In the process analysis over two hundred items, either verbal or action elements, were counted. Every verbal repartee of the double was considered a unit, and every action was considered as a unit, whether it was accompanied by words or not. In the course of replaying the record the subject warmed up again to her own attitude during the session and scored the responses of the double as correct (agreement), incorrect (disagreement), or probable. The score was 82% correct, 10% probably, and 8% inaccurate. By this method an objective estimation as to the accuracy of double experience was possible.

Another design that proved useful was the introduction of a double near the stage as a control to the double in action. The double control, a trained auxiliary ego, attempted to warm up to the subject: a sort of mute audience double. As the production went on she scored the actual double's responses as to agreement, disagreement or probability with her own. She scored on a sheet of paper the difference between her own double experience and the experience of the double actor on the stage. A 68% agreement between the double actor and the double was found.

Chapter 2

Early Pioneers

1949–1965

Role Reversal

If you and me
each other can be
will it not rob each
of individuality?

Oh, no,
we decree,
to the contrary.

If I can be me
sufficiently,
I can enter into
your identity.

Then, if you can be
yourself equally,
you can learn
to be me
eventually.

From *Love Songs to Life*
Zerka T. Moreno

Article 8

History of the Sociometric Movement in Headlines

Toeman, Z. (1949) *Sociometry, A Journal of Inter-Personal Relations* XII, 1–3: 255–259

Zerka's comments

1948 and 1949 were milestone years for me personally. In 1948 my parents came to the USA for a three-week visit. It was the first time we'd seen each other since my departure from England in 1939. In that intervening time I had found my career.

Moreno's divorce became final in 1949. On December 8 of that year, he announced, "Well, tonight we're getting married." He had obtained a special permit. The ceremony was held at 7:00 p.m. at a Justice of the Peace in Cold Spring, NY. I was surprised by the suddenness of the decision. Not only was he thinking of my welfare after his death, but also of the work we had been building. Neither of us wanted that to be jeopardized. After the wedding we went back to the office. So we were married between two lines of a manuscript.

This article reflects my role as "recordkeeper and documentarian." I did the major reporting job for the journal. I not only wrote, but edited the articles in each one. This was sometimes a challenge because many contributors were refugees and their first language was not English. I supervised the mailing of the journals, and many times had blisters on my fingers from putting them in envelopes. Often patients would help us get out the mailings. It gave them a chance to be part of the community.

The history of the sociometric movement falls naturally into three periods: (a) the period during which Moreno lived in Europe and was the only writer on the subject, preparing the foundations for inter-personal theory and the experimental study of small groups, from 1905 to 1925; (b) the period during which he lived in the United States, and found here a growing number of collaborators and co-creators in the development of sociometric theory and practice, from 1925 to 1941; (c) the period during which sociometry and sub-disciplines came to be generally accepted and universally applied, from 1941 up to the present.

Moreno is the founder of sociometry, psychodrama and group psychotherapy. But it may well be that he will be longer remembered as the creator of social inventions without which these new disciplines might never have reached the scientific stage. He invented the *open, multidimensional, circular stage*, without being an architect. He invented the *living, dramatized newspaper* without being a newspaperman. He brought it to the United States in 1925 and the idea of instantly transmitted news reached wide popularity through such newsreels as the *March of Time*. Only a few scientific writers are aware that it was first introduced by Moreno in Vienna in 1924, as a segment of the Theatre of Spontaneity.

Moreno invented the electric "*psycho-recording*," the idea of transcribing and "playing back" sound phenomena for exploratory and therapeutic aims. He proposed this idea in 1925, as spelled out in his *Application of the Group Method to Classification*, 1931, and has been for years its persistent advocate. Psycho-recording is now universally applied and has become an almost indispensable tool in the hands of the psychotherapists. Non-directive counselors, psychoanalysts, and group psychotherapists have been using it since 1941.

He invented, among other procedures, the *sociogram, psychodrama, sociodrama*, and the *psycho-therapeutic motion picture*. These inventions have one thing in common: their artistic character of conception, initiating a new era in the development of the social sciences, the arts coming to their rescue and aiding towards a synthesis.

First period, 1908–1925

1908–1912	Group psychotherapy applied to children, Vienna.
1911	Theatre of Spontaneity for children, Vienna.
1913–1914	Group psychotherapy applied to deviates, Vienna.
1914–1924	Development of inter-personal theory.
1917	Letter to the Department of the Interior, Austro-Hungarian Monarchy, suggesting a sociometric scheme for reorganization of Mittendorf, a resettlement community near Vienna. The term "sociometry" used for the first time.
1921	Psychodrama at the Komoedienhaus, Vienna, the first large-scale public session.
1922	Opening of the Stegreiftheater (Theatre of Spontaneity) in Vienna.
	Invention of the inter-action diagram.

1924 *Das Stegreiftheater*, a publication. It opened the way for sociometric study as a whole, spontaneity research, role-research, and action-research.

Die Lebendige Zeitung (The Living Newspaper), Vienna.

1924 First exhibit of the multi-dimensional, circular stage at the Internationale Ausstellung Neuer Theatertechnik (International Exposition of New Theater Technique) inaugurated by the city of Vienna.

1924–1925 Invention of the electro-magnetic recording disk (influenced by the work of a Norwegian engineer named Paulsson). Resembling a phonograph record, it records sound on one side and images on the other. Later leads to the idea of recording psychological processes.

Second period, 1925–1941

1925 Moreno comes to the United States on a two-year contract to General Phonograph Corporation, Elyria, Ohio. He tires of working with machines and returns to New York.

1925 Plymouth Church, Brooklyn, NY. Psychodrama applied to a Sunday school; demonstration of psychodrama at Mount Sinai Hospital, Department of Pediatrics.

1929–1930 Impromptu Theater, Carnegie Hall, combining group psychotherapy with psychodrama sessions. Among its visitors were many who later applied psychodrama and group psychotherapy to various social situations.

1931 National Committee on Prisons and Prison Labor convenes during the meeting of the American Psychiatric Association in Toronto. Moreno suggests program on Group Psychotherapy for prisons, mental hospitals, and schools.

The Living Newspaper presented at the Theater Guild.

Sociometric Study at Sing Sing Prison.

1931 Publication of *Application of the Group Method to Classification*. Coining of "group therapy" and "group psychotherapy."

1932 First Round Table Conference on Group Psychotherapy during the meeting of the American Psychiatric Association in Philadelphia, with William A. White, MD as moderator. Dr. White had shown interest in Moreno's inter-personal theory since 1929. Group psychotherapy, sociometry, and role-playing are discussed.

1932–1934 Long range sociometric study at the New York State Training School for Girls, Hudson, New York, in collaboration with Helen H. Jennings.

Sociometric study of a complete public school, P.S. 181, Brooklyn, NY, in collaboration with Helen H. Jennings.

1933 Exhibit of over 100 sociometric charts at the meeting of the Medical Society of the State of New York, held in New York City.

"Psychological Organization of Groups in the Community," an experimental study of small groups, paper read by J.L. Moreno during a joint meeting of the American Association for Mental Deficiency and the American Psychiatric Association, at Boston.

1934 *Who Shall Survive? A New Approach to the Problem of Human Interrelations* by J.L. Moreno, with a preface by William A. White, covering dimensions of community organization, especially home and industrial relations. Published by the Nervous and Mental Disease Publishing Company. First appearance of the sociogram.

1935–1936 US Department of Agriculture and Department of Interior sponsor sociometric research related to subsistence homesteads.

Showing of the therapeutic film *Spontaneity Training* during the meeting of the American Psychiatric Association at Washington, DC.

Development of social microscopy and microsociology, dynamic sociometry, sociodynamics and role playing.

1936 Publication of the *Sociometric Review*, containing among other articles Dr. Winifred Richmond's sociometric research of nursing students at Saint Elizabeths Hospital, Washington, DC, and studies of laissez-faire, authoritarian, and sociometric structure of groups, initiating group atmosphere exploration – since then widely treated and discussed.

1937 First Theatre of Psychodrama built in Beacon, NY.

1937 Founding of *Sociometry: A Journal of Inter-Personal Relations*, first scientific journal bearing this title. Editor: Dr. Gardner Murphy. The first journal contained the following articles:

(a) Inter-personal influence and public opinion research (Moreno, Lazarsfeld).
(b) Sociometry and sociometric status (Lundberg).
(c) Sociometry and leadership (Jennings).
(d) Sociometry of race cleavage (Criswell).
(e) Sociometric analysis of resettlement (Davidson and Loomis).

1937 Round Table Conference on Sociometry held during the meeting of the American Sociological Society, at Atlantic City, NJ. Moderator: Dr. George A. Lundberg.

1938 Sociometry in a Cooperative Community, Hightstown, NJ.

1941 Opening of Theater of Psychodrama at Saint Elizabeths Hospital, Washington, DC. (Pivotal in its implementation were Dr. Winfred Overholser, superintendent, and Margaret Hagan, director of the Red Cross, both at Saint Elizabeths.)

Founding of a publishing house, Beacon House, for sociometric books and monographs. Publication of *The Words of the Father*.

1941–1945 Recognition of group psychotherapy and psychodrama by the United States War Department, Technical Bulletin 103 and War Department Bulletin TBMED84.

1942 First meeting of the American Society of Group Psychotherapy and Psychodrama, New York City.

Founding of Theater of Psychodrama, Psychodramatic and Sociometric Institutes, New York City.

	Introduction of *action* research methods, techniques, tests, and practice.
1942–1944	Sociometric selection methods in the British Army.
1943	Audience research and role analysis (Toeman).
1944	Psychodrama applied to problems of alcoholism.
1944–1947	Psychodramatic Institute, Denver University.
1945–1946	Founding of the American Sociometric Association.
1946–1948	Initiating of psychodrama and role-playing in Veterans Hospitals: West Brentwood, Los Angeles; Lyons, New Jersey; Winter General Hospital, Kansas; Little Rock, Arkansas; etc.
1947	Pastoral psychodrama, pastoral group psychotherapy; Department of Theology, University of Chicago; Church of the Brethren, Illinois.
	Psychodrama at New York University and UCLA.
	Founding of *Sociatry: A Journal of Group and Inter-Group Therapy.*
	Psychodrama in France.
1948	Sociometric Institute, Paris.
1949	Sociometric anthropology (French Oceania).
	Psychodramatic anthropology (Eskimo, Alaska).
	Convention of the American Sociometric Association, New York ASA, Member of the World Federation for Mental Health.
	Spontaneity research in parapsychology (CCNY).
	Psychodrama in prisons (San Quentin, California).
	Spontaneity theatre and psychodrama at Boston Psychopathic Hospital.

Theater of Psychodrama, Harvard University, Henry A. Murray, Director.

1950 Sociodrama session at the Mansfield Theater, New York City. Psychodrama Directors: Anthony Brunse, MD, James Enneis, Ernest Fantel, MD, Robert B. Haas, Helen H. Jennings, Leona M. Kerstetter, J.L. Moreno, MD, Justus F. Randolph, III, Zerka T. Moreno.[1]

Psychodrama in a Well-Baby Clinic

Moreno, Z.T. (1952) *Group Psychotherapy, Journal of Sociopsychopathology and Sociatry* IV, 1–2: 100–106

Zerka's comments

As Moreno's reputation grew, we were invited to hospitals and universities all over the country. In addition to lectures, people wanted to see some practical applications. This is a recounting of our visit to a major university in Georgia. They were particularly interested in Moreno's theories of child development. His main message was that the building of the psyche is done through relationships; the individual must be studied in relation to other human beings.

While Moreno was visiting one academic department, I was invited to the clinic. The doctor and I did not work out ahead of time what would happen; as I state here, at one point he turned to me and this was the spontaneous result.

What was striking for me was that the women were willing to accept this obviously white woman stranger as their baby. They became able to role reverse with their babies and had some significant realizations, like the woman who actually admitted waking her baby up at night because she herself felt lonely. Sometimes we're not aware of what we're doing until it's pointed out to us. The doctor was thrilled because everyone was smiling at the end. Perhaps that was not the norm for these group clinics.

As it happened, I had just found out before this trip that I was pregnant with Jonathan.

Psychodramatic methods have a great field of application in maternity and pediatric clinics. During a recent seminar at a southern university hospital the writer demonstrated the use of such techniques to a pediatrician just engaged in examining a group of babies whose mothers brought them to the clinic for the first check up; the infants were all between four and six weeks old.

In this clinic the only feasible approach to the babies was a group psychotherapeutic one because of the large number who came to the hospital at one time. Each staff member took from six to ten mothers with their babies in one group. They were seated in a circle, with their babies on their laps. The physician and I were seated among them; he asked the mothers to remove the babies' outer clothing.

We had been informed that they were all colored mothers, a number of them unmarried, and that they might be confused by my clipped speech since this was unfamiliar to them. They were new to this entire process – it was their first visit with their babies in arms – and the doctor felt they might be reluctant to confide in him in the presence of a stranger. I began, therefore, to warm up to the group as if I were a part of it, just as the members of a group do in a psychodrama session.

The physician first examined the babies, then interviewed each one of the mothers in turn, and when the initial rapport had been established he inquired whether they had any questions to ask. One or two came forth with a few remarks about minor eruptions on the babies' skin. Some suitable medications and methods for dealing with the irritations were given. I looked around and noticed that the mothers and children were mostly of fairly dark color, with few wedding rings in evidence.

There was one mother–infant pair whose skins were considerably fairer than that of the others. For lack of any better name I shall refer to this mother as Mrs. Jones. She was furthermore neatly and expensively dressed, had on a wedding ring, some costume jewelry and looked and acted very tense. The group's talk came around to diaper rash and this time Mrs. Jones, who had been very reticent up to that point, stated that her daughter had some eruptions she could not deal with and which might be diaper rash. The physician asked her to show them to him and as she opened the diaper of her little girl she turned away her nose in disgust at its odor. The physician had told me that in general these mothers were extremely loving, very permissive, feeding their children whenever necessary without much attention to time or place, and I did indeed see several mothers breastfeed their babies in the course of the session. Not so Mrs. Jones. Her child was examined as was each one of the others for similar difficulties. Again some suitable recommendations were made by the physician who then sat down once more, becoming a member of the group.

He looked around the circle and asked the entire group: "Do you have any feeding problems with your babies?"

Most of the mothers shook their heads: "No."

"What remarkable children, or maybe you are all remarkably fine mothers."

This double-headed dart from the physician reached its mark.

One mother, the one seated at his immediate right, spoke up: "Well, I did have some trouble with her, she was spoon-fed some vegetables this week and she spit them out."

At this point the physician looked at me inquiringly and challengingly, as if to say: "What does a psychodramatist do in such a situation?"

I fell into line and *took the part of the baby*. In a very soft, rather weak but appealing voice I said: "Well, those vegetables don't taste so good after the milk. I'm not used to them yet. They're kind of rough on my sensitive mouth. I don't like them so I spit them out, I don't know what else to do with them, it hurts me to swallow them. After all, I'm only a month-old baby." The mothers looked at me, surprised at my entry into the situation and startled by this turn of events. Slowly I saw one after another beginning to smile, especially the mother who had brought up this problem.

The physician asked her, "Do you think your baby could be thinking this?"

"Yes, she could."

"Do you think she might resent you if you continue to do this?"

"Yes, she might."

"What made you start her on vegetables?"

"*I* did not start, it was my mother."

In the south certain feeding customs prevail and generally the grandmothers take an active part in the rearing of children, especially if the child's mother is very young and has to work.

The physician then asked, "Was it her own idea or was it someone else's, a friend of your mother, who had urged her to try to give your baby vegetables so soon?"

The mother answered, "I don't know."

"Perhaps the baby is not ready for such food yet. Maybe you had better wait a while until we tell you about solid food and what to give her."

This was met with general approval from the group and the particular mother said: "Alright, I will tell my mother not to try vegetables any more."

The ice began to break very fast now and the warming up process spread from mother to mother. Several women began simultaneously to speak of feeding problems. One said, "I don't give my baby vegetables yet, I breast-feed her and I give her very little milk at one time. And still she throws it up, you see?" She had been feeding the child and held the baby up to the physician to show him what had just occurred.

He asked her, "Do you burp her sufficiently?"

She replied, "I think I do."

Again the physician looked at me as he were prompting me to step into the breach. Taking the role of the baby I said: "She puts me down too fast. I can't eat that quickly, so I bring up the milk with the burp."

The physician looked away from me at the actual child whom I represented. "Yes," he said, "it looks more like a wet burp than vomiting. (*To the mother*) Why don't you give the baby more time? I'm sure that is what she needs, now that I see her do it."

The mothers all smiled at this and the guilty one looked lovingly and apologetically at her baby. The physician grinned at me as if we were in cahoots and I continued, in the role of the baby: "After all, I'm not as much of a hustler as she is and besides, I have all the time in the world. She forgets, I'm still very small and helpless, it takes me some time before I can bring up a burp."

"Alright," said the mother, "I'll take it easier with you from now on." She addressed the baby and the group at one time. The mothers began to smile directly at me as if I really were their baby and the talk began to deal with another problem, that of sleeping.

One mother stated, "You know, my baby frets at night, although he sleeps beautifully during the day. But at night I don't know what to do with him, he's so fretful and restless. I have to get up early in the morning and can't always wake up and caress him and play with him during the night. I'm so sleepy I often can't hold him. Once or twice I fell asleep again before he did and I could hear him cry and fret in my sleep."

This was my cue again, especially as we saw how several mothers warmed up very much with the last speaker who was, incidentally, sitting close to me. "What's the matter with mothers," I said, again in the role of the baby, "I am a little tiny baby, I don't know night from day, whether it's early or late. All I know is that when I wake up and everything is so quiet, I'm lonely. Every one else is asleep or dead or something and it's dark. Then I get scared and I start to cry. I want my Mummy and I want some companionship and comforting. During the day I see things and people moving and I hear voices of people or grownups or somebody and people come to me; they talk to me or smile at me or pick me up and love me. I don't feel the same way at night, only I don't know it is *because* it is night, I'm just scared to be all by myself in the world, I feel so lost."

At this all the mothers shook their heads affirmatively. The majority of them started to talk rapidly, confirming the fact that during the day their babies were quiet and happy. One mother raised her voice and said slowly, "That's true. I guess they don't know day from night." Another chimed in, "I don't mind taking care of the baby if I'm not asleep or tired, I pick him up and make him feel good, play with him and all."

The physician asked, "Maybe you all would not mind turning night into day." Several answered him to the effect that they would not mind "if they could only sleep during the day instead."

The mother who brought up the problem had become pensive and suddenly came out with "You know, come to think of it, I myself feel lost at night when I'm not asleep and I wake him up to play with me."

The mothers smiled again. The physician asked them, "How many of you feel lost and alone when you wake up at night and everyone else is asleep?" Quite a large number conceded they did feel that way, although they "do not always wake up the baby to keep them company."

The discussion lasted for some time until one mother said, "Well, I understand all that, but sometimes my baby cries and I don't always know why, or what to do about it."

This was quite a challenge, so I tried to warm up again to the mother who had raised this point and to the role of her baby and said, "Sometimes I just like to cry, not because I'm unhappy, but because it makes them pay attention to me. It is not always fun to be left alone. Other times I cry because I'm uncomfortable. I want to turn over and can't do it all by myself. Or my clothes are creased and that hurts me or my diaper rubs me sore. Of course *they* think it is good for a baby to cry, that it helps his lungs to develop. I don't know about that, I just cry."

The physician asked the mothers, "What do you think? Could that be how the baby feels when it cries and you don't know why?"

They nodded their heads affirmatively, smiling at me. The whole session was now running entirely on its own momentum. Unfortunately the period allotted was coming to an end. Quite unpredictably – and we know that the warming up process is responsible for this total contagion – Mrs. Jones, who had all this time remained more aloof than the other members stated, "I don't know, there have not been any babies in my family as far back as I can remember. I should feel better about her. I was a schoolteacher before I married, but somehow I just can't seem to get adjusted to having a baby around the house. Everything seems to be going wrong, mostly in the way I feel about her. I can't get used to her at night *or* by day. I sometimes have to go out for some errands during the day and when I return everything seems to be more difficult than before I left."

At this point the physician suggested that Mrs. Jones return for an individual meeting with him, when he would work out her difficulties more intensively and an appointment was made to this end.

The rest of the group now began to tell the doctor how much they had enjoyed this visit.

He asked them, "Did you learn something from this meeting?"

The mother with the night owl baby said, "I think she [looking at me] helped us a lot. Now I, anyway, understand better why my baby acts as he does. Do you feel that way too?" She turned to her neighbors and looked about the group. They nodded their affirmation.

One mother said to me, "I hope you will be here again the next time I come."

Article 10

Psychodrama in the Crib

Moreno, Z.T. (1954) *Group Psychotherapy, A Quarterly Journal* VII, 3–4: 291–302

Zerka's comments

This article was written when Jonathan was a little over two years old. In some ways our home and family life was a perfect laboratory. We wanted to share whatever we discovered there that we felt would be useful for people to know.

The problem is that our classical academic learning process (extracting experience from content) is totally wrong. In the psychodrama context, first comes experience, then comes learning.

The infant, when he enters the world, passes from the womb into the crib, which becomes his first shelter. According to Moreno's theory of the Matrix of Identity (Moreno, J.L. 1943) he soon discovers two crutches, (a) the *mother-subject* in the various roles of protector, nurse, co-sleeper, etc., and (b) the *mother-object* in the various forms of bed, pillow, blanket, etc. The "mother-object" is a neglected phenomenon in psychological literature but every mother knows how long children, often into their third and fourth year, cling to some object, a blanket for instance, treating it like a fetish and carrying it around wherever they go.

It has been found useful to differentiate in the development of the infant three trends: the stage of the double, the stage of the mirror, and the stage of role reversal (Moreno, J.L. 1952). The technique used by the mother or mother-surrogate to act as the double of the infant is a counterpart to the double technique in adult psychodrama. It is postulated that the body–mind recognition in the physical mirror is a forerunner to the self-recognition in the psychodramatic psychological mirror technique. They can well be interpreted as "identity dynamics," expressions of the infant's effort to sustain and reinforce the satisfactions attained in the original matrix of identity.

By means of psychodramatic techniques the veracity of the above-mentioned states can be tested and emotional as well as social disturbances in the infant's world corrected.

The dramatis personae in this report are a mother, a baby, a daddy and a doll.

The double and the mirror

At the age of five and a half months, when placed before a large mirror in which he could see himself, Jonathan crawled up to the mirror, placed his right hand with outspread fingers on the mirror, moved the hand back and forth, tried to match every mirror finger with one of his own, finally hitting with the flat of his palm against the mirror and watching carefully what the mirror hand was doing. Then he proceeded to do the same thing with his left hand, repeating his effort, and finally combined this activity with both hands at the same time, simultaneously examining intently the baby's face in the mirror. When this was all over he kicked with both legs at the mirror legs. It was a total involvement of his actions with the counter-actions of the mirror baby. He was amused at the simultaneous and symmetric character of the operations and the fact that one digit seemed to correspond to the other, something that he had not seen with any of his dolls. It was a double and a mirror experience although he obviously did not realize that the other baby was himself. What seemed to puzzle him was the simultaneity of the collateral bodily actions of which he was the author and changer.

The next step in this mirror imagery took place some six weeks later, at seven months, when Jonathan tried to hand the mirror baby a piece of bread that he was holding. He made several such attempts, first with one, then with the other hand. When he sensed a separation between himself and the other baby he tried to find out what the separation consisted of, put his face on the mirror, particularly his mouth, and tried to explore it. He bumped his forehead against the mirror several times in the course of these attempts, tried to reach for the glass with his lips, laughed and enjoyed this experience. He looked up at his mother who stood behind him, studied her image in the mirror for a while, and then proceeded to hand the bread to his mother's mirror image. The final step in this development occurred when Jonathan at the age of fourteen months recognized himself to be the baby in the mirror. He did this by pointing at himself and at the photographs of himself that he was holding while standing before the mirror, as well as indicating pictures of himself on the wall. Then he began to roam around the house to try and locate other pictures of himself and when he did, recognized them as representations of himself. Before mirror recognition is reached the child cannot put himself in the place of another, reverse roles and become a fully fledged member of a social group.

Auxiliary ego and role reversal

The need of co-acting and co-living with an auxiliary ego[1] was evident when Jonathan was a very small baby, clinging to his mother's breast. As soon as he was able to grab food in his fist and eat in this manner he would stretch out his hand to the person who offered him the food and offer a bite in return. The baby was about nine months old when he became sensitive to role reversal and extending his identity. The next step in this development occurred with toys. When given one of his favorite playthings, he would take it without playing with it and hand it back to the auxiliary ego who gave it to him. To test out whether this was a mere accident, the same or another toy would be given to him and the child went through the same motion of accepting and returning it, as if to say "I don't want to play with it now. You play with it." When he tired of this repeated interchange he turned his head away from both the toy and the auxiliary ego, the same way in which he later refused food when he had had sufficient.

In a more articulate stage of development, when Jonathan was twenty-eight months old, he hit his head against a projecting drawer while picking up a dropped toy. When he realized what had hit him he grabbed his mother's head and tried to push it, too, against the objecting object. His mother stopped him from doing so and asked him, "Did the drawer hurt you? Do you want me to 'bump my head' too?" Jonathan replied "Yes, Mummy bump head too." The auxiliary ego thereupon lightly bumped her head against the drawer, called Jonathan's father and he, too, in turn "bumped his head." All this took place to Jonathan's great delight. The meaning of this is that the child obviously required some co-experience of the hurt he had innocently suffered. The auxiliary ego did not permit a blind acting out of this co-experience by letting him vent his anger and hurting her in turn. Instead, she stopped his aggression, faced him with her willingness to experience the same hurt voluntarily, on the spot, and with his acquiescence repeated the "bump on the head," then called in his father as another supporting ego. This is a "deliberate" technique, permitting the child to share his experiences, whether traumatic or joyous. In the case of a traumatic experience the delight of this co-living is evident and in the subsequent laughter the child's hurt is washed away.

Baby language

At approximately the same time as mirror negotiation reaches a climax (ten to fourteen months old), the baby language becomes more nearly structured. It is a psychodramatic language, without logical structure and without grammar. Jonathan's babbling at this time had specific and repetitious sound configurations, which were the matrix upon which gradually the meaningful words of the mother tongue are built. At this time also, the use of the baby's own language towards him by parents and nurses becomes obviously useful as a form of speech communication and arouses in the infant not only repetition and imitation but actual repartees. Adult and infant now speak to one another, via the baby language, the adult by using the child's technique of babbling deliberately and employing the sound configurations that the baby has devised. This babbling of the infant associates with anger, fear, denial, protest and approval of all sorts. Now that he is in the stage of role reversal, his ability and striving to learn the actual words spoken by the adults toward him will become very strong; the beginning of learning the adult language. It is also at this time that his independence from an auxiliary ego in the feeding situation is growing. He tries to feed himself, and also at this time, his favorite form of locomotion becomes walking instead of crawling or being carried by an auxiliary ego. Encouraging the systematic use of baby language and sharing the baby language with the child to the point of socializing it helped Jonathan to emancipate himself with comparative ease from the baby language ("nature's tongue") into the mother tongue.

Psychodrama *in situ*

As the child grows older, particularly from about the second year on, the drive towards self-realization of projects becomes more and more insistent. "Let me sit here," "Baby do this," "Shall we go bye bye new car?" "Want to go out," "Sit Mummy lap," "Want to see Daddy," and so forth. There are two customary ways in which parents approach the child in such situations. Either they *agree* with him and take him for a drive, let him go out in the fresh air, let him see Daddy, take him on their lap, or they *oppose* him. The "yes" approach leads to more and more, and apparently endless demands for the realization of the little projects and may not always be possible or convenient, requiring more attention than can be made available. The "no" approach leads to repeated frustration, disappointment and finally rebellion.

There is a third method, the psychodramatic approach. It is based on the well-founded hypothesis that a child does not always require the realistic living through of a project. His act hunger can be frequently satisfied equally well by a shortcut, with playing it through. This means playing through the situation in every detail, but on the imaginary level. It is of a therapeutic and cathartic nature, a deliberate, dramatized extension of what the child does when he plays alone. The mother picks up the child and says: "Let's play 'going downstairs.'" She now goes through the motions of going down the stairs without moving but a few inches forward. It is a shortcut of going down, a first step towards it, and parallels what the child expects when he actually goes down, but he is satisfied with a fragment. Now the mother goes to the next step: "Here we are downstairs, and here is Daddy," pointing at a distance in space. "How are you Daddy?" The baby throws back his head and laughs, "falling into the role" and playing his part. He plays his part without resistance because this is positively what he expects to happen after he goes downstairs to "see Daddy" and so he is satisfied. The inventive mother then says, "Now let's say goodbye to Daddy, throw him a kiss and say good night." That he may not always expect. It is a negative interpolation. This is something he may at times resent, but he is now sufficiently warmed up and involved in playing it through, so that he also does this with a gesture of tolerance, at times with enjoyment.

Now the mother proceeds to return to the room "upstairs," going up the steps, walking down the corridor, rhythmically proceeding towards the crib and gently caressing him while returning him to bed. *All this takes place in the child's room.* Such exercises are an important training in the perennial struggle during one's lifetime between the fantasy and reality dimensions. Analytically, there is here a distinction to be made (a) between the child's playing by himself or (b) playing with other children, (c) the mother's playing with the child and (d) this kind of playing which is designed to overcome an immediate difficulty; it is remedial or "emergent" playing, "Psychodrama *in situ*." Therefore, *it has to be carefully structured on the basis of clues that the child provides.* It is not only a matter of diverting the child's attention, this rarely works. Rather, it provokes the child to insist upon realization. A mother or nurse who knows the child well and has some psychodramatic training and insight will be able to structure the scene effectively. The first alternative of permitting a child always to attain his act hunger's aim results often in unhappy and untherapeutic conduct of the child. The mother then (and in later years the world) "must" do what the child wants; otherwise there is a temper tantrum. This kind of utter permissiveness is love without insight and guidance.

Another illustration of the same technique is the following: Jonathan resisted going to sleep when his bedtime arrived or when his sleep had been prematurely interrupted and would insist upon "come downstairs." The situation would usually terminate in insistent weeping, often lasting for a considerable period when his request was not complied with. Since it was not considered advisable to permit him to warm himself up away from sleep as it might result in a poor sleeping pattern in the long run (letting him have his way had been tried and it usually meant a two-hour play period before he was again ready for sleep), the auxiliary ego decided to insist upon his remaining in his bed, or, at the very least, in his darkened room. But always, when it came to the point of covering him up, he would return to his demand obstinately, until his mother said one morning (2:00 a.m.) "I cannot bring you downstairs because it is still dark outside" (lifts the shade to prove her statement true and show him) "and Mummy and Daddy are also going to sleep now" (rolls shade down again) "but we will pretend you will go downstairs and say good night to Daddy." (Daddy was in the room with us and he immediately fell into line, placing himself on a chair and waiting for us to appear.) The auxiliary ego picked up Jonathan's pet blanket, wrapped it around him – the same way in which he is usually prepared for bed, after the bath or when not fully dressed, etc., picked up the child, carried him on her arm, started to walk. "Here we are, we are going through the door" (walking around the room and not leaving it) "here we go down the stairs, slowly now, hold on to Mummy" (the way we usually proceed on the steep stairs) "down the last step" (making a sharp right turn to indicate the twisting step) "and here we are in the living room. See, it is quite dark. Look at the windows. It is still night. There is Daddy, sitting at the head of the table in his usual chair. Let's go over to him and say good night to him." Daddy now enters into the action. "Good night, Jonathan. It's time to go to bed." Mother carries Jonathan over to Daddy. Jonathan bends down and gives Daddy his cheek. "Good night, Jonathan." "Good night, Daddy." "Now we go back up the stairs to bed, here we go up the steps. Hold on to Mummy. Here we are at the top of the stairs (circles room again). Here is the door to your room and here is your bed. Let's put Jonathan in bed now." She places child back in his bed.

"Come downstairs," Jonathan insists, but not quite vehemently as he had done prior to the psychodramatic episode, with a smile on his face. Mother answered, "Let's not spoil our little play acting now. Tomorrow morning you can come downstairs." Jonathan laid down easily without further protest, repeated "Tomorrow morning? Oh" and put his head down on the pillow. At this point his father slipped quietly out of the room and Jonathan, quick to notice his departure and to make capital of it, made another attempt. "Daddy, come downstairs?" but seeing no immediate results from this request, he again laid down when his mother asked him, "Do you want to cover yourself, or shall Mummy cover you?" Calmly and confidently he replied, "Mummy cover you." There was no further scene, which was in stark contrast to a few previous nights when this method was not applied and when his batting average for insistent crying ran anywhere from one to two hours. Furthermore, the demand did not recur for a number of days since this psychodramatic enactment, although prior to it, was a regular feature of going to bed. When he repeated his demand a few more times, psychodramatic enactment satisfied him entirely.

Another application of this method occurred about two weeks later when upon the occasion of being put to bed for his afternoon nap, Jonathan asked me, "Mummy dress you." "I cannot dress you now, not until after you have had your nap. But shall we play the little game we did the other day? You can pretend to say 'good night' to Daddy." "Alright," he answered with relish. The mother and child went through a very similar performance as above described, with several significant features added: (1) The child now knew what to expect, and realized he would not actually go downstairs (the initial surprise element was gone) but he willingly cooperated, (2) Daddy was *not* present in the room, and (3) Jonathan threw a kiss at the imaginary Daddy when informed by the auxiliary ego "Here is Daddy, throw him a good night kiss." The child is now able to produce an "absent" person psychodramatically and interact with him as if he were present. The latter enactment had the result of removing this delaying tactic from Jonathan's behavior repertoire when going to bed.

At a later occasion, when he awoke from sleep and asked to "go downstairs," he cried bitterly when told he could "play going downstairs" instead. His mother picked him up nevertheless and started the by now familiar motions, rocking him rhythmically at first. Although he was quite resistant and said "No, no, no," the auxiliary ego persisted, bringing Daddy into the situation *in absentia*. It is to be noted that this time his resistance was far greater. His protest was longer, and yet his warming up process took hold and carried him along into co-living the psychodramatic situation. He responded to Daddy, and when the auxiliary ego said, "Now I will be Daddy" and spoke in a deep masculine voice to the child, asking him for a good night kiss, the child bent over and kissed his mother on the cheeks. From there on the warm up was complete. He accepted a cookie that had been brought to him before the psychodramatic enactment and that he had violently rejected when it was offered as a pacifier, and nibbled contentedly on it when put back into bed. This was, in effect, an extension upon the previous enactments because (1) he had a completely negative warm up to overcome, (2) he accepted his mother in the role of his father and interacted with her on that level and (3) he accepted a previously rejected "real" object. This is like a test of ability to overcome interpolated resistances, and a demonstration of bodily contact (kissing) in imaginary warm up.

Reconstruction of "basic" language as a therapeutic tool

Psychodramatic work with stutterers and speech difficulties has often pointed to a faulty warming up process in the formation of language patterns. Such difficulties arise from a number of sources, one of the main ones being anxiety in speech production. Individuals learn to stutter and stammer, often by having contents that cannot always be put into words or meaningful context fast enough. We have noted that Jonathan has a tendency to lisp and slur over words, half swallowing them, in order to put over his point. It is evident that he knows and cogitates and experiences a great many more things than are possible to fit into the straitjacket of language. Even fairly sophisticated adults are frequently at a loss to find *le mot juste* or even to express simple emotions in suitable language forms. How much more difficult it is then, for small children whose spoken, grammatic language is still in formation.

As we found Jonathan to be a particularly rich producer of basic and baby language prior to his learning to speak, we decided to experiment with basic language as a mode of reducing the restraints and stresses that come with learning to speak, to eliminate anxiety, to make him feel complete master of the language, and to assist him to lose the lisp, stutter and stammer, if possible, by "practicing his spontaneous baby language." It was a remarkable experiment, for although it has been found very difficult to make adults fall into this apparently meaningless form of communication, it is quite evident that young children have not developed this barrier and are still close to the threshold upon which they so firmly stood but a short while ago. Jonathan, for instance, fell into line at once, laughed heartily at the auxiliary ego's sound production, and responded there and then. He did not slur or swallow any sound, though the same cannot be said for the lisp, which continued to appear from time to time. We communicated in his language for quite a little while. We made jokes, and I referred to his favorite blanket which he calls "badum," to anchor the conversation around a tangible object. He answered in his own language, also speaking about badum. On several subsequent occasions when this language was employed the child immediately responded with pleasure. Of late, he has even initiated this type of speech. We are continuing to use this spontaneous sound patter as a guide towards the foundation for good adult speech.

Locus nascendi and the warming up process

It has been hypothecated that the reconstruction of the psychological geography (which includes the physical geography) will assist the protagonist in the warming up to a psychodramatic recall. Although this is clinically demonstrated, it is interesting that confirmation of this phenomenon can be found in children. For instance, Jonathan was sitting with me, side by side in the car, going to the bank. This is a bank with a drive-in window and one day, while waiting our turn at the window, I turned to him, patted him on the arm and said, "You're my little sweetheart." Since then (I do not claim this to be the only time I said this to him, but it appears to be the *first* time that it had recognizable meaning for him) he never fails to make the same gesture and tell me the same thing, "You're my little sweetheart," whenever we go to this same bank, and, strangely, always at the very same locus where the endearment arose, as we enter the corridor leading to the window. This particular space has become connected with this remark and appears to have the special significance for him that makes him return to the completion of the act each time.

The second example is another corner on Main Street. Turning from a northbound street around the corner one day, Jonathan asked me, "Where's Heika?" I did not immediately recognize the connection, but after explaining to him that she was not with us I began to search my mind for an incident which might have occurred at this locus, and indeed, remembered that a friend by this name was given a lift into town one day, and let out of the car at this very corner. Returning to the same spot a few weeks later made him remember this configuration of events, and thus arose the question.

These findings vindicate the psychodramatic director when he is asked by questioners why he takes so much trouble to pin a protagonist down to a particular point in space and time, and why he asks the apparently meaningless questions, focusing upon them, when assisting the subject in his preliminary warming up process, as he enters upon the psychodrama stage. It is additional evidence that such *loci nascendi* have a dynamic meaning for the subject, although in adults the direct connections are often lost.

Toilet and going to bed training

While encouraging a twenty-eight month old baby to use the potty, a psychodramatic doll technique was applied to "use the potty" ahead of him. The doll was held upright or in the sitting position, over the toilet seat or potty, in the same way in which a human being would use it. Auxiliary ego method was applied in verbalizing for the doll what it was doing. "Dolly has to go to potty now; here I am, I have to make wee wee" (sound of gushing water). "There, that's done. I'd better wait a minute and see if I have some more coming. Hmmm, hmmm" (sound of pushing) "I'm a good boy, Mummy, I made." The toddler thereupon proceeded to do his part. Recently, without the aid of the mother, the child picks up the doll spontaneously and helps it to "make on potty," making all the appropriate sounds himself. When the dolly has finished he sits down himself and reports to his mother "I'm a good boy, Mummy" when the task is completed. It is obvious that the doll technique becomes unnecessary as soon as toilet training becomes a routine, and the auxiliary ego takes her cues for ceasing to use the technique from the child as it develops from stage to stage, just as the cues for using a new technique come from his needs.

Warming up the child to gentle sleep after he was put in bed, the auxiliary ego picked up one of his dolls or bed companions (stuffed animals, etc.) and began to ask it, "How do you feel today?" Speaking in a different tone of voice the doll (spoken by the auxiliary ego) would answer. In this case it asked, "I'm fine, but Mummy, why don't I have any clothes on? I'm as nude as the day I was born." Mother: "Well, dolly, when you first came into this house your clothes were taken off by Jonathan because he loved to feel your smooth, soft skin." (Strokes skin of the baby gently, then hands doll to child while doll continues to speak to Jonathan) "Did you like to stroke my skin? Do you want to feel it now?" Jonathan nods affirmatively, strokes baby's skin, and says: "Nice." Hands doll back to auxiliary ego who continues to explain, "And then, when he was teething he used to love to chew on your hands, arms, feet, legs, to help the teeth push through the gums." Doll: "He did? How did he do that?" Mother takes doll's feet in her mouth and chews on them, then hands doll to Jonathan who does the same thing, making a wry face. This technique differs from "telling a fairy tale." In the fairy tale the child gets involved and warms up in his mind only, but by means of the psychodramatic method he does not only "hear the story" or "see" it as a motion picture or in a picture book. Here he acts it out with someone, not in a monodramatic form by playing it himself, but in collaboration with significant members of his group, his mother, his father, his toys.

A few days later a more elaborate scene took place. Both mother and child are holding a baby doll on their lap.

JONATHAN: Mummy, speak to baby.

MOTHER: (*turning to doll she is holding*) Well, how are you today, baby?

BABY DOLL: (*mother takes its part and uses a high, babyish voice, different from the one in which she addressed the doll before*) I'm fine mother, but would you tell me something? Why does everything seem to go wrong on certain days? Why does everything seem to happen all mixed up?

MOTHER: Why, what happened, baby?

DOLL: Oh today I put my left sock on my right fist, then I tried to put my right foot into my left shoe. I put my shirt on inside out and my hat on upside down.

The child laughs hilariously at this.

MOTHER: (*to baby doll*) Well, we all have off days like that once in a while. The most important thing is not to take yourself too seriously and to remember that everything is all right as long as you and I love each other. Isn't that right, my child? (*both mother and baby doll look at Jonathan*)

CHILD: Yes, that's right.

Child then hands mother his own doll, says, "Speak to the baby, Mummy." Mother and child exchange dolls.

MOTHER: And how are you feeling today?

DOLL: (*again in a somewhat different voice, not as high pitched as the first doll and still not in the auxiliary ego's own voice*) I'd like to take a trip around the world, Mummy. I'd like to see something of the world while I'm still able to.

(Mother is preparing the child for the fact that a new doll will soon have to replace this one that is falling to pieces and hard to keep together. As this may involve some feeling of loss on Jonathan's part, the auxiliary ego thought it might be wise to weave this theme of "going away" into the game.)

MOTHER: That's a fine idea. Where would you like to go?

DOLL: Everywhere. By airplane, ship, train, to see the whole wide world.
MOTHER: I think we can arrange that for you and send you on a worldwide trip, and, at the end, to some other little boy or girl to make them happy.

The child was intrigued at this notion and asked his mother: "Put baby to bed for me now."

DOLL: But first I want to go to Jonathan. (*mother helps doll to walk and hop and jump over to child, doll cuddles close*) Good night, Jonathan.
JONATHAN: (*being placed into bed beside baby doll*) Good night, baby.

The child is thirty months old. What intrigues him about this technique is that this mute, mechanical doll with which he plays becomes animated through the voice of an auxiliary ego; that it is being given life and reality, a life and reality akin to his own, different from the mechanical kind of animation given to dolls that open and close, wetting of the diaper when given the bottle, walking when stood on their feet, etc. As soon as the child uncovers the mechanism behind these tricks he is disappointed, but what the auxiliary ego gives to the doll is a "psyche," a new dimension, ever new, unexpected and adventurous. It is a calculated "return of the unconscious animism of the illiterate."

The child asks for this game spontaneously. "Speak to baby," he demands. He may not understand all the words spoken by the doll through the mother's voice, but he understands the rules of the game. It opens up new forms of communication between mother and child. On the reality level the child may say "No, no Mummy" to this or that, going to bed, eating, or any activity that might interfere with his present aspiration or activity. But the "Speak to baby" technique removes these barriers. Mother and child walk hand in hand through their fantasies in a psychodramatic land in which everything is possible. The chair talks and the table sings, and the doll speaks, and the dog doll suffers pain and barks. The division between real–unreal, which adults have accepted after a long struggle, the child cannot quite accept and he is anxious to fall into any system of activity that brings these two worlds into unison. It may well be that the age-old dream of every woman to become a mother is linked to the equally old dream to be a child again. And so two things happen to every mother and are encouraged by this technique: the mother teaches the child to become an adult and the child teaches the mother to become a child.[2]

Article 11

Note on Spontaneous Learning "*in situ*" versus Learning the Academic Way

Moreno, Z.T. (1958) *Group Psychotherapy, A Quarterly Journal* XI, 1: 50–51

Zerka's comments

When I had my amputation I read Helen Keller's story and was inspired. She was so courageous in the face of so many things against her. Miss Sullivan became her perfect auxiliary ego. That moment of recognizing water – the arousal of the senses in the action of learning – seemed to speak directly to the principle of spontaneity.

In *The Story of My Life* by Helen Keller[1] it is repeatedly stressed that Helen Keller made such remarkable strides in her learning abilities that the question was raised to her teacher Anne Sullivan Macy whether all of her rapid progress could be ascribed to her talent and intelligence. Miss Sullivan herself states in this book, "Helen is a wonderful child, so spontaneous and eager to learn" (p. 263). Then she describes the method by which she was able to teach her and reach her so deeply and fast, which, indeed, has all the earmarks of "*in situ*" learning, using the child's spontaneity as her guide. Quoting again from Miss Sullivan's reports: "I am beginning to suspect all elaborate and special systems of education" (p. 260). "Since I have abandoned the idea of regular sessions, I find that Helen learns much faster" (p. 261).

There is ample evidence throughout Miss Sullivan's reports in the book that the method was an "*in situ*" method, closely related to the principle of spontaneity training in psychodrama. Miss Sullivan used Helen Keller's own indicators, her spontaneity, as her guide; this showed the teacher where Helen needed to be led in order to make her potentials awaken to further develop them. There is, for instance, the following incident described by Miss Sullivan (pp. 256–267): "This morning, while she was washing, she wanted to know the name for 'water.' When she wants to know the name of anything, she points to it and pats my hand. I spelled 'w-a-t-e-r' and thought no more about it until after breakfast. Then it occurred to me that with the help of this new word I might succeed in straightening out the 'mug-milk' difficulty. We went to the pump-house and I made Helen hold her mug under the spout while I pumped. As the cold water gushed forth, filling the mug, I spelled 'w-a-t-e-r' in Helen's free hand. The word coming so close upon the sensation of cold water rushing over her hand seemed to startle her. She dropped the mug and stood as one transfixed. A new light came into her face. She spelled 'water' several times."

This illustration of action learning and action insight is quite indicative of the method intuitively followed by Anne Sullivan Macy. There is a more striking illustration: "Whenever it was possible she was made the *actor* in the lesson [emphasis added], and was delighted to stand *on* the chair, and to be put *into* the wardrobe" (emphasis in original, p. 279). This was done to teach Helen the difference between *on* and *in*.

If psychodrama would be used systematically in the teaching of deaf–dumb and blind children we feel sure the results would be equally gratifying and productive as were those used so gropingly by Miss Sullivan in the case of Helen Keller. She reports about a visit to a little school for the deaf in which the academic method of blackboard instruction was used via painful construction of simple sentences not spontaneously produced by the children. "They were astonished at her command of language. Not a child in the school, they said, had anything like Helen's facility of expression, and some of them had been under instruction for two or three years" (p. 292). This was reported on May 15, 1888. Miss Sullivan arrived at the Keller home on March 3, 1887. Therefore the total instruction period at the time of this report was a little more than one year.[2]

Article 12

The "Reluctant Therapist" and the "Reluctant Audience" Technique in Psychodrama

Moreno, Z.T. (1958) *Group Psychotherapy, A Quarterly Journal* XI, 4: 278–282

Zerka's comments

I was intrigued by the report of a psychodrama therapist working with an at-risk juvenile who continually resisted the proposed scenes in sessions. At one point the therapist just walked out. It seemed to have a positive impact, because the adolescent began to cooperate. I remember Moreno doing something like this with a drug addict in a state hospital in the Midwest. Besides being non-compliant, the patient was collecting marijuana on the hospital grounds and distributing it to his peers. Moreno confronted him, asking, "Why should the staff bother with you if you do not want to change?" The protagonist was stunned. Moreno ended the session there. This was true "reality therapy." He later discussed this patient with the staff and recommended that the boy be discharged. We were not informed whether this recommendation was carried out.

The psychiatric literature is replete with examples of patient-produced resistance to the therapeutic process and, particularly in psychoanalysis, this problem and its various approaches form a substantial part of such literature. In psychodrama this problem is dealt with in a head-on, direct manner. The resistance is systematically enacted, in psychodramatic episodes and interaction with the therapist–director, the auxiliary ego therapist and the audience carrying the load of hostility, aggression and negative warm up. Resistance may take the form of hostile silence, refusal to participate in the preliminary interview or to portray a role – his own or that of another person involved in his problem – inappropriate laughter, side remarks irrelevant to the situation to be portrayed, acts which are destructive of a cohesive warming up process leading to an integrating action catharsis. The literature of psychodrama too is replete with descriptions of this type of resistance and how to assist the subject or patient to work it out *in situ*.

Sometimes the protagonist is not a single individual, but a group of patients. They may be resistant as a total group. Then it is the task of the director to work through the group's reluctance, to help clarify distorted perceptions and false expectations, before therapy can take place. The process of interaction in which the protagonist, single or plural, is engaged with the therapist who directs the session is like a subtle interchange between new-found lovers; there is a gradual process of seduction going on, which the director hopes will bring him to the goal of a psychodramatic production leading to total involvement.

The reluctant therapist technique

Not so well acknowledged is the phenomenon of the "reluctant psychotherapist." It is met with very frequently and we believe that it occurs far more often than the therapist in the one-to-one therapy situation is aware or willing to admit. Since there are no observers of the proceedings, it is easy to ascribe the resulting interpersonal dynamics to the occurrence of negative transference – usually on the part of the patient. However, the needs of the patient frequently fail to be met by the therapist and here we come to the part that the therapist plays, consciously or unconsciously, in the patient–therapist relationship.

Sociometry has taught us that transference is a one-way process, unilateral, based on projectional fragments carried into the present situation and, according to psychoanalytic tenets, patterned on parallel interpersonal experiences from the past. According to Moreno, transference is the pathological aspect of a far more inclusive phenomenon which he called "tele," a two-way "feeling with" another that binds together – either positively or negatively – an attraction.

Therapists who are not aware of or refuse to face the fact that they may have "negative tele" for a patient are deluding themselves and the patient. How could it be otherwise? Sociometry has taught us how highly selective humans are in the choice of partners for innumerable daily activities – indeed, it has uncovered and studied such selectivity also for the subhumans (Moreno, J.L. 1958b) and that this choice process is not a one-sided affair, but one in which both partners have equal responsibility. To continue filling books with lengthy descriptions of painful negative transference dynamics and to speak of counter-transference is to deny the existence of a vast sociometric body of knowledge, painstakingly gathered over a great many years. It is in the field of psychotherapy particularly that neglect of sociometric knowledge of the structure of human interrelations is doing damage to those who are seeking "expert" help. Without sociometry we are not filling that need. What would be the status of physical medicine today, for instance, without the use of the microscope? Yet, there are psychotherapists who continue to ignore the most up-to-date instruments in social science to uncover social microscopy.

The therapist – let us face it – makes choices too. He decides whether or not he likes a patient and whether he can give him of his best. When his decision is or becomes a negative one, it is the therapist who becomes the reluctant participant in the therapeutic process, thus preventing the patient from deriving those benefits to which he is entitled. It would be more ethical to interrupt treatment at the point where this occurs, freeing the patient to find a more productive therapy situation for himself, at the same time making the therapist available for another patient with whom positive tele relations might be established. We know from sociometric research that a person may be rejected by one or another person, but wanted by someone else. We have ample evidence to note that a patient may be rejected by one or another therapist or carried in an unproductive relationship until not even a willing therapist is able to reach him. If a positive patient–therapist tele relation can be established early in the therapy-seeking, much harm can be avoided.

It has been especially Moreno who has pointed out the implications of this patient–therapist relationship (Moreno, J.L. 1954). It was also he who had the courage to stand up to an audience of more than three hundred individuals who were filled with hostility and aggression, and to reject them as his protagonists in a psychodrama. It may be said that these were not unanimously rejecting individuals. Nonetheless, the positive relationships within the group were not sufficiently strong to carry the audience to a productive level. The director–therapist faced them with this fact and refused to be crucified by them (Ben Ali 1958). The writer was never faced by a group like it; it was a perfect, classic example of the enraged mob. The theme of the day which, parenthetically, had come forth early in the session, was: "How can we help patients to face hostility in themselves?" Physician – Heal Thyself!

The reluctant audience technique

A further elaboration of this theme occurs when, as is sometimes the case, an *audience* rejects a patient–protagonist. Such was the situation we faced with a patient whose exhibitionist tendencies reached alarming proportions in the course of his therapy. The patient suffered from a series of massive tics, which involved his entire body, resulting in tonic and clonic movements. He had first developed these symptoms at the age of seven and they had become progressively worse. He had been under psychotherapy on and off since the appearance of his symptoms but resisted the uncovering types of therapy. There had been but one fairly long period when his symptoms subsided, during his last year of high school. He was well accepted by his peers, participated fully in school life and gained particular recognition as a comic performer on the stage. After graduation he was admitted to college and during the beginning of his freshman year developed an exacerbation of his symptoms, which subsequently led to withdrawal from school and hospitalization. He was referred to us for psychodrama therapy because of his preoccupation with fantasies, which involved his inclination towards the drama, and because it was assumed that psychodrama is better suited to treat such psychomotoric disturbances than the verbal methods.

Dick (not his real name) enjoyed the psychodrama sessions and appeared to benefit from them. He particularly relished the fact that he had an audience. The audience members began, in the course of his treatment, to develop very distinctive relationships to Dick and he found much warmth and responsiveness on numerous levels. His fear of failing, however, forced him repeatedly into the role of the clown, especially when this role was most inconsistent with the demands of the situation. For example, we placed Dick into a situation with an auxiliary ego in which he was being interviewed for a job. His enactment of the role of the prospective employee was so destructive of the correct warming up process that the audio-egos became more and more irritated with his performance. It was evident that he used the comic approach to cover up his own deficiencies and to deviate attention from this area.

One could interpret this as resistance to therapy but that would be only the partial truth, for in fact, Dick loved his psychodrama sessions. He would feel rejected if he were not the protagonist in a session and was unable to sit through the performance of another protagonist as a spectator, though he was willing to participate as an auxiliary ego. He had been the exclusive subject in a number of previous sessions, when the audience finally became restive and refused to become the scapegoat for his narcissistic destructiveness. In other words, they were physically present, but emotionally absent. At this point one of Dick's most ardent supporters (she had frequently taken the role of his mother in earlier sessions) whispered to the director, "What would happen if he had no audience? What if we all left the auditorium, one after another?" The director nodded his consent – it seemed the same thought had occurred to him as well as to several other audio-egos at about the same time – *and the audience quietly withdrew.*

Dick remained behind, together with the director–therapist and the few auxiliary egos necessary. He reacted with a strong show of real emotion, resentment and hostility at the audience's fickle behavior, but for the first time during that session was able to go into a realistic portrayal of a job application. Whereas the mere perpetuation of permissive support produced no real heat in him, forcing him back into the action portion of the session without the gallery to play for was of essential therapeutic value.

The meaning of the "reluctant audience" technique is clear. If therapy is to be a true learning situation, no efforts should be spared to assist the patient in a re-evaluation of his behavior patterns, and to offer restraint where mere permissiveness would inhibit growth and integration. Permissiveness in such a situation would defeat its own purpose. The withdrawal of support at a crucial moment when the audience felt itself abused was a necessary step in the therapeutic process, thus interrupting a rigid behavior pattern, which was bound to lead to disaster for the patient.

Article 13

A Survey of Psychodramatic Techniques

Moreno, Z.T. (1959) *Group Psychotherapy, A Quarterly Journal* XII, 1: 5–14

Zerka's comments

I lost my right arm to cancer in January, 1958. Three days after the surgery I had my husband bring in my typewriter. One of the best ways for me to recover was to get back to work as quickly as possible. This is one of the first articles I wrote, although it was not published until 1959. It occurred to us that there was no up-to-date listing of the techniques that had been developed up to that time.

I recently came across a paper that concluded, after an "extensive review" of the literature, that Hannah Weiner, one of our students, is the originator of the Magic Shop, as evidenced by a paper she co-wrote with James Sacks in 1969, among other less concrete substantiation. As the reader will note, I refer to the Magic Shop technique in this paper, not as a new phenomenon, but to describe a technique that Moreno originated and had long been using before the publication of the article. I hope this settles the origination question.

The psychodrama is not a single technique. It is a methodology, a synthetic method in which many dimensions of experience are mobilized on behalf of the patient. We will enumerate a few of them, adding some brief illustrations. These are by no means all of them. Directors are frequently forced to invent new techniques or to modify old ones on the spot so as to meet a challenging situation presented by the patient.[1]

Soliloquy technique

This is a "monologue" of the protagonist "*in situ*." The patient enacts a scene in which he is on his way home from work, for instance. He is walking from the subway station to his apartment. In life itself his thoughts would not be verbalized as he is alone, but he is thinking about himself. The psychodramatic therapist–director instructs him to use the soliloquy technique: to talk out loud as he walks what he is thinking and feeling at this moment, here and now. The patient uses the large, bottom level of the psychodrama stage. He walks and walks, shaking his head, warming up to the situation, one which he encounters daily. His face is frowned, his head tucked between his shoulders, drooping halfway on his chest. He is very despondent. His voice is low, barely audible as he speaks: "I am sick and tired of my life. I enjoy my work, it is true, but oh, how I hate to go home at night. I know just what is going to happen when I get there. There is my old mother with her complaints, and endless series of aches and pains that no doctor is able to cure. And then there is my sister, Jane, a sour, unhappy old maid who resents having to dedicate her life to mother because life is passing her by. But she does not have the get-up-and-go to change the situation and find another life for herself. And here am I, her male counterpart, resenting both of them because I have to support them."

Technique of self-realization

The protagonist enacts the plan of his life, with the aid of a number of auxiliary egos. The patient believes himself to be Adolf Hitler. His former identity has dropped away and the psychotic structure has replaced it. In order for him to free himself from psychotic production, he needs helpers who embody for him the personages who interact with him as his new self. The patient is unable to complete this self-realization alone in the world of reality, but at the same time he is convinced that his psychotic world is the real one. Indeed, it has become the only real world for him. The auxiliary egos who during the therapeutic sessions take the roles of Hess, Goering and Goebbels, among others, become midwives, assistants in the birth of his psychodrama. They make it possible for him to bring his psychodramatic pregnancy to fulfillment and, once the psychotic baby has been completed, to be delivered of it.

Hallucinatory psychodrama

The patient puts his delusions and hallucinations to a reality test. Hallucinations do not follow the law of physical gravity; they may rise into space or come down from above. They disregard the laws of sensory perception. They may speak to and touch the patient. In the following scene the patient is sitting at the dining room table. The director [ZTM] decided to have the psychodrama session deal with this everyday situation because it was a stressful one for the patient as well as her table partners, most of whom were present and taking their own roles. One of the patient's neighbors speaks to her: "Carolyn, please pass me the salt." Carolyn does not move. Another one addresses her: "Carolyn, please give Mr. Stone this glass of milk." Again, Carolyn remains frozen. She is physically present but otherwise absent from the reality of the scene. She gazes fixedly into space. Director: "What are you looking at, Carolyn?" Carolyn (in a hushed and fearful voice): "Don't you see them?" Director: "Yes, I do, but how many are there?" Carolyn: "Three of them." Director: "How are they dressed?" Carolyn: "They are dressed in black, but cloaked like members of the Ku Klux Klan." Director: "Can you see their faces?" Carolyn: "No. They are completely hooded." Director: "Just where are they?" Carolyn: "Hovering on the ceiling." Director: "Do they represent anything?" Carolyn: "Yes, they are the spirit of hate, fear and death." Director: "Hate, fear and death. Are they alone?" Carolyn: "No, each one is standing in front of a coffin." Director: "Are the coffins empty?" Carolyn: "No." (Throughout this interchange she does not stir. Her answers are given in concise form. It is evident that she perceives all this very clearly.) Director: "Are there figures in them?" Carolyn: "Yes."

Director: "Get up, Carolyn, let us pick from among the people here the spirit of hate, fear and death." Director takes Carolyn by the hand. She assists in the choices of the auxiliary egos – all patients who have experienced hallucinations – and places them on the stage. Director: "And now, Carolyn, who is the first figure?" Carolyn: "I see my mother lying in the coffin of death." Director: "You go now and lie down in the coffin of death." Carolyn does so, representing the figure which is under the spell of this particular spirit, that of death. Her actions and use of the coffin correspond with the feeling-tone emanated by the spirit. Here she lies with her eyes closed, arms relaxed at her sides, the image of sweet repose.

Director (addressing Carolyn as her mother): "Mrs. Smith [not family name], I am sorry to see you here. What happened?" Carolyn (in sepulchral tone): "I am better off dead. That daughter of mine, she killed me. That Carolyn, she used to upset me so, she gave me heart attacks. I am better off this way." Director: "I understand, but where is Carolyn now? What is she doing without you?" Carolyn: "She is dead, too." Director: "Is she in a coffin?" Carolyn: "Yes, she is a murderess and had to die too." Director: "You are Carolyn now, there in the coffin?" Carolyn: "Yes. This is me." Director (turning to the spirit of death): "What do you feel about this, oh spirit of death? Do you have anything to say?" Patient (a very regressed schizophrenic who was rarely able to warm up to any role other than his own fragmentations): "She is too young and pretty to die." Director: "Shall we forgive her her sins and let her live?" Spirit of death: "Yes." Director: "And will you restore her mother to life also?" Patient: "Yes." Director: "Carolyn, come with me. The spirit of death will relinquish his claims on you. Leave the stage, spirit of death." Patient does so.

Director and Carolyn now turn to the next coffin. Director: "Carolyn, which coffin is this?" Carolyn: "The spirit of fear." Director: "Get in the coffin and show us how it is in this coffin." Carolyn crouches on the floor like a frightened animal, her back arched over her knees, her arms crossed over her head. Director: "Who are you?" Carolyn: "I am all the patients in mental hospitals, especially state hospitals." Director (turning to the spirit of fear): "What do you think of this, spirit of fear?" Spirit (another very disturbed patient): "I only show her the fears she creates for herself." Director: "Is this true, Carolyn?" Carolyn: "Partly. I can't help it and the others don't help me." Director (signaling to all those present to join in speaking to Carolyn, as in a chorus): "We promise to help you, Carolyn. Please have no more fear." (The chorus speech is repeated several times, more loudly and insistently.) Director: "Come out of that coffin now, Carolyn, for we will do our best to help you. And therefore, the spirit of fear may depart." Spirit leaves the stage.

Director, taking Carolyn to the third coffin: "And here is the final one, Carolyn." Carolyn: "The spirit of hate." Director: "Get into that coffin and show us how hate feels." Carolyn lies down, her arms and legs twining around her body like self-imprisoning bands of hate. Director: "And who is this?" Carolyn: "This is me when I don't get what I want." Director: "What, for instance?" Carolyn: "When I want them to stop using electric shock on me." Director: "Spirit of hate, how do you feel about this?" Patient, as spirit of hate: "They use electric shock when it is necessary. It is supposed to help patients." Director: "Has it helped Carolyn?" Spirit: "I suppose so, or else they would not have given it to her." Director: "What do you think about that, Carolyn?" Carolyn: "It's too dreadful a treatment." Director: "Did you ever have it here?" Carolyn: "No." Director: "How long ago is it since you had it?" Carolyn: "I think about one year ago." Director: "We all promise you will not get it as long as you are here, Carolyn, so you may rise and the spirit of hate will depart."

Multiple double technique

The patient is on the stage with several doubles of himself. Each portrays part of the patient. One auxiliary ego acts as he is now, the patient acts himself as he was when he was little, and as he was soon after his father's death. Another auxiliary ego acts as the patient maybe thirty years hence. The masks of the patient are simultaneously present and each acts in turn. With psychotic patients the multiple double technique has been usefully employed when the patient suffered from numerous delusions involving parts of the body. Each of the auxiliary egos then represented a different organ, responding to the delusional stimuli produced by the patient.

Role reversal technique

In this technique the patient, in an interpersonal situation, takes the role of the other person involved. Distortions of perception of "the other" in interaction may thus be brought to the surface, explored and corrected in action, in the fold of the group. Role reversal has been used effectively with infants and children as a technique of socialization and self-integration. An illustration is the role reversal between a mother and a three-year-old child, the child assuming the role of authority. Jonathan was fearful of a very large black dog which used to appear on the grounds as if out of nowhere. The dog would make attempts at being friendly with the child, trying to come close, to lick his hand, jumping around him. Jonathan became so fearful of him that he would cling to his mother's skirt even when the dog remained at a considerable distance. Verbal assurance was unable to assuage this fear. It was decided to work it out in the following manner:

MOTHER: Jonathan, there is the big black dog again. (The dog was nowhere in sight.)

JONATHAN (*runs to this mother, hides his face in her skirt, exclaims*): I'm afraid of him, Mummy, I'm afraid.

MOTHER: But honey, there is nothing to be afraid of. First of all, I'm here and wouldn't let him hurt you. Besides, he really wants to be friends with you and play with you. Wouldn't you like to pat him on his back?

JONATHAN: Will he bite me?

MOTHER: Of course not. If you are nice to him he will be nice to you. And besides, I'm with you. (*Takes Jonathan's hand who reluctantly allows her to use his hand to pat the back of the dog.*)

MOTHER: Now, you will be me and I will be Jonathan.

JONATHAN (*as mother; his voice taking on notable strength, his posture becoming far more erect*): Jonathan, here is that black dog. Now, don't be afraid of him.

MOTHER (*as Jonathan, crouching low on the ground, clinging to his mother*): Mummy, I'm afraid, I'm afraid, I'm afraid.

JONATHAN (*as mother*): Honey, there is nothing to be afraid of. (*Puts his hands tenderly around his baby.*) Don't forget. Mummy is here with you and she wouldn't let you get hurt.

Dream technique

Instead of telling the dream, the patient reenacts it. He takes his position in bed, and when he is able to reconstruct the dream, he rises from the bed and represents it in action, using auxiliary egos to enact the roles of the dream characters. This technique further makes use of retraining the patient, giving him an opportunity to "change" his dream. This is the unique contribution of psychodrama to dream therapy: to go into enactment over and beyond the actual dream, including actual and latent material, but even more, to retrain the dreamer rather than to interpret. Interpretation is in the act itself.

Symbolic realization technique

Enactment of symbolic process by the protagonist using soliloquy, double, reversal or mirror for their clarification.

Analytic psychodrama

An analytic hypothesis, for instance, that of the Oedipus complex, is tested out on the stage in order to verify its validity. The patient takes the role of his mother in a situation with his father (coming home, fired from his job because of a heart ailment). The analyst sits in the audience and watches. Analysis of the material is made immediately after the scene.

Auxiliary world technique

The entire world of the patient is restructured around him "*in situ*" by the aid of auxiliary egos. William has been classified as a dementia praecox. He calls himself Christ and has written a proclamation to the world that he wants to save it. The auxiliary egos around him live in his world and are completely guided by his needs. One auxiliary ego becomes the apostle John. Christ asks him to kneel in a corner of the room with his head bowed. He does not want him to kneel in any other room or in any other corner. Another auxiliary ego becomes the apostle Paul with whom he prays. A third is the apostle Peter who is the only one he permits to bathe him once a month. He does not permit members of his family to come to visit him. The only persons he accepts are those who people the world of his psychosis, according to his instructions.

Treatment at a distance

The patient is treated *in absentia*, usually without his knowledge. He is replaced by an auxiliary ego who is in daily contact with him and is the go-between between patient and therapist. He acts out in the clinic all crucial episodes in which the patient is involved. Other members of the immediate environment are drawn into the action, for instance the parents of the patient.

Warming up techniques

Used to induce spontaneous states.

Techniques of spontaneous improvisation

The protagonist acts out fictitious roles and tries to keep his personal character uninvolved from his fictitious characters.

Therapeutic community

A community in which the disputes between individuals and groups are settled under the rule of therapy instead of the rule of law.

Mirror techniques – behind your back

Many mirror techniques are so constructed that the individual can "see" and "hear" himself through other people's perceptions of him.

In the classic mirror technique as described above, the protagonist is physically present, but psychologically absent. The auxiliary ego "acts as if" the patient were not present, so as to challenge the patient when he realizes that the person portrayed on the stage is a radically truthful expression of himself.

There are other mirror technique forms that are used by Moreno and his associates at the New York Institute, as follows.

(a) The behind your back audience technique

The entire audience is instructed to leave the theatre but actually they are permitted to remain seated, pretending that they are not present, so as to give the protagonist full freedom of expression. The patient tells each member of the group how he feels towards them. The audience members are not permitted to respond, no matter how much he provokes them. The members of the group are now put on the spot; they see themselves in the mirror of the protagonist's world. This is frequently the starting point, the warming up period preceding a psychodrama. It is often effective if the members of the group *actually* turn their backs.

(b) The turn your back technique

Protagonists are frequently embarrassed to present a particular episode face to face before the group. They are then permitted, if unavoidable for the warm up, to turn their back to the group and to act as if they would be alone, in their own home, or wherever the episode takes place. The director, too, may turn his back to the audience so as to observe the protagonist or protagonists. Once the protagonists, for instance in the case of a matrimonial couple, have reached a high degree of involvement, they become ready to face the audience.

(c) The black-out technique

The entire theatre is blacked out although all actions continue as if there would be full daylight. This is done so that the protagonist may go through a painful experience unobserved, to retain for the protagonist the experience of solitude.

Improvisation of fantasy

Since the early days of psychodrama, improvisation of fantasies has been usefully applied in order to attain therapeutic aims (see "Bulletin of Psychodrama and Group Psychotherapy," *Sociometry, A Journal of Inter-Personal Relations*, Vol. VI, 1943, p. 349).

A popular technique was and still is the *Magic Shop technique*. The director sets up on the stage a "Dream or Magic Shop." Either he himself, or a member of the group selected by him, takes the part of the shopkeeper. The shop is filled with imaginary items, values of a non-physical nature. These are not for sale, but they can be obtained in barter, in exchange for other values to be surrendered by the members of the group, either individually or as a group. One after another, the members of the group volunteer to come upon the stage, entering the shop in quest of an idea, a dream, a hope, an ambition. They are expected to come only if they feel a strong desire to obtain a value which they cherish highly or without which their life seems worthless.

An illustration follows: A depressive patient, who was admitted after a suicidal attempt, came to the Magic Shop requesting "Peace of Mind." The shopkeeper, a sensitive young therapist, asked her, "What do you want to give in return? You know we cannot give you anything without your willingness to sacrifice something else." "What do you want?" the patient asked. "There is something for which many people who come to this shop long," he replied, "Fertility, the ability and willingness to bear children. Do you want to give this up?" "No, this is too high a price to pay. Then I do not want peace of mind." With this she walked off the stage and returned to her seat. The shopkeeper had hit on a sensitive spot. Maria, the protagonist, was engaged but she refused to get married because of deep-seated fear of sex and childbirth. Her fantasy preoccupations involved images of violent suffering, torture, death, etc. in the act of childbirth.

This illustration indicates the diagnostic value of the Dream Shop technique. The crux of the technique is for the shopkeeper to demand of the client what he wants to give in return; what price he is willing to pay.

Another fantasy technique is the dramatization of fairy tales as described in Moreno's *Das Stegreiftheater* (Moreno, J.L. 1924: 35–37; Moreno, J.L. 1947). The tale remains entirely unstructured so that the protagonists are required to fill in with their own fantasies around the theme.

Still another fantasy technique is improvisation of early childhood experiences. In the process of acting them out the protagonists go far beyond that which they actually remember.

Many psychodramatic techniques, however odd and fantastic they seem, can be traced back to the rituals and customs of ancient cultures and are found in the classic writings of world literature. Moreno has merely rediscovered and adapted them to psychotherapeutic objectives. *Their real inventors are the mental patients of all times.* The number of applications of the psychodrama method is practically unlimited, although the core of the method remains unchanged.

Article 14

Psychodramatic Rules, Techniques, and Adjunctive Methods

Moreno, Z.T. (1965) *Group Psychotherapy, A Quarterly Journal* XVIII, 1–2: 73–86

Zerka's comments

Moreno was good at creating ideas, but they were not always organized or presented in a lucid manner. I worked at giving some form to them, wanting him to be understood by as large a population as possible.

By this time I was doing most of the training, so this article was part of the organization of a curriculum that could be understood, especially by the newcomer. We didn't have extensive course handouts as they do today. The emphasis was on doing, not on reading about doing. This article was a brief summary to pull the practical experience together in an organized way. Moreno had groups of students come to the house in the evening for more free-ranging philosophical/historical discussions. I saw to it that there was an organized part of the training that could be grasped and learned.

The growing demand for skilled workers in psychodrama has awakened us to the need to structure a comprehensive statement of fundamental rules (Moreno, J.L. 1959) in the practice of this method, and a brief survey and explanation of the numerous versions of psychodramatic intervention. Other surveys of methods have described some of these (Moreno, Z.T. 1959) but a number of basic rules to serve as guidelines for the practitioner are vital.

Rules

I

"The subject (patient, client, protagonist) acts out his conflicts, instead of talking about them."

To this end, a special vehicle or psychodrama stage may be used, though the process may have to take place in any informal room or space whenever no such specially designed vehicle is available. Ideally, the special vehicle makes for more intense involvement. The process requires further a director (or chief therapist), and at least one trained auxiliary ego (though the director may be forced to act also as an auxiliary ego where no one is available). Maximum learning is achieved whenever such trained assistant–therapist–actors are used.

It should be borne in mind that psychodrama may be applied as a method of individual treatment – one patient with one director and auxiliary ego, or one patient and the director. Where it is applied as a method of group treatment, other patients in the group may very well serve as auxiliary egos for one another. In this fashion even individual-centered sessions involve in action other members of the group, who, in turn, derive therapeutic benefit from this auxiliary ego function. This further intensifies the learning of all those present.

II

"The subject or patient acts 'in the here and now,' regardless of when the actual incident took place or may take place, past, present or future, or when the imagined incident was fantasied or when the crucial situation out of which this present enactment arose, occurred."

This is also true of situations that have not taken place and may not ever take place. One of the notable experiences in psychodrama is the ineffectual, weak, incomplete and distorted fashion in which recall and re-enactment are produced. This has been experimentally verified by the immediate re-enactment of scenes that took place only five minutes earlier, using the identical persons involved in the original scene. Both verbal and action recall, as well as interpersonal perception were impossible to reproduce, even though all actual partners tried systematically and honestly to recapture "what actually happened."

The subject speaks and acts "in the present," and not in the past, because the past is related to memory and speaking in the past tense removes the subject from the immediacy of experience, turning him into a spectator or a storyteller rather than an actor.

The inability to recall perfectly indicates that such recall is a practical impossibility. Absolute recall does not exist and correct reproduction is hardly an attainable ideal. Furthermore, spontaneity and "presentness" are subjugated to correct reproductions and thus disappear. To release spontaneity and increase presentness in the here and now, the protagonist is specifically instructed to make time his servant, not his master; to "act as if this is happening to you *now*, so that you can feel, perceive and act as if this were happening to you for the first time."

III

"The subject must act out 'his truth,' as he feels and perceives it, in a completely subjective manner (no matter how distorted this appears to the spectator)."

The warming up process cannot proceed properly unless we accept the patient with all his subjectivity. Enactment comes first, re-training comes later. We must give him the satisfaction of act completion first, before considering re-training for behavior changes.

IV

"The patient is encouraged to maximize all expression, action, and verbal communication rather than to reduce it."

To this end, delusions, hallucinations, soliloquies, thoughts, fantasies, projections, are all allowed to be a part of the production. Again, restraint has to come after expression, though it should never be overlooked. Without, however, getting expression *in toto*, restraint can at best be only partial.

V

"The warming up process proceeds from the periphery to the center."

The director will, therefore, not begin with the most traumatic events in the patient's life. The commencement is on a more superficial level, allowing the self-involvement of the patient to carry him more deeply towards the core. The director's skills will be expressed in the construction of the scenes and the choice of persons or objects needed to assist the patient in his warming up.

VI

"Whenever possible, the protagonist will pick the time, the place, the scene, the auxiliary ego he requires in the production of his psychodrama."

The director serves as dramaturg in assisting the protagonist. The director and protagonist are partners. At one moment the director may be more active, but the protagonist always reserves the right to decline the enactment of, or to change a scene. Furthermore, when the interaction between the patient and director becomes negative, the patient resisting the director as well as the process, the director may: (1) ask the patient to designate another director – if more than one is present or (2) ask the patient to sit down and watch a mirror production of himself by auxiliary ego or egos or (3) turn the direction over to the patient himself, who may then involve others in the group as auxiliary egos or (4) ask the patient to choose another scene or (5) explain to the patient why he chose a particular scene and, even though it may not be carried out now, the patient should understand his rationale in making the choice or (6) return to such an enactment at a later time if he continues to believe the patient needs this or (7) insist upon its enactment if he believes that the benefits to be derived thereby for the patient are greater than his resistance.

VII

"Psychodrama is just as much a method of restraint as it is a method of expression."

The repressiveness of our culture has attached to "expression per se" a value that is often beyond its actual reward. Methods such as role reversal or enactment of roles that require restraint are greatly underestimated and disregarded applications of psychodrama for retraining and/or reconditioning of excitability in patients.

One thinks here especially of the chronic bad actor in life, the delinquent or psychopath, whose ability for self-restraint has not been strengthened by his warming up to stresses in life.

VIII

"The patient is permitted to be as unspontaneous or inexpressive as he is at this time."

This may seem to be a contradiction of the Fourth Imperative above, but only apparently so. Thus "maximizing of expression" may also refer to the patient's inability to express, his withdrawal, his submerged anger, etc. First we must accept this inability, and assist him to accept himself. Gradually we try to release him from his own bonds by various methods as asides or soliloquies, the use of the double, etc.

The fact that a patient lacks in spontaneity is not a block to psychodramatic production. That is the reason for the existence of auxiliary egos who are trained to support, assist and strengthen the patient. Thus, also, have developed techniques such as the soliloquy, the double, the mirror, role reversal, etc. The person who is unable to be spontaneous as himself in his own roles may become extremely spontaneous in role reversal as his wife, father, baby, pet dog, etc. His expressiveness will grow as his spontaneity increases. Expressiveness at any price is not necessarily spontaneous. It may be a cover-up for genuine feelings, for instance, by producing a steady flow of words and actions. A patient may be entirely spontaneous while sitting quietly in a chair or observing others around him.

IX

"Interpretation and insight-giving in psychodrama are of a different nature from the verbal types of psychotherapy."

In psychodrama we speak of action insight, action learning, or action catharsis. It is an integrative process brought about by the synthesis of numerous techniques at the height of the protagonist's warm up. Psychodrama is actually the most interpretative method there is, but the director acts upon his interpretations in the construction of the scenes. Verbal interpretation may either be essential or omitted at the discretion of the director. Because his interpretation is in the act, it is frequently redundant.

X

"Even when interpretation is given, action is primary. There can be no interpretation without previous action."

Interpretation may be questioned, rejected or totally ineffective. The action speaks for itself. Furthermore, interpretation is colored by the orientation of the individual therapist. Thus, a Freudian will interpret from a different framework than an Adlerian, Jungian, Horneyan, etc. But that does not in any way change the value of the production itself. It merely puts interpretation into a lesser rung of importance. At times, indeed, interpretation may be destructive rather than constructive; it may be that what the patient requires is not analysis, but emotional identification.

XI

"Warming up to psychodrama may proceed directly from culture to culture and appropriate changes in the application of the method have to be made."

It may be impossible to start a psychodrama in the Congo by verbal exchange; it may be necessary to start with singing and dancing. What may be a suitable warm up in Manhattan may fall flat in Tokyo. Cultural applications must be made. The important thing is not how to begin but that we begin.

XII

"Psychodrama sessions consist of three portions: the warm up, the action portion and the post-action sharing by the group."

Disturbances in any one of these areas reflect upon the total process. However, "sharing" may at times be of a nonverbal nature. A silence pregnant with emotion is often the most suitable way of sharing with a protagonist, or going out to coffee together, or making plans to meet again, or whatever.

XIII

"The protagonist should never be left with the impression that he is all alone with this type of problem in the group."

The director must draw from the group, in the post-action discussion phase, identifications with the subject. This will establish anchorages in the group for mutually satisfying relations among group members, increase cohesion and broaden interpersonal perceptions.

When there is no one in the audience who openly identifies with the subject, the protagonist feels denuded, robbed of that most sacred part of himself, his private psyche. Then it is the task of the director to reveal himself as not merely in sympathy with the protagonist, but as being or having been similarly burdened. It is not analysis that is indicated here, but love and sharing of the self. The only way to repay a person for giving of himself is in kind. This will frequently warm up other persons in the audience to come forward in a similar manner, thus involving the audience in a genuine warming up that once more includes the protagonist, and helps to establish closure.

XIV

"The protagonist must learn to take the role of all those with whom he is meaningfully related; to experience those persons in his social atom, their relationship to him and to one another."

Taking this a step further still, the patient must learn to "become" in psychodrama that which he sees, feels, hears, smells, dreams, loves, hates, fears, rejects, is rejected by, is attracted to, is wanted by, wants to avoid, wants to become, fears to become, fears not to become, etc.

The patient has "taken unto himself" with greater or lesser success, those persons, situations, experiences and perceptions from which he is now suffering. In order to overcome the distortions and manifestations of imbalance, he has to re-integrate them on a new level. Role reversal is one of the methods *par excellence* in achieving this, so that he can re-integrate, redigest and grow beyond those experiences that are of negative impact, free himself and become more spontaneous along positive lines.

XV

"The director must trust the psychodrama method as the final arbiter and guide in the therapeutic process."

This imperative is so universal that it finds confirmation among psychodramatic director–therapists. When the warm up of the director is objective, the spontaneity of his presence and availability to the needs of the patient and the group, or conversely stated, when there is no anxiety in his performance, then the psychodramatic method becomes a flexible, all-embracing medium leading systematically to the heart of the patient's suffering, enabling the director, the protagonist, the auxiliary egos and the group members to become a cohesive force, welded into maximizing emotional learning.

Techniques[1]

Therapeutic soliloquy

The portrayal by side dialogues and side actions of hidden thoughts and feelings, parallel with overt thoughts and actions.

Patient is confronting her superior, who has called her on the carpet for participating in civil rights demonstrations. The auxiliary ego, as the superior, asks her to account for her whereabouts the previous evening. Patient tells her she went to visit a sick friend. Auxiliary ego states she has evidence that this is not the truth. Director stops the overt action, asks patient to express how she feels, explains that her superior won't hear her and will not react, since she could not have known what was going on inside of the patient in the real situation. Patient states, "I really *did* go to that demonstration. She can't really do anything to me because I have tenure, but she can make it unpleasant for me." Director: "What do you want to do?" Patient: "Give her a raspberry, but of course, I can't." Director: "Here you can." Patient belches lustily. Director asks her now to continue the scene as it was and end it on the reality level.

Self-presentation

The protagonist presents himself, his own mother, his own father, his brother, his favorite professor, etc. He acts all these roles himself, in complete subjectiveness, as he experiences and perceives them.

Double

The patient portrays himself. An auxiliary ego is asked also to represent the patient; to "establish identity with the patient," to move, act, behave like the patient.

The patient is preparing to get up in the morning. He is in bed. The auxiliary ego lies down on the stage alongside of him, taking the same bodily posture. The double may start speaking: "What is the use of waking up? I have nothing to live for." Patient: "Yes, that is true. I have no reason for living." Auxiliary ego: "But I am a very talented artist. There have been times when life has been very satisfying." Patient: "Yes, but it seems a long time ago." Auxiliary ego: "Maybe I can get up and start to paint again." Patient: "Well, let's try and get up first, anyway, and see what will happen." Both patient and auxiliary ego get up, go through the motions of washing, shaving, brushing teeth; all along moving together as if they were one. The auxiliary ego becomes the link through which the patient may try to reach out into the real world.

Mirror

When the patient is unable to represent himself, in word or action, an auxiliary ego is placed on the action portion of the psychodramatic space. The patient or patients remain seated in the group portion. The auxiliary ego re-enacts the patient, copying his behavior and trying to express his feelings in word and movement, showing the patient or patients "as if in a mirror" how other people experience him.

The mirror may be exaggerated, employing techniques of deliberate distortion in order to arouse the patient to come forth and change from a passive spectator into an active participant, an actor, to correct what he feels is not the right enactment and interpretation of himself.

Future projection

The patient portrays in action how he thinks his future will shape itself. He picks a point in time – or is assisted by the director to do so – the place and the people, if any, with whom he expects to be involved at that time.

The patient is studying to be an English major and has his bachelor's degree. He has been working on his MA for almost eight years and is unable to complete it. The future projection shows him three years hence, teaching his first course in English at the university. The entire audience is his class. He is asked to face them and inspire them with the beauty of the English language. "My name is Mr. Johnson. It is a very ordinary and yet beautiful name. I should like to welcome you here today by asking you all to introduce yourselves to one another. But remember, the name stands for you. Try to present it in such a way that it sings, that it reaches out to the other as if to say 'here I am, who are you?'"

Adjunctive methods

Hypnodrama

Hypnosis is induced on the psychodrama stage portion. The hypnotizant is free to act, to move about, and is given auxiliary egos to help portray his drama. Hypnodrama is a merging of hypnotherapy with psychodrama.

Psychodramatic shock

The patient is asked to throw himself back into the hallucinatory experience while it is still vivid. He does not describe it; he must act. He puts his body into the position in which it was then, in the space he was in, at the time of day or night when this actually occurred. He may select a staff member to recreate the hallucinatory involvement (Moreno, J.L. 1939b).

The patient may show resistance against being placed again into the horrifying experience from which he had just emerged. His natural bent is to forget, not to talk about it and to leave it behind. He is full of fears that his newfound freedom may be shattered. The mere recall frightens him, and the idea of enactment still more. The psychodramatic director explains that it is to learn control, not a mere reliving, that this reenactment will help him build resources against recurrence.

Once the patient has warmed himself up again into the psychotic state and has thoroughly enacted it, the director stops him, to assist the patient in the realization that he can construct his own inner controls.

Improvisation for personality assessment

The subject is brought into the psychodrama theater or the life situation without any prior preparation. The director has structured the situation in advance with the aid of auxiliary egos. The subject is asked to warm up to the situation, as he would do if it were actually happening to him.

The subject is told he is in his car driving on the highway. He is alone. Suddenly he hears a siren and a police car comes alongside, then ahead of him. The policeman stops him, walks over to him, demands to see his license and gives him a tongue-lashing because he was driving 20 miles per hour over the speed limit. He gives him a ticket for speeding.

Or: the subject enters a cafeteria. An auxiliary ego, obviously the worse for indulgence in alcohol, approaches him and asks for money.

Numerous sets of standard situations have been devised and they enable the director and group members to get a profile of the action potential of the individual which paper and pencil tests are unable to uncover (Murray 1947).

Didactic psychodrama and role playing

Used as a teaching method, auxiliary egos, nurses, social workers, psychologists, psychiatrists, are taking the role of a patient in a situation of everyday occurrence. For instance, the patient who refuses to obey rules as they are applied in the hospital or clinic setting. The students learn to take both roles, those of a patient as well as their own professional role. The training situations are structured according to typical conflicts with which they are familiar, or that they are likely to face in their professional roles. Several versions of how to deal with the obstreperous patient can be represented by various students. The patient is usually portrayed by an auxiliary ego, a staff member, so that real patients need not be involved.

Another teaching application is to have staff members sit in on actual patient sessions, becoming involved as seems necessary. In this event, the patient represents himself, the staff members themselves. Role reversal between staff member and patient will intensify learning, with each getting a new perception of their relationship and of the responsibility in being a staff member, and the agony of being a patient.

Psychodrama combined with narcosynthesis, LSD, etc.

Under the influence of drugs, the patient relives certain experiences or, after having undergone drug therapy, needs to integrate his monodrama as it unfolded inside of him while he was unable to communicate those experiences.

There are two variables: the drug, for instance sodium pentathol, and the enactment of the inner worlds. The question here is which variable contributes what to the treatment.

Family psychodrama and family therapy

Husband and wife, mother and child, are treated as a combination rather than alone, often facing one another and not separate, because separate from one another they may not have any tangible mental ailment (Moreno, J.L. 1945a; Moreno, J.L., Z.T., and J.D. 1955).

In the course of this approach the family members may reverse roles, double for each other, and in general, serve as each other's auxiliary ego.

Summary

The important question that remains to be answered is the scientific evaluation of psychodrama. Does psychodrama, with or without group psychotherapy, beyond the subjective reports of therapists and their patients, produce behavior change? According to John Mann, forty-one studies have substantiated that fundamental changes in behavior take place (Mann 1965).

Article 15

The Saga of Sociometry

Moreno, Z.T. (1965) *Group Psychotherapy, A Quarterly Journal* XVIII, 4: 275–276

Zerka's comments

I found this totally unsolicited modern day example of Moreno's "parent test" in a popular magazine. We wanted to point out anything from everyday life – in this case the popular media – that offered an example of sociometry and reflected its history. We received no report of results from McCall's.

Sociometric tests have come of age. They go back as far as 1910, to the romantic "Kingdom of the Children" in the Viennese Augarten, when the children at a family picnic were asked by J.L. Moreno to designate whom they wanted as their parents, regardless of blood ties. This, the original "parent test," at which the children moved towards those adults they designated as their choice, was a more-than-mild shock to many a parent, for here they experienced dramatically their offspring's overt rejection or admission of mutuality of choice. Some parents found themselves joyfully surrounded by large hordes of children – their own among them. Others were amazed to have acquired "sociometric offspring" – not their own flesh and blood, but the children of other parents, while their own were having a fine time with their newly adopted parents. Still others found themselves entirely without children – a foretaste of things to come!

Since that day of the First Sociometric Revolution, the sociometric test itself has undergone numerous modifications and adaptations. In 1932 at the New York State Training School for Girls at Hudson, New York, the "parent test" was extended to include not only choices by new girls for housemothers they wanted and in whose cottages space was available, but also the choices by and for the sociometric stars in the cottages, representing the peer-sibling group of the newcomer. Thus, adjustment and acceptance of the newcomers were greatly facilitated and their integration into the community speeded up.

Sociometric testing has been used in school systems from kindergarten to university, the military (of which one notable adaptation was the "Buddy Test" used especially in Korea), industry, government, prisons, mental hospitals, institutions of all types, to return again in newer forms. And of late, students at Yale, New York University, the College of the University of the City of New York, among others, have been asked to "rate" their professors. We assume that, like the parents mentioned above, the professors may be subjected to a few eye-openers.

This brings us to one of the most sophisticated applications yet uncovered on the popular level. *McCall's* magazine for January, 1966 has come out with the following closing statement and questionnaire, on page 10, under the column entitled *Sight and Sound.* We are copying it below by permission of the editor of *McCall's*, Mr. Robert Stein.[1] We are eager to have your ratings of your own children, and of any other youngsters in your social atom for their parents. Please let us have the responses right away. *McCall's* will integrate them with all those they receive and publish the results. In addition, we would be interested in your own comments as to the meaning of this procedure, as it is actually a "sociometric mass test." Such mass techniques can be applied to other problems of national and international scope, such as the Negro–white problem, or the war in Vietnam. [Editor's note: The following text and survey are reproduced from *McCall's*.]

Heirs apparent. Inspired by the countrywide tendency to have college students grade their faculties, we decided to bring this frightening practice right into the home. Below, a form for youngsters from 6 to 16. If you are a parent, why not be daring and hand this to your offspring? After all, you do have tenure – and won't it be fun to find out what the kids think? (Kids: Give it to us straight.) We'll publish the results this spring.

BOYS AND GIRLS: GRADE YOUR PARENTS!

A parent-rating system for modern children. (Fill in and mail to Sight and Sound, McCall's, 230 Park Avenue, New York, N.Y., 10017. Results to be published in a later issue. Note: You may omit your name and address if you wish.)

FATHER		MOTHER	
(CHECK ONE)	(CHECK ONE)	(CHECK ONE)	(CHECK ONE)
Wonderful ☐	*Too strict* ☐	*Wonderful* ☐	*Too strict* ☐
O.K. ☐	*Not strict enough* ☐	*O.K.* ☐	*Not strict enough* ☐
Just all right ☐		*Just all right* ☐	
Annoying ☐		*Annoying* ☐	
Do you argue?	*Yes* ☐ *No* ☐	*Do you argue?*	*Yes* ☐ *No* ☐
About what? ______		*About what?* ______	
______		______	
Best quality ______		*Best quality* ______	
Worst fault ______		*Worst fault* ______	
Does he understand you?	*Yes* ☐ *No* ☐	*Does she understand you?*	*Yes* ☐ *No* ☐
Do you understand him?	*Yes* ☐ *No* ☐	*Do you understand her?*	*Yes* ☐ *No* ☐

Would you like to change your parents in any way? *Yes* ☐ *No* ☐

If yes, how? ______

______

Do you feel they are giving you a good start in life? *Yes* ☐ *No* ☐

Explain ______

______

Name ______ *Age* ______ *School grade* ______

Street ______ *City* ______ *State* ______ *Zip Code* ______

Chapter 3

Transitions

1966–1974

The Right to be Me

I am not you
or he
or she
I'm Me.

I am not short
or tall
or big
or small
I'm Me.

I am not good
or bad
or gay
or sad
I'm Me.

Oh, let me Be!

Don't you know?
Can't you see?
First of all
I'm Me!

From *Love Songs to Life*
Zerka T. Moreno

Article 16

Sociogenesis of Individuals and Groups

Moreno, Z.T. (1966) In J.L. Moreno (ed.), *International Handbook of Group Psychotherapy*, New York: Philosophical Library, pp. 231–242

Zerka's comments

I presented this paper at the Third International Congress of Group Psychotherapy in Milan, Italy, 1964. It was well received, and the comments reflected positively on our institute. As usual Jonathan, age 12 was with us. Other conference-goers had brought their children, so he had playmates. Thus, two of my major roles flowed together.

The sociodynamically oriented group psychotherapist views the development of the individual and of the group according to certain "sociogenetic laws." One of the first of these is that the group has a structure of its own which can be studied and measured, and another, that group organization develops from early, simple forms into more complex and higher forms. The group, like the individual, has a skeleton that can be made visible by sociometric and psychodramatic microscopic intervention. A description of the sociometric skeleton of the group includes the following findings which have been discovered and verified to exist in all groups so studied: individuals who form no relationship, they do not choose and are not chosen, these are called isolates; individuals who choose but are not chosen in turn, these are called unchosen or neglected; individuals who are rejected, rejectees; individuals who form mutual pairs or dyads; individuals who form incongruous pairs, one choosing the other who rejects him in turn; individuals who form chains and clusters of mutual choice or of mutual rejection; individuals who form "interpersonal networks" of mutual relations though not necessarily on a face-to-face basis, but through links of key individuals who act as junctures for numerous sets of mutual relationships.

The instrument used to bring to light these skeletal structures is the sociometric test, and the findings are always in relationship to a criterion on which the choices are based, and only relate to a particular group at a specific time and place and in reference to a shared function within the group.

Groups develop from a non-specific, horizontal type of structure without a top or bottom to highly differentiated substructures which propel the individuals within the group towards choice, isolation or rejection, and with leaders on top of the pyramid. Various types of leadership have been uncovered as well as various types of isolation. These findings are being confirmed by researchers all over the globe and in varying cultures.

The psychodramatist extends the sociometric test. He views man as an improvising actor, living in roles. Some of these roles may be productive and integrative, others deficient or weakly developed, and some actually destructive to himself and to others. The actor emerges slowly from a non-specific mold into an individual with his own particular, private set of roles; but even these private roles partake of and are shaped by collective elements within the culture in which he shares. The child from birth until about the twenty-sixth week of life lives in what is called in sociometry "a stage of organic isolation." He does not recognize his peers and is not recognized by them in turn. In psychodramatic terms, he lives in what Moreno has called the "matrix of all-identity." He experiences his universe as a totality of himself. Only gradually does he become aware that he is not the entire universe, that his being has limits and that other beings move to and fro in this universe.

Once he begins to be aware of separation between himself and other beings and objects, his psychodramatic and social role repertoire starts to form. What is usually described as the ego grows out of the roles enacted by the human actor. The psychodramatic view of man states that the neonate is not given an ego or an identity from the start, but that he works on it, slowly, painfully. It is molded, assisted or distorted by the world around him, his co-actors. He starts with the physical organism that has been endowed to him, using it as the interaction of his spontaneity with his environment allows. His ego emerges from the roles and not, as is usually claimed, the other way around.

Roles are divided into three major categories: (1) psychosomatic roles, which are active from birth on, such as the eater, the sleeper, the walker, etc.; (2) psychodramatic or fantasy roles, as God, the angels, devils, gremlins, etc.; and (3) social roles, as the policeman, the judge, the soldier, the teacher, and so on. Every culture can be studied from the framework of these roles and each culture produces the roles that are relevant for it. The role of the astronaut, for instance, now so important in our technologically advancing era, certainly has no place as yet in the heart of the Congo.

The family, too, has been investigated from both the sociometric and psychodramatic viewpoints. The same dynamics operate within the hierarchy of the family as operate in groups at large. There are the highly chosen, the medium-range, and the under-chosen or rejected individuals. The sociometric hierarchy does not necessarily parallel the official, authority-based structure and may at times run completely counter to it.

Such families tend to fall apart as family units or to congeal into substructures which are anathema to good parent–child relations. They may, for example, show close sibling-to-sibling relations or warm parent–parent relations, the other generation being left out of the socioemotional contact so necessary for family cohesion.

The factor responsible for mutuality of relationships between individuals and in a group is called "tele." Tele is made up of the reality-based feelings that individuals have for one another in relationship to their interaction in roles and situations they share together here and now. The existence of tele, its effect upon group structure as deviating from chance, has been experimentally validated. Without tele, groups cannot cohere and will fall apart. Transference, in this orientation, is the dissociative factor and the pathological branch of tele. Transference is always a one-way process of projection. Transferences cannot meet, since they are totally subjective. Even if they occur between two people simultaneously, it is never a case of transference/counter-transference, but rather separate subjective states.

The sociometrist speaks of another law: "the sociodynamic law," which is basic to our understanding of the sociogenesis of groups and of individuals. In a given group, a percentage of individuals will be over-chosen, obtaining more love than they can give or consummate (the sociometrically rich, sometimes referred to as the sociometric capitalists). Another, larger percentage will represent the sociometric middle class, giving and receiving approximately an equal amount of choices, about as much as they can use productively. Another percentage will represent the sociometric proletariat, the unwanted, unchosen or rejected individuals, who obtain and give far less love than they need for emotional growth and integration. It may shock this audience to know that in many groups studied so far, especially in groups of school children, the percentage of unchosen individuals runs between twelve and fourteen percent. Think of it. More than one tenth of the entire population of our globe may be found to fall within this category, and these are only the extremes on the scale! A far larger percentage will have to be included if we think of those who hover on the edges of isolation in our societies.

The accident- or injury-prone fall into the sociometric category of isolated, unwanted or rejected individuals. Recently, in New York State, an intensive campaign was waged against repeaters in driver-caused accidents. Their frequent involvement in such accidents made them poor insurance risks. The only satisfactory approach to them – and many were tried, including individual psychotherapy – was group psychotherapy. A report by the Governor of New York State quite emphatically pointed out that the follow-up on these individuals made this mode of psychotherapy the treatment of choice in their case.

Just as we have little control over time or place of our birth, so we have little control over the sociometric family structure into which we are born.

These sociometric family structures pre-exist us; every child has to find his place within them. The sociometric structure in the family is different for every child. Hence, we are able to observe how some children thrive and others do not, within one and the same family. There are good sociometric reasons for these differences. Some of the variables that influence our sociometric situation are: culture, race, sex, religion, economic status, position in the family ranking, and, as we grow older, age. An individual who is born male, for instance, when the sociometric choice of the mother is for a female child, immediately is confronted with a major setback with which it may well take him his entire lifetime to learn to deal. How does one cope with the existential fact that one is not of the desired sex, race, religion, culture, age, etc.? We know the impact of these problems and their compounded effects only too well. The sociometrist sees the seeds of these conflicts within every family, in every group and in every culture, though their outward expressions may differ.[1]

The sociometrist has more than diagnosis to contribute to the amelioration of these existential conditions. After the diagnosis has been made, sociodynamic theory can be used to restructure the groups more along the lines of their spontaneous responses.

For instance, in the seating order around the table in the so-called "normal family" in our western culture, the baby sits nearest to Mama, so she can supervise his prowess. However, sociometrized families have taught us that this typical seating order is often the worst arrangement possible for the baby, whose first choice for the table partner is frequently Daddy and not Mummy, this being the one time of the day he can get close to Papa. Disorderly, rebellious behavior in the family, with the concomitant disturbed atmosphere so bad for digestion and emotional health – and what can be a more devastating situation than one that recurs with such deadly certainty in all families at times more than once daily? – has been rectified by the simple maneuvering of the seating arrangement, in accord with all the choices of all the partners involved. Even in a democracy – a much-abused term – how often is the baby's choice as heavily weighted as that of his authority figure?

Sociometry is pure democracy in action; but it is more than that. We are by now used to the idea of transplanting our vegetation in accord with its needs. We analyze carefully the elements that make up the soil in which our crops will thrive. We build special hothouses, artificially regulated as to light, temperature, moisture, etc. The same general approach is used for our livestock. By comparison, our manipulation of humans is, to say the least, exceedingly crude. Sociometry finds the suitable group soil and then proceeds to so transplant individuals that their growth, integration and equal participation in group life are insured, by scientific means.

In the philosophy of spontaneity–creativity, every man is viewed as a potential genius; one whose spontaneity and creativity, if permitted to grow closer to its potential, will produce levels of integration that are rarely achieved, at least in our western culture. This is not to say that more primitive cultures are likely to produce more spontaneous individuals. Rather, that a culture based on spontaneity–creativity will produce a different type of personality development than is now possible. Most known cultures regard highly such qualities as intelligence, memory, mechanical skills, motor coordination, etc. But spontaneity–creativity for their own sake are not considered of equal importance. It has taken the psychodramatists a long time to make the spontaneity–creativity axis acceptable and we are still struggling with having its essential features understood and appreciated.

Spontaneity is defined varyingly as an adequate response to a new situation, or a new response to an old situation, or further qualified, a response of varying degrees of adequacy to a situation of varying degrees of novelty. The only truly spontaneous individual is the neonate at the moment of birth. He is entering for the very first time into a situation that is entirely novel and his adequacy of performance in it will determine whether he will live or die. He will go through numerous kinds of learning from that point on, but this response makes all the others possible. We may, therefore, think of the neonate as the true genius of mankind. Psychodramatic therapy revolves around restoring some of the neonate's spontaneity to persons whose later learnings have cramped, distorted, submerged or denied it. But spontaneity in one person meets or fails to meet counter-spontaneity in the other. Therefore, spontaneity training has to deal with all the persons involved in a relationship. It was Moreno who first stated that, for instance, a marital couple represents not two, but three entities: the husband, the wife, *and* the relationship between them. This third entity, the relationship between them, is the particular expression of their interaction in numerous roles, the arena in which they meet as actors, co-actors and inter-actors.

Actors do not act alone, but with others, in concert or disharmony. The disharmony may start very early in the development of the infant. The neonate is entirely dependent in the first months of life upon auxiliary egos, helpers who do for him what he is unable to do, and who assist him in gradually doing those things he can begin to achieve alone. We have assumed too long that parents are born, not made. We know now that the mere biological production of a child not yet a mother makes. The role of the mother is exceedingly taxing and one in which we could all stand training.

Psychodramatic training of motherhood proceeds from the basis that every mother carries within her collective experiences of babies in general, besides the individual experience and images which she has of her own baby. She has also private experiences of her specific mother, and collective experiences of the mother role besides those of her own role as a mother.

Learning takes place in psychodrama through enacting these collective experiences but with the special reference to her own baby as embodied by a trained auxiliary ego. These action images and feelings may differ from culture to culture.

The psychodramatist views the child as the chief protagonist in the mother–child drama, because it is he who needs most help. The mother is tested in action and assessed in terms of her spontaneity, adequacy of performance and ability to serve the child's needs. Because the child is incapable of giving full expression to his experiences, a trained auxiliary ego who has had the chance to observe the mother in action with her own child will step in when training commences, taking the "role" of the baby, warming up as intensively as possible to the perceptions she feels the mother has of her child. The auxiliary ego will "speak" for the baby, even if it is a neonate, trying to come close to the mother's action perception. She will think and express and do things which the mother may feel about the baby, even though the baby is not capable of doing so. It is the mother's perception of the child that may be weak, totally or partially distorted, incomplete or negative, that the auxiliary ego attempts to arouse and confront, in order that change may take place. It is action learning in a non-threatening situation, which, though molded after life, is more plastic. The auxiliary ego child will not be damaged by the mother's mistakes, and in turn, the auxiliary ego is objective enough to assist the mother's attempts to change. The auxiliary ego is a go-between; he operates between the chief therapist and the protagonists; an actor, interpreter and guide all in one.

There is another, subtler aspect to the need for motherhood training that psychodrama has uncovered. Every female bears within her, from early infancy on, an imaginary, or psychodramatic, fantasy baby. In some this fantasy baby is weaker, in others stronger. This baby exists within her and continues to do so, in varying stages of dormancy or development, whether she actually bears children or not. The "psychodramatic baby" is a universal phenomenon, occurring in different cultures, as sociogenetic studies indicate. In some women this idealized baby is such an intensive experience that it may interfere with and overlie the actuality of her live child. The psychodramatic baby is then "real," the live child but a phantom to her.

Therapy lies in helping the mother to bring the perception of the psychodramatic baby and that of the real baby closer together, first by permitting the psychodramatic baby to live in the retraining situation. Once it has been "born" and is outside of her, finished like a real child, she can begin the separation from it. We cannot let go of those precious things with which we have not yet finished. Therapy consists for all our patients, in whatever category, in learning to complete unfinished business and then settling down to the tasks at hand that require our attention here and now.

Once she has been able to deliver herself of the fantasy baby, she will be more ready to become available as the mother to her live baby.

Lest we psychodramatists be accused of favoritism towards the child in all parent–child conflicts, allow me now to present a situation in which psychodrama is used, not as a method of *expression*, but as a method of *restraint*. It is our contention that where restraint is indicated, it should be so presented as to come from within the child, rather than having it imposed from without. Imposition of restraint from without may lead to still greater rebellion or may increase the barriers between mother and child rather than reduce them. Psychodrama presents opportunities for built-in spontaneous restraint via the use of the role and role reversal.

In role reversal, the parent takes the role of the child, while the child takes the role of the parent, thus borrowing the status, dignity, authority, actions and feelings which the child experiences in the parent. Psychodrama, like charity, should begin at home. The following illustration deals with a role reversal that took place between my own son, Jonathan, at two and a half years of age, and myself. He had become very adept at using role reversal to strengthen his own ego several times, and it looked at times as if the role playing and role reversal game might deteriorate into an "I-can-do-everything-I-want with this role reversal business" on his part. However, the psychotherapist in me would not permit abuse of either a method or a person. One day, when he was just getting ready to go upstairs for his afternoon nap, he waited at the bottom of the steps to be carried to the second floor of our house. In his most precious-baby tones he stated with much conviction, "I'm a little baby. You're Mummy now," like a psychodramatic director who doles out the roles at the beginning of a new scene. He looked at me with great big beautiful shiny orbs and commanded, "Carry me, Mummy." "Oh," I replied in my most charming manner, "You be Mummy and I'll be Jonathan." We reversed roles and changed places in space. Now I, in the role of Jonathan, stretched out my arms to him and commanded, "Carry me upstairs, Mummy!" Jonathan, as Mummy, replied with more dignity than subtlety, "You are a big boy now and very heavy. Walk up the steps by yourself." We reversed roles again and he walked proudly upstairs, without assistance or complaint.

Role reversal is based on a very ordinary, diurnal idea. How often have we said in the midst of a heated argument with another person, "But what do you want from me? Just put yourself in *my* position!" Psychodrama is scientific, for it is organized common sense personified. Instead of merely talking about this, we actually do it, by means of role reversal. There is an old American Indian saying which states, "Let me not judge another man until I have walked a mile in his moccasins." Role reversal is what parents must learn to do with their children, what marital partners must learn to do with their mates, what every person should learn to do in order to become the well-balanced, well-rounded, properly integrated, satisfactorily-interacting, spontaneous being for which he has the potential. We may well start with our children because their spontaneity and wisdom is closer to the truth than our own.

In the sociometrically organized world of the future we will live by the commandment: Be Spontaneous!

Article 17

Evolution and Dynamics of the Group Psychotherapy Movement

Moreno, Z.T. (1966) In J.L. Moreno (ed.), *International Handbook of Group Psychotherapy*, New York: Philosophical Library, pp. 27–35

Zerka's comments

It was necessary to constantly set the record straight about the beginnings of the movement. For us, it wasn't a question of competition or recognition. It was more an issue of keeping the method intact so that it could retain its potency and effectiveness. We weren't interested in turf, but due recognition was also important.

Group psychotherapy is a creation of the twentieth century. It is an American movement.

Group psychotherapy became a "historic" event through the leadership of a Viennese psychiatrist, J.L. Moreno, who came to the USA in 1925, and through the efforts of a few American-born pioneers. We are fully aware that scattered efforts in the direction of group therapy have been made under different names in other countries, but they did not crystallize into a movement. This happened only in the United States.

It is comparatively easy to determine the origins and history of the group psychotherapy "movement" as it relates to *events, dates* and *places*. This is the main task of this introduction.

It is far more difficult to trace the origins of various methods and their inventors. We have been only partly successful in this. Further research is necessary to clarify more completely the emergence of one or another method and its influence upon the movement. A method may have loomed important in 1921 but appear overrated in 1935. Methods that emerged in 1935 may appear two decades later as negligible. It is up to future historians of science to explore further.

Defining and naming the field

Looking over the literature of the last thirty years one would get the impression, because of the growing number of modifications, that group psychotherapy is a "leaderless" movement. Actually, there was clear leadership visible in the beginning, of which sight was lost. The situation was like not seeing the forest because of the trees. Whatever changes a movement may undergo in the course of time, it is important to know its *status nascendi*.

The inspiration of a new idea or movement is often expressed in the name by which it becomes known and by which it is identified. "Group therapy" and "group psychotherapy" have become the all-encompassing key phrases representing our field. It is significant that the combination of *group* and *therapy* survived. The combination of the term *group* with *analysis, psychology, treatment* or *guidance* did not last on the global level. It was the emphasis on therapy, rather than on research or analysis, that made history.[1]

The group psychotherapy "movement" must be differentiated from the group "methods" that developed from it. An organized movement is expressed in the creation of institutions, societies, scientific journals, teaching and training centers, and in its tendency to spread among the laity. Examples of organized movements are Christianity, Marxism, and psychoanalysis. A distinction is made between the idea and the organization dedicated to its propagation. Christ was the carrier of the idea, but Peter was the founder of the Church of Christianity. Marx was the author of *Das Kapital*, an important scientific work, but he and Engels became the founders of the communistic movement when they organized the "First International." Freud developed psychoanalytic methods, but he became the founder of the psychoanalytic movement when he sponsored the First Psychoanalytic Society, the first psychoanalytic journal and psychoanalytic institutes.

There are scientific methods that do not lead to the development of an organized social movement; for instance, the Mendelian theory of heredity and the conditioned reflex system of Pavlov. They remained laboratory- and university-anchored.

Group psychotherapy belongs to the category of social movements. It has developed institutions, societies, etc. all over the globe.

In the historical account of the group psychotherapy movement we shall present the authors in chronological order. They are recorded one by one as they emerge in history with their ideas or methods in specific publications traceable in literature. The authors are treated as historical phenomena rather than in a summary manner. Because of space limitations we shall apply this principle particularly to the crucial early period (1908–1935), during which the basic and lasting orientations developed. This period may be called the era of the pioneers, an era usually associated with the names of Moreno, Pratt, Lazell, Burrow, and Marsh. We trace the work of these men back to the places where they began – Moreno to Vienna, Pratt to Boston, Lazell to Washington, DC, Burrow to Westport, and Marsh to Long Island.

Several versions of ranking are possible according to the point of view:

1 According to date of first publication: Pratt and Moreno rank first, Lazell, Burrow and Marsh rank second.
2 According to treating problems of mental hygiene, mental disorders, etc.: Moreno, Lazell, Burrow and Marsh rank first, Pratt ranks second.
3 According to concepts still dominating the field: Moreno and Burrow rank first; Pratt, Marsh and Lazell rank second.
4 According to continuity of productivity: Moreno ranks first; Pratt, Lazell, Marsh and Burrow rank second.
5 According to originality of therapeutic philosophy: Moreno and Burrow rank first; Pratt, Lazell and Marsh rank second.

An interdisciplinary process

Group psychotherapy is an interdisciplinary process. It is related to several disciplines: psychiatry, psychology, sociology, anthropology, and education, to mention a few. But it has become a scientific and therapeutic discipline in its own right based on a growing science of the group. It is not an adjunct to any other discipline, such as to psychoanalysis or social psychology. "I am a group psychotherapist" sounds as respectable today as "I am a psychoanalyst." Group psychotherapy means simply to treat people in groups.

The literature of modern group psychotherapy is practically sixty years old (1907–1965) but the movement itself is only thirty-four years old (1931–1965). Sufficient time has elapsed for an objective appraisal of its pioneers, organizers, and methods.

A new revolution in psychiatry is taking place in our country, called by Moreno the "Third Psychiatric Revolution." (The first, suggested by Zilboorg, was symbolized by the emancipation of the insane from chains; the second by psychodynamics and psychoanalysis.) This Third Psychiatric Revolution has transformed the meaning and practice of psychiatry, largely due to the impact of social forces.

Appraisals have been made from time to time by numerous writers (Giles W. Thomas, Joseph I. Meiers, Raymond Corsini, etc.), but the actual data have come to the fore only gradually.

Beginnings of an organized movement

Group psychotherapy as an "organized" social movement originated in the USA in 1931. It was in August of that year that the National Committee on Prisons and Prison Labor published the first edition of Moreno's *Plan for the Transforming of Prisons into a Socialized Community*. The book was distributed widely by the National Committee on Prisons and Prison Labor throughout the USA, Great Britain and Europe. The Committee sponsored a research program at Sing Sing Prison. The New York State Training School for Girls at Hudson, NY sponsored research there. The objective was the transformation of a prison and a mental hospital into therapeutic communities, and "the therapeutic regrouping" of the occupants of the Hudson reformatory on a sociometric basis (sociometric group psychotherapy based on diagnostic sociograms).

During the annual meeting of the American Psychiatric Association in Philadelphia on May 31, 1932, a "Conference on the Group Method" was initiated by Moreno under the sponsorship of the National Committee of Prisons and Prison Labor. The topic of the conference was Moreno's book, which had just appeared in March, 1932 in its second edition entitled *Application of the Group Method to Classification*. More than one hundred psychiatrists, psychologists and sociologists took part in the conference. Its moderator was the late Dr. William Alanson White.

The book contained sections on group therapy, describing its application to delinquents, prisoners, children, and mental patients, fields in which the method from then on continued to have its widest application. The method had further applications in other fields as well. *The Application of the Group Method to Classification* was not only Moreno's first American book but also "the" *first book on group psychotherapy*. Quoting from Dr. Walter Bromberg's foreword, "There seems little historical reason to doubt his pioneership." In this book the terms "group therapy" and "group psychotherapy" were used for the first time in several places and defined in the meaning that is now universally accepted: "One man the therapeutic agent of the other, one group the therapeutic agent of the other" (Moreno 1931: 103). Thus, these terms were put into circulation and the subject was studied within the framework of empirical science. It was the beginning of "scientific" group psychotherapy.[2]

The definition of group psychotherapy in its current meaning was spelled out two years later in Moreno's *Who Shall Survive?* that further developed its principles (Moreno 1934: 301): "Group therapy treats not only the individual who is the focus of attention because of maladjustment, but the whole group of individuals who are interrelated." This definition referred to both clinical group therapy and family therapy.

Sociometry and group psychotherapy were sponsored by Dr. William Alanson White at Saint Elizabeths Hospital, Washington, DC in the autumn of 1934. The application of the group method to resettlements was encouraged by Franklin D. Roosevelt in 1935. These combined activities accomplished the first stage in the group psychotherapy movement.

Summing up, it seems that scientific group psychotherapy is indeed a creation of the twentieth century. The field was initiated and named by J.L. Moreno when he introduced the terms "group therapy" and "group psychotherapy" in 1931 and 1932. He has been given credit for fathering the movement. Credit for the "methods," however, should be given to each pioneer according to merit.

Early application of group psychotherapy to prisons, hospitals, schools and child guidance

As already pointed out, the first book on group psychotherapy was Moreno's *Application of the Group Method to Classification.* It has been overshadowed by *Who Shall Survive?* which appeared three years later and developed further its principles. As the first English presentation of scientific foundations of group psychotherapy, *Application of the Group Method to Classification* introduced several methods of classification. Its main thesis was the study of group formation and its relation to group structure. It started "a study of inner structures of (small) groups which can be compared with studies concerning the nuclear nature of the atom or the physiological structure of the cell."

In order to accomplish this aim, Moreno introduced a number of methods:

1 *The sociometric experiment.* "The objectives of these experiments are to add to the knowledge of group structure. In classes with an average of 25 to 35 pupils the children were instructed to choose spontaneously those pupils they would prefer to be associated with . . . These experiments corroborated the importance of the sociometric choice factor in any system of classification which leads to group assignment." These data were then presented in sociometric diagrams and analyzed. They were the first sociometric diagrams published, preceding the sociograms in *Who Shall Survive?*

2 *The spontaneity test.* "The intelligence tests have been made after the standard of formal interview. But to answer set questions and to meet reality are two different things. We need in addition to what we have, a method of testing which is patterned after a life situation. This is what the spontaneity test attempts . . . The initial attempt to *warm-up* was crowded in their memory and they experienced resistive conflictive tendencies for the first time."

3 *Role playing.* "A number of persons were placed opposite one another in a situation whose pattern was unknown to them before the moment of start and in roles and states which were equally unknown to them. The writer's first suggestion to them during the initial phase of experimentation was to let loose, unconcerned about involuntary remarks and gestures, faithfully relying upon the spontaneous aptitudes to act and react on the spur of the moment." The spontaneous responses were recorded in interaction diagrams which were then submitted to measurement and analysis.

4 *An objective analysis of interrelation attributes in small groups.* "Group formation is to be on the basis of the interrelationship attributes of men. When we observe that the same individual is intolerant and demonstrative in one group, tolerant and abiding in another group, that the same individual takes the attitude of a solitaire in one group but is cooperative and suggestible in another group, we begin to suspect that a great number of these traits are falsely labeled individual and are truly interrelationship products."

In a section entitled "An Illustration of Group Therapeutics," the application of these four methods was demonstrated. "A ten year old girl was sent to us because she used to bite her nails ruthlessly. In the first phase we shifted her from one group of playmates to others, having in mind to acquaint her with a wide range of children. Then we let her *choose* any playmate she liked, as we do not interfere if the patient can shape a remedial situation for himself . . . We laid our emphasis on the *present* because we realized that the products of our interrelations were *new*, constellations resulting from the clash of their individual mechanisms, interrelation effects . . . Every situation into which the child was placed was well defined and well prepared, but for the child, each was an impromptu situation. The behavior during each situation was afterwards analyzed, but the analysis and the therapeutic process did not run parallel and were kept apart . . . Group therapy is thus the result of well calculated spontaneous therapy plus proper social assignment. In other words, psychological treatment is projected away from the clinic into real life situations, and techniques for a proper procedure to be used on the spot are developed. The leader is within the group, not a person outside."

These group methods were similarly applied to a mental hospital and at Sing Sing Prison, breaking up the population into small groups of seven. Group therapy was based therefore upon a combination of observations, interviews, discussions, spontaneity tests, sociometric tests, role playing, and objective analysis of interrelations.

Corsini (1957) made the following comment: "In 1931 he [Moreno] suggested a new method of prison classification, arguing that if prisoners were grouped sociometrically the interactions would be beneficial. In a monograph on this thesis he used the magic words 'group therapy' for the first time, although, as stated before, in a somewhat different sense from that currently employed. Actually the group therapist did not even have to come into contact with the group members, since groups were to be constituted on paper in terms of analyses of their own strengths and weaknesses."

This comment gives the impression that Moreno introduced a new method of classification exclusively for prisoners. Actually, the method of classification was applied, as quoted above, to numerous social settings, schools, child guidance clinics, and mental hospitals, in addition to the prison situation. It also conveys the impression that Moreno formed groups merely by placing patients together on the basis of their "sociometry," without considering their subjectivities, their confrontation with each other, and their therapist. This, obviously, does not make sense. How could there be any sociometric test without the most intensive interpersonal contact between the group members and their therapist?

This well-intended but misleading comment has been repeated by other writers and has spread a false picture of the methods used by Moreno in group formation, and of the meaning of group therapy. Actually, the current trend in the forming of small therapy groups increasingly follows the lines Moreno laid out in his first book.

Another significant aspect in Moreno's first book is his early emphasis and reinforcement of the "analytic trend" in group psychotherapy. (He is frequently labeled as anti-analytic.) He was the first to use the term "group analysis" in the current sense. He criticized vigorously "the lack of a group analytical basis." In the following words he opposed the inspirational method: "Spontaneous formation of social groups based on the enthusiasm of the participants or on common interests and aims achieves often miraculous results but cannot be called grouping in our sense, as most of the interrelations remain unanalyzed."

Therapy groups are small groups. They exercised a dominant influence upon small group research. The group therapy movement and small group research developed simultaneously and are closely interlocked.

Article 18

The Seminal Mind of J.L. Moreno and His Influence upon the Present Generation

Moreno, Z.T. (1967) *International Journal of Sociometry and Sociatry, A Quarterly Journal* V, 3–4: 145–156

Zerka's comments

It was important that Moreno be put properly into the picture of the evolution of group psychotherapy. I came up with these questions by role reversing with the person who didn't know anything about psychodrama – what would they want to know?

A new development since the writing of this article is that I was contacted in March 2004 by Dr. Robert Waldl, a philosophy student in Vienna whose PhD research compares a totally new and idiosyncratic use of the German language in Moreno's 1918 paper published in Der Daimon *to Buber's use of almost exactly the same words in* Ich und Du, *published five years later in 1923. The intent is not to build a case for plagiarism, but rather to establish the source of a point of reference, one which has had a profound influence upon our culture and mode of thinking about significant areas of human concern.*

In the social sciences, more than in any other branch of the humanities, it is particularly difficult to assess, as a contemporary, the sources of inspiration and the channels they have traveled on their way to becoming absorbed by the culture. Indeed, history itself is written from a subjective and biased point of view and one of the most persistent problems, even in elementary education, is the frame of reference that determines it. Religion, for instance, may at times "bend" the truth as seen by the scientist, if not force outright distortion of fact. Thus no one, not even the scientist, is above suspicion in staking claims or pointing out sources.

As a participant actor in one of the major revolutions in social science, therefore, the author is in a particularly vulnerable position, and the writing of its history, even when supported by objective evidence, dates of materials in print, and so forth, is often called into question. Nevertheless, it is profoundly satisfying to watch the spread and growth of ideas and to see them being carried forward by contemporaries, not merely as a confirmation of findings, but because of the assistance thus rendered in establishing the new frontiers of thought. In this manner we see these ideas moving from the private and personal to the general and universal. Many of Moreno's ideas have reached such a level of universality that they are becoming widely accepted as if they had always been, a fact that may be of interest to the members of the ASGPP and to the readers of this journal.

In my various roles as teacher, researcher, practitioner, editor, author, etc., I have tried to trace the development and influence of Moreno's ideas upon the group psychotherapy movement, on existentialism, behavioral techniques in psychotherapy, and psychodrama. The most recent of these efforts appeared in the *International Handbook of Group Psychotherapy* in a chapter entitled "Evolution and Dynamics of the Group Psychotherapy Movement" (Moreno, Z.T. 1966a). To my satisfaction, this chapter provoked numerous discussions and inquiries, some of which I will try to answer in this paper.

1. Who introduced the concept of "the encounter," as used by the existentialists today?

The best way to answer this is to quote from Professor Paul E. Johnson's book *Psychology of Religion* (Johnson 1959):

> In the spring of 1914 Moreno published in Vienna the first of a series of poetic writings entitled *Einladung zu einer Begegnung (Invitation to an Encounter)*, which is evidently *the first literary definition of encounter*, the concept which has become central to the existentialist movement . . . During the years 1918–20 Martin Buber was a contributing editor of *Daimon*,[1] and his articles appeared side by side with Moreno's, prophetic of the role each would have in the history of interpersonal theory.

It is clear, therefore, that Moreno should be credited with having first introduced the concept of the encounter, and not Martin Buber who was, however, a powerful force in spreading it.

2. What relationship is there between the concept of the encounter and "the encounter group," whose recent spread arouses curiosity?

In the past few years the National Training Laboratories for Group Development in Bethel, Maine, and many of its followers throughout the country, have increasingly discarded the terms "T-group" and "T-group training," and replaced them by "encounter group." This term and concept were first suggested by Moreno in *Group Training vs. Group Therapy* (Moreno, J.L. 1958a: 80):

> I differentiate natural groups, like the family, from synthetic groups like therapy and training groups and further, the *encounter group* which is neither, although it has elements of both. In the encounter group the private as well as the collective individual, both are eliminated.

This leads directly to the question as to who put forth first the idea of "training in groups." This too can be traced to Moreno; see *Who Shall Survive?* (Moreno, J.L. 1934: 321–331).

3. One hears the term "interpersonal therapy" used these days. Whence does it stem?

This concept is increasingly used in the therapy of dyads, intimate ensembles and small groups, in conjoint therapy, family therapy, matrimonial therapy, etc.

Dr. R. Grinker Jr., in an article entitled "Complementary psychotherapy" in the *American Journal of Psychiatry* (Grinker 1966), speaks of "associated pairs." In the May, 1967 issue of the *American Journal of Psychiatry*, p. 1463, Moreno commented on this article as follows:

> It is a hopeful sign of the times that a psychoanalyst of Dr. Grinker's reputation has shown an open mind toward the treatment of "associated" pairs. But it is unfortunate that authors referred to by him in his references are limited to psychoanalytically-oriented workers, since the implication is that the "leaders for change" have come from the psychoanalytic establishment. Dr. Grinker fails to mention contributions from other sources. But as in many other areas of community-related psychiatry, the original and continuous insistence upon interpersonal and joint treatment of marriage partners (Moreno, J.L. 1937, 1939c; Solby 1941) has not come from the representatives of the classic psychoanalytic school but from other schools of psychotherapy (Biddle and Thomas 1966: 5–19; Spiegel and Bell 1959: 136). The development of community-related psychiatry is, for instance, greatly indebted to interpersonal therapy, interactional group psychotherapy, sociometry, psychodrama, group dynamics, and reality practice. This should not be obliterated from the consciousness of the younger generation of psychotherapists.

As an observer of history in the making, I might add a fact that shows some of the networks of influence at work in our own lifetime. Dr. Grinker, in the above-named article on associated pairs (husband–wife, mother–daughter, etc.), lists among others in his references, articles by Dr. Bela Mittelman, "The Current Analysis of Married Couples" (Mittleman 1948) and "Simultaneous Treatment of Both Parents and Their Child" (Bychowski & Despert 1952: 103–118). Dr. Mittleman's publication dates are the earliest in Dr. Grinker's reference list: 1948 and 1952. These dates are significant. Dr. Bela Mittleman was well known to the author, as he had been a student enrolled in a seminar at the Psychodrama Institute in Beacon, and a regular attendee at open sessions at the New York City Psychodramatic Institute at 101 Park Avenue from 1942 and throughout the middle forties. Indeed, he was much intrigued by psychodrama and became involved as auxiliary ego in psychodrama sessions with a *mother–daughter pair* then under treatment in Beacon by Moreno. He often stayed after sessions in the theater at 101 Park, entering into long discussions with me on the interpersonal dynamics operating between patient and auxiliary ego, showing particular interest in the "double" technique which we were in the process of subjecting to severe clinical and experimental tests, as I have previously reported (as Zerka Toeman) in *Sociometry, A Journal of Inter-Personal Relations* (Toeman 1946) and again in *Sociatry, Journal of Group and Intergroup Therapy* (Toeman 1948).

The history of a science is permeated with such direct but meaningful interpersonal contacts that frequently change the direction of a man's thinking. They are too often overlooked and even more frequently they are not put on record.

4. How did the concept "interpersonal sensitivity" emerge?

Moreno's life was permeated by the idea "that some real process in one person's life situation is sensitive and corresponds to some real process in another person's life situation and that there are numerous degrees, positive and negative, of these interpersonal sensitivities." He was especially concerned with defining and measuring interpersonal processes and arrived at a system of quantifying the choice process, establishing mathematically, clinically and experimentally, via the choice–rejection axis, that there is a factor which is responsible for the two-way attraction and rejection interaction between persons.

The interpersonal sensitivities were subjected to careful scrutiny, in action, in spontaneity testing and training. The reader is referred to the following publications: "Statistics of Social Configurations," (Moreno, J.L. and Jennings, H.H. 1937); a detailed description of how interpersonal sensitivity operates, for instance, between husband and wife, is given in Moreno's "Inter-Personal Therapy and the Psychopathology of Inter-Personal Relations" (Moreno, J.L. 1937).

5. When was the concept of "group cohesion" first suggested and discussed?

The first edition of Moreno's *Who Shall Survive?*, 1934, contains the following statement on p. 103 about research conducted at the New York State Training School for Girls in Hudson, NY:

> We had found that the desire to remain in the present cottages – the ratio of interest summed up for all the cottages – is 44.81%. Hence it is evident that *the cohesive forces at work in Hudson were stronger than the forces drawing the girls away from their groupings.*

In "Statistics of Social Configurations" (Moreno, J.L. and Jennings, H.H. 1937, p. 363) Moreno states:

> The study of the cohesion of forces within a group can be made through an analysis of choices made and choices received, the choices going to individuals inside and to individuals outside of this constellation. A different study of cohesion is based upon the configurational aspect. It considers, instead of single elements, choices, the interpersonal structures and the degree of cohesion produced by them. Cohesion would be very low, for instance, if a larger number of choices going to the individuals of a group were unreciprocated.

The principle of group cohesion formulated by Moreno also in *Who Shall Survive?*, second, revised and enlarged edition, 1953, is on p. 454, as follows: "The larger the number of mutual pairs the wider will be the rate of interaction and the probability of a high group cohesion. The larger the number of individuals involved in positive tele communication the greater the group cohesion."

The superiority of Moreno's hypotheses on interaction to those of George C. Homans, who many years later wrote a book, *The Human Group*, largely based on sociometric findings (Homans 1950), has been demonstrated by many leading authorities in the field of human relations. For one of the most recent critiques of Homans, see Professor P. Sorokin's *Sociological Theories Today* (Sorokin 1966).

6. When were motion pictures and television first used in a therapeutic setting?

In this area, the following references are available: *Psychodrama, Vol. I*, 1946, Section IX, "Therapeutic Motion Pictures," pp. 385–420. From p. 402 to p. 420 the chapter deals specifically with the *television* medium. We quote from p. 403:

> One of the most important aspects in the study of interpersonal relations is the interactive performance of a group of persons in a medium which is continuously changing, and in which the attention of the participants is shifting from one task to another without warning. Under these conditions, split-second judgment and responsive spontaneity will be most rigorously challenged. Television is a medium in which interpersonal action of the moment is the final desideratum.
>
> A new opportunity for testing interpersonal productivity is given in television broadcasting, since it can combine in a unique fashion spontaneity of human interaction with the flexibility of a technical instrument well attuned to such intent. The human organism, singly and collectively, has in the past been so overconditioned and made so responsive to cultural conserve stimuli that new methods and procedures must be investigated in order to develop new reaction-patterns.

Motion pictures of psychodrama with genuine protagonists were first introduced by Moreno in Hudson, NY in 1933, while he was Director of Research at the New York State Training School for Girls. This film dealt with the spontaneity testing and training, and role training of girls for vocational goals. It was shown at the Department of Psychology, Columbia University, where it was seen by Professor Gardner Murphy and Dr. Kurt Lewin, to mention but two disseminators of ideas who were present. The production of motion pictures with and by patients was continued in Beacon, NY, throughout the forties.

Films specifically made for television were produced by us in Paris, for the French Radio and Television Center in 1955 and 1956, and were repeatedly shown on public television. We had the amazing experience one night of walking innocently into the entrance hall of the Hotel Lutetia in Paris, only to see our own faces staring at us from the television screen. It was being watched with rapt attention by numerous guests who recognized us at once!

Films of patients, actual protagonists in psychodrama, were made in the forties at the Psychiatric Department of the Medical School at McGill University by Dr. and Mrs. René Hartogs. At the University of California at Los Angeles Robert Haas made a film, *Psychodrama in Guidance*, in 1948.

A television breakthrough in this country came when in 1953 Dr. Verna Minear made a television broadcast for the general public using psychodrama with alcoholic patients. She reports this in our journal, *Group Psychotherapy*, under the title "An Initial Venture in the Use of Television as a Medium for Psychodrama," from which we quote: "A psychodrama session was televised for the first time on Station WTOP in Washington, DC on the 19th of April, 1953. It was one of a series of thirteen programs produced by the Committee on Education of the Alcoholic Rehabilitation Program of the District of Columbia" (Minear 1953: 115–117).

Following Dr. Minear's pioneering venture, Drs. Abel Ossorio and Leon J. Fine, of the St Louis State Hospital, made a television film in 1959, shown publicly through the courtesy of the CBS Network, in the series called *Montage*. This series won the Albert Lasker Award for outstanding television programs.

The next original venture came in the use of closed circuit TV for patients' benefit at the Camarillo State Hospital in May 1964. Moreno was televised while conducting a psychodrama session with patients and the entire patient population watched from their screens throughout the institution. The production was recorded on videotape as it proceeded and is shown weekly on the closed circuit to the patients. The complete protocol of this production was published in this journal, *Group Psychotherapy*, under the title "Psychodrama in Action" (Moreno, J.L. 1965).

Another first came about in September 1964 in Paris during the First International Congress of Psychodrama when, unbeknownst to Moreno, a complete motion picture set-up was organized in a large reception room at the old Faculté de Medicine. When he entered the room there it was, and a group of several hundred participants were breathlessly waiting, expecting a psychodrama demonstration right there and then, and . . . they got it. This production, also on film, was the psychodramatic treatment of a marital problem, with both partners participating in the psychodrama.

This film, too, was under the sponsorship of the French government, the same Radio and Television Center of France that had so graciously been involved in our two earlier undertakings there during the fifties. The complete report of this film is contained in *Group Psychotherapy*, which is part of the proceedings of that memorable First International Congress of Psychodrama, under the title "Psychodrama of a Marriage" (Moreno, J.L. 1966).

The film is especially noteworthy because its second reel consists of the "Psychodrama of a Dream" – of the wife – also a first of its kind. In psychodramatic dream production the dream is enacted by the protagonist, with the aid of auxiliary egos who closely follow the directions of the protagonist, moving and speaking only when the protagonist directs them to, like wax figures that spring to life at the touch of the good fairy's magic wand. According to recurrent reports from France, this film is repeatedly shown on the public television network and is a great favorite with the French public, who are proud that Paris was the scene of this unusual event.

Several of Moreno's associates have also appeared on national television in this country. In November 1965 on the Hugh Downs Show *Today* NBC broadcast a live production entitled *Alcoholism, America's Greatest Failure*. Psychodrama was one of the methods dealt with, and a psychodrama was conducted on the program, with an actual patient and auxiliary egos, by Hannah B. Weiner, one of the Directors of the Moreno Institute.

In 1966, Dr. Lewis Yablonsky televised a live psychodrama production with a group of patients in Los Angeles in a series called *Therapy*. Two marital partners are shown in interaction, attempting to resolve some of their difficulties, besides a number of scenes dealing with patient–adolescent conflicts involving several other members of the same group.

It is, therefore, rewarding to read in the *American Journal of Psychiatry*, Vol. 123, May 1967, dedicated to Innovative Approaches in Therapy, that other workers are rediscovering the usefulness of videotape in closed circuit TV. Drs. Ian Alger and Peter Hogan describe their application of the medium in "The Use of Videotape Recordings in Conjoint Marital Therapy" (Alger and Hogan 1967). Such confirmation of findings is absolutely imperative if we are to achieve growing understanding of person-to-person and person-to-group relations. It is noteworthy that the non-psychodramatic workers have restricted themselves largely to videotape recording for closed circuit television, whereas the action therapists have been involved from the onset in both closed and open circuit television broadcasting.

The pioneer in the field had something to say about the future of television broadcasting. As early as 1942 he was speculating about how the media would affect human interaction and spontaneity (Moreno and Fischel 1942: 7–28). He envisioned television's use not only for closed circuits, but also for open circuits for large scale, therapeutic purposes, making the mass media of communication serve the public interest rather than helping to line the pockets of commercial producers. To quote once more from *Psychodrama, Volume 1*, p. 420:

> I foresee that in the not too distant future theaters for therapeutic television and motion pictures will be just as commonplace as newsreel theaters are today (1946). Each will have a psychiatric consultant. They will provide the most effective vehicle for mass psychotherapy ever devised. 'Localized' group psychotherapy will have found a counterpart through which millions of local groups can be treated en masse.
>
> (Moreno, J.L. 1946c)

7. Considering the constant fact of Negro–white problems in the USA, who was the prophet of the present race crisis?

Moreno's systematic investigation of interracial tensions was begun and published in *Who Shall Survive?* in 1934, ten years before Gunnar Myrdal's book *An American Dilemma, The Negro Problem and Modern Democracy* (Myrdal 1944). On the basis of extensive sociometric research of small groups (schools and small communities) Moreno predicted that the latent social and emotional tensions between white and colored will eventually lead to violent outbreaks. He showed, on the basis of sociometric analysis of groups, that "there is a sociometric point of saturation of a specific homogeneous group for a specific other contrasting element under given conditions. In the case of social groups the point of saturation may change with the organization of interrelated groups."

This work was further elaborated by Dr. Joan H. Criswell in 1935 and reported on by her in an article "Racial Cleavage in Negro–White Groups" (Criswell 1935).

8. Personality researchers, psychotherapists and educators are emphasizing the involvement of the body more and more. Who was responsible for this direction away from the word, to the act?

At the risk of being repetitious, it must be said: Moreno. In his *Psychodrama*, Vol. 1, we find the following on p. 216, under the heading "Psychodrama Without Words, the Dance and Psychomusic:"

> We approach here new realms of the psychodrama, the realms of pantomime, the realm of rhythm, dance and music, and the realm of the (apparently) nonsensical. Methods for the exploration and development of a language-free, non-semantic psychopathology are needed. An illustration of such a method is the experimentation with the spontaneity states, with the warming up process, and with the body moving into space. We did not deal with the word association primarily. No verbal process was expected.
>
> (Moreno, J.L. 1946c)

And on p. 140, under "Spontaneity Training of Children:"

> Education through action and for action has been neglected. The Spontaneity Theory and Method is an answer to this demand. Founded on known facts of physiology and psychology it offers a simple practical method for the direction of those forces which determine the development of personality.
>
> (Moreno, J.L. 1946c)

On p. 142 he speaks of "Body-to-Mind training" and of "Mind-to-Body training." He repeatedly emphasizes throughout his writing that we are engaged in "body-therapy, just as much as in psychotherapy." One of his most profound disagreements with Freud arose out of his observation that "The word is not the royal route to the psyche, in fact, there are parts of the psyche which are language-resistant." On p. 11 of *Psychodrama*, Vol. 1, we read:

> A psychology of action is more akin to the Americans (as opposed to Europeans), a motorically minded people, trained by a history of pioneering and the philosophy of pragmatism to favor motoric ideas, and drama means action. "Going places and doing things" is a more popular notion to them than "sitting in a chair and reading a book." It seems easier for them to accept a psychotherapy which is a battle of acts.
>
> (Moreno, J.L. 1946c)

From body-therapy of the individual it is a logical next step to move into bodily contact, applying physiodramatic techniques, especially to non-cooperative patients who are not reached or moved by words. With them, the psychodramatists enter into combat, wrestling, boxing, hitting, pinching, slapping, caressing, gymnastics, ball games, dancing, rhythmic movements of all kinds, embodiments of animals, plants, objects, parts of the human body, etc.

During the early fifties we admitted to the hospital in Beacon a mute catatonic adolescent male, who had been in this condition for seven years during his stay at a state hospital. He was given a psychiatric aide, a young, strong and athletic male who was his constant companion. They attended sessions in the theater together, ate together, went for walks, in short, did everything together. Although Richard liked his "auxiliary ego" and did not resist him, he remained mute. Moreno then devised a program for him. He scheduled boxing and wrestling matches for Richard twice a week. The theater was turned into a ring. Patients, students and staff came to watch while the two young men showed their physical prowess. The auxiliary ego was instructed not to be "soft" with him; to counter every blow as he normally would when engaged in such a fight.

Richard responded positively to this. After six months of this completely non-verbal approach, he began to participate in psychodramas with other patients, first making astute but sparse comments as an observer, gradually as an auxiliary ego on behalf of other patients. Although always a "man of few words," he was extremely effective, sensitive, and to-the-point as an auxiliary ego, but it was impossible to get him to cooperate in the production of his own psychodrama. Nevertheless, he was discharged as much improved and returned to the community after approximately fourteen months having achieved a fair social recovery.

Moreno pioneered yet another undertaking in the area of body movement: the scientific study of boxers (which led him to the above-described form of treatment). He observed boxers in action in the ring, and, on the basis of this and numerous other areas of research which I shall describe later, predicted the outcome of the championship fight for which they were preparing themselves. He was hired repeatedly in this capacity by the Associated Press between 1935 and 1958. He went to the boxers' training camps, made action studies of the boxers while they were sparring with their partners, counted the number of times they connected per minute, recorded the complete set of movements used, measured blood pressure, breathing rate, checked the amount of perspiration both in action and while resting. To understand the psychological pressures they were enduring – besides their physical hardship – he tirelessly investigated their sociometric relationships to their trainers, promoters, members of their families.

Psychodramatically he explored their perceptions of themselves and of their opponent while in action in the ring, their fears of losing and how they manifested themselves in their dream and wake states, etc. He was even interested in what they read, ate, and their belief in God. I went along with him on a great many of these occasions and assisted in the recording. He thus investigated all the major champions and made very acute predictions about their performance – even to the number of rounds they would be able to carry. The Associated Press carried worldwide releases on his findings concerning the championship fights of Joe Louis, Max Baer, Max Schmeling, Jersey Joe Walcott, Rocky Marciano, Ezzard Charles and others. Even such famous sportswriters as Damon Runyon listened with awe to his predictions and came to rely on them for betting purposes!

Moreno made a fascinating series of discoveries while doing all this, not the least of which was that trainers intuitively chose sparring partners who represented the fighting style of the opponent their boxer was training to encounter. He designated the sparring partners – naturally – as auxiliary egos, stand-ins for the real person and the real event, very much the way the psychodramatic chief therapist proceeds to prepare his patient by means of auxiliary egos for his eventual return to his own real life partners and the inevitable encounter with them.

I attended Joe Louis's final championship fight at Yankee Stadium in 1949, and observed at first hand the various phenomena Moreno had trained us to look for. Regrettably, neither of the two aged champion-protagonists was at the height of his action power. The event left its mark in my memory nevertheless, in a heightened awareness of the multiple psychodramas that had preceded this final "physiodrama."

A number of the younger, eclectic psychotherapists, such as Fritz Perls and William C. Schutz, are using these body methods. For a long time we stood alone. It was assumed by others that all this bodily involvement was harmful for the patient, especially as it changed his relationship to his therapist from an objective to a highly subjective one. The use of auxiliary egos as go-betweens was never completely appreciated or understood. Moreno stuck to his guns. The only concern, he preached, is whether all this is done for the welfare of the patient. It is never intended to fill needs of the therapist. After all, how could a dentist, a surgeon, a gynecologist or obstetrician, or a dermatologist, practice his skills without "touching?" Is the psyche more, or less, sacrosanct than the body? Where does one begin and the other end?

We are happy to see that this barrier, too, is finally being surmounted.

9. There is a general trend in psychotherapy away from the negative view of life, to an affirmative, positive position. Who is responsible for this mood?

A social psychologist, William Schutz, recently had the courage to re-emphasize one of Moreno's cardinal ideas: to replace the therapy of negativism and depression with the therapy of gaiety and joy. This can be seen from his book *Joy: Expanding Human Awareness* (Schutz 1967). In a now classic quote, Moreno, when he met Freud, told him in 1912, "You analyze their dreams. I try to give them the courage to dream again. I teach the people how to play God." Elsewhere on the same page he continues, "Psychoanalysis had developed an atmosphere of fear among young people. Fear of neurosis was the measure of the day. A heroic gesture, a noble aspiration made its bearer immediately suspect" (Moreno, J.L. 1946c: 6).

Existential validation came to us from a practicing psychodramatist, Dr. Marvin Wellman, then Clinical Director of the Northeast Florida State Hospital at Macclenny, who wrote me in a letter on October 15, 1963:

> I think the greatest contribution which Dr. Moreno has made to medicine is the possibility of treatment with joy. We have all known the burden of therapy both on the physician and on the patient, but frequently enough in the Moreno therapy, and no place else in medicine, there is joy which is as spontaneous and as deep as the burbling of a baby. Unfortunately, Hamlet has more prestige than the Merry Wives of Windsor.

Thousands of participants in sessions of the Moreno Institute will remember one of the oldest, most persistent sayings of Moreno: "I would like my tombstone to carry an epitaph which reads 'Here lies the man who brought joy and laughter into psychiatry.'" He may well have his wish fulfilled.[4]

Article 19

Psychodrama on Closed and Open Circuit Television

Moreno, Z.T. (1968) *Group Psychotherapy, A Quarterly Journal* XXI, 2–3: 106–109

Zerka's comments

We did some very daring things and encouraged others to do so as well. Moreno asked the psychodrama group at Saint Elizabeths if psychodrama could be done on television. The hospital had the wherewithal to make it happen. Dr. Verna Minear televised a session with a female alcoholic patient on local television. Her mother at home witnessed her daughter's work on TV. This resulted in the mother and daughter having a real in-depth face-to-face conversation (not televised) for the first time.

J.L. Moreno was the first to break the orthodox rule of treating only one person in the family. He treated concurrently both parties in a marriage as early as 1923, as reported in German (Moreno, J.L. 1924). The first English report of this approach appeared in 1937 (Moreno, J.L. 1937). It was natural, therefore, that Moreno would look for a medium which permitted a more effective approach for the treatment of intimate ensembles as well as for larger groups. With this in mind, he began to weigh the possibility of using the mass media of communication. He was the first to evaluate and use motion pictures and television in the treatment of marital couples, families, and groups in combination with psychodrama (Moreno, J.L. and Fischel 1942). Reports on the television medium for teaching, training, therapeusis and research via psychodrama have appeared in this journal from time to time.

In 1966, while Moreno was conducting a seminar at the State Hospital, Pueblo, Colorado, his psychodrama session with patients was simultaneously televised on closed circuit as a teaching device for the staff, a large number of whom were gathered in the room especially set aside for this purpose. The advantages of televised psychodrama sessions have been enumerated so often that it does not seem necessary to repeat them here, but what was especially noteworthy about this occasion was the fact reported to us by the staff, namely, that we were able to involve in the psychodrama a number of patients who had been intractable on the ward and unreachable by usual methods employed.

The session began with Moreno's usual warm-up, addressing the group members, introducing himself, shaking hands with a number of group members, and establishing an atmosphere of intimacy and mutual respect. Then he addressed one of the patients who had been watching him closely, and began to ask her where she came from. She told him – it was a remote mountain area, known for its poverty and desolate isolation from the world. When he asked her "Why did you leave your home?" she launched into a tirade against her niece Violet who, according to her, had unjustly accused her of being in cahoots with the devil, stating Violet to be a witch who practiced the black art, etc. Before she could go into further details, Moreno constructed a scene in which Emily, the patient, confronted Violet, who came to visit her in the cabin to which she had returned, the role of Violet being taken by a trained auxiliary ego. Emily described her home, a bare hut up in the mountains, at the end of a narrow, winding, uphill dirt road.

At the very start it was clear that Emily lived in a world of religious hallucinations within a well-structured and frozen paranoid system. In role reversal as Violet, the auxiliary ego as her, she at once began the accusing train of thought, how Emily was scheming with the devil against God and the world, to destroy it and rule it thereafter, as the Queen of the future, implying that Emily was trying to involve her, Violet, in the plot. The auxiliary ego attempted to defend herself but this only added fat to Violet's fuel. At the height of their battle of wits the roles were reversed and in her own role Emily revealed her inability to deal with these accusations and her hatred for her niece whom she, in turn, accused of seducing her husband and turning him into an alcoholic.

None of this was produced in coherent form, but in the typical fragmented and dissociated manner of the schizophrenic, which somehow becomes coherent in the course of psychodramatic processing. In interview, this type of patient is not able to communicate, or to relate specific experiences and their contents. Within the psychodramatic context the inner drama is revealed and somehow makes supreme sense to the group members, even to those who have up to this moment been unable to put the scattered psychotic pieces of the patient's puzzle into a whole.

One of the post-session discussion questions raised by a staff member was: How do we know that this is actually the content of the patient and not the by-product of the psychodrama? Does not psychodrama have an influence over the patient's production?

Here psychodrama on the television screen becomes not merely an excellent introduction to the psychodramatic method as such, but is revealed as an equally powerful teaching instrument for giving insight into what constitutes psychopathology. So completely severed are the psychotic's experiences from those of the so-called "real world" that the depth of involvement in his own cannot be perceived until it is psychodramatized. Because this world of the patient is not transparent and cannot be penetrated by other means as thoroughly, we must not assume that psychodrama *produces* this world. This would be tantamount to accusing the microscope of *producing* microbes. Obviously, ascribing this kind of magic power to psychodrama is as unscientific as the microscope-as-microbe-producer accusation. We must learn to think in terms of the inner world of the patient, whose invisible but enormously involving processes have replaced the world of the "real," and psychodrama is its microscopic exploration.

The value of this kind of learning for the staff members can only be assessed in practice when the staff and patients take up the process of wrestling with the various demons in subsequent sessions, for now they can "see, feel and live in" Emily's world. The patients who have been made aware of Emily's ability to reveal her world can take heart and begin to reveal their own.

We do not wish to deny the influence of psychodrama upon psychotic patients, but anyone working with the type of patient represented by Emily knows that influencing for change is a very difficult process indeed. We are already very satisfied if we can just break through first, having the patient take us by the hand so that we can get to know her inner world. This is merely the beginning. Changing her world takes more than one session, if, in fact, it can be done at all.

Another session of psychodrama in closed circuit television, which was simultaneously taped, took place at the Southern Florida State Hospital at Hollywood in February, 1968. This session involved the problems of a volunteer worker at the hospital and his difficulties in translating his learning about mental illness at the hospital to persons in the community at large, whose ignorance of the trials facing the returning mental patient and of the "talent for making one another sick" – a condition so prevalent among the so-called normal population in the community – was a depressing experience. This session touched a larger number of persons in the group, a total of around 600 who were present in the large hospital auditorium.

This type of session and the tape made serve admirably to enlighten members of the lay community, to assist in sensitizing them to the changes needed to bring about greater general mental health within the ranks of the populace itself.

Article 20

Moreneans, The Heretics of Yesterday are the Orthodoxy of Today

Moreno, Z.T. (1969) *Group Psychotherapy, A Quarterly Journal* XXII, 1–2: 1–6

Zerka's comments

This article was written out of a growing concern that psychodrama was being separated from its philosophy and methodology and no longer grounded in Moreno's ideas. I don't know how effective it was, but I felt it needed to be stated. We prepared the soil. Even if only taken up in small pieces, psychodrama and group psychotherapy changed the profile of psychotherapy.

We, the Moreneans,[1] were the heretics between 1910 and 1950. Today, on the eve of 1970, the picture has changed. We are now respectable, almost orthodox. Everybody under many flags is doing what we started. Many of the concepts that we have introduced have become the "Mardi Gras" of psychiatrists, psychologists, educators, religionists and philosophers. We must protest, therefore, against uncritical use of our methods and techniques.

Freudianism

It is not so long ago that Freudian concepts and methods were sacrosanct. "Id, ego, super-ego, subconscious and unconscious, cathexis, the couch, and free association" were on all lips. Today, these terms and processes are used more and more critically or disregarded. For id, ego and super-ego, we have substituted creativity, spontaneity and the cultural conserves. For psychoanalysis, group psychotherapy; for free association, the role; for the couch, the stage or open action space; for interpretation, the warming up process and psychodrama; and for verbal communication, the act.

Behaviorism and behavior therapy

It is not so long ago that behaviorist concepts, borrowing their ideas from various schools of thought and diluting them, from Pavlov, Watson, Thorndike, Dollard, and others, were overhauled in the name of behavior therapy but the vogue for it is also beginning to lose its appeal, because behavior itself is only a symptom, which must be grounded in a meaningful philosophy of life.

Existentialism and existence therapy

The third and more recent step in this evolution of programs is academic existentialism. But what is existence? Where is the existentialist? Where are the "Christs of our time?"

Super eclecticism and the "*lingua psychiatrica*"

At the end of a long chain emerged the present condition of psychology, psychiatry and sociology: unlimited numbers of pseudomodifications, hundreds of so-called "new" techniques, thousands of "new" terms and prescriptions, a super-anomia, an anomia "without end." A new *lingua franca* of mental hygiene has developed; a mixture of terms borrowed from all schools; the *lingua psychiatrica.*

Morenean position

Moreno did not invent such methods and techniques as encounter, groups, sensitivity training, role reversal and others, for their own sake. They are based on a theory of life, without the comprehension of which they are meaningless, even harmful. According to Moreno, the roots of life are simple. Let us quote from his oldest book, *The Words of the Father*, and other books that followed.

> The universe is infinite creativity. It is not sufficient to define creativity by its semantics, as for instance: "Cause to be or to come into existence; or to make a new form out of preexisting substance." Creativity can only be defined by its inner dynamics. It requires that we enter into its dialectic opposites so as to make clear what it means. One way of defining creativity is by its maximum condition, maximum creativity – the fullest penetration of the universe by creativity, a world that has been creative from beginning to end and that never ceases to be creative. The opposite condition of creativity would be then zero creativity – a world that is entirely uncreative, automatic, that has no past or future, no evolution or purpose, absolutely changeless and meaningless.
>
> Spontaneity–creativity is the problem of psychology; indeed it is *the* problem of the universe. Creativity is *the* problem of the universe; it is therefore, the problem of all existence, *the* problem of every religion, science, the problem of psychology, sociometry, and human relations. But creativity is not a *"separate"* mystic, aristocratic, aesthetic or

> theological category; if it is on top, it is also on the bottom; it is everywhere; if it is in the macrocosmos, it is also in the microcosmos; if it is in the largest, it is also in the smallest; it is in the eternal and the most transitory forms of existence; it operates in the here-and-now, in this pencil and in this paper, as I am writing these words to the reader
> (Moreno, J.L. 1941b: 126)

> When the nineteenth century came to an end and the final accounting was made, what emerged as its greatest contribution to the mental and social sciences was to many minds the idea of the unconscious and its cathexes. When the twentieth century will close its doors that which I believe will come out as the greatest achievement is the idea of spontaneity and creativity, and the significant, indelible link between them. It may be said that the efforts of the two centuries complement one another. *If the nineteenth century looked for the "lowest" common denominator of mankind, the unconscious, the twentieth century discovered or rediscovered its "highest" common denominator – spontaneity and creativity.*
> (Moreno, J.L. 1934: 49)

Moreno's ideas of a science of human relations

An adequate science of human relations did not exist before the advent of sociometry.

> Comte's Hierarchy of the Sciences, (1) mathematics, (2) astronomy, (3) physics, (4) chemistry, (5) biology, and (6) sociology, has become obsolete. His assumption that all sciences can be treated by the same basic methodology is an error. The social sciences need – at least in their crucial dimension – different methods of approach. The crux of the ontology of science is *the status of the "research objects."* Their status is not uniform in all sciences. There is a group of sciences like astronomy, physics, chemistry and biology in which the research objects are always mere "objects." Their actions speak for themselves and the generalizations concluded from them are not threatened by any metaphysical protest or social revolution of their kind.
>
> Then there is another group of sciences, the social sciences. It is because of a chronic inertia in their development that sociometry has raised the question: *how are social sciences possible?* It has found that the social sciences like psychology, sociology, and anthropology require that their objects be given "research status" and a certain degree of scientific authority in order to raise their level from a pseudo objective discipline to a science which operates on the highest level of its material

> dynamics. It accomplishes this aim by considering the research objects not only as objects but also as *research actors*, not only as objects of observation and manipulation but as *co-scientists* and *co-producers* in the experimental design they are going to set up.
>
> (Moreno, J.L. 1934: 63–64)

Our two chief experimental designs are sociometry and psychodrama.

Diffusion, lack of unity

A large number of derivatives and outgrowths of Moreno's work have sprung up, as: body therapy, contact therapy, joy therapy, behavior therapy, sensitivity training, encounter groups, etc. It may be to the point, therefore, to bring some historic facts to the attention of the reader, dealing with their origins.

A long list of these ideas was originated, initiated and disseminated long before the birth of the present generation: the concept of the encounter and encounter groups, 1914; group therapy and group psychotherapy with their natural extensions as family therapy, conjoint therapy and community psychiatry, 1913, 1931, 1932 and 1934; the interaction diagram, 1924; the sociogram, 1933; the concept of interpersonal sensitivity and sensitivity training, 1937; the concept of acting out and psychodrama, 1937; the permanently ongoing psychodrama marathon, 1950s.

That psychologists are not entirely unaware of these roots is borne out by a letter from Dr. Abraham Maslow to the editors of *Life* Magazine, August 2, 1968 issue:

> Sirs: Jane Howard's article on Esalen and other new developments in education and psychology was excellent. I would however like to add one "credit where credit is due" footnote. Many of the techniques set forth in the article were originally invented by Dr. Jacob Moreno, who is still functioning vigorously and probably still inventing new techniques and ideas.

Behind many breakthroughs in sociology, psychology, psychiatry, education, and theater peers the cryptic image of Moreno. Think of the inspiration and influence of Moreno upon Buber's concept of "encounter" and "I and Thou" (1914). Think of the influence and inspiration of Role Theory in the writings of T. Parsons and E. Goffman (1934). Think of the pervasive influence of the role concept and of spontaneity and creativity in the entire literature of modern education; the beginnings of play therapy in the early work of Moreno, directly or indirectly influencing Anna Freud and Melanie Klein (*Die Gottheit als Komdiant*, 1919; *Das Stegreiftheater*,

1924). Think of the concept of "playing for adults," or "kindergarten for adults" that he postulated, which is now exemplified in game theories and the games – formal and informal – that people play.

The Living Theatre and Open Theater

Think of Moreno's influence upon the so-called Living Theatre and Open Theater: participation of the audience, removal of barriers and differences between actor and audience members, the stress upon here-and-now, which is neither here nor now in these theaters. Think of the frequent misrepresentations of Shakespeare as a psychodramatist. True, Shakespeare described role-playing techniques within the context of a number of his plays. But it is one thing to use role-playing techniques as part of a finished script for a theatrical play; it is something very different to use role-playing in the here-and-now with real people.

The role-playing of Hamlet or Falstaff as part of the script is a different phenomenon from a "live" psychodrama. Moreno has been the mighty exponent of the "Age of Ad Libbing," which is now current on radio, television, in theater and films. Around 1920, for instance, improvisation and spontaneity were taboo, and even today many actors state that security is knowing every word in the script. Many great theater and motion picture producers abjure the destruction of the script, plead for the restoration of classic structure and the complete submission of the actor to its directives. Everything else stands for death to the theater in their opinion.

It is not so important that Moreno's school did these things first. That is merely one aspect of the problem. But we want to pierce the vanity and outrageous bravado of our many good friends and enemies who, under the broad mantle of science, have disowned and absorbed these ideas and are brazenly trying to get away with it. The problem is not "getting a bigger bag of better working tricks." The problem is far more serious; the disowners undermine a system of thought, a view, a philosophy of the world, a synthesis of methods that hang together and whose breakup produces confusion instead of enlightenment, invites disaster instead of producing cohesion.

Freud's dilemma was holding his ideas tight to himself, therefore his rejection of everyone who did not recognize his priority and adhere to his dogma: Jung, Adler, Rank, Stekel, and Ferenczi, among others.

Moreno did the opposite. He is tolerant and devoted to his students. His secret weapon was "giving away" his ideas. His strength lay in letting people use his ideas, encouraging them to try them out, making them their own. There was considerable risk in this. Losing the priority claim was only one small part; the deeper conflict arose out of separating the methods from the philosophy. Substitute theories and philosophies are false and misleading, as they abrogate or abort the complete execution of the methods.

Moreno's position was, therefore, take my ideas, my concepts, but do not separate them from their parent, the philosophy; do not split my children in half, like a Solomonic judgment. Love them *in toto*. Support and respect the entire structure upon which they rest. Make them your own as completely as I do. Role reverse with me and put yourself entirely into my position.

Many have not done this. They have split the children and separated them from their true parent, as the false mother before Solomon intended. But an ever-growing number are becoming aware and the recognition gap is slowly narrowing. If Moreno continues to make his students aware of this gap, his way may yet prove to be the winner.

All of the above-listed concepts and ideas have a serious purpose, leading up to the philosophy of a world system; to the ethical prospect of a "therapeutic world order," a unity of mankind, as foreshadowed in 1934 in the opening sentence of *Who Shall Survive?*: "A truly therapeutic procedure can not have less an objective than the whole of mankind." A therapeutic world order is mandatory. It is the cosmic imperative if our world is to survive.

In view of the escalating anarchy of all values and ideas, it is paradoxical that Moreno is now beginning to be honored in many places all over the world, but the most astonishing is that he has been honored in an unusual manner in Austria, his spiritual soil.

Moreno has been in contact with many of the great men of his time, shared and exchanged ideas with them: Trotsky, Freud, Adler, Buber, Stekel, John Dewey, William Alanson White, Gardner Murphy, Pitirim A. Sorokin, Henry A. Murray among them. But academia was rarely approving of men of the caliber of Freud and in this respect the University of Vienna was no exception.

This can, however, no longer be said in connection with Moreno, who saw a great change of attitude take place in his own lifetime. 1. Laboratoire d'Experimentation Sociometrique et Psychologique, Sorbonne, Paris, 1951. 2. International Committee of Group Psychotherapy, 1951, Paris. 3. *Sociometry* becomes an official journal of the American Sociological Association, 1956. In 1964, the Faculty of Medicine of the University of Paris saw fit to sponsor the First International Congress of Psychodrama; the same occurred in 1968 when the Fourth International Congress of Group Psychotherapy took place under the sponsorship of the Medical Faculty of the University of Vienna. In 1968 the Faculty of Medicine of the University of Barcelona extended a Doctor Honoris Causa to him. The Medical Society of the State of New York awarded him in 1967 a citation for Fifty Years of Medical Service. In 1969 the Faculty of Medicine of the University of Buenos Aires made him their guest of honor and sponsored the Fourth International Congress of Psychodrama and Sociodrama. In 1970 the Medical Faculty of the University of São Paulo is doing the same thing on behalf of the Fifth International Congress of Psychodrama.

In May 1969 we undertook a pilgrimage to Austria that had as its primary purpose two events: the ceremony at the Medical Faculty of the University of Vienna, Moreno receiving the Golden Doctor Diploma, and the ceremony in Voslau, the unveiling of a plaque in Dr. Moreno's honor. Though modest in themselves, they may yet prove to be of considerable historic consequence.[2]

Article 21

Practical Aspects of Psychodrama

Moreno, Z.T. (1969) *Group Psychotherapy, A Quarterly Journal* XXII, 3–4: 213–219

Zerka's comments

Besides the work in situ, *the journal was the main guide for director training. This article was meant to present exactly what it says. I first presented it at the Fourth International Congress of Psychodrama and Sociodrama, Buenos Aires, Argentina, August 24–31, 1969.*

The postulate of "sociatry" is that what needs to be healed is not individual psyches alone, but *all of society*. The word has two roots: Latin *socius* ("the other fellow") and Greek *iatreia* ("healing") (Moreno, J.L. 1953: 90). The focus of attention is upon the interaction between psyches, between group members, their adhesions to other groups and the nature of interaction between groups.

The following are guidelines for the director of psychodrama by which to conduct the session.

Rule I

The director (or chief therapist) must be the most spontaneous member of the group, that is, more spontaneous than the other professional group members as auxiliary egos and even – and this is often the most challenging and difficult – more spontaneous than the patients or protagonists. According to Moreno, the personality of the therapist–director is his greatest skill (Moreno, J.L. & Moreno, Z.T. 1959: 236). The more spontaneously or flexibly he can deal with the protagonists and other therapeutic team members, the better he will be able to guide the group interactions. Spontaneity and anxiety are linked and are functions of each other. Anxiety will increase if spontaneity recedes. Conversely, anxiety will decrease if spontaneity is allowed to rise. Spontaneity has been defined as "a new response to an old situation" or "an adequate response to a new situation" (Moreno, J.L. 1956b). *New* in this context means fresh, novel, creative, in the here and now, not foreordained or predetermined, but arising out of the immediate situation with which the group is struggling; a genuine rising to the occasion in a fluid manner.

Thus, if the protagonist is rigid, compulsively repeating his old type of behavior in the psychodrama, the director must offer the protagonist the opportunity to try out a new set or order of skills here, now, on the spot, as a rehearsal for life. Psychodrama is a living laboratory for experimentation with life, with all its encumbrances *except* punishment; for trying out new ways of living it. Some of the immediately effective techniques are: role reversal, the mirror, the protagonist as his own spectator, as-his-own double, as-his-own-director, as-his-own-counselor, to mention but a few. He might, for instance, observe himself in role reversal, or in his own role watching from the side as the auxiliary egos repeat before him the scene he has just completed, duplicating the essence of his own portrayal, either in his own role or in the role reversed position as the other person (or persons) involved in the interaction. He may be placed in the role of the therapist by the director: "What other ways could you recommend for Jack to try out here? Make whatever suggestions you may have for him to change his behavior." This forces him to devise new channels of warming up for himself. He shapes his own therapy.

Rule II

The director must be aware of his own psychodramatic needs, as against those of his protagonists. Be sure you are not foisting your own views and needs on them. We frequently see directors whose religious or moral imperatives make it difficult for them to deal with those of their protagonists and group members who carry different imperatives. The parallels and similarities should not trap him, but neither should the differences.

A recent example of this was experienced during a training seminar in which a student from a foreign country was misperceived and misinterpreted by his student-director. The foreign student's behavior in the group was based upon his desire to be a good ambassador for his country – a troubled land in the Near East – and he worked diligently at this sociodramatic role in order not to cut off interaction with students who might otherwise reject him. He wanted to build goodwill for his country while abroad. The student-director accused him of hypocrisy, stating with conviction that his protagonist's behavior was hypocritical, that there was no way any human behaved except on the basis of "individual dynamics."

During the group members' sharing in the post-action period, a number of group members revealed their own feelings of loneliness and isolation in strange groups, with the consequent loss of feelings of identity as a person. One very perceptive group member then stated that it was not even necessary to go abroad to feel this way. One could feel cut off and suffer anomia in one's own country, but how much more emphatic this experience must be when one's own background, language and culture, mores and views of life, have to be replaced by a completely new set.

The student-director stated he had never been abroad and claimed to be unaware of such sensitive sociodramatic experiences on that basis. But beyond that, he denied ever having had such discomforting experiences, in any groups into which he moved. This aroused much protest from the group members, who pointed out to him that he had been noticeably withdrawn in this very group, having remained without meaningful personal contact with others and he, in fact, emerged as "the stranger," the sociometric isolate, within it.

For a psychodrama director a little modesty goes a long way. One may quote Shakespeare's Hamlet for this rule: "There are more things in heaven and earth than are dreamt of in your philosophy."

Parenthetically, this is just one more indication of how much role testing, role training and role sensitivity is needed for our diplomats. These methods would produce fruitful results if applied to them before they are sent abroad to represent our country.

Rule III

The director must put himself into a subjective relationship with the protagonist, so to speak. Borrowing terms from the field of sports, be in the protagonist's corner with him, as a partner, at least at crucial moments.

This is not the posture of the analytic person, rather that of a lover of mankind. The director must make his emotional equipment available to the protagonist as much as his intellect, as one human being with another. Once the protagonist senses the director to be genuinely "with him," the director is free to move again into a more objective position, whence he can survey the further needs of the protagonist and those of the other group members. This delicate balance of the subjective–objective relationship is one of the most crucial demands on the director for effective achievement of his task. It is the basis of true "tele contact" between himself and the protagonist, himself and the group members. Tele should sustain the director even when initial contact with the protagonist is difficult.

To illustrate this rule the following experience in a recent session is relevant. In an open session conducted in Manhattan attended by a large number of persons, the majority of whom are professional workers who have come for a didactic session, the psychodrama director, a woman, is attacked loudly by a group member, a female therapist in the group. She starts off by violently accusing the director – whom she has never seen before – of being intolerable in every respect. She rejects her face, clothing, shoes, speech, manner, and, even at considerable distance, her body odor.

The director, caught by surprise, asks her quite calmly nevertheless, to step upon the stage, to show her what she wants to do about her.

The protagonist leaps aggressively upon the stage, apparently desirous of taking over the session. The audience is shocked into stunned silence at the violence and completeness of the attack. Because of the irrationality of the protagonist, they are deeply puzzled and begin to fall into several subgroups, as is often observed in groups: some for the protagonist with whom they identify, some for the director for the same reason. A large number assume a careful wait-and-see-how-she-handles-this position, anxious because of its potential dangers, wondering how they would handle such powerful, abject rejection.

The director has recovered her balance and invites the protagonist to use an empty chair on the stage to represent the director and to do anything to and with it that she wants to. The protagonist, whom we shall call Nora, kicks the chair viciously on the legs. It slides off the stage and collapses. Nora bursts out, "I feel exactly the same way towards my mother. In fact, you resemble her."

Now the director moves the protagonist into various confrontations with her mother, taking her scene by scene from the present into the past, at the most crucial turning points in the relationship, as indicated by the protagonist, from step to step.

Nora sees her mother as a cold, controlling, critical, superior, manipulative, dishonest person. She has hardly anything positive to convey about her. She relishes taking the role of her mother in role reversal and pushing her "auxiliary ego Nora" around with her awesome power over her. Nevertheless, in this embodiment of her mother she becomes gradually a very statuesque, gracious albeit somewhat distant and impersonal woman. The director asks her, "Now that we understand you better and your feelings toward your mother, would you tell me whether you ever had a better or substitute mother? One who, though not your biological mother, was emotionally close to you and met your needs better?" "Yes," Nora states and eagerly warms up to this new relationship. To psychodramatize it, she chooses from the group present as auxiliary ego the professor who brought her and her classmates to this session.

The climax of the session now proceeds fast, as we see Nora go through the psychodramatic paces. The "real" mother is her governess. They are all German Jews. Nora is a refugee from Nazi Germany. The governess – also a Jewess – is her constant companion in her childhood, protecting her lovingly from all shocks and pain in the pre-Nazi period. When that period erupts, when Nora is thirteen years old, the governess becomes emotionally ill and is hospitalized, leaving Nora doubly abandoned. She schemes to get her out of the hospital and to smuggle her out of the country, whence her family is planning to depart. Her plan almost succeeds, but once again the "mother" is taken away from her into the hospital, completely out of contact with the world. Soon afterwards, the Nazis emptied all such institutions in their infamous "cleanups."

Nora, having re-enacted all such these scenes, breaks down and sobs uncontrollably. At this point she allows the director to comfort her, even permits her to put her arm around her. When she has calmed down sufficiently, the director gives her an opportunity life did not give her: to complete the rescue of her good mother, without whom her life is meaningless. Nora once more meets her "Mutti" and psychodramatically carries out to a successful conclusion the deeply buried rescue fantasy. Nora is a very attractive woman in her forties, married; with two children. She works in a clinic for the emotionally disturbed doing nonverbal, body and movement therapy. One may, of course, look at her professional role as an attempt at self-therapy as well as making good the rescue failure in life, but apparently it is too indirect and diffuse to remove the scars she has been carrying around with her for over thirty years. The psychodrama is meant to assist in the healing process, over and beyond that which she could achieve on her own in life itself. It supplies emotional need satisfaction.

When the session ends, Nora looks at the psychodrama director with amazement and kisses her warmly. There is an overwhelming sense of relief in the audience. The silence in the group is pregnant with emotion. There is a sense of existential anguish so deep that no words can suffice. The director closes the session. What has occurred, in spite of all the difficulties with which this session began, is a genuine "encounter."

Rule IV

The psychodramatist emphasizes the warming up of the protagonist, encourages and assists him to focus on action and interaction. To prevent the protagonist from "interpreting himself" – which leads too much to being his own spectator rather than being his own actor – instructions should be clearly stated in simple terms: "Here we do *not* talk about how we feel, here we *act out* how we feel. It is happening *now, here*. Let's live it through together. *Show* me, *do not* tell me."

We give the protagonist the freedom, the license to go into action, including embodiments of all dimensions of his world: positive, negative, real, fantasied; it is immaterial. He must have the freedom to feel at home in his own world.

This is one of the biggest stumbling blocks for many therapists who insist upon analysis and teaching patients to stop and think, those whose own training has come from different orientations. They fear that teaching their patients this way of achieving catharsis is going to turn them into delinquents or criminals; that it will teach them to behave irrationally in life. Our position is exactly the opposite: that to prevent this from happening in the therapeutic setting where the patient can learn from it, is to invite disaster on the outside, where there are no controls.

Psychodrama is similar to a vaccination: it is a small dose of insanity given under conditions of control.

Rule V

The director's own "surplus reality" awareness should stimulate him to follow the protagonists without fear, to enter into their own world of "surplus reality." Surplus reality is that realm beyond reality in which the protagonist may live most deeply, his fantasy world.

A recent example follows: The protagonist, a patient we shall call Neil, is a teacher, married, devoted to his wife, with three adolescent boys. He is at present engaged in research on the west coast involving educational processes, completing his doctorate.

His presenting symptom is violent sadomasochistic sexual fantasies which he states interfere with relations to his wife, although she is not aware of them. Because of his fear that she will discover them or that he will force her to carry them out with him, he has decided to relieve himself through psychodramatic enactment. He is allowed to choose those persons in the group whom he wants to have present. The sociometric group construction before the session helps to strengthen his feeling of trust. He also chooses a male director.

The bizarre, Genet-type fantasies which occur in the protagonist's mind when he is in bed with his wife are reproduced with the assistance of a female auxiliary ego, a group member chosen by the protagonist. The director guides the process very sensitively, without stimulating exhibitionism, but delicately exploring, side by side, in action, the dual situation: the actual one taking place with the wife, and the fantasy one simultaneously occurring in the protagonist's mind. It becomes clear that the protagonist is more intrigued by his fantasies than involved in the lovemaking of his wife. The resulting split becomes disastrous for his real performance. When he is permitted by means of psychodrama to *complete* his fantasies, instead of fighting against them as he tries to do in life, he begins to be better able to control and integrate the fantasies, intensifying his being in the-here-and-now in subsequent performance with his wife. This intensified warm-up in the real situation in turn increases their mutual satisfaction; a classic "catharsis of integration."

In the post-action sharing of the session, the members of the group are aware and state that they have had some fantasies of a similar sort, though not as intense as those produced by the protagonist who is, however, delighted and much relieved to know this. The director especially remarked that his own experiences along these lines helped him to appreciate the nature of these phenomena in the protagonist. He felt that this was one of the reasons he did not consider them bizarre and was not afraid to enter into the psychodramatic exploration. Instead, he was gratified to see that this type of fantasy experience lends itself so well to psychodramatic processing. The most important thing was that he did not "fall out of the role of director," but made his own sensitivity available to the protagonist.

The psyche of man is not transparent. Action methods such as here described are the most suitable instruments for dealing with the multiple, invisible dimensions in which all of us live in life by ourselves, but which we learn to open and share through the psychodrama.

Psychonauts of the world, unite!

Article 22

Beyond Aristotle, Breuer and Freud: Moreno's Contribution to the Concept of Catharsis

Moreno, Z.T. (1971) *Group Psychotherapy and Psychodrama, A Quarterly Journal* XXIV, 1–2: 34–43

Zerka's comments

I made up the myth of Barney for the paper, which was read at the ASGPP. People loved it, and it was refreshing to inject a bit of fun into a serious subject. I used the quote from Pearl Buck because I liked her writing, especially the fact that she talks about other cultures. One thing I emphasize about catharsis is that our protagonists do not owe us one.

Social scientists have traditionally been looked down upon by physical scientists and, to a considerable extent, they are so today. The reasons are numerous, the major one being that according to the detractors, social science continues to be an admixture of art with science, therefore not "pure" science.

To illustrate the fallacy in this type of thinking, allow me to share with you a small fable I have written *à la* Aesop or Jonathan Swift, with, of course, proper apologies to these illustrious poets. It is called "Barney, the Insightful Bumblebee."

Once there was a little bumblebee known as Barney who spent all his waking life flying and being lightwinged. One day he made friends with a mathematician. This mathematician really enjoyed his friendship with Barney but gradually Barney noticed that his friend was frequently more and more morose. So he decided to ask him what he, Barney, had done to upset him. "Well," the mathematician shook his head, which was so full of wise thoughts, "Well, yes Barney, to tell the truth, there *is* something about you which upsets me deeply. I love you and value your friendship and do not want any harm whatsoever to befall you. But you see, I have made careful studies of all known mathematical laws and *there is simply no way of excusing your ability to fly. It is against all laws of aerodynamics.* The plain truth is, Barney, you just ought not to fly around like that! It is dangerous! Because there is no way of figuring out how you are able to fly, you ought not to be doing it. Your body and wingspread simply are not properly geared to it. I often have nightmares about it and wake up in a cold sweat when I realize that you and all your relatives and friends are literally taking your lives in your wings every time you take off. I cannot tolerate the idea that one of my friends lives and flies in constant danger." And he shook his wise old head again in dismay.

Barney was astounded, to say the least. Imagine! He and all his relatives and friends were endangering their lives by doing just that for which they had been created! He was deeply shocked. "Well," he told Mr. Mathematicus, "I will have to go and warn them and we will have to hold a family council. I know you are my good friend and want to save us all from a fate involving death." He tried to fly away – which was, after all, his normal mode of transportation – and found to his own dismay that, spread his wings as he would, he could not lift his large, bulky body off into the air as he had been doing almost since he was born. What suffering! What misery and anguish of mind, heart and body that poor Barney underwent! He saw no way out to save himself and his own kind. He began to lose weight and became so deeply depressed, even suicidal, that he had to undergo psychiatric treatment. But there are no psychiatrists anywhere trained to deal with so existential a problem. Try as he might, going on foot or on the shoulder of his very best friend Mr. Mathematicus, from one type of therapist to another, representatives of all the different schools – of which there exist quite a few – none and no one was able to cure poor Barney.

Mr. Mathematicus now had real reason to be concerned about the welfare of his friend and besides, began to feel more and more guilty, responsible for the fading away of his friend. Periodically he would sit down again and try to refigure the laws he was so familiar with, but try as he would he could not find a rational basis for encouraging Barney to undertake such a dangerous task. What a dilemma! He could not lie to his friend convincingly because he saw no way out. The mathematical truth was Barney really *should* not be able to fly and therefore it was dangerous!

Out of the depth of their mutual despair, they decide to leave no stone unturned and, having made a long odyssey all around the globe, they take their strange case for consultation to a psychodramatic therapist. After all, they have nothing to lose and a great deal to gain.

In difference from all other specialists previously consulted, the psychodramatist is not at all amazed. Barney's problem is one he has long been encountering, every day, in myriads of forms. He listens and watches very sympathetically and intensely as Barney re-enacts the entire story of his sad debacle from the moment he gained insight into his "dangerous condition." "Barney," says the psychodramatist, "I want you to sit very still, here, right by me, for a few minutes and concentrate very, very deeply." The psychodramatist darkens the theater, turning down the lights until only a glimmer of blue is visible. "Concentrate upon your dream, my friend, give it everything you've got, and when you are warmed up to represent it in action, just start *doing* it. No more words or thoughts or puzzlements. Just be silent, sink into your innermost and then begin to act on the very wildest dream you have ever had or ever will have in your life."

Barney does exactly as he is told and, lo and behold, to the astonished eyes of Mr. Mathematicus, Barney spreads his wings, ever larger and larger, so wide as to make his bulgy body appear a lot less impressive, takes a few faltering first steps but, encouraged by the psychodramatist, lifts his heavier-than-air bulk up, up into the ocean of air and FLIES! The more he flies, the more his heart lifts up and the more that happens, the better and higher he flies. "Barney," says the psychodramatist while opening the door of the theater wide for him onto the great, beautiful world, "Forget about all your past troubles. They cannot be changed. Just live as you feel is best for you. And when well-meaning friends warn you of your foolishness, remember this moment. Remember all your hopes and dreams of the wildest schemes; never let go of them and put them into action to the best of your ability."

And Barney flew away so fast, he even forgot to say goodbye to his good friend. Off he went, into the azure blue sky.

That is how Barney was cured of his crippling insight forever.

We are not apologists for the social sciences. On the contrary, there is overwhelming evidence to convince us that no one can be truly called a scientist who does not, in fact, embody both science and art, whether he be physical or social scientist. Indeed, the history of the physical sciences is replete with human errors, blindness, mythology and intuition. To quote Einstein, "Imagination is more important than knowledge." This same Einstein was so overwhelmed when he first heard Yehudi Menuhin play, when Menuhin was fourteen years of age, that he embraced him and said, "You have once more proved to me that there is a God."

In his book *The Sleepwalkers*, Arthur Koestler declares that if Galileo had been truly "scientific," that is, basing his opinions on knowledge of astronomy available in his own lifetime, the history of his own life as well as of science *could* have been very different. First, he might not have been condemned for his views and second, more importantly, he could have speeded up man's knowledge of the physical universe enormously, simply by thoroughly acquainting himself with the work of Johannes Kepler, a contemporary genius and visionary, and by acknowledging his contribution. Instead, due to his narcissism, he brought about his own disgrace at the hands of his inquisitors and impeded progress in the area of physical sciences. According to the same author, Galileo's real, immortal contribution to science rests on his work on dynamics and not on his sketchy knowledge of astronomy. Yet it was the latter that earned him his worldwide reputation. Indeed, it was his "ill-conceived crusade which had discredited the heliocentric system and precipitated the divorce of science from faith."

Incidentally, Kepler had apparently a wake-dream dealing with moon flight and moon landing described in his *Somnium*, published posthumously.

It was the first science fiction book ever produced and influenced later authors on interplanetary flight. The *Somnium* appeared in 1634, although he commenced work on it in 1609 and even sent in his fanciful description to Galileo, according to Lewis Mumford's report in *The Myth of the Machine*. Koestler reports that Kepler worked on the *Somnium* until his death and adds, "All Kepler's work, and all his discoveries, were acts of catharsis; it was only fitting that the last one should end with a fantastic flourish."

In our own time we need but to look at the level of care given by the medical profession who specialize at that apex of the physical sciences – medicine of the body – to recognize the inadequacy of the coldly scientific approach.

All this by way of saying that the stamp of a good scientist is a synthesis between art and science, giving equal weight to both. They not only have common roots in religion but one cannot long survive without the other. A most fortunate instance of the happy marriage between the two is the little known fact of the birth of the phrase "count down," familiar to all who are part of the space age. This phrase, all assumptions despite, was not coined by anyone even remotely connected with astronautic engineering or mathematics. Instead, it was created by Fritz Lang, a famous German film producer–director. It occurred in 1929, while shooting the takeoff to the moon for a movie called *Die Frau im Mond* or *The Lady in the Moon*. It was a science fiction story of the moontrip of two male astronauts and one very beautiful blond lady astronaut – a new twist to the eternal triangle – and a film for which Willie Ley, the rocket expert, was technical adviser.

Lang conceived the idea as the scene was built up to enormous tension, while the spaceship is preparing for takeoff on the pad and the count one to ten is about to begin. Lang stops the actor portraying the counter of the final ten seconds, saying, "This counting is dull, predictable and anticlimatic. Let's do it backwards, let's *count down*, from ten to one!" This has since then become the standard term as well as accepted procedure in preparation for space travel. By the way, I was twelve years "young" when I saw the film and, believe me, it made the actual recent moon landings appear like science fiction. It was a superb, pioneering creation of cinematographic art.

No other social scientist embodies, in our time, the requirements stated above as succinctly as does Moreno, whose pioneering ventures in both branches of the sciences as well as in religion have been wellsprings of inspiration. The eventual effects of his work upon mankind are far from being predictable. History and posterity will, I am certain, be better able to evaluate this than we, his contemporaries. It is a peculiarity of human nature to make respectful genuflections at the genius of the past and to belittle, deny, detract from, overlook and even ridicule the genius in our midst. If we here are truly to be considered social scientists, let us be so consciously, systematically, objectively and intuitively.

One of Moreno's fundamental contributions to the knowledge of man's emotional life is the concept of mental catharsis based upon action. For the term and description of catharsis itself we must go back to Aristotle, who in his *De Poetica* describes the effect of tragedy upon the spectators in the theater of his day. Aristotle goes into great detail on the structure of comedy and tragedy. His frame of reference was, of course, drama in its *conserved* form, although he does state quite clearly, "It – tragedy and comedy – certainly began in improvisations." However, he does not dwell any further upon its beginnings. He concentrates his attention on what happens in the audience as the play unfolds and defines tragedy as follows, "Imitation of an action, in a dramatic, not in a narrative form; with incidents arousing pity and fear, wherewith to accomplish its 'catharsis' of such emotions." Catharsis, then, is a purging, an emptying, a cleansing. Many of us remember from our childhood an unpleasant medication, the purgative, which was popularly labelled as "cathartic."

Aristotle described the phenomenon from the point of view of the *spectator*. This is important and should be borne in mind, as it has a bearing upon the particular interpretation Moreno gave, as well as upon his unique contribution which has carried us beyond Aristotle and beyond Breuer and Freud, to whom we shall now turn our attention.

Breuer and Freud both first used hypnosis with patients. As we know they later parted ways and Freud then developed his technique of free association, dispensing with hypnosis altogether. It is not the purpose of this paper to dwell on the reasons for these developments; they are not germane to it. Rather, we must concentrate on our central theme, catharsis.

Breuer and Freud observed that when their patients under hypnosis described particularly painful scenes in their lives they often burst into tears, showed anger, even rage, or succumbed to the stress of those scenes in visible ways. Breuer called this phenomenon "catharsis" and attached the label "the cathartic method" to this use of hypnosis. However, because the patients *reported* the scenes, that is, verbally recalled them, they were still *observers* in the sense in which Aristotle spoke, namely of "incidents arousing pity and fear wherewith to accomplish a catharsis of these emotions." True, the drama was not written by a playwright and the fact that these were scenes in their own lives made the feelings genuine and more explosive, but from the point of view of the *method*, Breuer and Freud did not go beyond Aristotle. Like him, they did not move the person out of the seat of the observer.

However, Aristotle does make the distinction between poetry and tragedy when he says of the latter, "in a dramatic, not in a narrative form." The *narrative* form, he implies, is a form of *poetry*. Aristotle did not deny that catharsis can be evoked in the listener of the narrative, but he stressed the *quality of drama* as especially provocative. We may say, therefore, in Aristotelian terms, that Breuer and Freud's hypnotisands were, at least methodically speaking, at best poets or songsters, narrators of their own lives. Lacking the actorial dimension, one may wonder whether Breuer's designation of the term catharsis or cathartic method obfuscates rather than clarifies the underlying process.

Beyond the above quoted reference as to the early beginnings of tragedy in improvisation, Aristotle himself did not deal with the function of the actor in more detail or depth. His observations did not include the dimension of the actor's contribution to the process. Indeed, he never clearly envisioned the distinction between actor and spectator, nor does this arise in the thinking of Breuer or Freud. Their observations simply are not in this realm; the actor has no part in their system.

Therefore, whenever we use the terms "spectator catharsis," "actorial catharsis," "actor's catharsis" or "catharsis of action," it is always in the sense of Moreno. It is entirely due to his penetrating insight into the totality of the processes of drama, conserved or spontaneous, whether dealing with the function of the actor or that of the spectator, that we have gained this multidimensional vista.

If Moreno had been satisfied with the *word*, he would not have been able to move beyond the spectator. It was his absorption in and involvement with the concepts of spontaneity and creativity, with the moment, the here-and-now, with the idea of immediate creation, that led to the new dimension of catharsis, the "catharsis of the actor *in situ*." His concern was not the past but the living present, the encounter, the moment as a dynamic, pulsating, arising category, not already experienced.

Methodologically, this made Moreno turn away from the frozen, given moments of creativity whose products he called "cultural conserves," away from the rehearsed form of the drama, away from the recalling of the past however intensively recorded, perceived and experienced. His first step was to remove the actor's script. He tore off the mask of the actor and forced him to reveal himself, placing his own, private person on center stage. This "liberation of the actor from the script" took place first in the classic theater and led to the development of a new form of theater, the theater of pure spontaneity, spontaneity as an esthetic form, an art of the moment. When this art of the moment was established, the catharsis of the actor *in situ* became a visible reality. Now the actor was no longer the slave to another's creativity; he could be the master of his own. The peeling off of psychological layers of himself, of his own masks, made him helpless, vulnerable, weak, dependent. It simultaneously forced him to rely upon his spontaneity and creativity. All his earlier crutches were taken away. It was a most painful process.

In place of them, Moreno asked him to trust his inter-actors, to throw himself not merely upon his own resources of spontaneity and creativity, but also upon those of his co-producers, the other actors in the evolving drama. Thus he was made to deal with the "counter-spontaneity" evoked in the interaction with his partners. It was a humbling experience. It involved not only the words but the motions, the actor's total mnemo-technical equipment. Whenever an actor began to freeze his better motions, lines, facial expressions, at the cost of his continuing creativity, Moreno subjected him to exercises of "deconservation," forcing him into new modes of contacting his spontaneity, to keep it in ready, liquid form. This was such a difficult task that it may have been largely responsible for the fact that the actors, disillusioned in their own spontaneability, returned to the classic form of the conserved drama in a majority of cases.

Nevertheless, this was, and remains today, one of the most profound revolutions in the domain of theater. It has led far beyond Stanislavski, to the eventual development of Second City, the Premise, the Happening, the so-called Living Theatre, Open Theater, Guerilla Theater, Theater of the Streets, etc. However, not a single one of these later offspring is as pure or essential a form of spontaneous–creative theater as was the Theatre of Spontaneity. Each has given up part of or bastardized both spontaneity and creativity of the actors.

Besides leading the actor back to his own spontaneity–creativity, Moreno helped him to focus on the role. In liberating the actor from the script Moreno gave him the leeway to try a variety of versions of the same role. The role of the father, for instance, was no longer subject to a single interpretation. The actor could try out any number of versions to his soul's content. Thus, the tyrannical father, the gentle father, the strong-but-patient father, the weak, dependent father, the cold, critical distant father, the warm, responsive, companionable father all fell into the realm of possibilities of action. His co-actors' repertoire too was thereby enormously expanded as the above variations of roles required the complementary son role for their completion.

Each individual actor now became the carrier of almost limitless possibilities. When, for instance, one of Moreno's actresses in the Theatre of Spontaneity developed a "histrionic neurosis" – another of Moreno's diagnostic terms – that is, a neurotic condition due to her spontaneity being channelized only into roles of "pure, virginal womanhood" which caused her to behave like a wild virago in her private world as reported by her husband, Moreno hit upon the idea of "role-range expansion." Henceforth he had her take roles of women of the lower depths in the Theatre of Spontaneity. Not only did she do them well, but the process enabled her to effect a more complete integration of both kinds of womanhood within herself. This then, was the conscious turning point of the Theatre of Spontaneity as an art form into the Theatre of Catharsis, the Theatre of Therapeusis. Step number one, *the catharsis of the actor*, was assured and completed.

Moreno discovered early in his work with the children in the gardens of Vienna that even a role conserve can be catharsis-producing for the actor, provided the role dynamics parallel those of the actor, that they are "the right fit," do not crush his spontaneous–creative function and help him to expand and intensify this function.

A striking example of this type of actorial catharsis, though merely as an observation and happy accident, not as a central theme of her book, may be gleaned from Pearl Buck's autobiography *My Several Worlds*, from which I quote:

> That spring a little dramatic group among the foreigners gave a play for the English-speaking community. It was *The Barretts of Wimpole Street*. I do not remember the other actors but only the little frail creature, whose name I have forgotten, but who played the part of Elizabeth Barrett. She was a missionary, I was told, a shy virginal woman, not young, not old, whom nobody knew. But she had great dark sad eyes and a small olive skinned face and heavy dark hair, and a soft stealing footstep. Upon the stage she became Elizabeth herself, the beloved of a poet, and before our amazed eyes she gave a performance so passionate, so true, so utterly astounding in the perfection of its sensitive comprehension of a poetic love, that I have never forgotten it. And indeed when later I saw our own great Katherine Cornell play the same part in revival, I felt the little missionary had surpassed even her performance. Yet when the play was over that small creature shrank away again, and when she was tried in another play was quite mediocre, I was told. Something in that play and in that one character fitted, I suppose, the emotional need of her own life at that moment.

What happens to the catharsis of the spectator when the catharsis of the actor is being unfolded? For a truly magnificent exposition of spectator catharsis I am indebted to St Augustine, who, describing his early and, to him, most sinful youth in Carthage, states in his *Confessions:*

> Stage-plays also draw me away, full of representations of my miseries and of fuel to my fire. Why does man like to be made sad when viewing doleful and tragical scenes, which yet he himself would by no means suffer? And yet he wishes, as a spectator, to experience from them a sense of grief, and in this very grief his pleasure consists. What is this but wretched insanity? For a man is more affected with these actions, the less free he is from such affections. However, when he suffers in his own person, it is the custom to style it "misery;" but when he compassionates others, then it is styled "mercy." But what kind of mercy is it that arises from fictitious and scenic passions? The hearer is not expected to relieve, but merely invited to grieve; and the more he grieves, the more he applauds the actor of these fictions. And if the misfortunes of the characters (whether of olden times or merely

> imaginary) be so represented as not to touch the feelings of the spectator, he goes away disgusted and censorious; but if his feelings be touched, he sits it out attentively, and sheds tears of joy.

As St. Augustine so beautifully sums it up: you don't *do* anything as a spectator, you just sit and watch it all happen.

It is quite a different experience, for an adult at least – children are easily captivated by dramatic magic if they have not yet estabished the break between fantasy and reality within themselves – to go from knowing the play to be "as if," a fiction, and the actors merely players, mask bearers, to being shocked into an awareness that the actors in *this* theater are real people, without their masks, truly experiencing what they are now living, before one's very own eyes. *Their* suffering and joy is actual, here; *their* tears are what they are; *their* laughter is the genuine article.

Moreno distinguished three forms of catharsis: (1) the esthetic, that is, the experiencing of beauty; (2) that of the spectator, already dwelt upon; and (3) actorial catharis or catharsis of integration. It is the actorial catharsis, the catharsis of integration, which is his particularly momentous contribution. It was born when he turned the protagonist into the *actor of himself* rather than the narrator–spectator. The transposition of the actor from the level of "as if" and his transformation into the *primary source* of catharsis itself, moves the spectator from the level of "as if" to the level of "is," from the recognition of "he is" to "I am." This shock of awareness of real others creates a parallel shock of real self-recognition in the spectator and astronomically intensifies it. But Moreno was not content with leaving the spectator there either, in his seat, merely being the receptacle of other people's spontaneity–creativity. He proceeded to propel the spectator, too, out of his seat, demanding him to turn into an actor, here, now, just as had the others before him. This was the completion of the catharsis of the actor, coming from the level of former spectator, and taking central stage in due course. Thus, the spectator represented not merely the watching, judging world as public opinion, but the larger all-inclusive world of total creativity and total involvement. The audience as actors and interactors could now complete the final round: that of therapeutic actors.

We know from psychodrama that the greatest depth of catharsis comes not merely from re-enactment of the past, however traumatic or instructive, but from embodying those dimensions, roles, scenes, and inter-actions which life has not permitted, cannot permit and probably never will permit. It is in the realm of surplus reality that the catharsis of action, of both individual and group, is achieved in its purest form.

And who is there to predict with absolute certainty and foreknowledge, which of man's dreams and visions are capable of realization? Freud's concept of the dream was that it is a wish and wish fulfillment. Yet, Kepler's dream became reality four hundred years later.

In Freud's work the encounter is an intellectual phenomenon. In Moreno's work encounter between I and Thou results in a direct, mutual catharsis. To quote Ramon Sarro in his Foreword to Ann Schutzenberger's book *Introduccion al Psicodrama* just published in Spain: "The essence of the act, its final meaning, is to provoke an encounter, not only a catharsis."

The work of Freud was based on atheism. There is no significant, fundamental relationship between atheism and catharsis. The atheistic position is without promise and hope.

Moreno's work is based on religion. This gives catharsis a religious anchorage.

In conclusion, this then, is the lesson we learn from Moreno: "Throw away the old script. Redo it, here, now. Act yourself as you never were, so that you may begin to be what you might have become. Make it happen. Be your own inspiration, your own playwright, your own actor, your own therapist and finally, your own creator."

Article 23

Note on Psychodrama, Sociometry, Individual Psychotherapy and the Quest for "Unconditional Love"

Moreno, Z.T. (1972) *Group Psychotherapy and Psychodrama, A Quarterly Journal* XXV, 4: 155–157

Zerka's comments

This was written around the time when it was discovered that some psychotherapists were sleeping with their patients. I was shocked and considered it totally unethical. This was my rebuttal. Beacon during the sixties was not quite as way out as other places. It was very exciting because we were getting students from all over the world. Perhaps that served to rein in a certain amount of the permissiveness or "anything goes" attitude that seemed to go along with that era.

It has long been asserted by psychotherapists that the patient is really coming to psychotherapy because of unfulfilled or incompletely filled needs for love. The conscientious psychotherapist must, at one time or another, question himself or herself as to whether this need is truly being met in his or her role of therapist. We know that sociometrically there are patients we prefer to others; it would be dishonest not to declare this to ourselves, even if we do not do it to the patient. One solution to this problem has been advocated by the practitioners of the "love therapy" school, who go the whole way with their patient, even to the point of becoming lovers.

What is the psychodramatist's view of this approach? One of the problems we face is that, by being psychotherapists to others, we are also vicariously being therapeutic to ourselves. How, then, is it possible to know when we are transgressing from the professional role into the personal? This problem becomes more and more acute as ever-greater freedom of bodily contact is being permitted.

We find, in practice, that the existential pain for the great majority of people who come to us out of their need, is not to have had "unconditional love" as a child. It is every child's natural birthright but very few of us ever receive it. How many of our patients come then, in search of this unconditional love which makes no other demand of them than that they be themselves, whatever they may be? Our task is largely one of "healing the hurt child" inside. Do hurt children want sexual contact with adults?

Hardly. On the contrary, this is one of the most frequent areas of their pain. They have had relationships, sexual or otherwise, for which they were not prepared, and into which they did not enter as "consenting adults," foisted onto them by their parents. This is not merely a legal or ethical problem. It is routine fare for the psychotherapist. How, then, can we rationalize that this hurt child needs a good sexual partner? How is it that we overlook completely the need to be first unconditionally accepted, loved and cherished, not merely in a cold, therapeutic relationship, but as two human beings facing their common pain.

How and where can this best be attained? What is the most productive setting for achieving this worthy goal? And who and what are the forces that best bring it about?

The hurt child who comes to us is looking for a way to correct past and present misfortunes in not finding suitable parents, a loving home, compatible siblings, warm lovers, etc. That these may be found in a group has been common knowledge ever since Moreno began to work on the premise that the problems of living are interpersonal and intergroupal and set about organizing groups sociometrically, that is, on the basis of mutual choices. Each person in the group was there because he so decided, not because he was tolerated or pushed into the group. This group, and others to which he chose to belong on the basis of the criterion extant in the group, became his "sociometric family." Today, encounter groups speak of "The Second Family" group, but since they do not organize these groups sociometrically, it is still not what the sociometrist has in mind, and falls short of maximizing involvement and mutual responsibility. Assignment is not made on the basis of mutual choices for partnership in the group, but on whoever enrolls for it, hit or miss. The assumption is that whatever happens in the group is productive. Moreno has long pointed out the fallacy of this type of thinking. It has little more to commend itself than the natural family group has now, to which the cosmos assigns us hit or miss and which may or may not be a good sociometric assignment for us.

Nevertheless, the group psychotherapist, even without sociometry, has great advantages over the individual therapist, just because he functions within a group. In the group setting the therapist's behavior is constantly being assessed, and provided he is a peer and not merely a superior in the group, the members of the group will soon let him know if he betrays himself as being seductive or hostile to one or another group member. The psychodramatist has the additional advantage of being a protagonist in the group as well as being in the role of director or guide or facilitator. Thus, when he or she is confronted by the group about his or her behavior, it is the director's right to request a session as a protagonist, in order to deal with this recurring problem.

One interesting aspect of this assessment process was brought to my attention by a patient who actually did not like groups. She was the oldest child of a large family with much neglect and a great deal of suffering because of incomplete relationships with her parents, especially her mother. She came to psychodrama therapy after thirteen years of individual therapy which had helped to keep her out of mental hospitals, but which still left her feeling unfulfilled. After shopping around for a number of months, she chose to join one of my psychodrama therapy groups. She explained to me that, although she was not a "group person," she decided to join this one "because that way, if I see you are honest with all the others, I shall trust your honesty with me. Without being able to weigh this, I could not trust you."

I think this is one of the best recommendations for group treatment, though I realize many therapists question the validity of patients' evaluations. However, they must use it for themselves; how else could they gauge the effect of their own work? Especially in individual therapy, such evaluations are largely subjective. In the group, the other members help to keep an open eye and ear for the ongoing process.

Is it, then, not fair to say that the therapist should question him or herself before entering into what he chooses to interpret as a "love relationship"? To what extent is he basing this enterprise on his own needs? Are we being honest if we undertake this without remembering the "hurt child"? Are we adding to the child's hurt by entering into such a relationship? Is this not a repeat performance? Shouldn't we be as severe with ourselves as the child was with the original parents?

I believe that psychodrama goes far in resolving these questions. It makes possible a level of involvement over and beyond the sexual, on the part of all participants in the session, which puts the child who is questing for unconditional love into the most favorable limelight. In the past-action sharing the group members reveal their own hurt child and in so doing, again are able to obtain a small part of that unconditional love within a warm family group for which every human being hungers.

To a considerable extent this phenomenon may account for the growing number of adherents and practitioners of psychodrama.

Article 24

Psychodrama of Young Mothers

Moreno, Z.T. (1974) *Group Psychotherapy and Psychodrama, A Quarterly Journal* XXVII, 1–4: 191–203

Zerka's comments

We held role-training groups for young mothers twice a week at both the Beacon and New York City locations. I've always felt that we should train parents as well as parents-to-be in these methods. Our children come into the world bearing such gifts of insight for us if only we would become auxiliaries in their world rather than expect them to conform at first to ours. The specific mothers herein mentioned were grappling with their own issues of life and death in anticipation of bringing life into the world. Separating these issues from the births of their children eliminated one potential barrier to forming a primal bond between mother and child.

Psychodrama offers systematic action training for the most important role in the world, "the role of the mother." Mother role training is designed to assist the new mother in finding herself in this delicate, entangling and often frightening relationship to the expected new human being, a being in whose creation she has the leading part.

The psychodramatic method can be usefully extended to mother–infant situations with adolescent girls long before they go through the actual experiences of marriage and pregnancy, delivery and motherhood. Psychological babies preoccupy their minds considerably. Psychodramatic techniques can help to liberate them from and correct distorted perceptions. If distorted perceptions, false anticipations and morbid presentiments are left unresolved, they may become the kernel of deep-seated mother–child conflicts later on. Psychodrama with a pregnant woman may be contra-indicated in the normal course of events unless the subject has a special problem to work out for herself, and volunteers to do so. Even so, every precaution must be taken not to traumatize her.

Some of the problem areas uncovered by means of psychodrama are: *anticipation* of (a) stillbirth, (b) premature birth, (c) crippled babies, (d) blue babies, (e) twins, (f) a specific sex – boy or girl, (g) looking like cultural prototypes, the Moses baby, the Jesus child, (h) resembling father or mother when they were children, (i) looking like a phantom, a monster, a beast or bird, (j) rejection of child by father, (k) rejection of child by her, (l) rejection of her by husband while pregnant, with concomitant delusions as to his sexual behavior and fear of losing him, (m) fears that the husband believes the child is not his. We have dealt with such areas as *perceptions* of herself: (1) grotesqueness of appearance during pregnancy, (2) fear of injury during birth, (3) fear of death in the course of delivery, (4) fear of bleeding to death after delivery, (5) fear of labor starting somewhere and being left unattended, (6) fear of being deserted by husband and having to take care of the child alone.

It is difficult to resolve such conflicts on the verbal level when they are so deeply rooted in the actional framework of the psyche. The motoric aspect of the psyche demands acting out.

Psychodramatic therapy and training

Although the more advanced "natural childbirth" programs include lectures and group instruction on the care of the neonate, they cannot bridge the gap which psychodrama can fill in the area of multi-dimensional mother role training.

We usually commence our mother role training with a selected group of pregnant women who volunteer. The most common reason for desiring training is unfamiliarity with newborns, insecurity in handling them; the mothers-to-be state that they do not want to practice on their own babies, they want to have the security of knowing what to do in advance. One declared that she was very impatient and, since her husband was in the Navy, she had little to occupy herself with during the waiting time. She wanted to "enjoy" her pregnancy rather than fritter the time away on inconsequential chitchat with neighbors.

To enable our mothers to begin to feel the "reality" of the baby, we decided on the "rehearsal for the future," a scene in which each group member projects herself forward into time, about one year, and warms up to her baby as one already born. As a warm-up scene, the director asked each member of the group to visualize their baby's sex. "Here you are, it is a year from now, and your baby is about six months old." "Mary" (to one of the group members – not her real name), "would you like to come upon the stage?"

Mary steps up.

DIRECTOR: How old are you?
MARY: I'm twenty-four, oh, no, twenty-five, since this is next year, I forgot.
DIRECTOR: And your husband's age?

MARY: Twenty-seven.

DIRECTOR: What does your husband do?

MARY: He is a teacher of mathematics in a boys' high school.

DIRECTOR: What do you do?

MARY: Before I married and had the baby, I also taught, English, for foreigners.

DIRECTOR: You say you have a baby?

MARY: Yes.

DIRECTOR: Boy or girl?

MARY: (*falling out of the future situation due to her preoccupation with the present*) Well, I'm glad that came up because I'm quite disturbed today. Before coming here this morning, my husband told me he was sure the baby is going to be a boy.

DIRECTOR: Why are you disturbed? Now that the child is here, what is it?

MARY: Well, I, too, want a boy, but suppose it is not?

DIRECTOR: But the child is here already! You are falling out of the role!

MARY: Yes, I am. That is because I can't seem to visualize it clearly now.

DIRECTOR: This morning, before your husband discussed it with you, what did you visualize then?

MARY: A boy.

DIRECTOR: Very well, then, you have a boy.

MARY: (*trying to warm up to the future projection again*) Yes, he is a big, husky fellow.

DIRECTOR: What is his name?

MARY: Carl, after my brother.

DIRECTOR: An older brother?

MARY: Yes, we lost him when I first conceived, in a dreadful skiing accident, and I wanted my baby to be named after him.

DIRECTOR: That was too bad about your brother. It's nice that you have a namesake for him now. May I see him?

MARY: Sure. He's in the playpen, trying to crawl. Here he is.

DIRECTOR: I'll tell you what I'd like you to do. We will do a role reversal. You, Mary, be Carl now, and lie down on the floor of the playpen. This way we can all get to know him better and see what a nice boy he is. And I will call our auxiliary ego and ask her to be Mary. (*motions to auxiliary ego, who comes up on the stage*)

(*Mary lies down and crawls, as if in playpen*)

AUX. MARY: Hello there, fellow. How're you making out with crawling? (*bends over Mary who is now baby Carl, crawling and drooling and grinning at mother*)

CARL: Grrh. (*grins and grabs at mother's hair*)

MARY: You know what, Carlie boy? I think you're teething. Hey, let go of my hair and let me pick you up so I can see. (*goes through the motions of picking up the baby*) Open your mouth, honey, and let me see.

(*Carl grins and grabs at mother's hair again*)

MARY: Baby, dear, let me see, maybe you've got some ivories peeking out. Come on, now (*tries to get him to open his mouth, while trying to untangle her hair*), say Oooh, or Aaah, or something.

CARL: Grr, da, da, da. (*continues to play with mother's hair*)

MARY: (*cuddling the baby*) Oh, well, maybe Mummy is asking too much of you. But we're so proud of you, and Mummy and Daddy love you so much. I thought maybe we could surprise Daddy with the good news when he comes home tonight. (*caresses baby's hair*)

DIRECTOR: Good. Now, Mary, get up and be Mary again, and you (*to auxiliary ego*), you are the nurse. Here you are, we are going to do something a little bit different. Now, Mary, let's return to the present for a moment. When do you expect to have your baby?

MARY: In about five months.

DIRECTOR: All right, here you are; it's June, June the?

MARY: Oh, the 20th or so.

DIRECTOR: June 20th. You're in the hospital; the baby has just been born and the nurse is with you and the child. You have not seen it yet. (*prompts auxiliary ego as nurse that the baby is a girl, whispers so Mary does not hear*) You are in bed, the nurse comes in with the baby.

NURSE: Well, you have a fine, eight-pound baby. Aren't you proud?

MARY: I sure am! Let me see him.

NURSE: Him? It's a girl! A beautiful, bonny, round baby girl.

MARY: A girl? Are you sure? (*looks questioningly at the director who shakes his head affirmatively*)

NURSE: (*indignant*) Of course I'm sure. Are you all right?

MARY: Oh, do let me have her. I want to see and hold her. (*nurse hands her the baby*)

DIRECTOR: Now you (*to auxiliary ego*) become the baby. You see, Mary, although the baby cannot speak yet, it is obvious that you are putting all kinds of things into the situation, what the baby might be feeling and thinking. The auxiliary ego will represent the reflection of these things in your relationship with the child. Go ahead.

BABY: (*in high pitched voice*) Mummy, I hope you love me.

MARY: Sure I do, but it's sort of sudden.

BABY: Why? Didn't you expect me?

MARY: To tell the truth, we thought you'd be a boy.

DIRECTOR: Now reverse roles. Mary, you be the baby and the baby becomes Mary.

AUX. MARY: (*repeats last sentence of Mary to help her warm up*) To tell the truth, we thought you'd be a boy.

MARY (*as baby*): Oh, and I'm a girl. I'm so sorry but I can't change that.

AUX. MARY: Of course you can't. I don't mean to seem displeased, but I had wanted a boy to name Carl, after my dear brother.

BABY: Uncle Carl?

AUX. MARY: Yes, but he is dead, you see. And I loved him very much. I always wanted to be like him; in fact, I wanted at one time to be a boy myself. (*this is a piece of information not given by the subject, but produced out of the situation, and later supported as true by the subject*)

BABY: I'm sorry, Mummy, but you could call me Carolyn. That's a nice name?

AUX. MARY: Yes, dear. I never thought of that. A girl? Oh dear, it is true that boys and girls wear similar things these days when they are small, or you'd look like your own brother in all the blue things we bought for you.

BABY: Maybe one day I can have a brother and then you can call him Carl. And I'll help you bring him up.

AUX. MARY: Yes, darling, that's a lovely idea.

BABY: And you do love me, don't you?

AUX. MARY: Oh, yes, I do. You're my little girl.

BABY: And do you think I'll be all right with Daddy?

AUX. MARY: I think Daddy will just be happy it's all over and we're both well. Now he'll have two girls instead of one.

DIRECTOR: Thank you, Mama and baby. Now let's sit down and discuss what just occurred.

The other members of the group, although they did not have such a traumatic incident to account for it, shared to a considerable degree this rigidity of "future imagery," being tied either to male or female child, and unable to shake off the conviction as to the sex of their baby. Needless to say, this future projection is a dynamic approach to this very common problem. Mary was enabled, by simultaneous role reversal, to feel what it means to be a mere newborn, and more or less rejected because of being the "wrong sex." As this problem affected such a large number of the members of the group, we decided to continue the production part of the session by constructing a few other test–training situations.

The second mother, herself the oldest of five girls, admitted always having dreamt of having a boy. But, she stated, her husband wanted a girl. A scene was set up in the hospital with Diana in bed, and her husband coming to see her and the baby, a girl. In this scene the husband (again acted by an auxiliary ego) declares his joy at having a daughter and gives for his reason his fear of not being as good a father to a boy as he would to a girl, because: (a) he himself never got along well with his parents, but his sister had much better relations with them and (b) he feared the competition for her affection which he assumed a boy would cause.

The third mother, whom we will call Patricia, was placed into a situation with a nosy neighbor who deprecated her boy because "boys are noisy and dirty and so much harder to bring up" (a fear which she herself had expressed and which she had declared made her want a girl). Patricia was now forced to defend her boy child. The group members again discussed these scenes and reflected their own feelings in reference to the problems they raised.

There are, obviously, non-private factors involved in these obsessions, cultural values placed upon having a boy, etc. But the private configurations as they affected the members of the group were intense and meaningful conflict areas that lend themselves to deeper exploration by means of the psychodramatic future projection and role reversals.

The fact of having to face themselves in the role of the mothers they are likely to become to their own child, *in situ*, is often so revealing as to make further analysis irrelevant. The learning in action is of an all-inclusive nature, and matures them for the next step of learning without the need for insight-giving on the part of the therapist.

There are two other applications of psychodrama to young mothers which we have used: namely that of treating the traumata of the labor itself, and of the problem of spontaneous abortion. Regrettably, our physical hospitals are not geared to the emotional needs of patients. This is true in hospitals across the nation. Nurses, aides and even physicians are not trained to deal with the emotional upheavals attendant upon surgery, diagnosis of malignancies, terminal disease, loss of babies, or whatever, and they are terrified of allowing patients their emotional release. The patient is expected to be a "good" patient, which simply means submitting himself or herself to the dulling routine of the hospital and not making waves, no matter what ill fate awaits or meets them *en route*.

One such incident occurred when a young mother came to us with her three-month-old baby boy. She had terrible memories of her labor. She had requested that her husband be allowed to be present at her labor but the hospital in which her doctor worked had no facilities for this. She wanted her baby by natural childbirth, having had four previous ones that way and suffering no ill effect whatsoever. Again, this was denied. Her older children were born in England, whence she had come into this country while pregnant; she and her husband had immigrated six months earlier. She re-enacted first the experience as it was, with all its horrors, isolation, brutal treatment, such as being given medication without explanation, being heavily sedated without her consent and a number of other insults. When she stated her demands, she was told to stop being "neurotic" and finally became so hysterical that several nurses were needed to hold her down so she could be sedated by injection! We allowed her to ventilate her spleen upon all these torturers and then re-do the entire process as she wished it would have happened, with her husband present and the kind of non-interference she had expected to be allowed during labor, to be treated for what she was, a normal, sensitive adult whose needs were respected and met according to her choices. We did not assume the prerogative of knowing more and better what she needed than she did herself.

The auxiliary egos were very effective, especially the young man she picked to play her husband. Her husband, too, had been traumatized by the way he had been shut out. All his efforts to avert this had been met with physical force to keep him out of the labor room. We expected her to have a catharsis and that she would be able to put the whole series of unfortunate events behind her instead of brooding obsessively about them as she had been doing. This did happen. But far more important things happened. She had been so involved with the emotional deprivation she had experienced that she had not been able to warm up properly to her role of new mother. This aspect she had not uncovered before the psychodrama session. Indeed, we assumed that, as she was breastfeeding her baby quite successfully, there were no deeper disturbances in the symbiotic relationship. The protagonist astounded us, therefore, when she reported to us the next day that for the first time since she had the baby she experienced him as "real." She became aware that he had a body, a presence, a personality. Whereas before she could not experience him, she now had a complete perception of him. There had been a total reorganization of perception since her psychodrama. She felt confident once more in her ability to be the mother she knew herself capable of being. One session was all that was needed to bring this healing about.

Another type of trauma or rather series of traumata we were able to deal with successfully was that of a young woman who had lost four pregnancies. The last one had been of longer duration than any of the previous ones and the loss was therefore even greater. As she was the wife of a physician, she was expected to perform in the role of the exemplary patient in the hospital and every time she wept at her loss the nurses would chide her and make denigrating, feelingless remarks such as, "Oh, we don't want to cry now, do we?" "This isn't the end of the world, you know. You can always have another one." "Aren't you indulging yourself?" She became extremely depressed and when first presenting herself doubted her ability to ever bear a child to term. We re-enacted the last and most painful loss and when it was completed, permitted her all the grieving she wanted, right then and there. No nurse came and chided her; instead, her doctor, her husband and the family members and friends she wanted around, attended her, cherished her, wept and mourned her loss with her. These were all represented by auxiliary egos of her choice, from among the group members present. The end result of this session, again a single one, was that she conceived within the month and has since given birth to a full term healthy child.

Conclusion

The psychodrama teaches mothers in a simple, direct way how to accept life as it is, in whatever environment, to become more relaxed in relation to their infants, to learn to help themselves and their children by becoming more effective auxiliary ego mothers, and to achieve more harmonious interaction.

Chapter 4

On Her Own

1974–1997

To J.L.M. May 23, 1974
Upon listening to The Words of the Father record for the first time since your death.

What shall I say
of death
when man's technology
restores your voice?
I hear it, disbelieving,
in deep shock
and realize your presence
in great pain.
I weep
and weep again.
My loss is sharp, is here,
in being, now,
alone.
Your voice is real,
yet gone.
Your spirit's immortality
a painful newness brings.
I cannot bear it.
Tears are not enough,
I want to stay and yet
to run away.
The telephone's ring
breaks through my spell.
I answer it and weep,
no longer keep it
secret.

In the dark
we share our sorrow
Dee and I.
She knows and stands by me,
along the wire,
another man-made thing.

In writing this
again in agony I mourn
and sob and moan
as I have never done before,
in animal intensity
which grips and seizes me.

Is this **my** *voice?*
It has an unfamiliar sound
yet universal.
I realize: This is
the morning of my mourning,
the living of my loss
and that of all the world's,
the "Farewells" still unsaid,
unspoken.
Across the years
my link with you remains,
unbroken.
I need the comfort of my tears.

You who have given me
my life anew,
again and again,
Oh God, how many times?
And also ripped my guts
with pain.

Last night
my students shared lovingly.
They had no fears,
they stood around,
they sensed your presence,
very near.
Ann held me
in her comforting embrace
and wept with me,

as did they all.
Some wiped my face.
Meinolf supplied a handkerchief,
all new, a virgin cloth,
for me to blow my nose,
absorb the tears.
And Jannika in privacy revealed
she saw tonight
a fog at edge of Hessian Lake.
We'd wandered there together,
the group and I.

This fog contained a shadow
which hovered
at my side.
She thought it might
be you.
I did not see or feel you there.
I needed this, your voice,
to have you close,
once more reliving
our first journey in 1941.
Your voice, dynamic, young
and ringing, there
in the Pullman car,
presenting then these very Words,
a gift, only to me.
The railroad's roar
mingling in
my ear's delight,
the galleys of your book
spread on the seats,
your giant hands,
your eyes, your presence,
reading, only to me,
out loud,
with stentor's voice.
How do I convey
the singing in my soul
when it joined yours?

There simply is no way.

Before you died
I promised
you would never lose me.
"I'll find you again,"
I said.
You heard, nodded, gave sign
that you approved.
But there is no
limit for all this
in time.
Now I must live
while you are so removed.
My life still runs its course,
full charged with loving.

Who knows what oceans
I must cross
what lives touch,
what companions meet and
cherish yet,
before I once again
am there with you?

The cosmos is our home
and no one shall be
there
alone.

From *Love Songs to Life*
Zerka T. Moreno

Article 25

The Significance of Doubling and Role Reversal for Cosmic Man

Moreno Z.T. (1975) *Group Psychotherapy and Psychodrama, A Quarterly Journal* XXVIII: 55–59

Zerka's comments

This article came out fully shaped. Moreno's death stimulated me to think in cosmic terms. I began rethinking his ideas, teasing out what I had learned, and what I wanted to focus on.

Merlyn Pitzele came into my life in July of 1974. This was totally unexpected. Although he had declared even to Moreno that he was in love with me, it never occurred to me that it would happen so fast. He moved to Beacon late in 1974. Merlyn's background was so totally different from mine – he was New York City intelligentsia, aggressive and passionate in his questioning and examination of issues. His questions stimulated me to reformulate our ideas. He had undergone analysis and in listening to him, I was challenged to establish Moreno in his own right. This made me stronger and more independent in what I knew and what I had experienced. Eventually Merlyn began to understand, joining me in my work.

Marx postulated the economic man, Freud the psychological man, Moreno the cosmic man. Man's cosmic nature is evident at his birth. Of this, motherhood brings its own intimation. One of the most potent experiences of the mother (and of the father, in role reversing with his mate) when she first sees and holds her newborn child is of great wonder, awe, a sense that this is a gift, this child, an inheritance, that she could not possibly have produced it, that there are forces at work that have caused this to come into being, over and beyond the biological. It is as if this child is "loaned" to the parents by the cosmos for a certain period of time, eventually to be returned to it when an adult. The mystery of this is overwhelming, rarely completely grasped.

The behavior of the neonate and young infant, with total involvement in body movements, has been observed and described by a large number of specialists. Moreno named this phenomenon "the act hunger syndrome." He concluded that the organism of the child is driven by a hunger for action. As the child develops the movements become more refined, better controlled and focused, but he continues to exhibit what appears to be to adults at times irrational behavior, moving into space, running about, looking, listening, touching, smelling, tasting, searching. He hungers to know what is going on about him, who and what is out there. He also wants to define his own position in space and to be affirmed as an entity. The multiple stimuli he encounters are so challenging and arousing, their bombardment requires a great deal of his energy and attention to sort out. To an adult this behavior may seem exaggerated, purposeless and irritating. For the child it is sheer necessity. There may, however, be a deeper reason for all this activity, a need to re-integrate himself with the cosmos, to become once again united with it.

If, as the idea of the cosmic being suggests, the child has been lifted from the universe, given human embodiment (or to speak in oriental–mystical terms, if he has chosen this embodiment for karmic purposes) and loaned to his parents, one may assume that this rupture has been more or less a shock and that the behavior described is a consequence of this separation. It is not merely separation from the mother's body, described in psychoanalytic terms as the "trauma of birth," which is the shock, but separation from the totality of the universe. Moreno viewed birth as first of all a victory. He thought the traumata came later, in life itself. But this present view may form a bridge between the two concepts, that of the birth trauma *and* the victory of birth, provided the journey into life is properly guided. This is the thesis of the present paper.

There is also increasing awareness among us of the "traumata of death" and an entire section of our psychological practice is bent in dealing with death and dying in a more wholesome, integrative fashion, at the other end of life's spectrum. Approaches to death and dying can be greatly enriched by the introduction of psychodramatic techniques into this sensitive arena.

Moreno described the child's first universe as the "matrix of all-identity," the phase in which the child experiences himself as the total universe, without any separation from it. In the next phase, that of differentiated all-identity, persons and objects are perceived as separated from one another but he is not yet aware that he does not control them. The third phase is that of the break between fantasy and reality. This is when the child suffers one of the deepest existential shocks: he becomes aware that he is not the total universe, that he does not have control over other beings and objects, that they move to and fro in space and are not totally at his command. This is also the phase in which, to bridge the shock, fantasy may replace reality, the fantasy being preoccupied with restoring power to himself. When these preoccupations lead to a complete break between perception of reality and fantasy, profound pathology may develop. Because this experience of the centrality of the human organism never quite leaves him, man suffers from "normal megalomania" which it takes him a lifetime to evaluate and deal with. For the child it is magic medicine. With it he is restored to his rightful place in the center of the universe.

When the child discovers himself capable of moving independently in space, he begins to experience the world as friendly or threatening, interesting or amusing, painful or entertaining, according to encounters along the way. One of the most demanding tasks of his significant adults is to assist him to have integrative rather than traumatic experiences. Before the child can integrate himself into the world, then, he needs to be assured that being himself is a positive category. He requires self-affirmation above all. This is of the essence because without it he is not able to role reverse adequately or later on double as will be necessary, with all the significant others in his world. Spontaneity–creativity must first be affirmed in him. To that end, we have found that it is essential that the parents at first, later extending to others such as siblings and more remote relatives or friends, learn the essence of affirmative doubling and later of non-injurious role reversal.

If our assumption is correct that the child has been lifted from the cosmos, given human embodiment and loaned, it is the parents' responsibility to make the child's transition from the cosmos to the terrestrial world as integrative as possible, up until such time as the parent is himself ready to be yielded to the cosmos and the child can prepare himself and his child for the elder's return to the cosmos. Doubling and role reversal are basic in this circular development.

We have found the earliest suitable moment for the parents to double with the child to be at the time when the child starts to make sounds, reproducing the baby language or pre-verbal language. Shucking off her own identity, the mother takes on the bodily position and makes the same sounds as the baby. When this doubling is started early, the baby delights in it, responds to it and enriches his basic vocabulary. I have myself done this with our child and we have never, before or since, told one another more beautiful fairy tales. And the laughter and joy we co-experienced! Later the parents can double with the child as a day-by-day process, to understand the child's needs and meet them better, to assist in emergencies, or merely to invigorate diurnal contact. Children so affirmed are able to reach the next level, that of role reversal with significant others, earlier and with greater depth. The child is not able to role reverse with others until he recognizes his separateness. He cannot yield what he does not own. Lack of ability to role reverse indicates deep lack of early self-affirmation.

The parent precedes the child in the world. Regrettably, he cannot pass on his experiences of that world to his child. It is the tragedy of the human race that every child and each generation needs to explore life from the very start. Very little experience or wisdom can be passed on. But through doubling first and later through role reversal, some of these gaps can be bridged.

We see this ability of the child first to accept doubling, still later to role reverse with the parent, and in the final stage to double the parent, as essential and clearly indicated for emotional growth. It has attained a firmly needed position in the developmental thinking in psychodrama.

I have begun to see the Seven Stages of Man in these terms. In the first stage it must be the parent who is the child's auxiliary ego and doubles with that child; in the second the parents role reverse with the child. The child begins to take the role of the parents versus himself. In the third stage he can take the role of his parents versus siblings and significant others. These may all still take place up to this point on the psychodramatic level, that is, within the confines of the family setting. Simultaneously he starts to become his own parent more consistently.

In life itself meanwhile, the child has learned to role reverse with his peers and has begun to test himself out in that form of relationship. In the fourth stage, somewhere in the late teens, he desires to be seen as a peer to and by his parents. If the earlier stages have been successfully mastered by both parent and child, it will not be difficult for the parent to begin to see the child growingly as his peer. But it is frequently at just this stage in their interaction that the parent may fail the child by continuing to take the role of the parent in a fashion more suitable to the earlier phases. In the fifth stage he is totally independent of his parent and begins the cycle all over again versus his own child. In the sixth stage he can role reverse and double with the parent, divining the parent's needs as once his parent did for him when he was unable to speak. In the seventh and final stage he is able to completely assume responsibility for his parent and for himself in terms of dealing with the end of the parent's life, returning the parent to the cosmos and also starting to deal with his own eventual return there. If he has learned his lesson well, his child will now go through the same stages and in turn become his auxiliary ego, role reversing and doubling with him as he may require.

Incomplete doubling and role reversal lead to a great number of intrapersonal and interpersonal conflicts. With increasing longevity we are seeing in our clinical practice a growing number of problems stemming from the lack of orderly development. When the child has not been sufficiently affirmed in the early stages, the problems are enormously augmented at the time when the parent becomes dependent upon the child. If he then demands role reversal and doubling from a child who is being forced prematurely into the parent's responsible position before he has had good parenting himself, depression, guilt, resentment and even outright hatred and rejection or neglect may ensue. Self-recrimination and emotional upheaval are frequently seen in such deprived adults, bringing in their wake great torment for all concerned.

The adult normally precedes the child into eternity. If in the course of their life together the doubling and role reversal have taken place on a satisfactory and sequential basis the child will be enabled to yield up the parent to the cosmos without experiencing separation anxiety, guilt or remorse. He will want to double for and with the parent and give him of his own power and status, support and assistance. The child must first become his own complete parent before he can become the parent of his parent.

Much of our psychodramatic clinical attention is now spent in bringing back the dead so that the protagonist can complete the relationship that has never been completed in life itself. The psychodrama has to provide via the auxiliary ego that which has been denied in life. The psychodrama is the treatment of choice for this type of need. But we see its most productive application to be in life itself with the parents actively participating in the circular process with their own children.

Moreno pointed out that death takes place around us in our social atom long before it takes place in our own organism. Even children encounter death throughout childhood and adolescence, in the form of death of a pet, a beloved friend or relative, or the death of a relationship although the person involved remains alive. They are, therefore, already sensitized to some extent to the idea of death. But adults are familiar with the tremendous fear children suffer at the mere idea of their parent's death. I believe it is not merely that they are dependent upon them. They intuit that the relationship would remain incomplete, unfulfilled, and therefore they cannot relinquish their parents yet. They cannot permit them to return to the cosmos whence we all came.

Studies on death and dying have not taken the sociometric and psychodramatic aspects of the life and death cycle sufficiently into consideration, largely because of a lack of awareness of the significance of doubling and role reversal, and of the contribution sociometric approaches can make in these areas.

In view of the "cosmic shock" that being born may bring about, we may also revise our attitude toward suicide. It may be a *contradictio in adjecto*, but we have all witnessed "therapeutic suicides," i.e., suicides whose eventual effect was not destructive to the survivors and may even have been salutary. In view of the cosmic shock, we may conjecture that suicide is a form of returning to the cosmos without waiting for the life span to complete itself. It may be, viewed in that light, a healing effort at restoring the unity with the cosmos.

The psychodramatist has a valid contribution to make to child development on one hand and to gerontology on the other, by teaching the process of doubling and role reversal to both young and old. In addition, he has the opportunity to make the path of cosmic man here on earth that much more rewarding.[1]

Article 26

The Function of the Auxiliary Ego in Psychodrama with Special Reference to Psychotic Patients

Moreno, Z.T. (1978) *Group Psychotherapy, Psychodrama and Sociometry* XXXI: 163–166

Zerka's comments

Moreno originally identified three functions of the auxiliary ego, and I added the fourth and fifth based on my experience in that role. Moreno never stepped out of the director role, although while he directed he did bring out some notions of what the protagonist might be feeling. The refinement of the auxiliary role was my area of expertise. It should be noted that the fourth and fifth functions as applied to work with psychotics differ slightly in work with what we called "normotics" (i.e., normal neurotics). Whereas the goal of the fourth function with psychotics was, as I say here, "to bring the various parts of the protagonist to greater integration," with normotics we want to feel our way under the surface of the auxiliary role and offer an interpretation: "I've never told you this, but . . ." Sometimes this is done in the sharing afterwards rather than during the action. The fifth function with psychotics was specifically to help them return to the group and to the world at large. With normotics, the fifth function is to provide guidance for the director as to what is needed, or how the protagonist can best deal with the issue at hand.

Introduction

One of the reasons why very few psychotherapists undertake to treat the psychotic person is that it requires personal traits of great versatility and creativity to stay ahead of the fantasy world of the psychotic. The practitioner is often swept away by the majesty and horror of the patient's production, fascinated but immobilized. Even though psychodrama can deal with this fantasy world more satisfactorily and completely, there is so much awareness of the pitfalls that even its practitioners stay away from this area of application. This is altogether regrettable. Since Moreno first introduced the psychodramatic approach to the major psychoses, no new reports have come from others and no practitioners have established themselves in this arena. With Moreno's death in 1974, there is a large gap that no one seems able or willing to fill.

One may refer to John N. Rosen's attempts to apply dramatic action methods but even these did not partake of the multiplicity of techniques and subtleties pioneered by Moreno. One of Rosen's greatest problems was that he made himself the main auxiliary ego in the process, bringing about role confusion. Rosen still functioned within the psychoanalytic framework, at least for his interpretations. Thus he was not only the analyst, he mixed his roles and became embroiled in the psychotic drama. One may say that he thus muddied the transference more by so doing, or at least contributed to confusion in the patient as his role was no longer external to the patient nor clearly defined.

Moreno stayed out of the drama of the psychotic so as better to overview the patient's needs and to be able to determine the indicated therapeutic interventions. This further allowed him to remain free of some of the more deleterious aspects of the transference. Transference was broken up into multiple parts and carried by the auxiliary egos actively engaged in the treatment process with him and the patient. Another aspect of Moreno's inventiveness was that he introduced the auxiliary ego therapist, thus his treatment became a team operation rather than that of one mastermind.

Having been privileged to work closely with Moreno for more than thirty years, I shall always feel greatly indebted to his genius in devising psychodrama which, particularly with the psychotic patient, has taught me more about the labyrinth of the human mind than I could otherwise have hoped to know. Some of the most profound learning it produced was my ability to deal with madness, my own and that of others, with considerably greater equanimity. Moreno's students were taught not to fear, through the way he dealt with his own fears as well as those of his charges, the fringes of lunacy in all of us. Indeed, he felt these areas of his own psyche to be one of the chief sources of his creativity. He trusted that he could be living proof that a man could be, for all intents and purposes, at times considered insane yet able to be productive, creative and contained. That this is not an easy task is immediately grasped. The human actor is not a monologist, but an inter-actor with other actors against whose counter-spontaneity he bounces; this may hurt him and he may cause hurt to the others in turn.

It was always a privilege when very distraught patients allowed me entry into their world. It was as if they stretched out a hand, saying, "This is my world. I trust you. Come and be with me inside it. Live my pain, my sorrow and my joy, that you may know me better." This leads to becoming a genuine auxiliary ego, eventually able to stretch out one's own hand to that person, indicating, "Now that I have been with you in your world, let me take you into mine." At that point the final task of the auxiliary ego becomes that of reintegrating the patient into the world of so-called reality.

The five functions of the auxiliary ego

Let us review the several functions of the auxiliary ego because it is precisely in this realm that Moreno created a new modus operandi. The first function is to take on a role required by the protagonist to complete the drama, either a significant absent other, real or imaginary, alive or dead, past or present, or future, or an hallucination or delusion. Sometimes it may be that of a body part or an object, an aspect of the self, a fear or an emotion with which the protagonist is struggling. Obviously the closer the auxiliary ego is to the ethos of the patient, the easier his task becomes. But as patients are unique in their psychotic production, the challenges are numerous.

The second function is to approximate the perception held by the protagonist of him/herself, to give it flesh, for without this the protagonist "falls out of the role and situation" and fails to become involved.

In the course of representing the absent other, the third function is to explore and assess the protagonist's perception of the relationship to this absent other in the role-playing context.

The fourth is to interpret this absent other as well as their relationship to the protagonist over and beyond the protagonist's ability to do so. Thus, certain distortions may be clarified and corrected within the role-playing context.

The fifth, which is built upon the foregoing, is to act as a therapeutic guide for the protagonist, to greater intrapersonal and interpersonal harmony or, if indicated, to a separation of the relationship with the other.

The term "auxiliary" is most apt, as it describes the instrument; the auxiliary ego is an extension of the protagonist who is incomplete without the significant other(s), an extension of the director who does not move into action, of the absent others who need interpretation, and of the group of co-participants who need to understand the dynamic interaction. Particularly with the psychotic, the auxiliary ego functions as a bridge to assist the protagonist's return to the world at large. The function of the auxiliary ego as a double to psychotic patients cannot be overestimated; the more bizarre the patient is, the more a double can be effective in this process. Often a protagonist is unable to communicate what is going on inside and around him, but the double can and does. Eventually family members are brought into the therapy whenever possible; they may, in turn become auxiliary egos for a while, or be treated as co-protagonists, learning about the part they have possibly contributed to the patient's difficulties.

There is another, highly privileged manner in which the auxiliary ego operates, namely that of the "double" or as a "mirror." Here special sensitivity is needed to be accepted as a recognizable representation of the patient, as the functions are intrapersonal instead of interpersonal: First, to represent invisible dimensions of the patient who is present, or the patient at various chronological or developmental points, or body parts. To this end the patient serves as the guide and the double becomes, in every aspect, a true double, emulating the physical motions, body language, stance, facial expression, vocal tone, etc. Second, to feel into the patient how he/she feels about him/herself, and to bring that out into the open. Third, to interpret the protagonist to him/herself. Fourth, to act as a catalyst to bring the various parts of the protagonist to greater integration. Lastly, to help the protagonist to return to the group and to the world after having reached a deeper level of self-revelation and self-affirmation.

The mirror ego differs from this only in that, as a rule, the protagonist sits among the group members, watching him/herself "as if in a mirror." Some of this mirroring or reflecting back also takes place in the work of the double, but in the mirror technique the protagonist just watches himself being enacted. Thus, he/she can survey the self from a non-actorial, non-engaged position. This later function has been taken over largely by the use of videotape replay, which removes the need for the mirroring actor and thus eliminates possible distortion as the patient views himself. Hence the protagonist cannot hide behind any excuses as to his/her performance since he/she is truly able to see him/herself as others see him/her, revealed by a non-judgmental, non-human object agent – the tape.

When Moreno first began to deal with and describe the auxiliary ego's operations, he sometimes spoke of the "alter ego." He later discarded this term because "alter ego" is a phenomenological term dealing with an intrapsychic phenomenon, that of "the other," the inner voice. As such, it is often confused with the function of the auxiliary ego as the double. He wanted it to be clear that the auxiliary ego is an objective instrument in the hands of the psychodramatic director and not a subjective entity. Even in the function of the double, the auxiliary ego's best performance encompasses more than that inner voice. The operation might involve opposition, encouragement, challenging, denying, exaggerating, exploring, supporting, exposing, defending, attacking, etc., all within the context of self-confrontation. As the auxiliary ego was a new operational instrument as well as professional identity, we stopped using the term alter ego entirely.

Speaking subjectively, my own learning has been tremendously enhanced through the various doubling engagements in which I have been active over the years. To be able to transcend the limitations of the human body and psyche and join another human being in the realm of *una cum uno*, if only momentarily, is enspiriting and enriching.[1]

Article 27

The Eight Stages of Cosmic Beings in Terms of Capacity and Need to Double and Role Reverse

Moreno, Z.T. (1980) Unpublished paper

Zerka's comments

A student of mine had been reading Erik Erikson's idea of stages of development and given what she knew about psychodrama, said she thought it was incomplete. I wrote this article to address the stages from a psychodramatic perspective.

Stage	Child	Adult
Stage 1 First six months approximately	Neonate is in the Matrix of All-Identity; does not distinguish between self and other, human or object. Begins to babble at about five months. Holds up its head.	Parent or caregiver as auxiliary ego doubles with child to learn about child's needs, enabling him/her to meet these, speaks in child's own babble.
Stage 2 Six months to one year approximately	Child is in the state of Differentiated Identity, has become aware of its own organism by exploring extremities; begins to move about in space; attempts first sounds, then words. Crawls, attempts to stand.	Parent or caregiver as auxiliary ego doubles with child to support child's growing separateness and identity; continues to speak child's speech and starts to teach it the adult's speech.
Stage 3 One year approximately to eighteen months approximately	Child may develop separation anxiety if significant others' absence is prolonged; continues exploring space, able to move about independently; communicates wants by pointing, later speaking.	Parent or caregiver continues doubling with child; supports its growing independence and awareness, helps expand and strengthen child's identity.

Stage	Child	Adult
Stage 4 Eighteen months to two and a half years approximately	Child begins to be aware of having a separate identity; reaches out into first exploration of identity of significant others and can double with others.	Parent or caregiver doubles with child to assist exploration of significant others and helps establish relationship to others.
Stage 5 Two and a half years to five years approximately	Child is able to role reverse with significant others, adults, pets, peers, and objects.	Parent or caregiver role reverses with child, continues to support the child's growing independence and ability to assume responsibility for self, accept authority, its understanding of and relating to peers.
Stage 6 Five to eighteen years approximately	Role reversal with adults leads to gradual acceptance of greater responsibility for self; can act at the later stage as authority figure for self and peers as well as younger others.	Parent or caregiver doubles and role reverses with child to learn to accept child increasingly as a peer and to ease child into adulthood; prepares self to separate from child.
Stage 7 Eighteen to thirty years approximately	Doubling and role reversing with parent in preparation for yielding parent to the cosmos; begins cycle as full adult and parent to its own offspring.	Parent prepares for maturity and eventual return to the cosmos; allows child to double and role reverse with self on behalf of support for self, as a peer.
Stage 8 Thirty years and beyond	Completes unfinished business with parent, role reverses with parent to complete cycle in readiness to yield parent back to the cosmos.	Parent permits child to take responsibility as needed for himself/herself; prepares self to return to the cosmos.

Article 28

Psychodrama

Moreno, Z.T. (1983) In H. Kaplan and B. Sadock (eds), *Comprehensive Group Psychotherapy*, 2nd edn, Philadelphia: Lippincott, Williams & Wilkins, pp. 158–166

Zerka's comments

I was invited to contribute this chapter to Kaplan and Sadock's book. By then I was being recognized for my own contributions to the field.

Introduction

Psychodrama represents a major turning point away from the treatment of the individual in isolation and toward the treatment of the individual in groups, from treatment by verbal methods toward treatment by action methods.

Psychodrama and universals

The objective of psychodrama was, from its inception, to construct a therapeutic setting that uses life as a model, to integrate into the setting all the modalities of living – the universals of time, space, reality, and the cosmos – including all the details and nuances of life.

Time

To what extent does time enter into and function in psychotherapeutic settings? Man lives in time – past, present, and future. He may suffer from a pathology related to each dimension of time. The problem is how to integrate all three dimensions into significant therapeutic operations. It is not sufficient that they figure as abstract references; they must be made alive with treatment modalities. The psychological aspects of time must reappear *in toto*.

The past

In orthodox Freudian psychoanalysis, time is emphasized in terms of the past. Freud found going back and trying to find the causes of things of particular interest. Psychoanalysts went back further and further – into the womb and, if possible, even beyond that – until they tired of this futile search.

The present

However important the past is as a dimension of time, it is one sided, neglecting and distorting the total influence of time upon the psyche. Time has other important phases, one of which is the present, the here and now. In 1914, Jacob L. Moreno began to emphasize the dynamics of the present and all its immediate personal, social, and cultural implications from the viewpoint of the therapeutic process as it takes place in connection with patients in patient groups – the encounter.

The encounter is a telic phenomenon. The fundamental process of tele is reciprocity – reciprocity of attraction, rejection, excitation, inhibition, indifference, and distortion.

The future

Until recently, the future has also been neglected as a dimension of therapeutic time. Yet it is an important aspect of living: we certainly live a good part of our lives with an eye on the future.

It is one thing to consider the expectancies of future happenings and another to simulate them, to construct techniques that enable one to live in the future, to act as if the future is on hand. With therapeutic future techniques, one can act out a situation expected to happen tomorrow, a meeting with a new friend or an appointment with a prospective employer, to simulate the morrow as concretely as possible so as to predict it or to be better prepared for it.

Many patients suffer from an employment or an unemployment neurosis. They are anxious about getting a job, or about an interview with a boss to ask for higher wages. In psychodrama, the therapist rehearses such a patient in advance for what may happen; it is a rehearsal for life. This rehearsal-for-life technique is also effective with patients concerned over affairs of the heart – whether it be a prospective marriage, a divorce, or a new baby. The problem is how to integrate these expectancies and concerns of the patient into the therapeutic operation as actualities, to be of value for both client and therapist.

Space

Space, too, has been almost entirely neglected as a part of the therapeutic process. If you go into a psychoanalyst's office, you find an abstract bed, a couch, but the rest of the office space is not related to the therapeutic process. The patient is language centered, and the therapist is centered to listen. If you go into an office in which one of the current varieties of psychotherapy is practiced, you may find only a chair. The space in which the patient experiences his trauma has no place in that setting.

The idea of a psychotherapy space has been pioneered by psychodrama, which is action centered and which comprehensively tries to integrate all the dimensions of living into itself. When a patient steps into the therapeutic space, the therapist insists on a description of the space in which the ensuing scene is to be portrayed – its horizontal and vertical dimensions, the objects in it, and the distance and relationship of objects to one another. The configuration of space warms up the protagonist to be and act as himself in an environment modeled after that in which he lives.

Reality

Reality has undergone quite a change in the last 40 years. As psychiatry takes place more and more in the community, rather than in hospitals, reality begins to attain new meanings. The trend is very much along the lines of confrontation and concretization.

Infra reality

The reality of a psychoanalyst's office, from the point of view of therapy, is reduced, an infra reality. The contact between doctor and patient is not a genuine dialogue but is more of an interview, a research situation, or a projection test. Whatever is happening to the patient – for example, a suicidal idea or a plan to run away – is not a phase of direct actualization and confrontation but remains on the level of imagining, thinking, feeling. To an extent, this is also true of the reality in the office of the patient-centered, existential, or interview therapist.

Actual reality

The next step is the reality of life itself, of the everyday lives of all people: how they live in their own homes, in their businesses, and in their relationships to all those who affect their lives – their husbands, wives, children, employers, teachers, clergymen – and to the world at large.

The manner in which they live in reality, their relationships with the significant people in their lives, may be defective or inadequate, and they may wish to change, to attempt new ways of living. But change can be both threatening and extremely difficult, to such an extent that they stay in their familiar ruts rather than risk a calamity they cannot handle. Thus, a therapeutic situation is needed in which reality can be simulated so that people can learn to develop new techniques of living without risking serious consequences or disaster, as they might if they first tried the techniques in life itself.

Surplus reality

Surplus reality represents the intangible dimensions of intrapsychic and extrapsychic life; the invisible dimensions in the reality of living that are not fully experienced or expressed. The therapist uses certain operations and instruments to bring out these dimensions in therapeutic settings.

Role reversal

One of the most popular surplus-reality techniques in psychodrama is that of role reversal. If a husband and wife fight in the reality of everyday life, each remains in his own role, in his own life situation. The perceptions, expectations, fears, and disappointments of each remain unchanged. And even if both parties come to some point of agreement, they still maintain the same relative status: the husband remains the husband, the wife remains the wife. But in role reversal the wife takes the part of the husband, and the husband takes the part of the wife. Not only must they do this nominally, but also each one must try to feel his way into the thinking, feeling, and behavior patterns of the other. This technique is particularly useful in situations that are provoked by stress.

It is not always easy to establish identity with one's own self at a certain time in one's life, to recapture one's own feelings and behavior in a crucial episode – as a child or adolescent, for instance – but it is at least plausible. How then can one establish identity with another person, as one is requested to do in a role reversal? It is possible, especially with two people who have lived a long time in intimate ensembles, such as husbands and wives, mothers and children, fathers and sons, sisters and brothers, or very close friends.

Auxiliary ego

One of the basic instruments in constructing a patient's psychodramatic world is that of the auxiliary ego, the representation of absentee people or of delusions, hallucinations, symbols, ideals, animals, and objects. They make the protagonist's world real, concrete, and tangible.

Bodily contact

In the course of making the protagonist's world real and dynamic, numerous problems emerge, as in the use of bodily contact, for instance. Bodily contact has been, to some extent, a taboo in all psychotherapies. Yet, when a nurse sees a patient suffering, she cannot help but touch him and say, "Now, Jack, don't worry; it will be all right." Her touch may mean more to the boy than the words she speaks – not in a sexual way but as a maternal, protective approach to him.

A psychoanalyst who would become in any way physically personal with his patient would be ostracized. But in the psychodramatic approach to human relations, the therapist is interested in following the model of life itself and, within limits, in making therapeutic use of the bodily-contact technique. This technique is obviously contraindicated if it is used to gratify the need of the therapist, but it is indicated if it gives the patient, not only in words but in action, the warmth and immediacy of pulsating life in an area in which he is in need.

Role playing

This is another important surplus-reality technique. Here a person may be trained to function more effectively in his reality role, whether he be employer, employee, student, instructor, parent, child, mate, lover, or friend. In the therapeutic setting of psychodrama, the protagonist is free to try and even to fail in this role, for he knows he will be given the opportunity to try again, to try another interpretation and another, until he finally learns new approaches to the situations he fears, approaches that he can then apply in life itself.

Other techniques

There are still many other effective surplus-reality techniques, such as the empty chair (empty crib, empty pew, empty bed, etc.), the high chair, the magic shop, dream enactment, God technique, existential validation, and the therapeutic community.

Warming up

It would be difficult to find an adult who has not witnessed at some time or other an act of warming up. An automobile engine warms up when it is started; track athletes warm up prior to a race; some people make circular motions before signing an important document; singers vocalize before singing a solo. Every act of man begins with warming up.

There is a circular quality in the relationship of warming up and spontaneity. Warming up initiates spontaneity. Spontaneity, in turn, shortens the period of warming up. At times, warming up and spontaneity are so entwined that they seem to be both cause and effect. In a sense, the shorter and more controlled the process of warming up becomes, the greater the degree of spontaneity. Also, the shorter the period of warming up, the more efficient the personality becomes in meeting life situations. The more quickly one can make adjustments prior to beginning a task, the less trial and error is involved in shifting gears, especially in proceeding from one task to another.

One of the goals in creating a good personality is to be aware of and to appreciate the effect of warming up. Efficient warming up may also reduce emotional anxiety. Take, for example, the ubiquitous intrusion of the telephone call. Answering a telephone permits very little opportunity for warming up to the voice on the other end of the line. The usual reinforcement clues, such as the speaker's appearance and the location of the conversation (one expects to talk of bowling in a bowling alley), are absent. The abrupt ring of the telephone, the voice not always clear, the face unseen, and the disruption of one's activity are not designed to aid the answering party in warming up to the conversation. Emotional anxiety may result, therefore, if the individual does not possess adequate spontaneity and an efficient warming-up technique suited to telephone conversation.

Warming up does not mean the same thing as conditioning. Conditioning implies a set relationship between a stimulus and a response. A person may become conditioned to respond to the telephone's ring by arising and answering the call with little or no apparent thought. However automatic that response becomes, he is still confronted with a warming up task the moment he picks up the telephone. In his conversation he makes preliminary adjustments, and the manner in which he makes them produces reciprocal adjustments in the person calling him. Both prior to the calling and during the call, the warming-up process is operating. A conditioned response produces only a singular behavior pattern. Warming up both prepares the subject for the act and is highly involved in structuring the act as it proceeds from singular act to singular act. As the individual warms up to the telephone conversation, he becomes more spontaneous. As he becomes more spontaneous, he continues to warm up to the situation.

Creativity–spontaneity–cultural conserve triad

Creativity

Creativity manifests itself in any series of creative states or creative acts. One example is the creation of new organisms capable of surviving on land at the time that animal life was confined to the sea. A new animal organism arose when it underwent, through the evolutional process, certain physical changes. This process may be called biological creativity. A second example is the Sermon on the Mount as it emerged, however unformed, for the first time from the mind of Jesus. This is a form of religious creativity. A third illustration is musical creativity, such as the music of Beethoven's Ninth Symphony at the moment it was being created by him in contrast to the same music as a finished product, separated from the composer himself.

Spontaneity

Creativity is a sleeping beauty that, to become effective, needs a catalyzer. The arch catalyzer of creativity is spontaneity, a form of energy that is unconservable. It emerges and is spent in a moment, it must emerge to be spent and must be spent to make place for new emergence, like some animals that are born and die in the love act. It is a truism to say that the universe cannot exist without physical and mental energy that can be conserved. But it is important to realize that without the other kind of energy, the unconservable one, the creativity of the universe could not start and could not run. Creativity would come to a standstill.

Spontaneity operates in the present. It propels a person toward an adequate response to a new situation or a new response to an old situation. Thus, while creativity is related to the act itself, spontaneity is related to the warming up, to the readiness for the act.

Here follow three types of spontaneity. The first type is a novel response to a situation that is not adequate for that situation. Psychotics, for example, may state that two times two equals five, certainly a novel response but hardly adequate. Children, too, burst with spontaneity and have a wide range of novel experiences, but the creative value of their responses is often doubtful, at least from the point of view of the adult world, just as the creative value of the novel responses of psychotics is doubtful from the point of view of normal people.

The second type of spontaneity is a stereotype variety. It consists of a response that is adequate to the situation but that lacks sufficient novelty or significant creativity to be fruitful for the situation. The comedian's repetitive reaction to a situation soon loses its novelty, and although it may continue to provoke some laughter, it loses spontaneity with each repetition.

The third type of spontaneity is the high-grade creativity variety of genius. In this type an adequate response is accompanied by characteristics that are both novel and creative. The resulting phenomenon may be in the form of an act or a substantive article, such as a poem, story, art object, or piece of machinery. To be truly spontaneous, the results must be in some way new and useful for some purpose.

Cultural conserve

The finished product of the creative process is the cultural conserve, the latter word coming from *conservare*, to guard. The cultural conserve is anything that preserves the values of a particular culture. It may take the form of a material object – such as a book, film, building, or musical composition – or it may appear as a highly set pattern of behavior – such as a religious ceremony, theatrical performance of a written play, fraternity initiation, or inaugural ceremony for the President of the United States. As a repository of the past, cultural conserves preserve and continue man's creative ego. Without them, man would be reduced to creating spontaneously the same forms to meet the same situations day after day. For example, a cultural conserve such as the dictionary makes it unnecessary for men to redefine words every time they wish to communicate. In addition to providing continuity for the heritage of human existence, the cultural conserve plays an even more significant role as the springboard for enticing new spontaneity toward creativity.

There is a danger in the over-reliance of mankind on the cultural conserve. This danger is inherent both in the conserve's state of finality and in its abuse by mankind. Once conserved, spontaneous creativity – however supreme it may be in itself – is, by definition, no longer spontaneous.

Encounter

In the center of the group process is the concept of the encounter. The term "encounter" covers numerous areas of living. It means to be together, to meet one another, the contact of two bodies, seeing, observing, touching, feeling the other person, withdrawing and uniting, understanding one another, intuitive insight and through silence or movement, language or gestures, kiss or embrace, becoming one.

Encounter is a unique experience that occurs only once and is irreplaceable. A touch and contact between two bodies, as in a psychodrama session, is a personal outburst of interaction that is unrehearsed. It is a challenge not only to the acting protagonist but also to all the participants. They witness an experience in the making. Encountering is, therefore, at the core of psychodramatic experience. The encounter comes first. Perception or interpretive analysis comes second. It cannot be exchanged through other forms of expression, other individuals, a book, or a letter.

Encounter means that two persons not only meet but also experience and comprehend one another, each with his whole being. It is not a circumscribed contact like a professional meeting of a therapist with a patient, nor is it an intellectual contact (teacher and pupil) or a scientific contact (a transaction between an observer and an object). The participants in an encounter are not pushed into the situation by an external force. They are there because they want to be there. The encounter is unprepared; it is not conducted or rehearsed in advance. There is in every encounter an element of surprise.

Encounter is essentially different from what the psychoanalysts call transference, and it is also different from what the psychologists call empathy. It does not negate transference, and it does not negate empathy. Rather, it includes transference and empathy and gives them their natural function in the entire process. It moves from I to Thou and from Thou to I. It is two-feeling. It is tele.

Tele

Tele, a term introduced by Moreno (1934), describes such affects as group stability, group cohesion, and group integration. Previously, it has been used not as an isolated term but always in various combinations: telencephalon, telepathy, telephone, television, and the like. Taking over such concepts as transference from the individual situation would not have satisfied the requirements of the group situation. By definition, transference tends to produce dissociation of interpersonal relations. In contrast, tele strengthens association and promotes continuity, security, stability, reciprocity, and cohesiveness of groups. In the construction of a conceptual framework, it is advantageous to introduce concepts that are indigenous to the field, rather than to force alien concepts on a new situation.

Tele is the constant frame of reference for all forms and methods of psychotherapy, including not only professional methods of psychotherapy like psychoanalysis, psychodrama, and group psychotherapy, but also nonprofessional methods like faith healing, and methods that have apparently no relation to psychotherapy, such as Chinese thought reform.

Neither transference nor empathy could explain in a satisfactory way the emergent cohesion of a social configuration. Social configurations consist of two or multiple ways of interaction. They are social wholes, not the point of view of one particular person. Empathy and transference are part of a more elementary and more inclusive process, tele. It is an objective social process functioning with transference, a psychopathological outgrowth and empathy as an esthetic outgrowth. The process of reciprocation does not enter into the meaning of empathy, and transference is considered the factor responsible for dissociation and disintegration in social groups. Tele is the factor responsible for the increased mutuality of choices surpassing chance possibility, and responsible for the increased rate of interaction among members of a group.

Tele is the interpersonal experience growing out of person-to-person and person-to-object contacts from the birth level on and gradually developing the sense for interpersonal relations; some real process in one person's life situation is sensitive and corresponds to some real process in another person's life situation, and there are numerous degrees, positive and negative, of these interpersonal relations.

Role

Role can be defined as the actual and tangible form that the individual self takes. The role is the functioning form a person assumes in the specific moment and reacts to a specific situation in which other persons or objects are involved. The symbolic representation of this functioning form is perceived by the person and by others. The form is created by past experiences and the cultural patterns of the society in which the person lives, and may be satisfied by the specific type of his productivity. Every role is a fusion of private and collective elements. Every role has two sides, a private and a collective side.

Role versus ego and self

It has been hypothesized that understanding human behavior is more easily facilitated by means of the role concept than by any other concept. It is a more operational concept than the concept of the ego, and more descriptive than the concept of self.

The tangible points of crystallization of the ego are the roles in which it manifests itself. The roles and the relations between them are the most important phenomena within a given culture. It is simpler to speak of the roles of a person than of his ego. Ego has mysterious, metapsychological side orientations. But the expression of behavior in terms of roles is not new. The universal cultivation of drama has made this a part of our common-sense knowledge. Dramatists have repeatedly described in literary terms what today is defined in technical terms. However, such roles as King Lear, Macbeth, and Romeo are not created before the eyes of the audience. The step from the texts of the playwrights to scientific texts requires a return to the original formation of a role in *statu nascendi*.

The approach to the problem of verifying the role process is most promising in experiments with roles in laboratory settings. In such settings, persons are placed in an experimental climate with the task of improvising and creating roles on the spur of the moment. The people who are used for these experiments are required to use their spontaneity, rather than their memory. A psychodramatic theater can be easily transformed into a laboratory setting by the adequate selection of subjects, controls, recordings, and trained observers.

Role-playing comes before the emergence of the self. Roles do not emerge from the self; the self emerges from roles. This is, of course, a hypothesis that appeals only to the sociometrist and the behavioral scientist, and that may be rejected by the Aristotelian, the theologian, and the metapsychologist. The sociometrist will point out that the playing of roles is not an exclusively human trait, that roles are also played by animals. They can be observed taking sexual roles, roles of nest builders, and leader roles, for instance.

Role reversal

Role reversal is important both as a learning technique for children and adults, and as a method of therapy for individuals and social groups. Role reversal is the heart of role-playing theory as demonstrated in psychodrama and sociodrama.

Here are some hypotheses about the nature of role reversal.

- Role reversal increases the strength and stability of the child's ego. Ego is here defined as identity with himself.
- Role reversal tends to diminish the dependency of the child on the parent, but it tends also to increase his ability to dominate the parent because the child has gained a profound knowledge of him through inside information.
- Frequent role reversal of the child with persons superior in age and experience increases his sensitivity for an inner life more complex than his own. In order to keep up with them on their internal role level, which is far above the overt level of the role, he has to be resourceful. He becomes prematurely skilled in the management of interpersonal relations.
- The excess desire to reverse roles with the mother is due to an early appreciation and perception of her roles. Frequency of role reversal with the father increases as the perception of the father's roles becomes clearer to the child.
- The technique of role reversal is more effective the nearer in psychological, social, and ethnic proximity the two individuals are: mother–child, father–son, husband–wife.
- Role reversal is an effective technique for socializing one ethnic group to the other. The greater the ethnic distance between social groups is, the more difficult the application of role reversal.
- The empathy of individuals or representatives of groups for the internal experiences of other individuals or representatives of groups – what they feel, think, perceive, and do – increases with the reciprocal perception of the roles in which they operate. Therefore, the training of auxiliary egos and doubles, as well as of psychotherapists in general, is in the direction of increasing their sensitivity.
- The empathy of therapists increases with their training in role perception and role reversal.
- Role reversal is a risk, and is at times contraindicated when the ego of one person is minimally structured and the ego of the other maximally structured. Psychotic patients like to play the part of authorities – nurses, doctors, policemen – or of ideal persons – for instance, they like to play God. But when faced with an actual person who embodies authority, they resent interaction and role reversal.

- Role reversal is without risk when the two persons who reverse roles with one another are solidly structured.[1]

Conclusion

Psychodrama is a form of psychotherapy which is modeled after life. It offers great flexibility for growth and emotional learning. Man, in the psychodramatic situation, is free from the fetters of facts and actualities, although not without the highest respect for them. He has a good foundation to believe that things are changing, as science has repeatedly taught us. In psychodrama, he can take his own dreams, hopes, and aspirations and create his own new world. This is not a plea for escape from reality but just the opposite – a plea for creativity in a psychodramatic world which one day may become true.

Much of this chapter is based on the original work of the late J.L. Moreno, MD, as it appeared in the first edition of this textbook.[2]

Article 29

J.L. Moreno's Concept of Ethical Anger

Moreno, Z.T. (1986) *Journal of Group Psychotherapy, Psychodrama and Sociometry* XXXVIII, 4: 145–153

Zerka's comments

This article was written after a period during which I wrote less and traveled and taught more, much of the time in Europe. We sold the Moreno Institute and the publishing house in 1982. The new owners took over the training programs, and I continued to hold a residential psychodrama training there for two weeks every summer. At first it was a huge change for me not to have a daily routine of eating, drinking and sleeping psychodrama. However, life did go on.

Merlyn suggested that I write this article after I had talked about it in a speech at Lesley College. I wanted to get across the point that there are forms of anger that are not destructive or "bad."

The expression of anger in our society is normally frowned upon. The therapist has to deal with anger in his everyday practice. However, there is a form of anger which J.L. Moreno described as "ethical." This article deals with some of the ways in which anger can be viewed as having an ethical basis.

The German poet Goethe said that the greatest happiness of mankind is the personality. Personality is constantly in formation during our lifetime. Among the endowments of the human personality are the emotions and our ability to express them. The expression of love has usually found support in our Western societies, whereas the expression of anger has been looked upon with disfavor.

Perhaps primal scream therapy was a rebellion against the repressiveness of our culture, but it could have been the need of the therapist rather than that of his clients.

The waves of humanistic psychology, including certain forms of Gestalt therapy, have invested much energy in getting clients to express anger. This became an end in itself and was supposed to be the aim of therapy. What often resulted was that patients could not get beyond the anger. They were not getting purged, which was assumed to be the positive outcome; they were merely learning to be angry. There are no rewards for this type of learning. An extreme case I came across was that of a young man who had been treated in this fashion. Thereafter, whenever he met situations in life that upset him, he needed to run away, to go somewhere where he could scream – hardly either a creative or new or adequate form of expression, or one that serves interpersonal contact. In psychodramatic terms, he was stuck in this warm-up of screaming, unable to lift himself out of that track. It took a good deal of hard work to get him out of it. His first session dealt entirely with his expression of impotent rage at the former therapist.

This article deals with a special kind of anger, a concept postulated by Moreno, which he called "ethical anger." This concept points to the fact that there are not only many sources for anger but also many different forms. The literature on anger has not dealt with "ethical anger," which is that kind based on a value system that has been affronted in the individual. It may arise out of a collective situation or a personal one. In this country, for example, we are confronted with issues such as a mother's right to end a pregnancy by abortion vs the child's right to live; maintenance of life after brain death vs the right to die; the right to possess arms vs gun control; the idea that homosexuals are unfit for public office vs equal employment opportunities for all; the right to consume alcohol before a certain age vs the enactment of laws to prohibit it; the superiority of the white race vs the idea that all human beings, given the same opportunities, are potentially able to reach similar levels of achievement, and so on. One can create more items for this list. There are those who would deny us the right not only to speak out, but even the right to carry ethical anger when others are being denied privileges or rights that we deem to be the lot of all. I am not referring to righteous indignation. I am indicating how ethical anger is able to resist the corrosion of our value system.

We are all aware that there are circumstances in which the expression of anger, no matter how justified, will seriously damage a relationship or wound another person so as to do other kinds of damage, sometimes irreparable.

We deal openly with such situations in all forms of therapy. Psychodrama is especially suited to allow expression of this type because it provides a lifelike but safe setting, with auxiliary egos present, not necessarily the original target. The advantage over scream therapy is that it is not directed to a non-present shadow figure or a symbol, but to a real person, with the additional factor of a chance to reverse roles, the protagonist becoming the recipient of this anger, to learn from this more than is possible by remaining in his own role. This is done especially when there is strong need to repair a relationship.

Several outcomes may result: the protagonist has been given the desired relief and now finds it unnecessary to replicate the expression of anger in life itself, or the protagonist realizes that this behavior is unacceptable or destructive and wants to practice in action alternative ways of handling the conflict, or the protagonist realizes that there is no possibility for repairing the rift and decides to let the relationship end; or the protagonist may be ready to accept a scene of healing, with the offender making up for his transgression. Sometimes a blending of several of these outcomes takes place. Subsequently the protagonist can be guided into, or personally find, alternative ways of dealing with the situation in life itself.

There are occasions when the release of anger will be of benefit to all concerned, but it is difficult to determine in advance what the outcome will be. Testing it out in a neutral setting is one way we can assess it to some degree, by having the protagonist enact not only his own role, but also that of all the others involved who are going to be affected.

The problem is often, whose idea of justice are we promoting? Are there certain standards? The *Random House Dictionary of the English Language* defines ethical as "pertaining to or dealing with morals or the principles of morality; pertaining to right and wrong in conduct." There is usually a fairly broad consensus that some social conduct is wrong, but the idea of ethical anger may have to be applied to circumstances either of which we have not been aware or to which we have given insufficient thought or attention.

Now, what did Moreno mean by ethical anger? It was not a cold, dispassionate kind. No, indeed. A striking example he was fond of giving was that of Christ's action in chasing the moneychangers out of the temple courtyard. This is, obviously, a far cry from turning the other cheek.

We can explain these two opposite positions in terms of man's multiple role repertoire in which some roles may lie dormant for a time until they are challenged to come forth, pushing themselves into the foreground. When this awakening comes, actions may take place that appear to be in contradiction to previous behavior. There are actions and interactions that are suitable in one context and totally unacceptable in another.

Moreno's concept of ethical anger gives us a new category for understanding as well as for behavior itself: namely, that there are moments in life when we are justified to be angry, and that not all anger is pathological or in need of treatment (Moreno, J.L. 1946c; Moreno, J.L. & Moreno, Z.T. 1959). Such moments are those in which things occur that our conscience cannot allow and in which we act upon its prompting. At such times we are, in fact, role models for others to think about and possibly to emulate in some fashion.

We do not know what words, if any, Jesus used in the action quoted above, but we have found that the expression of ethical anger is often most effective when done nonverbally. Childhood and adolescence are periods in our lives when we are acutely sensitive to injustice; we are often made hot under the collar when encountering it. Early indoctrination frequently inhibits expression and, in addition, we develop thicker skins as we get older. But when children are able to convey their feelings to adults, and when they listen, the children feel affirmed. Often the adults are able to learn much from such interchange, but regrettably, more often they resist and resent such confrontations.

Inspired by the young, let me report several psychodramatic explorations of problem situations they have experienced. A third grade elementary school teacher wished to introduce social learning by role-playing. The children were asked to volunteer situations with their peers that they found difficult to handle. The problem chosen by the children from among several presented was that of a little girl who, practically in tears, told how she had been snubbed recently by another girl whom she had considered one of her dearest friends. What more threatening situation is there for anyone, young or old, than to be rejected for no spoken or even apparent reason? The situation was re-enacted as it took place with the girl in question choosing a classmate, a stand-in, for the real friend, who was not present. If she had been, it is doubtful that the protagonist would have been able to bring up the scene at all. The teacher, realizing its importance because it had been chosen as a central concern by the students, asked who had an idea how to handle the situation, as the protagonist herself was unable to mobilize her own energies to redo the scene. She suggested to the protagonist that she sit down and watch how others might have handled it. She was thus employing the mirror technique.

Children make remarkably good improvising actors and several students were eager to confront the one representing the offending person, who, by the way, was thoroughly enjoying her role. Clearly, she, too, had met such interactions and was getting her own catharsis in this manner. Some of the new protagonists became quite verbal and aggressive. The teacher asked if there were perhaps other ways to handle such a painful scene. A tiny girl shyly put up her hand. This little one, in encountering the offending friend, stood and looked at her for a moment, tossed her head up in the air without a word, and walked past her. Her performance was voted by all odds the most powerful of all. This is truly a nonverbal psychodrama. What power was in that little slip of an eight-year-old, what wisdom and depth! And how could one teach this type of superior behavior without seeing it in action? Several of the more verbal protagonists got into the act by trying it out for themselves. Without the courage and spontaneity of the original actor this learning could not have taken place.

Certainly all of us have experienced situations of this sort, in which we ourselves or someone else was a striking example of behavior that was either in accord or discord with the demands of ethical anger.

Another example of how to handle anger also came out of a social learning class with fifth grade children, mostly ten years old, in which another nonverbal example was presented by a girl. Possibly these incidents teach us something about handling constricting situations: namely, that nonverbal behavior may be more telling than pouring out a plethora of words.

The scene is a park where the children go and play after school. The usual cliques of boys and girls are there. Tina, the protagonist, comes to the park and finds her usual afternoon companions there. But instead of welcoming her to join the game, the girls, all five of them, scurry like mice away from her towards each other, and, as if by prearranged signal, link arms and march from her in a single line. One of the girls is especially well known to Tina, as she lives across the street from her. This girl has been an indoor playmate on days of inclement weather. They have played in both their homes and there has never been an angry exchange between them. Nevertheless, Tina, a sensitive and intuitive child, senses that this particular girl is the instigator of this group behavior as she is the one closest to her in a relationship. In the re-enactment Tina is asked to soliloquize out loud what she feels while the auxiliary egos are representing the offending rejectors and how she accounts for it. Tina now recalls that this girl's mother always praises her loudly when she comes to the house and poses her as a model to her own daughter. She realizes at this moment that her friend may be suffering from unjust behavior by her mother.

Tina is in a true quandary at this point and recalls that this is not the first time that this friend has set other playmates against her. This last incident, however, is the most open rejection. Tina feels ethical anger towards her friend's mother for doing this to her child, as well as anger towards her friend for taking it out on her, an innocent bystander observing the difficult mother–child relationship. She knows that there are not words to defend herself adequately and surmises that her friend would deny the underlying situation if she presented it to her. So she takes a brave step and runs to catch up with that forbidding row of walking girls who snicker among themselves. She manages to reach them and links her arm onto the one of the end girls who is not her offending and offended friend. This girl may not be so involved in the situation as she is at the end of the line, whereas the co-protagonist is in the center. In any event, she does not pull away from Tina, perhaps also because she is amazed and taken by surprise.

There are a few tense, silent moments during which Tina continues to march with the others, silently, pretending not to have noticed the previous rejection, until the middle of the line breaks up and a new game is organized in which all are active, Tina included. This is how the original scene took place. The psychodramatic enactment went further as Tina was asked to reverse roles with each of the individuals involved to explain how this scene developed into the rejection she experienced. Especially in the role of her chief adversary, she found her earlier interpretation confirmed and the feelings of this girl deepened, enabling Tina to shift her set of perceptions about the girl and their relationship so that future contacts would be more mutually satisfying. It also was an affirmation of how well she handled what could have become a very explosive and damaging situation.

Sometimes ethical anger can lead a human being to death, as for instance in the case of resisting massive injustice. This is the altruistic side. I recall the story, after the horrors of the Second World War, of one of my closest Dutch-Jewish friends. The Germans were in Holland, conducting their nightmarish persecutions in rounding up the Jews. Robert, my friend, was himself in the underground and was saved innumerable times by his boss, a non-Jew who risked his neck to cover for him and get him out of trouble. Robert had a former classmate from high school who became involved in the underground network that expedited Jews or obtained false identity papers for them. He had recently married and become the father of his first-born child. His mother pleaded with him to cease his dangerous activities, stating that he now owed loyalty and support and care to his young family. "Mother," was his response, "I cannot stop. I go to bed at night and see the suffering eyes of all the Jewish mothers in the world and I am bound to continue for I cannot go on living otherwise." This noble young man was caught by the Nazis, with the inevitable result. Robert suffered not only severe trauma at his friend's death but also obtained a totally new vision of this particular young man. "You know," he told me, "he was very unremarkable while we were at school together. I would never have been able to guess at the depths within him." There are many, many others, all over the earth, about whom we know very little and who are capable of such noble actions when put to the test and are, in fact, behaving this way.

What is novel about the concept of ethical anger is that in the Christian tradition, anger is considered the very opposite of love. It is clear from the example I gave above of Christ's action in the temple courtyard that he would not have agreed with this interpretation. He was not the first teacher, nor will he have been the last, whose meaning has been misunderstood and distorted.

Our early indoctrination, against which we struggle all our lives, is that anger is *a priori* a bad thing to have, to carry, and to act upon. Anger based on the ethical principle is of a totally different order and must be recognized as such. It is an outgrowth of the twin principles that undergird Moreno's thinking: namely, spontaneity and creativity.

Spontaneity derives from the Latin *sua sponte*, "from within the self." The philosopher Charles Sanders Peirce described spontaneity as having "the character of not resulting by law from something antecedent . . . I don't know what you can make out of the meaning of spontaneity, but newness, freshness, and diversity" (Peirce 1931). Moreno coupled spontaneity with the principle of creativity. *The Random House Dictionary* defines "to create" as: "to cause to come into being, as something unique that would not naturally evolve or that is not made by ordinary process, to evolve from one's own thought or imagination, to make by investing with new functions, rank, character, etc."

Moreno described spontaneity as "a new response to an old situation, or an adequate response to a new situation, with creativity adding the element of inventiveness." Note that all three speak in terms of newness.

Ethical anger, then, is of a passionate nature, a new experience, meant to challenge and arouse. It upsets actions of persons who offend values we hold dear and which are evident to us. Under such circumstances we must ask ourselves whether we can allow our standards to be violated.

There are two poles to the experience of ethical anger: the first is its open expression and subsequent action when ethical anger is experienced by the protagonist or observer; the second is when one becomes entangled in a situation in which one is the innocent target of ethical anger that cannot be disposed of directly. The handling of both these poles is a delicate matter and certainly calls for spontaneity and creativity on the part of the persons so involved.

Willard Gaylin refers to Ernest Becker, writing in a symposium entitled *Emotions: Their Parameters and Measurement*: "The person reacts to assert himself, to show and feel that he is someone to reckon with. Anger generally has this function for the person, as a way of setting things in balance again" (Gaylin 1984).

Gaylin also remarks that:

> Freud failed to deal with anger and aggression and . . . this was one of the major deficiencies in early Freudian theory. As a theoretician who placed the Oedipal conflict at the center of all problems, Freud cannot have been unaware of competition, but he never adequately incorporated the dynamic role of the emotions into the theory of psychoanalysis . . . Since Freud dealt only peripherally with emotions, conventional psychoanalysis also ignored them.

If the opposite of anger is not love, what is it? I would state, as have many others, that it is indifference. And, indeed there has been some growing evidence in a number of quarters that we are shielding ourselves from too much pain in this manner, by becoming indifferent, partly because we feel unable to change the overwhelming amount of pain experienced around the globe, partly because there are immediate demands on our energy, which comes in limited amounts.

Anger is defined by Aristotle as "an impulse attended with pain to avenge an undeserved slight openly manifested toward ourselves or friends." He considered that persons who show insufficient anger are morally blameworthy, and that it is slavish to tolerate contemptuous treatment (Aristotle 1974).

One expert on anger, R.F. Richardson, feels strongly that one should have a working residue of anger on tap for when it is needed. "Good healthy resentment is at times a good thing and should be kept alive" (Richardson 1918). He also quotes Goethe as saying, "With most of us the requisite intensity of passion is not forthcoming without an element of resentment, and common sense and careful observation will, I believe, confirm the opinion that few people who amount to anything are without a good capacity for hostile feelings upon which they draw freely when they need it." And again, Aristotle observes that the only constrictions on anger are that it be "at the right time, place and right degree and duration." To which I would add that it should be directed at the right target.

Ethical anger, then, must be distinguished in its form, content, value, target, and purpose from other kinds of anger we deal with in therapy and should be recognized as dealing with conflicts of values, personal and extrapersonal.

Article 30

Psychodrama, Role Theory and the Concept of the Social Atom*

Moreno, Z.T. (1987) In J. Zeig (ed.), *The Evolution of Psychotherapy*, New York: Brunner/Mazel

Zerka's comments

At the very first Evolution of Psychotherapy conference sponsored by The Milton H. Erickson Foundation in Phoenix, AZ (December 11–15, 1985), it was my aim to put psychodrama in its proper context in the professional world.

*Although many of the group and family therapy "luminaries" who presented at this conference had their roots in our teachings, most never bothered to give a backward glance. Fritz Perls came often to our sessions in New York City. Imagine my surprise years later when he stated the need for "psychodrama" (*sic*) in his* In and Out of the Garbage Pail *but never mentioned Moreno.*

As for who thought up the empty chair technique, it was certainly not Perls. In 1958 an article appeared in the journal Group Psychotherapy *in which Rosemary Lippitt described her work with kindergarten children, using an empty chair as suggested by Moreno, to portray the "naughty child" in helping children identify and perhaps change their own place on the "class terror" spectrum. Moreno called the chair "the four-legged auxiliary ego."*

Historical background

Moreno first began by observing and joining in children's play in the gardens of Vienna, Austria, in the first decade of this century, while a student of philosophy, before entering medical school. He was impressed by the great amount of spontaneity in children and became aware that human beings become less spontaneous as they age. Why does this occur? he asked himself. What happens to us? The same process struck him when he started to direct the children in staged plays, rehearsed as they were in the legitimate theater. At the first portrayal whatever spontaneity was available to the children was mobilized. But the more often they repeated their performance, the less inventive, creative and spontaneous they became. They began to conserve their energy, to repeat their best lines, movements and facial expressions as these produced the greatest effect upon their audience. This produced a mechanical performance, lacking in reality. Clearly, this was the same phenomenon evident in age and in certain types of emotional disturbance, repetition without relation to the current situation, a freezing of affect and of memory.

How could this process be reversed or slowed? Looking at the world at large – and it is notable that most of Moreno's theories and concepts were based on observations from life and not limited to the clinical setting – he conceptualized that what is of essence in human existence is the twin principle of spontaneity and creativity. The end products of these he called "cultural conserves," attempts to freeze creativity and spontaneity of a past moment into a concrete product. He noted that conserved products are all around us: musical, literary, artistic, religious, cultural, technical and even biological. The principle of energy conservation, the freezing of a past moment of creativity, resulted in ubiquitous conserves.

To break these frozen patterns and to try to redirect energy back to the source of creativity, Moreno asked himself: What is spontaneity? How does creativity emerge? He decided they were inherent in the human organism, endogenous, but that the conservation of energy can block them and turn them pathological under certain conditions. What are these conditions and how can spontaneity and creativity be revitalized when lost? How docs this loss affect our relations with one another? How does learning via play differ from learning via the intellect? The last question has since been elucidated more by the studies of the left brain and the right brain, but this information was then not yet at hand.

In his magnum opus *Who Shall Survive?* Moreno dealt with creativity and spontaneity as *the* problem of the universe.

> The universe is infinite creativity. But what is spontaneity? Is it a kind of energy? If it is energy it is *unconservable*, if the meaning of spontaneity should be kept consistent. We must, therefore, differentiate between two varieties of energy, conservable and unconservable energy. There is an energy which is conservable in the form of "cultural" conserves, which can be saved up, which can be spent at will in selected parts and used at different points in time; it is like a robot at the disposal of its owner. There is another form of energy which emerges and which is spent in a moment, which must emerge to be spent and which must be spent to make place for emergence, like the life of some animals that are born and die in the love-act.
>
> It is a truism to say that the universe cannot exist without physical and mental energy which can be preserved. But it is more important to

> realize that without the other kind of energy, the unconservable one – or spontaneity – the creativity of the universe could not start and could not run. It would come to a standstill.
>
> There is apparently little spontaneity in the universe, or at least, if there is any abundance of it only a small particle is available to man, hardly enough to keep him surviving. In the past he has done everything to discourage its development. He could not rely upon the instability and insecurity of the moment, with an organism which was not ready to deal with it adequately, he encouraged the development of devices as intelligence, memory, social and cultural conserves, which would give him the needed support with the result that he gradually became the slave of his own crutches. If there is a neurological localization of the spontaneity–creativity process it is the least developed function of man's nervous system. The difficulty is that one cannot store spontaneity, one either is spontaneous at a given moment or one is not. If spontaneity is such an important factor for man's world why is it so little developed? The answer is: man *fears* spontaneity, just like his ancestor in the jungle feared fire; he feared fire until he learned how to make it. Man will fear spontaneity until he will learn how to train it.
>
> (Moreno, J.L. 1953: 19)

Though approaching creativity from another aspect, Otto Rank, in *Art and Artist*, had this to say about its end products:

> [the artist] desires to transform death into life, as it were, though actually he transforms life into death. For not only does the created work not go on living; it is, in a sense, dead; both as regards the material, which renders it almost inorganic, and also spiritually and psychologically, in that it no longer has any significance for its creator, once he has produced it. He therefore again takes refuge in life, and again forms experiences, which for their part represent only mortality – and it is precisely because they are mortal that he wishes to immortalize them in his work.
>
> (Rank 1968)

Clearly, one reason spontaneity is feared is because it is confused with irrationality, unpredictability. But anxiety and spontaneity are functions of one another; the more anxious we are, the less spontaneous we become, and vice versa.

There seems to be a paradox in the notion of training spontaneity. If it is trained, can it still be called spontaneity? Perhaps a better designation would be the re-evocation and retraining of spontaneity.

Looking at some definitions of spontaneity and creativity, we note the following: Spontaneity derives from Latin *sua sponte*, "from within the self." *The Random House Dictionary* defines spontaneity as, among others, "coming or resulting from a natural impulse or tendency, without effort or premeditation, natural or unconstrained, unplanned, arising from internal forces or causes, self acting." The philosopher Charles Sanders Peirce spoke of spontaneity as having "the character of not resulting by law from something antecedent . . . I don't know what you can make out of the meaning of spontaneity, but newness, freshness, and diversity."

Creativity in the above-named dictionary is described as "To cause to come into being, as something unique that would not naturally evolve or that is not made by ordinary process, to evolve from one's own thought or imagination, to make by investing with new functions, rank, character, etc."

For Moreno spontaneity was a "new response to an old situation or an adequate response to a new situation," with creativity adding the element of inventiveness. Both Peirce and Moreno stressed newness.

The question remains: By what route can we train spontaneity? When Moreno noted the children's repetition in a role, he instructed them to throw away the written script, to improvise within the rationale of the role and the interaction, not to remember the lines but the feelings, to practice newness. By cutting off the old route he forced the actors to find within and between themselves new ways of sustaining their roles.

During the early twenties Moreno began to apply his method to adult actors and out of that experiment the Theatre of Spontaneity as an art form was born. Moreno put his actors into a variety of situations, taking them by surprise and having them respond to one another. It was a freeing of their ability to act and interact on the spur of the moment; being accused of infidelity by a spouse, being fired from a job, being insulted or misjudged by a friend, etc.

He attempted to tap into the unconservable energy, spontaneity, from within the wellspring of the actor and to use it in the developing interaction, to see if some resolution could be found, either between the actors or within the actors themselves. The bonding that took place between them and which helped them to be more creative due to their co-creation he called "tele." Tele goes beyond empathy and transference and may be thought of as two-way empathy. It is feeling into and appreciating the reality of the other, mutually experienced and reciprocally involving. Tele is responsible for mutuality between persons, over and beyond their projections, and responsible for interpersonal and group cohesion. In a New York State training school for delinquent girls, a study was undertaken in which the residents were asked to indicate whom they wanted as dining room partners around tables seating four persons. The organization of the seating order was carried out according to these choices. Mutual choices far outpaced what had been projected on the basis of chance. The factor responsible for these mutualities was revealed to be tele. Moreno decided that tele is the cement that binds people together in a relationship that is reciprocally satisfying.

Tele is found in several categories: mutual positive, mutual negative, positive versus negative, and neutral. The sense for tele develops with age; in general, it is fairly weakly developed in children. It grows with social awareness.

Emergence of the therapeutic drama, or psychodrama

In the course of exploring the implications of his findings with his actors in the Spontaneity Theater, Moreno began to apply his ideas to interpersonal disturbances. He required his patients to show him, in action, how they had reached their current impasse, turning them into actors of themselves instead of reporters. He conceived of three intrapersonal phenomena: the director who tells the actor what to do, the actor who carries out the directions in action, and the observer who records, makes mental notes and either encourages or discourages the action and interprets what has occurred *ex post facto*. These could all be at odds with one another and thus disturb the smoothness of performance. In addition, each of these could be in discord with the others facing him, further diminishing spontaneity and increasing anxiety.

Moreno wanted to have the problem shown him in action for a number of reasons. There was often a discrepancy between the verbal representations and the actional one; he wanted to reduce this. To a greater or lesser degree patients display, as all humans do, incomplete perceptions of self and others, as well as perceptions which are lacking, weak, distorted or pathological, but especially one-sided and subjective. Where perceptions are clear and mutually confirmed, positive tele is at work. The enactment was for Moreno not merely a better diagnostic tool, but a more lifelike model, yet larger than life. Later he often called it "a laboratory for learning how to live." It incorporated not only action and interaction, therefore including the body, which was left out of the verbal approach, but also speech, mime, music, dance, and the dimensions of past, present and future, and space.

He did not trust the verbal method to be the royal road to the psyche. There is no universal language; each is culture-bound. He observed that there are, in fact, language-resistant portions of the human psyche, which can preclude or impede speech as when emotions are very deep or in turmoil. And, he asked, if speech were the central and all-absorbing sponge of the psyche, why do we have the various forms of art? These communicate to us in ways that cannot be replicated in speech. Indeed, the verbal method requires a secondary process of interpretation, in itself a product of the therapist's own philosophical orientation. In the dramatic form the patient was learning to interpret himself as well as the others with whom he was engaged.

Another reason was that many persons have difficulties in transforming insight into action. And perhaps even more basic a reason is that both ontogenetically and phylogenetically language is a fairly late development in man. But we are in interaction from the moment of birth, and much learning goes on in the first few years without language, in action. Moreno saw man as an improvising actor on the stage of life. He concluded that he needed to tap a more primary level than speech, that of action. Children and psychotics frequently devise their own language, incomprehensible to auditors unless carefully studied; even then it may elude interpretation.

Dramatic depiction allows for the uncovering of concurrent fantasies; a number of techniques were developed to enable the actors to concretize them.

What other basis could there be for the need of psychodrama? It was noted that developmentally every human infant goes through a stage, the first few months after birth, in which it is not yet aware that there are other beings around outside of itself. It experiences itself as the totality of the universe, everyone and everything is an extension of its own being. Hangovers from this period may manifest themselves in children's play. It is called "normal megalomania." The child uses it whenever it feels the need and may well provide its own therapeusis. This phenomenon is also related to Moreno's view of man as more than a biological being, reflecting his cosmic aspect. Here he approaches Otto Rank who spoke of a lost union with the cosmos in which present, past and future are dissolved, and hypothesized the trauma of birth as a final rupture of this union.

The child emerges but gradually out of this state of all-identity into a state of differentiated identity, wherein other individuals and objects separate and become distinct from the self. This later stage leads to a complete breach, making the child aware that there are several kinds of experience, subjective and objective. This final breach, which is a universal phenomenon, the realization of the world within and the world without, is usually brought about by some traumatic experience, some deprivation. From this time onward every human being lives in these two spheres, subjective reality and objective reality, the world of fantasy and the so-called real world. If the essential nurture needs of the child are met, the child will learn about the two realms and, aided by spontaneity, will integrate them and balance them.

To the extent that there is profound, continued deprivation or inadequate spontaneity, these two realms cannot mesh adequately. Then the child will withdraw into the subjective sphere where it is once again the entire universe, all-powerful. The pathological seedlings planted there may eventually manifest themselves in various forms of intrapersonal, interpersonal and socio-emotional disturbances. We all fall somewhere along this continuum; as long as we are able to manage to maintain homeostasis or sociostasis, we can remain functioning.

Moreno's attention was engaged particularly by the psychotic experience as one of the most advanced forms of this split and it challenged him to treat psychotic individuals through psychodrama. He conceived this method to be the bridge between these two spheres. Treatment should result in greater flexibility and creative adaptability.

Otto Rank wrote about play: "In every case play, by diminishing fear, liberates an energy which can ultimately express itself creatively." Through the dramatic format of a play we are able to enter into the subjective, albeit psychotic, reality of the patient–protagonist by using supportive actors known as auxiliary egos, who concretize with and for the patient all those personae, real and fantasized, who are needed to complete and enlarge the internal drama. The protagonist is seen as a creator whose self-creation has gone awry, his creativity has erred and he is stuck in his creation. It may be pathological creativity but it is creativity nevertheless. It is the therapist's task to turn it eventually into healthy creativity. To this end, helpers are needed, midwives, to bring the incomplete creation to birth. Then the patient can complete the work, develop distance from it and eventually release it. The midwives are the director, auxiliary egos and supportive staff. These are also the guides who bring the protagonist back into the objective reality.

In *Art and Artist*, Rank wrote, "A man with creative power who can give up artistic expression in favor of the formation of personality – will remold the self-creative type and will be able to put his creative impulse *directly* in the service of his own personality . . . The creative type becomes the creator of a self."

In the thirties, psychotic patients were considered largely untreatable, as they were unable to establish transference. In constructing a therapeutic approach Moreno thought it more productive for the psychiatrist to warm-up first to the patient, to establish the relationship by internally role reversing with the patient and with empathy and creativity feel himself into the reality of the patient's subjective world and assess his needs. As there were multiple personae, real as well as hallucinatory or delusional, in the patient's world, the therapist needed helpers. Thus a team of co-workers emerged for the first time in psychotherapy; up until that time it was deemed best for only one therapist to be actively involved in psychotherapy. It may be argued that active group psychotherapy was born here.

The auxiliary egos had to learn to put their own organism at the service of the patient, his drama and his world. For the patient this also represented the first step to re-socialization. One remarkable aspect is the ease with which the patient is often able to accept the therapeutic helpers as representatives of the personae in his subjective system and to engage with them in interaction. The auxiliary egos had to develop spontaneity, which helped them to move fast along the axis leading from objectivity to subjectivity and back again. In terms of the development of treatment teams, it was much like what had occurred in surgery. But it was a revolution in psychotherapy, as before this only the therapist was supposed to have meaningful access to the mind of the patient. Moreno knew he could not influence a delusion or hallucination directly but hypothesized that such influence could be introduced through the relationship established on the psychotic level first; his auxiliary egos became the go-betweens; these he could direct. As the protagonist began to leave his subjective world more, the auxiliary helpers were there to support and guide him into the larger world, on the basis of the trust established earlier. This pioneering effort took place in a small mental hospital, in Beacon, NY, in the latter half of the nineteen thirties.

In addition to the use of psychodrama as a comprehensive tool for treating the psychotic and neurotic patients, the families were brought into therapy with them before discharge, to assist them all with achieving and maintaining more balanced interrelationships.

In the year 1937 Moreno started other innovations, using himself as a go-between in marital conflicts, as well as having both husband and wife in treatment together at the same time. Reports were published in 1937 in the journal *Sociometry* and later in the three volumes of *Psychodrama.* In the September 1981 issue of *Family Process*, a Belgian psychiatrist, Theo Compernolle, published a paper entitled "J.L. Moreno: An Unrecognized Pioneer of Family Therapy," from which I quote:

> . . . From his earliest writings in 1923 J.L. Moreno developed an interactional view of psychotherapy that in 1937 already resulted in formulations of a true systems orientation and very concrete ideas about marital therapy, family therapy and network therapy. He probably is the first therapist who actually involved a husband's lover in conjoint marital therapy. His general theoretical formulations about the pathology of interpersonal relations as well as his practical suggestions for their therapy seem to be insufficiently known to workers and researchers in the field of family therapy.
>
> (Compernolle 1981)

The article referred to by Compernolle contains the following:

> Then the momentary structure of the patient's life situation, in the physical and mental make up of his personality, and, most of all, how this operated and interacted with members of his family, and with various members of his network, was the information needed for diagnosis . . . Considering the more complex forms of social neurosis, when two, three or more persons were to be treated simultaneously, the scenes enacted between them became a formidable pattern for treatment. Finally, all the scenes in their remote past, and all the remote networks, became important from the point of view of general catharsis of all the people involved. The solution was the resurrection of the

> whole psychological drama, re-enacted by the same persons in the re-creation of situations in which their association had begun.
>
> (Moreno, J.L. 1924)

The new technique, if properly applied, aided the patient to actualize during the treatment that which he needed to let himself pass through in a procedure that was as close to his life as possible. He had to meet the situations in which he acted in life, to dramatize them, to meet the situations which he had never faced, which he avoided and feared, but which he might have to meet squarely one day in the future. It was often necessary to magnify and elaborate certain situations which he was living through sketchily at the time or of which he had only a dim recollection.

The chief point of the technique was to get the patient started, to get him warmed up so that he might throw his psyche into operation and unfold the psychodrama. A technique of spontaneous warming up of the mental states and the situations desired was developed. The spontaneous states attained through this technique were feeling complexes and, as such, useful guides toward the gradual embodiment of roles. The technique demanded usually more than one therapeutic aide for the patient, to help in starting off the patient himself and as representatives of the principal roles the situation and the patient might require. Instead of one, numerous auxiliary egos were needed. Therefore it led to this: the original auxiliary ego, the psychiatrist, remained at a distance but surrounded himself with a staff of auxiliary egos whom he coordinated and directed and for whom he outlined the course and the aim of psychodramatic treatment.

The 1923 reference made by Dr. Compernolle was in fact to Moreno's first book dealing with problems of spontaneous production and improvisational drama, *Das Stegreiftheater* (1924), translated into English and published in 1947 as *The Theater of Spontaneity*, in which he dealt not only with the research aspect but also the therapeutic and philosophic areas. Again I quote:

> *But the true symbol of the therapeutic theatre is the private home.* Here emerges the theatre in its deepest sense, because the most treasured secrets violently resist being touched and exposed. It is completely private. The first house itself, the place where life begins and ends, the house of birth and the house of death, the house of the most intimate personal relations becomes a stage and backdrop. The proscenium is the front door, the windowsill and the balcony. The auditorium is in the garden and the street.
>
> Spontaneous role playing gives the 'meta-practical proof' of a realm of freedom, illusion is strictly separated from reality. But there is a theatre in which reality or being is proven through illusion, one which restores the original unity between the two meta-zones – through a

> process of humorous self reflection; in the therapeutic theater reality and illusion are one.
>
> Some of the most significant techniques refer to the domain of *forms*, of *interpersonal relationships*, of *presentation* and *the treatment of mental disorders.*
>
> (Moreno, J.L. 1924: 89)

In psychodrama repetition of a scene or interaction need not be deadly; because it is impossible to reproduce life exactly, there is already introduced an element of newness; it is living it again, but with a difference. The cultural conserve, on the other hand, such as the legitimate drama, does not allow for genuine deviation. But, states Moreno:

> The cultural conserve is not an inescapable trap. Its stultifying effects can be corrected. Instead of making the machine an agent of the cultural conserve – which would be the way of least resistance and one of fatal regression into a general enslavement of man to a degree beyond that of the most primitive prototype – it is possible to make the machine an agent and a supporter of spontaneity . . . Indeed, every type of machine can become a stimulus to spontaneity instead of a substitute for it . . . The reproductive process of learning must move into second place; first emphasis should be given to a productive, spontaneous–creative process of learning. The exercises and training in spontaneity are the chief subject of the school of the future.
>
> (Moreno, J.L. 1946c: 55)

Clearly, Moreno's concern was not only with the treatment of mental disorders but with a new model of education, from kindergarten on up.

Goethe's play *Lila* has the heroine treated for her insanity by having all the persons involved in her private life join her in her delusions by taking the roles as she envisions them. After having lived these out in life itself with her co-actors, she can now rejoin them and thus she is cured and returns to reality. Goethe pointed out in a letter to the director of the royal theater of Saxony on October 1, 1818: "The play *Lila* is actually a psychological cure in which one allows the madness to come to the fore in order to cure it . . . The best way to attain a psychological cure is by allowing the madness to enter into the treatment in order to heal the condition." Similarly, Moreno often spoke of psychodrama as a homeopathic remedy and as a "small injection of insanity under conditions of control." It is the control that is of importance; the madness being contained within it and the learning taking place in a non-threatening and protective setting. It may be noted that family therapies similarly induce crises in order to treat the family in therapy.

Psychodrama uses mainly five instruments: the patient or protagonist, the director or chief therapist, the co-therapists or auxiliary egos, and the group members, as well as a space or theater for action.

Psychodrama sessions proceed in three stages: the warmup and interview, the enactment and the closure. The warmup is intended to prepare the group for the emergence of a protagonist or, if a protagonist has already been designated, to become more relaxed individually and more cohesive as a group. There are a great many warmup techniques; some may be physical, such as doing some exercises, it may be done with music or dancing, by mingling, by introduction by name. Directors often devise new warmup techniques on the spur of the moment. There are group-centered warmups and sessions as well as individual-centered. The warmup is also to assist the protagonist to establish some level of comfort within the group. In the course of years, as patients have become familiar with this type of treatment, they are often ready to start when they come into the session, having been warmed up by the psychodramas of other patients, or by some recent happening in their own lives. As they start trusting the method and the therapists, warmup time is reduced.

A further warmup is the interview when the protagonist has come to the stage space. This interview is to elicit essential facts, and to help the group present to become familiar with the patient's need and mental set, as well as to prepare the protagonist for the forthcoming action. This part is greatly reduced in the treatment of psychotics once the director, auxiliary egos and group members are familiar with the patient's inner world, and action starts almost at once. The interview should set the stage for the protagonist, the place, the time, the persons involved as the action begins. It also enables the auxiliary egos to be prepared to step into the action as needed. If the group is homogeneous in terms of diagnosis, for instance drug users or alcoholics, the group members may bring up a related or unrelated topic and the protagonist may be self-indicated or group-chosen. The enactment follows, incorporating self-presentation, role reversal, doubling, soliloquy, shifting to more relevant scenes, real or fantasized, returning to the past or projecting into the future, as seen essential by the director with the cooperation of the patient, or as indicated by the patient himself.

A special adaptation in psychodrama, called the mirror technique, is the enlistment of the patient as a colleague, watching an auxiliary ego in the patient's role show the patient's behavior in relation to others, and helping the director to guide the direction. Another is role reversal with the director who becomes the patient, placing the protagonist in the role of therapist; this technique has been taken over by individual therapists of various orientations. The patient can also be interviewed as a colleague and asked how this patient might be treated. We have found one of the most useful role reversals to be one in which the patient is taking the role of the person with whom the conflict is to be explored and interviewing him from that perspective. The amount of data and the sort of data that comes out of this is frequently more valuable than that obtained by interviewing in the role of self.

One of the reasons patients appreciate psychodrama is that their autonomy is mobilized, respected and put to use on their own behalf, in a setting where mistakes, if any are made, are not punished but can be corrected on the spot, where the possible consequences of their interactions can be tested out. Another reason is that it becomes manifest to them that they know more about themselves than they realized and, especially in the beginning, more than the therapists. Even their homes and the way they live with others are unknowns to anyone but them. This changes their status in relation to the therapists and makes them equal partners in an exciting process of exploration and learning. This experience is important for the patients to overcome their fears of acting, giving themselves away and possibly losing control.

The function of director is complicated. Let me sum it up by saying that it takes about two years to train a director, who must be a combination of scientist and artist. The more fully the director lives, the better he can fulfill this function. He has to be aware of cues of all sorts as action by itself may not be enough; often a subtle cue must be followed up, the current scene dropped, for a catharsis of integration to take place. My sense is that family therapists are now so close to this role that they should more easily incorporate psychodrama fully into their armamentarium.

The auxiliary egos have five major functions: (1) to embody the role required by the protagonist of either an absentee, a delusion or hallucination, an animal, an object, an idea or value, a voice, a body part, or, as the double of the protagonist, various aspects of the protagonist himself; (2) to approximate, in taking the role, the perception held by the protagonist, at least to begin with; (3) to investigate the true nature of the interaction between the protagonist and the role being enacted by the auxiliary; (4) to interpret this interaction and relationship, and if possible, to bring that interpretation into the scene; (5) to act as therapeutic guide towards a more satisfactory relationship and interaction. It can be seen that the first three functions are genuine additions to what the psychotherapist has been doing all along in points 4 and 5, but it is exactly the nature of the interactional process which refines the interpreting and guiding.

The function of the auxiliary ego as the agent of action on behalf of the director, and, having been closer to the protagonist in the action, is the next important aspect. The auxiliary ego can assist the director in his own evaluation and guiding. The function of the auxiliary ego as a double to psychotic patients cannot be overestimated; the more bizarre the patient is, the more a double can be effective in this process. Often a protagonist is unable to communicate what is going on inside and around him, but the double can and does. Eventually family members are brought into the therapy whenever possible; they may in turn become auxiliary egos for a while, or be treated as co-protagonists, learning about the part they have possibly contributed to the patient's difficulties.

Auxiliary egos and directors are required to be protagonists in their dramas during the course of their training, not only to develop as therapists and as people, but to enlarge their role repertoire and increase spontaneity. This becomes especially necessary when there is some aspect of the patient's psychodrama which enmeshes the auxiliary ego in his personal psychodrama. The first rule, therefore, for directors and auxiliary egos is: Be sure you are not doing your psychodrama on your patients. There is always danger of this in any form of therapy; in psychodrama it becomes a little more evident as it takes place in a group. Such developments should bring the director and auxiliary egos to the stage as protagonists in psychodramas of their own. Whether to have patients present or not is a decision to be made. We have found it enormously useful for patients to attend such sessions, as they learn that therapists, too, have their human problems. Prophylactic use of psychodrama sessions as a prevention of burnout is also to be recommended.

The last part of the session is sharing. This consists of bringing the protagonist back into the circle of the group and having group members identify with the protagonist or with another role presented in the psychodrama. Group members should speak about themselves, not the protagonist; here we share our common humanity. It is not merely that we are all more human than otherwise, as Harry Stack Sullivan declared, but we are more alike than we are different. The differences do stick out, so that we often forget our commonality. Dialogue, discussion or interpretation and evaluation must come later, when the protagonist is not as vulnerable. At this stage he is, as in surgery, in recovery and must be handled gently, if firmly. The protagonist has denuded himself or herself before a group; this giving of self must be rewarded in kind, not by cold analysis, critique or attack, no matter how shocking the revelations may have been, but by becoming once again a member of the group.

Sharing has been found to be the most healing after-effect; when that has taken place, analysis and interpretation can take place. However, these are best done by the protagonist; many are eager to get this response so they can extract further learning, but it is not the primary aspect of sharing, or rather, not the first step. Analysis leads to intellectualization. Healing comes from the revelation of others. Insight by itself rarely heals anyone and in any case is also more readily achieved after the emotions have been stirred and acceptance has been made manifest.

The concept of role in psychodrama

In psychodramatic terms the role is a final crystallization of all the situations in a special area of operations through which the individual passes in interaction with others playing complementary roles. A role does not take place in total isolation from the environment or from significant others. It is thought of as a functional or dysfunctional unit of interactional behavior. The role can be defined as the actual and tangible form that the self takes. Self, ego, personality, character, etc., are cluster effects, not roles themselves. The role is a fusion of private and collective elements.

There was attached to the term "role playing" an unfortunate connotation during the 1960s in which the enactment of roles was not seen as an inherent function of the human being, but as something dishonest, a mask over the real person. This is a complete misunderstanding of the role concept in therapy.

The dramatic format of the Theater of Spontaneity led to the concept of the role and role formation. They are placed into three main categories: psychosomatic roles, relating body and psyche; psychodramatic roles or fantasy roles, and socio-cultural roles. The role is not considered separate from a person's essence, as the clothes he puts on or takes off, but an existential part of his being, the part that makes up his ego with other roles. The personality may emerge from the roles, as role enactment takes place before there is role perception. The psyche is an open system with the roles in various stages of development. It is not a container into which the roles fit, like pick-up sticks in a tube.

Every human being has a role repertoire far larger than normally used. There is great individual variation in the number of roles each one activates and in the value placed on them. Roles may be absent, latent, emerging or developing, incomplete, distorted, in full activation, descending, dying or burning out and replaced; they may be of central order or peripheral. Their condition and states are not fixed; they may move from one position to another. Inability to move, rigidity of roles have to be attended to by therapy and/or retraining. Rapid and extreme shifting of roles can create group upheaval. An example of this is that of Gauguin, who, in the midst of a successful career in the world of finance, gave it all up for the role of the creative artist, thereby upsetting his family's lives; his wife moved back to Sweden with the children. The role of the artist has no counter role except that of the art appreciator. It is probable that Gauguin was considered psychotic; such a dramatic arising of a hitherto latent role and burning away of all the others in its intensity is frequently experienced by interactors in the previous role, and observers of the process, as insanity because their own role responses and needs no longer fit.

We see similar events in our world of today, though not always in such extreme forms, in the giving up of successful careers for a second or third one by a growing number of persons. If there is no support for these changes within the family or social setting, no effective counter roles, the protagonist has to establish a completely new and different set of associates.

Our role repertoire is activated and enlarged as we develop, moving from the protection of the family into the larger world. Inadequate role development in a much-needed role can lead to unsatisfactory interaction.

Society rigidifies certain roles and we have to struggle to free ourselves of these preconceptions: male versus female roles, the older person in our society as a non-worker and a non-sexual partner, to mention but a few sources of societal disablement.

While certain roles develop and remain fairly stable throughout a lifetime, changing only in frequency, duration or intensity, such as the psychosomatic role of the sleeper, the eater, the walker, a certain other number cease to be as central. The role of the protective parent, for example, changes gradually as required by the growing child, for a relation of greater partnership. Failure for this to happen brings the growing child and the family into conflict. There are parents who so love small children and their own parenting that they cannot permit the small child to grow up. Infantilizing and overprotection result. If the child rebels, the parents feel threatened and react, often negatively. There are others who feel the burden of small children to be beyond their own role ability and these can become child abusers; or they push their children into early adulthood, sometimes requiring them to reverse roles with them, to become their ideal parent. Their own small needy child gets in the way because of its early deprivation. Such role distortions require attention. Role structure is a complex phenomenon.

An example of misperception of a socio-cultural role was reported to me by a teacher. The first day of a first grade in school one of the little girls did not sit down in her assigned seat but stood up, next to it, when the class began. Upon the teacher's request that she be seated she answered: "But I'm not tired." Evidently she had not perceived that in the classroom the teacher is the only one allowed free movement. Students are required to sit and must ask for permission to move about. She stayed aloft all day. But the next day she had grasped the student role and sat down with the rest. This may be an example of spontaneous behavior, but in the eyes of the teacher and the rest of the students, it was inadequate.

It can be seen that changing roles in our society require great strength of purpose and determination and while such changes may be seen afterwards as worthwhile, the actors in the ongoing drama go through much turmoil in the process.

There are three levels in role playing: role enactment, role perception and role expectation. Discrepancies between any of these create interpersonal as well as intrapersonal disturbances. Certain roles, specifically psychosomatic ones, require specific settings in our society; in the average middle class household, eating is done in the kitchen or dining room, sleeping in the bedroom, the bathroom is for dealing with the excreta and cleaning oneself, the den is for the family to gather in and watch TV, to mention but the bare outlines. Deviations from this pattern can be greatly upsetting to the managers of the household. We even demand proper toilet training from our small children and our pets; if they fail they are not housebroken. The wrong or rigid emphasis on the correct settings can lead to family turbulence.

The roles of the eater and sleeper in children are often distorted because their interactional matrix is inequitable. Mother's need to have her child eat at a specified time and the prescribed amount of food as she determines may impose itself on the child's wants in ways which create a struggle between them. The same may be true for the need of sleep; having the child asleep is often more the adult's need for rest and recuperation than the child's need. Problems at sleeping time may result. The stress lies in the varying enactments of the interlocking roles, needs and perceptions, in terms of quantity, length and time. Intensity, duration and timing all play a significant part in role interaction.

Sometimes a simple reorganization of the seating order around the table can resolve eating problems. The parents may not share each other's view of how the child's eating role should be handled. We have successfully managed such reorganization by having the siblings take over some of these supervisory functions and by increasing the physical distance between the parent and child. This indicates the importance of space in interpersonal role conflict.

Instances of intrapersonal conflict between two or more psychosomatic roles are known to us all. The eater role, for instance, may thrust itself into that of the sleeper, awakening the sleeper and making it imperative that it be satisfied. The sleeper gets up, has a snack to satisfy the eater, and is once again able to return to the act of sleeping.

On the psychological or fantasy level role conflicts are usually more difficult to resolve. There may be conflict between two or more roles in different categories. A very familiar one to persons in the helping professions is the conflict between private and personal roles, that of the therapist versus that of the paternal. A little boy of nine, the son of a psychiatrist came to therapy and was a striking example of this. When confronted with a male auxiliary ego in the role of his father, he angrily stamped his foot and said, "I don't want to be your son. I want to be your patient; then you'll pay attention to me." This was a self-fulfilling prophecy that could not, in the end, be fulfilled since the father was not able to treat his son himself. The entire family entered into treatment so that new interaction could create familial balance.

The auxiliary egos in such treatment are extremely valuable; they can double for each of the family members, assisting in the communication between them. Individual members can work with auxiliary egos to express safely their innermost conflict without fear of retaliation and with reduced guilt, in the absence of the offending family members. To begin with, if indicated, the partners in the conflict are treated with auxiliary egos first; the latter become familiar with the conflict and represent the absentees realistically. Only when the various partners are able to enter into more open, honest contact with one another will they be brought together in treatment.

We note role deficiencies at times. One or another partner in a conflict may not have the particular role required by another in the repertoire, or may not give it the same centrality. This can be the cause for breakdowns of the relationship; the dissatisfied partner may search for substitution with another partner who has the required function and with whom interaction is more complete and satisfying. Role repair and substitution with another partner may lead to dissolution of the earlier relationship and is often found in marital breakdowns. This does not refer only to sexual roles although these may be involved; it is often a hitherto underdeveloped or ignored role that becomes dominant in one of the partners.

The designation of a person having a weak or strong ego beclouds the issue. No one has ever seen an ego. At best we can observe that a person has a weakly or strongly developed role. It allows that individual to realize what this structure does to the counterstructure in the partner or partners. Putting these structures in better balance may result in stronger partnership. Few among us are equally strong in a great many roles; these are rather the exception than the rule. The majority of us are deficient somewhere in one or another role relationship. Identification and training in these areas require spontaneity and creativity.

There are roles whose anticipation makes us anxious and insecure about entering situations in which they will have to be embodied, such as the lover, the spouse, the parent, the teacher, the employee, the traveler, etc. Desensitization is called for, as well as some exploration of earlier history that has contributed to this anxiety, with needed repair in the present.

Role structure and interaction can be plotted on diagrams for diagnostic and guidance purposes and are especially useful in the treatment of families and small groups. Such diagrams may be drawn by each partner and then compared with those of each of the other group members for discrepancies of perception and further dramatic enactment and correction. Role reversal is the essential ingredient here. The more harmonious the interaction, the greater will be the areas of agreement as well as the number of roles perceived as mutually satisfying. These diagrams can vary from total disagreement to considerable overlapping. Longitudinally done they are good indicators of changes achieved and of those still needed.

The concept of the social atom

The position that emotional disturbance is largely a product of human interaction and is not restricted to intrapsychic phenomena led to the examination of the individual plus his relevant others as well as the relationships they shared. In the treatment of husband and wife, designated as the intimate social atom, the focus of treatment was upon three entities: the two individuals *and* their relationship. As with the psychotic patient, Moreno found it difficult to influence the psyche directly and thought it might be more effective to approach it through relationship.

He applied this frame of reference to the study of a residential school for delinquent girls in upstate New York. His findings were published in 1934 in *Who Shall Survive?*, the first sociometric investigation of an entire community. The sociometrist is not merely an observer–participant and interviewer; instead the active cooperation and collaboration of the group members are elicited; they become, in effect, co-researchers in the project. Out of this research came a large number of sociograms and charts depicting the living, learning and working space of the group members in interaction in these settings. From this study the concepts of the "social atom" and of "social networks" emerged, among others. The structures around and between individuals, which tied them together, Moreno termed the social atom; their role relationship was the "cultural atom" which complements the social atom on the role level. The social atom and the cultural atom are two formations within a more comprehensive one called the social network.

Definitions of the social atom are as follows.

1 The nucleus of all individuals towards whom a person is related in a significant manner or who are related to him; the relationship may be emotional, social or cultural.
2 The sum of interpersonal structures resulting from choices and rejections centered about a given individual.
3 The smallest nucleus of individuals in the social universe who are emotionally interwoven, emotional because even the highest spiritual or intellectual relationships are meaningless without some feeling.
4 The center of attraction, rejection or indifference; the interweaving of emotional, social or cultural factors eventually takes the form of attraction, rejection or indifference on the surface of human contact.
5 The ultimate universal "common denominator" of all social forms, not normative like the family or an abstraction from the group like the individual.
6 An existential category, it consists of individuals. Once brought to cognizance it is in immediate evidence and cannot be further reduced. Contrary to it, the physical atom is not in immediate evidence and can be further reduced. It is not a reality but a construct. The term *atomos*, any small thing, is a misnomer, for the physical atom is not the smallest and simplest elementary particle of matter. Electrons, neutrons, protons, etc. are smaller and in the course of time still smaller particles

may be found. But it cannot be imagined that at any time a smaller social structure than the social atom will be found, as it is nothing else but the most immediate social coexistence of individuals.

7 A pattern of attractions, repulsions and indifferences discerned on the threshold between individual and group.

Examples of role relationships that form cultural atoms are: employer–employee, employee–employee, stranger–native, majority–minority group member, government–citizen, father–female child, father–middle child, etc., and the same goes, of course, for the mother–child relationships and the female–female and female–male.

Of particular concern to psychotherapists are six relationships uncovered in this microscopic overview. The dyad or pair is the smallest unit of social interaction. The family consists first of this pair. The dyad and its treatment, as pointed out earlier, encompasses three entities. These structures become far more complex in their interrelationships when entire families are involved: triangles, squares, pentagons, etc., all considered with their substructures and bonds.

Within the dyadic organization the following are discernible.

1 Two healthy persons can have a productive relationship in that it is mutually satisfying and growth-supporting; this is a reassuring finding even if somewhat rare.
2 Two otherwise healthy persons can have a disturbed relationship; with other partners they would be balanced, but together they contribute to one another's disequilibrium, disturbance or destruction.
3 One healthy and one so-called sick person can have a healthy relationship; on this psychotherapy is based. This cannot last. It may eventually lead to an end, with release and independence of the dependent person. But it means a mutually beneficial and satisfying relationship.
4 A healthy person and an unhealthy person can have a pathological relationship, one that is mutually destructive.
5 Two so-called sick persons can have a healthy relationship when one of the partners is somewhat better integrated than the other; that is, well enough not to be disequilibrated by the weaker partner. Group psychotherapy and Alcoholics Anonymous are based on this, as are all the mutual self-help groups, each partner acting as a therapeutic agent for another.
6 Two disturbed individuals can have a disturbed relationship in that they contribute further to the disturbance.

In psychodrama, after dealing with the dyadic organization, the social atom not only is studied from the perspective of the two central protagonists, as for instance a couple, but includes the children and in-laws from both sides, and siblings.

The effects of birth within the social atom are often profound. In addition to the exploration of these effects on the intimate, work and sociocultural atom, psychodramatists began to look at death within the social atom. In an aging population and in a network of dying such as with AIDS, the deprivation by social and physical death becomes a major concern. Not only the aged are severely affected by death. Working with adolescents and young adults who have attempted or are depressed enough to contemplate suicide, treatment is directed at having the protagonist role reverse with a person they have recently lost, either through the ending of a relationship or through death. In the latter case we often find that the continued relationship with the deceased is more valued than with anyone alive. Thus another subset of relationships was revealed, those to the Dead vs those Alive.

Treatment here consists in having the patient role reverse with the dead person and facing himself portrayed by an auxiliary ego who firmly declares love for the deceased and the fervent wish to join the dead. In all cases thus treated the deceased has not wished the patient to join him in death. But in any case, completing the healing must be a restoration of balance in the social atom of life, which must defuse the relationship to the dead person. Often patients are not aware that there is potential help around them. The way to reach for help is to ask the protagonist: "Who will be most hurt if you should happen to commit suicide?" The person so selected by the patient becomes the next candidate for role reversal into that person's learning of the suicide. When one patient denied that anyone would care, the start of the psychodrama was with the person who would first discover her. This led to a chain of six persons, each of whose roles she embodied each time someone was informed of her death. She did not have "psychodramatic shock" and full realization of what consequences her contemplated act would evoke until she became her own mother.

The social atom is a rich source of diagnostic and therapeutic information; it can be used to help restore what is called "sociostasis," homeostatic balance in the social atom. Homeostatic balance is primarily linked to stability of relationships and not to stability of the individuals involved, nor to their characteristics.

In psychodrama, process is more important than content; although the content is reconstructed, the "How did this happen to you? Show me" is the focus rather than the "What happened to you? Tell me." Patients frequently repress or forget what happened, but they rarely forget how they experienced it and how this experience affected them. Thus, we tap into the process and, remarkably, the contents begin to emerge again, within the flow of the process. Protagonists may fall temporarily out of a scene by stating, "Oh, I had forgotten, this and that occurred here," thereby amplifying and intensifying the re-enactment. Because it is a flowing, life-connected process, learning can be carried from therapy into life itself; it affects the protagonist on the level of action, fantasy and reality. We start with the magic "as if" but after a while the "if" falls away and becomes "as."

Rank says about play:

> For play, after all, differs not only conceptually, but factually, from art. It has in common with art the combination of the real and the apparent; yet it is not merely fancy objectivized, but fancy translated into reality, acted and lived. It shares with art the double consciousness of appearance and reality, yet it has more of reality, while art is content with appearance.
>
> (Rank 1968: 104)

He also says, "The great artist and great work are only born from the reconciliation of . . . the victory of a philosophy of renunciation over an ideology of deprivation" (Rank 1968: 429). It strikes me that this applies to our patients who may have to reconcile themselves to a deprivation of their privacy to gain or regain themselves on another level and with larger dimensions. But to achieve this and not to feel deprived, they must find within themselves and their relationships, as artists find in their work, something of equal or greater value. Possibly some can even become artists at living. Our task is to guide them so that this can take place. Then they can achieve, as Eric Erickson put it in *Young Man Luther*: "This pure self is the self no longer sick with a conflict between right and wrong, not dependent on providers, and not dependent on guides to reason and reality" (Erickson 1958: 265).

Moreno ventured a prediction in *Who Shall Survive?*:

> When the nineteenth century came to an end and the final accounting was made, what emerged as its greatest contribution to the mental and social sciences was the idea of the unconscious and its cathexes. When the twentieth century will close its doors that which I believe will come out as the greatest achievement is the idea of spontaneity–creativity and the significant, indelible link between them. It may be said that the efforts of the two centuries complement one another. If the nineteenth century looked for the "lowest" common denominator of mankind, the unconscious, the twentieth century discovered, or rediscovered its "highest" common denominator – spontaneity–creativity.[1]

Article 31

Note on Some Forms of Resistance to Psychodrama

Moreno, Z.T. (1990) *Journal of Group Psychotherapy, Psychodrama and Sociometry* LXIII, 1: 43–44

Zerka's comments

By this time I was living in Beacon, traveling to teach, and holding a monthly training group on the stage at Boughton Place in Highland, NY. I wrote this article in response to questions from staff at various institutions, from students who brought up the issue, and from my own experience.

A number of us who work in institutional settings, regardless of philosophy of therapy, encounter resistance from staff members, most frequently nurses, who are disturbed by the fact that patients often seem disequilibrated after having been in psychodrama. The psychodrama therapist may be met with questions such as "What have you done to my patient?" or "Why are the patients so often upset when they come out of their psychodrama session?"

It strikes me as incumbent upon us to educate other staff members about the noticeable effects psychodrama might have upon patients afterwards. The anxiety that this condition arouses is not malicious; the nonparticipating staff member may not be aware of the implications of treatment. The patient may still be in what I have come to describe as the "recovery room." The simplest way to explain their state is to let the anxious staff member know that psychodrama is deep surgery of an emotional nature. They are familiar with the recovery room after surgical procedures with patients. Tender, loving, and highly individualized care is given there. Merely because emotional states are not as evident as physical ones makes them no less valid. The best way to handle the recovery period is by gentle, loving attention. Above all, the upheaval should not be handled by tranquilizing or administering other drug approaches. It must be allowed to be worked through and integrated. Also, the patient should not be scolded even for what may appear to an objective observer to be outrageous behavior, but rather gently guided to a more stable mood. A delicate approach is called for. Soft words may take away wrath.

Another form of resistance may be met in the psychodrama session itself, this time on the part of the protagonist. Most often it involves the patient's resistance to taking the role of the other with whom the protagonist is in conflict. This may appear to be a sociometric rejection. Actually, it is more than that and, from the point of view of psychodynamics, it is a good diagnostic clue. It means that the pain caused by the other has not yet healed. The protagonist needs more work in order to be purged of that particular hurt. Humans cannot give up what they do not own. The indication is, therefore, for the protagonist to work more on the conflict. The self has to be intact before it can yield itself to others in role reversal.

The absent other will have to be portrayed by an auxiliary ego, even if the portrayal is based on little or no information. Role reversal for specific needs, such as for correction of perception and portrayal, may be possible by the protagonist for brief moments. Sometimes the auxiliary ego is not sufficiently aware of the amount of pain that the other being portrayed has placed on the protagonist or in what manner it was inflicted. Once the protagonist has made this clear in role reversal the action can continue with the protagonist, back in role, working through whatever material is brought to light.

The protagonist requires validation in every respect. Validation comes before resolution.

Let me illustrate this by an experience of my own while in training. I was going to work on a scene with my mother when I was three years old. Although I had shown my mother as a tough lady to deal with even for an adult, the auxiliary ego was much too gentle in her interaction with me. I fell out of my role and began to laugh at the very point where, in life itself, I had begun to cry. When the director asked me what was happening, I replied, "If my mother had been like this, I would not now have to do this scene." I then reversed roles, corrected, and resumed my own role.

I did not reject taking my mother's role; the auxiliary ego perceived it as pejorative and, because she liked me, wanted to be kind to me. That was not only a bad start, it was not really kindness because it took the wind out of my sails. I certainly would have rejected taking my mother's role in the form in which it was being enacted. There again, the validation of my perception and experience had to be completed before I could deal with the hurt in an integrative manner.

The psychodrama must never be less intense than life itself. We need to enlarge the experience if catharsis is to take place; therefore, wholehearted validation must be our first concern.

Article 32

Time, Space, Reality, and the Family: Psychodrama with a Blended (Reconstituted) Family

Moreno, Z.T. (1991) In M. Karp and P. Holmes (eds), *Psychodrama: Inspiration and Technique*, London: Routledge

Zerka's comments

This family lived in the West. They had heard of our work and contacted us to ask if they could come as a complete family. They all stayed at our institute in Beacon. In addition to the work depicted here, we did some work with the parents alone. As reported to us several years later, relationships in the family had completely changed for the better.

Introduction

This chapter deals with a fairly rare set of circumstances in that an entire family made the decision to enter residential treatment and to spend a week – the only week available in their various summertime schedules – having an evaluation and some guidelines for further conduct. As they live far away, we cannot be in continuous contact. The report of our psychodramatic explorations has to be less detailed than might normally be the case, due to lack of space and because of the fairly large number of participants. Therefore, the sessions are given in somewhat skeletal form.

This is the second marriage for both parents. The father has five children; he divorced their mother three years earlier. The mother was widowed and brought one child with her.

The main focus seems to be to find a solution to some of the daily irritating interactions and to see where and what changes appear to be indicated.

If need be, the parents are willing to have the family continue in treatment when back at home with other therapists; alternatively, we may have to go to them to re-evaluate and guide further developments.

We decided to proceed as systematically as possible, examining together the facts, the individuals and their various needs, the structure of the family in terms of overall system and subsystems, the boundaries, the levels of intimacy and communication, generational and intergenerational conflicts, role interactions, ethical considerations, the pushes and pulls, past history and what some family therapists indicate as obligations and entitlements (Karpel and Strauss 1983: 26). "We" means J.L. Moreno and this writer, working as a team of co-therapists.

First contact

The long distance telephone call is our first contact. The family has searched for a residential treatment setting in which the entire family can be accommodated. The parents know about our work and the psychodrama process is one of the reasons they chose to contact us. The family is setting aside two weeks for this project from their summer vacation. One half of that time has to be for travel by family bus.

"Is it possible for you to admit all of us?"

"Yes, of course. 'Be glad to have you, how many of you are there?"

"Eight. Two adults and six young folks."

"What ages are the young people?"

"Ranging from 12 to 19."

"What do you see as the most pressing problems?"

"Increasingly violent conflict between the two boys. The other children are girls."

"Do you feel one boy is the main instigator, or are they equally responsible?"

"We have observed it is the older one."

We have the presenting problem and one identified patient. We know this is but the beginning.

Mutually satisfactory dates are determined and suitable housing preparations made. We already know not to place the two boys in a double room and beyond that, that the four remaining youngsters are girls. We are told that five of the offspring belong to the father, the only child of the mother being the 13-year-old.

First meeting and opening session

Soon after arrival, when they have settled in their rooms, we enter into the theater. Its uses are explained and how we proceed outlined. Clearly, the play aspect appeals to them; they are open and seem eager to start.

As they came in a rather large vehicle, and the journey took several days, much time was spent in its enclosure. We decided to start there, going from the so-called periphery to the center, but being aware that this may reveal some of the essential features of family members' interaction.

The director begins the session:

"Please step on the top level of the stage and set up seating arrangements in your bus." Soon done (see Figure 32.1).

Matthew (Father, Driver)	Felix (17 years)
Katy (Mother, Stepmother)	Susan (19 years)
Chuck (16 years)	Candy (15 years)
Maureen (12 years)	Vivian (13 years)

Figure 32.1 Seating in the family bus

Now we have a visible seating sociogram. The arrangement is how they chose to be together.

"Did the seating arrangement change at all during the trip?"

"No, but that, too, was the cause for arguments between the two boys, the only arguments."

Matthew is largely the spokesman, with Katy chipping in at times to give details; they have a harmonious interaction.

"Please proceed and let us see the essence of the interaction during your trip."

The argument is a fairly low key one, but it demonstrates the tug-of-war between the two sons, both vying for Matthew's attention and proximity. Matthew uses a light-handed approach, tries not to interfere too much, but when he does it is to pour oil on troubled waters.

Felix, the oldest of the father's sons, and Chuck are each other's absolute opposites. Felix is domineering, determined not to give way, aware of his position as the oldest son and using it with a good deal of machismo. His attitude of superiority reminds us of the Alpha animal. It is his major route in dealing with his siblings, but is especially in evidence towards Chuck.

Chuck, on the other hand, is a rather shy, delicate looking boy, somewhat undersized in appearance. He wheedles and tries to negotiate to exchange seats with Felix, but to no avail. Matthew evidently is aware that rearranging the seating will lead to a good deal of upheaval among all the others as they tend to be afraid of Felix.

As the argument between them develops, Susan begins to stiffen in her seat; she appears to become growingly disturbed. As she remains silent and is seated next to a protective figure, her stepmother, and all the others show no such external behavior, a double is assigned to her, and her function explained. It is intended to search and feel out the reason for Susan's obvious discomfort. The double's task is to bring to light the inner, silent processes in Susan. She notes that Candy's right foot is placed on Susan's back and seems to be pressing her. Feeling herself into Susan, the tension, the anger, the double suddenly turns around to Candy and explodes at her:

"Who do you think you are, pushing your foot into my back? Do you want me out of the way? It's not fair. I'm getting tired. Stop it."

The tension in the group shifts from what appeared to be a central problem of interaction to a new area, to everyone's amazement. Candy is dumbfounded and silent. The reason for the amazement comes out later in the post-action sharing.

Susan's face is flushed as she softly explains to Candy: "That's right. I've never been able to tell you, but I've felt your anger for quite a while. I don't understand it. I don't know what I've done to you to cause it."

Candy is unable to speak.

We recognize that this is a second area that needs further examination. The action is ended here. Sharing and dialogue commences. The amazement at that Susan–Candy interaction comes through: "The double did just the right thing. Candy is another bossy character in the family and Susan has difficulty with such people. But we did not notice what happened between them on the ride." Some of the not-so-visible conflicts are beginning to emerge.

Second session – divorce and after-effects

It is time to look into what the families were like before the divorce.

The interview reveals first Matthew's story, which, as he is the father of the large brood he brought into the marriage, is more complex than that of the mother–stepmother. Her only child is Vivian.

Matthew is 50 years of age, a successful professional. Lately he has begun to search for a new career, one which he feels will give him both greater satisfaction and be more useful. Financially, with his wife working, such a change might be arranged. Katy is 38; she is also a professional, but her career is of more recent date. Since her first husband's death when Vivian was a baby, she has been her child's only parent and sole support. Upon marrying the first time she gave up graduate studies. Her husband's insurance helped to sustain her and the child while she worked part-time, but her second marriage made her present career possible after completing her degree. Matthew wholeheartedly endorsed her achievement. They have been married for two years.

Katy's marriage was not of sufficient duration for anything remarkable to have occurred in the way of problems, except for her husband's illness and death at a young age. She has managed her life extremely well and is a warm, stable person.

It is time to explore the relationship between Matthew and his first wife, the mother of his children. We discover that there is yet another child, Allen, a five-year-old boy, still living with his mother.

The auxiliary ego for the first wife is the stepmother (second wife). She knows Victoria and all agree that she will be a fair representative; the director asks Katy if she will allow corrections from family members, with possible doubling for Victoria as they see fit. Katy agrees. The rest of the family is now well warmed-up and becoming more and more available for the psychodrama process. In fact, we are rather taken by surprise at the negligible amount of resistance we have thus far encountered with them. Clearly, they are eager to find peaceful resolution of some of their interactional irritations. In spite of their youth, the children seem to be aware of the psychological impact of their history and the game-playing aspect of psychodrama appeals to them. They are also learning a great many new things about themselves and each other.

Matthew confronts "Victoria" with his decision to leave her and the children and start living alone. This scene took place four years earlier. There is no other woman in his life, but the conflicts with Victoria have become too hard and his work suffers under the strain.

One of the essential elements in the dissolution of the relationship is that Victoria is reputed to be a seriously ill depressive who refuses to undergo treatment. She is not merely withdrawn, but also suspicious and hostile. She is especially hard on Candy, whom she accuses of all kinds of apparently unfounded misdeeds. Matthew tells "Victoria" that the main reason she rejects Candy is that she is a healthy version of herself, fortunately without the depression. The more accusing "Victoria" becomes, he explains, the more he tends to protect Candy and thus the fire gets fanned.

Although taking himself out of the field of action seems to be both callous and lacking in courage, he finds it absolutely necessary, if only for economic reasons. He must at least be able to earn a decent living for such a large family. When asked to turn his head and soliloquize he reveals how stupid he feels, not having recognized Victoria's illness earlier so that suitable decisions could have been made. But now it is too late and he must do what he can to salvage the family. He sees this as his only way out.

All of this is a true revelation to the children, who have, as is usually the case, never been let into the reasons for the family difficulties. At the same time, Matthew is not accusing "Victoria," but makes clear that he sees his own part in all this.

Katy, in the role of Victoria, accuses him of desertion, of being unfaithful, a bad husband and father and a poor example for the children. We are aware that this is also a way of purging Katy from the feelings she has absorbed from the reports given her about Victoria by Matthew and the young people in the last few years.

Her enactment meets with recognition by the others, who feel very little need to add, except for some of them stating that they have heard these kinds of remarks directly, especially since Matthew remarried.

It is often noteworthy that the various family members have different perceptions about some of the others, but that, given the evidence here described, the absent mother and ex-wife represents for them an insoluble source of conflicts. We de-role Katy and thank her for her good work.

Because of this and her own subsequent decision to leave her mother's home, Susan requests to be allowed to confront her mother as she has not been able to in reality, due to her mother's emotional state.

Now it is Susan who, tearfully and remorsefully, explains to her "mother" in the empty chair why she had to leave. She reports she can no longer tolerate the divisions in the family, the mother's attempt to get Susan on her side against Matthew, whom Susan loves, and her relationship with Felix, using him as her standby and agent in disciplining the younger children. Susan especially accuses Victoria of her rejection of Chuck and Candy, which she feels to be dreadfully unfair and unrelated to their behavior. It is true that Candy tries to fight back, but Chuck is completely subdued and frightened, as is the youngest boy, Allen, who becomes confused by the turmoil.

Here we are beginning to understand some of the behavior Felix has thus far displayed. He has been trained since the divorce to be the male head of the family and his behavior puts him now, in the new family, in opposition to Matthew, the true head of the family. He also maintains his stance towards Chuck, as earlier fed by Victoria.

Susan ends the scene by informing her mother that, for the sake of her own sanity, she must leave. She can no longer be of help.

In reality this scene never took place. It is an interaction in "surplus reality," but it should be recalled that in psychodrama, scenes, relationships, events that never took place are frequently the source of the deepest catharsis for the protagonist who needs them for healing. Essential to psychodrama is to remember its prosopopoeia which is currently a central idea in surplus reality as it means personification, as of inanimate things, representation of an imaginary, absent or deceased person as speaking or acting.

There is much sharing and discussing and the members feel they are beginning to do a lot of clearing up as to the various steps taken by each of them, with some relief of guilt expressed as they see that their actions were not made in bad faith, but had rational soil.

It becomes clear that the only one present not involved in conflict with Victoria is Maureen. She was still too little, though like her younger brother bewildered by the troubles; but she has learned to be everyone's pet, as compensation, fairly successfully. This innocuous behavior has stood her in good stead, but also weakens her emotional ties to the rest of the family. In a benign way, she is also an isolate, as much as little Allen. We store it away for future reference, if needed.

The striking contrast of images of masculinity represented by the two boys is another aspect we need to deal with.

We are seeing some of the substructures in this family: Matthew–Katy (mutual attractions); Felix–Chuck (mutual rejection); Susan–Candy (ambivalent); Vivian–Maureen (not yet clarified, but they seem to be together a good deal); Chuck–Candy (mutually supportive, very close in age, but with some ambivalence); Katy–Susan (mutually supportive); Katy–Vivian (mildly conflicted since the additional members have come); Matthew–Felix (ambivalent). No doubt further cliques will be revealed as we continue, possibly some triangles, for instance, as well as other pairs.

Third session – how did you meet?

The third session deals with the newly reconstructed family.

Katy and Matthew met at the house of friends after he moved out. The romance flourished rapidly. To show what the early period of the marriage was like, Matthew, Katy and Vivian, sitting at the dining table, complete with wine and candlelight, represent an unreal-seeming trio, with Vivian being warmed by their newfound happiness. She has no memory of her own father and gets along well with Matthew. He, in turn, has no trouble relating to a single, younger child, and shows himself in general to be a nurturing parent, also to his own troubled brood. Here the vivid contrast between the old and the new is sharply brought to our attention.

We are made aware that Vivian, once a little princess in the second marriage, is about to be displaced by the emergence of her stepfather's children and we need to gauge what this means to her. We have unveiled some of the strands that tie the past with the present.

The director ends this scene and asks, "How does this change? When do your children come to stay, Matthew?"

After a brief discussion the next scene is set.

The time is a day or two before Christmas of the previous year. School holidays have just begun. Matthew, Katy and Vivian are decorating their tree. The honeymoon stage has not yet ended and the joy in their being together is evident. Matthew's children have been coming for vacations and weekends on and off, but they return home in time for school. The new family has moved from the earlier home to a larger house, to accommodate the regular influx.

The procession starts: there is an unexpected visitor, Susan. She arrives loaded down with suitcases, on vacation from college. As soon as she enters she starts to cry. The three of them stand around her. Katy shelters her until she quiets down. In a still-tight, small voice, Susan announces she has permanently departed from her mother's house. After her first semester at college, she finds life at that very troubled place unbearable. She does not plan ever to return there.

We think we need to hear everyone's soliloquy. This is a very dramatic development that is going to create some juxtapositioning in the family.

"How do you feel about what is happening? Matthew, please start. You already know how to do that. We need to hear your reflections and feelings. Do not talk to the others. This is not a dialogue. This is a talk with the self that normally others do not hear. But here we do it out loud."

MATTHEW (*looking very worried, frowns at first*): Good Lord, how will Victoria take this? I'm glad to see Susan here, but it is bound to have other consequences. Will Victoria put still more pressure on the others?

I see Katy being helpful to Susan. I'd better go soon and see how the rest of the gang is doing.

KATY (*not in the least perplexed, concerned for Susan*): This was inevitable. Anyway, Matthew knows I was prepared for something like this happening. I did not know it would be so soon, though. Wonder how Vivian will take this! (*looks at her daughter who is standing by and watching with much interest*) It may be complicated, but we must be ready to stand by. I think I can manage it well enough. It's good to know Susan feels secure enough to come.

DIRECTOR: You, too, Vivian, let's hear from you.

VIVIAN: Wow, wonder what it'll be like, having an older sister. I rather like Susan; anyway, she's in college most of the time. Guess I can take it. Wait and see.

SUSAN (*at a nod in her direction by the director*): It went better than I thought. Hope the others are not going to be too upset, but I just can't stand it anymore.

We end the dramatic exploration here and find out that there was a hiatus of several months before the balance of the young people joined their father and Katy. It is decided to leave that for the next session. We ask the children to think about their own entrance into the household, not to discuss it yet, but to go out and relax somewhere. There has been enough dealing with upheaval for one day.

We now see some more complex substructures. Triangles have developed as well as a quadrangle: Matthew–Katy–Vivian, Matthew–Katy–Susan, Matthew–Katy–Vivian–Susan. We are looking forward to learning about the migration of the rest, but, like Matthew, feel for Victoria, who seems to be becoming more and more isolated.

Fourth session – the others follow

Felix is the second arrival and becomes our protagonist.

We see him alone in his room at his mother's house, fretful, brooding. He does not talk to anyone about his feelings so we ask that he, too, soliloquize. Felix is an athletic boy, of average height. While Susan has always been a good student, he manages to get by, preferring sports to studying. However, he has never failed any courses. Possibly he is more affected by the various distractions at home, which Susan has managed to overcome. In fact, she gives evidence of having delved into her studies to shut out the turmoil. Matthew has kept Felix at an acceptable level by insisting he make an effort in order for him to be allowed the athletic activities.

FELIX (*note we often resort to soliloquy in order to give the protagonists a chance to open up without having their revelations discussed or opposed, accepting them as they occur, since it is rare for family members to be sufficiently open with one another and such openness leaves them vulnerable*): Since Susan's gone, Mother depends still more on me. I miss Dad. I can't take his place. Besides, Mum is so demanding. I feel strangled (*puts his hands around his throat here*). Nothing I do is right. Wish I could do better. Mum is so unhappy. (*he goes outside, starts pacing up and down in the yard of his mother's house, playing with an imaginary basketball, tossing it into the area indicated as the basket. The movement and this activity seem to be easing him*) Wish Dad and Mum could've gotten along better and hadn't split up. Dad has a much better thing with Katy. And Katy really is trying hard to be a friend. I think I'll go and talk with them. (*he takes his bike and leaves*)

DIRECTOR: Let's hear what you're feeling as you cycle, or what you're thinking about.

FELIX (*on his bike, pedals while standing on the chair*): I'm worried about Allen. I like him a lot. He's still small and I'm too young to take care of him. I'm going to ask Dad what to do about Allen. (*note that he seems to overlook his two younger siblings nearest to him in age; there is a year between himself and Chuck, two years between himself and Candy. We record this and later find out more about this triad*)

FELIX (*stops*): That's about it.

DIRECTOR: Who's at home at your Dad's and Katy's house?

FELIX: Both and Vivian. Susan's at school.

DIRECTOR: Go ahead and talk with Matthew and Katy. Is Vivian there as well?

FELIX: I don't think so. (*they step up on stage*)

DIRECTOR: Let's just go into the meeting between you three.

MATTHEW: Hi Felix, come in. What brings you here? Is anything wrong? (*Matthew is always aware that the old family situation has a very tenuous base and that there are frequent problems*)

Katy looks apprehensive, different from when Susan arrived; clearly she feels her relationship with Felix is more complicated. Later exploration reveals some of Katy's emotional history related to this difficulty.

Felix tells them pretty much the same things as we have already heard in the soliloquy, but he suddenly bursts out, "I don't think I can take living with Mum any more. Can I move in with you?"

Here we ask each of the parents to soliloquize their reaction.

MATTHEW: Here we go again. It's just the way we have talked about it, Katy and I. Sooner or later this was probably bound to happen. When Susan came, Victoria was very bitter. This is going to hit even harder. Felix is her best support. Lord, this is becoming heavier all the time. She's very unhappy and we just don't seem to be able to help her.

The children are keenly listening; all these revelations are eye-openers for them and they are becoming more sensitive to their elders and their concerns about everyone involved.

KATY: I've never had a son before. Matthew and I are going to have to work together on this. Well, the youngsters do need help. Victoria is really not able to manage them. It's a large family and would be complicated under the best of circumstances.

DIRECTOR: Vivian, do you remember what you feel when this happens?

VIVIAN (*takes a moment before responding*): This may be interesting but I'm not sure how I feel about it. I've never had sisters and brothers. I feel a bit swamped at times. It's harder for Mum and me to be close like we used to be.

Now Felix confronts his father and asks what should be done about Allen. Matthew points out that he still needs his mother and conversely, she needs to keep him. Furthermore, he reminds him that, because of the age discrepancies, whenever Allen comes and visits, Katy is the one who has to take care of him, as they all have their own friends and do not give up their various activities. It would be grossly unfair all around to take such a drastic step as to remove him from the only home he knows and would totally deprive his mother, besides.

In the course of sharing and discussing we find out that Felix is the only child who still goes and visits his mother and Allen from time to time.

The director asks Felix to show him how such visits go and Felix chooses Katy to be his mother, Maureen to represent Allen. It is clear from his role reversals with Victoria that she does feel very deprived by his departure and accuses him much as she did Matthew of disloyalty. Felix has a good deal of residual guilt, but his need for emotional stability helps him fend off some of her accusations. A touching scene takes place when he role reverses with Allen who asks him what divorce means and, in that role, says to Felix, "I did not divorce Daddy."

This appears to be one of the most unsettling and unresolved areas for the family to face. The smallest child has put his finger on one of the most disturbing aspects of a family's breaking up.

We have unearthed another triangle: Felix–Victoria–Allen, and the absent dyad, Victoria–Allen. The family talks about how Allen defends his mother whenever he comes for a visit with them. Clearly, the little boy is very early made aware of some of the substrata of conflict and has become his mother's protector.

Fifth session – Chuck and Candy's turn

The two next eldest children, Matthew informs us, being so close in age, were brought up like triplets with Felix. He believes it was at this point that Victoria felt her burdens to become too great and the marriage began to unravel. This is what Matthew referred to earlier, blaming himself for not having understood how and when it occurred. It also throws new light upon the conflict between the two boys. As Felix was the much preferred child, emotional neglect of the next born was almost inevitable, and when Candy appeared, an energetic, feisty girl, the dissolution became even more obvious. Furthermore, Felix displays characteristics somewhat resembling his mother, perhaps learned, while Chuck is completely different. Having his younger sister as his best friend, and Susan as a protectress, his idea of how not to be a male is embodied by his taking a position at the opposite end of the pole from Felix.

It may be said that Felix was his mother's "psychodramatic baby," her ideal child. Evidently, she did not desire or need any others. But they came and here they are, little nestlings in need of care.

We next turn our attention to Chuck and Candy as we understand that they came to their father's home together. They step up on the stage and show us what happened. It is about 1:00 a.m. during Easter vacation. We find out that Chuck goes to a private school, having some minor learning difficulties. His vacation date differs by a day or so from Candy's, so she waited for his to start. They have talked about leaving and plan to do it now. They hastily pack a few clothes and run for it.

There's not much new information about their reason except that Victoria has become still more harsh with the two of them and they often have to be each other's helper. Thus far all the young people display intact self-protective mechanisms, although Chuck is least well endowed. Their arrival, although in the wee small hours, has been more or less expected and by now the transfers are becoming routine. Katy and Matthew were aware it was only a matter of time.

Technically, their mother has custody, but in their state, at a certain age, the children are permitted to choose with which parent they wish to reside.

The assumption is that Victoria is fairly relieved to be free of the two children she least wanted and with whom the relationship is most troubling to her. There are now only Maureen and Allen living with her; the consensus is that she can manage that rather better.

It is decided to let Chuck have his session now and we are again struck by the wondrous diversity in the family.

Chuck goes about, in monodramatic form, taking all the roles himself, to show how he spends his time as a junior counselor during summer vacation, at a camp for disabled children. He is a tender, nurturing counselor and it is clear that here he shines. At home, the evaluation is that he is a little bit of a misfit, but now, with everyone able to see him in a different setting, some of his true nature is revealed. It is evident that this is new information for the rest of the family. Although his parents receive positive reports about his work, they have not witnessed him in action.

The awareness that the adolescent has many roles, and that these potentials are not always activated in the family fold, is helping others to see him differently.

> One highly significant aspect of family structure is its role structure – that is, the roles that are assigned to and assumed by individuals in the family and the relationship between or among those roles. This discussion does not refer to family roles in the functional sense, i.e., the role of the mother or father, etc., but to roles in the sense of interlocking identities, such as the "little angel" or the "peacemaker." The term "role" is often used to describe those presentations of self that we all assume in social or work situations. These roles are usually fairly temporary and limited, and are consciously or deliberately assumed. In other words, there is actually very little overlap between who we feel we really are and whom we may act like with the corner grocer or a neighbor down the block.
>
> When we speak of roles in the family, however, we are discussing a very different phenomenon. The roles we are given and assume in our families are more permanent, less flexible, and usually less conscious. In these cases, there is a great deal of overlap between who we are in our families and who we feel we really are. We can move in and out of the roles we play with our neighbor as easily as we may put on and take off a coat, but trying to change our role in our families is more often like trying to struggle out of a straitjacket.
>
> (Karpel & Strauss 1983: 26)

The fact that Chuck has been seen in a position of strength helps us to decide to go into the actuality of the present problem, namely, the fights between him and Felix. We keep this plan in mind for the next session.

Sixth session – the boys and their conflicts

As the layout of the family's living quarters is unknown to us, Katy and Matthew drew a schema of the house and its residents. As in most families, there are sexual considerations in placing the young people together. But the difficulties between the boys make such proximity rather undesirable and may increase the problem between them. In the next scene we see how the "territorial imperative" works here.

We are informed that the worst scenes take place during evenings, at weekends and during holidays, periods when sharing time and space are particularly in evidence. Sociometrically, sharing time and space are dynamic living categories, opportunities for interpersonal contact of both positive and negative impact.

It is evening. The boys are upstairs in their rooms, doing homework or whatever needs to be done, each away from the other. They have separate television sets, a provision for reducing clashes. There are visitors downstairs in the living room, which makes the parents particularly eager to have some peace and quiet, another aspect of sharing time and space. The rest of the young people watch as this scene develops. At home, they are not only spectators but also involved actors. We decide to focus on the essential interactors.

Suddenly the fight erupts. Felix goes to the bathroom, comes out and shouts at Chuck because he has left the bathroom messy (has not hung up the towels, scrubbed out the tub, or mopped the floor, as he should have done, it being his turn). They have been alternately assigned these chores and Felix feels he does them well, while accusing Chuck of being neglectful and sloppy. Chuck tries to defend himself but Felix now becomes physically aggressive and starts to hit him. This is the pattern he learned at his first home, the only way their mother was able to handle what she saw as unruly behavior of the children. Katy dashes upstairs, tries to calm them down and to shield Chuck, but now Felix turns against her and takes a physically threatening stance towards her. While he has not actually hit her, it is clear that he comes very close. Katy appears frozen, unable to handle her response to this, calls for Matthew to come up and help, and this is how the scene ends, with father becoming the mediator.

According to the post-enactment sharing, this is rather a frequent series of events and very little impact has been effected by talking about it. What to do?

Reorganization of the living space

We return to the schema of the house and note that Susan is not home a great deal of the time, being away at college. What about trying the following: since proximity is such a difficult arrangement, why not move Chuck downstairs to her room and have Susan move into his? Susan is asked how she would feel about that and after thinking it over she agrees, noting that if that will bring greater peace in the house, she is willing.

Felix agrees to this, while we point out that now the care of the bathroom will be largely his very own responsibility. But as he and Susan seem to be more compatible and she is away a good deal of time anyway, he feels relieved. He will have more living space for himself and can determine his own obligations.

The greatest relief is evidenced by Chuck, who is clearly intimidated by the conflict with Felix. He, too, is now assigned to take his part in being responsible for the chores in the bathroom shared with Candy. They accept this and Candy makes it clear to him that she, too, will expect him to carry his part. Because of the better relationship between these two, this assignment appears to be a more positive one. It remains to be carried out at home and tested out.

There is a good deal of discussion and sharing at the end. We have noted Katy's fright at the fighting and decide to have a talk with the parents alone, so they can ventilate some of their own angers and concerns, before the next session.

Seventh session – interview with Katy and Matthew alone

We review together what we have thus far experienced together and the various dynamic underpinnings. We turn our attention to Katy to ask how she feels about the boys' conflict, of which the bathroom and bedroom proximity are merely a part, and particularly her response to the suggestion of separating them. She admits that this is likely to reduce at least some of the difficulty, but states that Felix's aggression is very hard for her and frightening. He is getting taller and stronger and she fears that this type of behavior may lead to further difficulties if not corrected, not only at home.

While not in any way mitigating the threat as such, we inquire whether Felix's wild behavior reminds her of anyone in her past. She admits that her father was an alcoholic, physically abusive to her mother and herself. He died of the consequences of his illness when she was an adolescent, but the fear remained.

Katy is given an opportunity to address the empty chair and releases a lot of feelings in her own role. When asked what she needs from her father now, she states that he ought to ask her forgiveness. We suggest a role reversal with him and she takes time to get into his role. What comes out instead is how much he regrets not having been a good father and how proud he is of the way she has developed and lived her life. Also, that he realizes that her own mothering of this enlarged family is partly due to her own experiences lacking such care. He further suggests she should not mix Felix up with himself.

It is not uncommon to learn in role reversal what protagonists really need to receive from the absent other, and that it is not quite what they thought they needed. The role reversal was actually a more complete encounter than mere asking for forgiveness.

We purposely do not ask Matthew to undertake the father's role for Katy in order not to confuse the relationship. It is hoped that Katy's empty chair completion will ease her interaction with Felix.

At this point Matthew remarks that he senses Felix is confused by his physical attraction to Katy. Katy is younger than his mother, energetic and pretty. Matthew adds how eager Felix is to show off his athletic accomplishments and disappointed if Katy cannot always be there to see his success. The classic father–son, daughter–father conflicts come to the surface as well as the father–mother–son triangle. Katy agrees that all these factors may play a part in her inability to be more receptive to the boy.

Further clarification comes when Matthew states that there are traces of character in Felix he sees in Victoria as well and they are not the ones that he finds most endearing. There is the situation with Allen already reported. Matthew feels that Felix is here in parental competition with him and wants to show him up as a failing parent. Triangle father–eldest son–youngest son, but also quadrangle father–eldest son–youngest son–mother are in evidence.

When role reversed as Felix, he is asked what about Matthew he finds difficult. He says he'll never be able to equal his father's professional achievement. He feels the need to break free of the family. He wants very much to go to a local private school, in which there is more stress placed upon athletics than in his present, public school. Back in his own role we ask Matthew what changes fulfilling Felix's desire would entail. Matthew says that financially it would mean that Chuck would have to go to a local school rather than the private school he now attends.

We point out that maybe Felix feels he should have a chance to attend a school of his own choosing and that this, too, may be another source of his rejection of Chuck. Could it be that he interprets Chuck's schooling as a preferment to which he is also entitled? This is discussed as a distinct possibility that did not occur to them since there appeared to be a good reason for that decision. We ask, is it conceivable that Chuck's current level of achievement may be good enough so that he can meet the local school's standards?

It is agreed that they will look into this. We talked about how such a change may decrease Felix's demands, give him a needed sense of accomplishment and support his need for individuation. In any event, the change gives the parents an opportunity to set limits in order for Felix to attain his goal.

Matthew ends the interview by taking Katy's hand and telling her, in an emotion-filled voice, how deeply he appreciates their marriage and her devotion to his children. He believes the children may never fully comprehend the adjustments and sacrifices she has made and continues to make to ensure their healthy development. We applaud this and add that it was nothing short of heroic, and how central her role is in the family. Katy is touched and a bit embarrassed by these accolades. For us, Matthew's love for Katy, his appreciation of her and his relief that she is his partner, are clear.

Eighth session – the last newcomer

Maureen is the youngest of the girls, the final immigrant.

Her soliloquy prior to her departure from her mother's house shows her unhappiness. She has been spending weekends and holidays at her father's new home, but the school weekdays are not happy ones for her. She is particularly attracted to the new family because of her relationship with Vivian and this is one of the big pulls in her case. She has never had such a close age mate in her family before. Vivian is by now quite used to the additions and good-naturedly takes to Maureen's presence with minor reservations.

When she has completed her scene of decision, which is timed before a long holiday weekend, we ask Maureen and Vivian to present us with a typical interaction between them.

Although they are fairly convivial, there are some irritations between them because Vivian, being older and more mature, has trouble dealing with Maureen's tendency to adulate and imitate her, clinging more than she is able to bear. There are some altercations between them about clothing and borrowing things. Role reversals are suggested, which help clarify feelings on both sides.

It is fairly remarkable that Vivian has been able to emerge in her own right without being altogether overcome. Possibly it is the piecemeal pace at which the father's children entered the family fold, or the particular way in which the parents have managed to steer the ship, as well as the fact that Katy sensed well before it happened that the family would some day be much enlarged, and prepared Vivian for that eventuality.

Maureen, on the other hand, has avoided conflict in the past as already indicated, by being generally well accepted and has managed to stay afloat in the formerly troubled waters. In the main, it is clear that what strikes us as a problematic earlier family life has not made as negative an impact as might be expected. Therapists may tend to see these difficulties too darkly; there may be more health than we assume. When Maureen was left alone with her mother and younger brother, however, she felt the impact of her mother's depression too much and, like the others, felt unequal to the task of helping lift her out of it. Besides, she was lonely for her siblings.

There is another sister pair that needs further work: Susan and Candy. We now focus on their interaction and ask them to have a good talk, such as they were never able to have before.

A very touching confrontation ensues in which Candy explains to Susan what she feels to be the source of her anger, brought to light in the bus scene. Susan protected her and Chuck against the severe attacks on them by Victoria and her departure made life especially untenable at home. Their protectress had left them still more vulnerable. Susan and Candy both weep and Susan asks Candy's pardon and tells her how much she admires her fighting spirit. She, Susan, sees Candy as stronger than herself in this respect and therefore unaware of how much her withdrawal from the scene of battle meant to the younger girl. Role reversal at this point reinforces the interchange. When back in their own roles they hug, and admit that they love each other and are glad to be reunited.

Sharing and further discussion lead to the statement that parents have power over their children and that is fine, as long as they do not abuse it.

As we have had a good deal of emotional revelation, it is decided that the next session will be dedicated to the "Magic Shop," it being the final one. This allows for a more cognitive way of looking at their needs and is often filled with laughter.

Ninth session – the Magic Shop

The Magic Shop is a place where people can come and express a wish for something they want to attain, nothing of a material nature, but goals or feelings or attributes they feel they want or need. In exchange, the shopkeeper will ask for something to be given, as the shop must never be depleted; it must retain a certain inventory so all those who enter there may find something they require.

Everyone steps up and some find resolution of their wishes. Exceptionally notable is that all enter into the spirit of the game, as is demonstrated when Matthew expresses his desire for new skills that will enable him to build a new career. When the shopkeeper asks him to yield in exchange the very skills that have made him successful because they are valuable and needed by others, he is willing, shakes hands with the auxiliary ego and declares it to be an acceptable bargain.

The element of what seemed to be pure play helped to make the closure a more lighthearted one than might otherwise have been achieved, as there was a good deal of laughter in the course of this session.

Follow-up

Contact three months later informs us that the changes for the rooms and schooling have indeed been made. In general, the atmosphere has greatly improved and the interactions are less charged with negative feelings. Matthew has begun to look into his special needs for training in order to be prepared for the eventual career change, which is, however, some years in the future.

During a meeting with the parents a decade later, we are told that the young people are pursuing careers, some of them abroad, and are doing well in their chosen paths. Matthew has reached his goal of a career change he aspired to and is more fulfilled in it.

Summary

We tried to proceed in a manner consistent with sociometric and psychodramatic principles, not imposing our own ideas, but allowing information to guide us from step to step. Soliloquy was used as a form of "surplus reality," largely because the kind of communication and information it highlights is rarely brought out in complex and intimate relations. It is also useful as an educational tool, to help family members become aware of what may not be communicated, but may have to be searched out. Other psychodramatic techniques were used sparingly. We were not training these people to become each other's therapists, but trying to sensitize them to their own needs and those of others. Full role reversal was used only twice, between the two sister pairs, to cement the relationship or to ease it. It was not used where it might be interpreted as a weapon to hurt another person through new insights of vulnerability or a misplaced sense of power or authority over another. Mostly, we used self-presentation to affirm, support and clarify.

We proceeded from a model of health, not of pathology. Where there is pathology that diminishes the ability of healthy aspects to come through, the best any therapy can contribute is to reach the autonomous healing center of the individuals concerned. This approach meant that, while the presenting problem was not to be overlooked, we wanted more background information before assuming that it was the most important problem. Therefore, we did not start there, but entered into the family organization with the most recent and common experience. The family members guided us and, hand-in-hand, allowed us to guide them.

The time and space interaction explorations had been used by us earlier in family guidance. Based upon the children's expressed choice for partners at the dining room table which was in discord with their assignments by their parents, we changed the seating positions around the table and thus eliminated the presenting problem: the throwing of food by two siblings at one another across the table. In a residential center for neurologically impaired children such seating arrangements, too, were changed according to the children's sociometric choices, altering the assignments made by the staff. The staff reported that, among other positive changes, the children had unanticipated weight gains (Moreno, Z.T. 1966b).

The idea that runaways often come in strings, not as separate occurrences, was clarified by sociometric investigation of relationships in a residential community of adolescent girls. These did not have to be, as was the case in our family described above, face-to-face relationships, but were an aspect of the network effect. Our family of protagonists was, therefore, at far greater intensity of interaction and influencing one another directly (Moreno, J.L. 1953: 441–445).

The question remains: would this family have done equally well without our guidance? What might have happened if they had not been ready to ask for help? It cannot be answered except to say that we truly do not know. It is conceivable, though not likely, that some felicitous and welcome changes could have occurred by themselves, or that other forms of therapy could have been effective. The fact is that changes were achieved in fairly short order where previously they had not, and that certain patterns related to both past and present appeared to make change difficult without some external intervention.

Roles and role interactions often become fixed and enmesh family members in ways hard to overcome without some outside help. Certainly, the illness of an absent family member hovered pervasively over various developments and that person remained outside of treatment and guidance.

One may consider some of the changes due to cognitive awareness as well as emotional satisfactions, catharsis and integration, or to "reframing." Perhaps one thing that was learned is that in order to *act* differently, one must first learn to *see* the world differently.

> . . . the problems we want to change are not problems related to the properties of objects or of situations – to the *reality of the first order*, as I have proposed to call it . . . but are related to the meaning, the sense, and the value that we have come to attribute to these objects or situations (their *second-order reality*). "It is not the things themselves that worry us, but the opinions that we have about those things," said Epictetus some 1900 years ago.
>
> (Watzlawick 1987: 96)

Therefore, if we were helpful it may well be because we were able to change some of the ways they viewed and experienced one another. This, in turn, led to changing their interactions, leading to achievement of better intrapersonal and interpersonal integration. Not only their inner world changed, but also their outer world, as well as their various fields of interaction.

Is this an artistic approach or a scientific one? Can we really make this distinction in psychotherapy? Is it not, essentially, a mixture or a synthesis?

General comments

Family therapists differ somewhat as to their various approaches. Some will deal only with the total family when all are together and refuse to see any of the members individually; others will combine these two forms of intervention. We leave ourselves the option to see one or another person individually or in subgroups, as the occasion may demand. We state this clearly at the outset, contracting for secrecy of what emerges there, as indicated by the person or persons involved.

The enmeshment of family members and their fear of retaliation outside of therapy may make constant openness difficult to achieve at times. The adults in the family, moreover, bring into the marriage their former life experiences which may have no bearing upon the current situation, yet manage to color it deeply and may distort it. Such findings force us to take a look at these experiences without the constraints of the presence of all the others.

Secrets are generally not supported in family therapy, there being a belief that openness makes for better relationship. We have found that this much-vaunted openness may, in fact, be dangerous and inflict wounds that are lasting and hard to heal. Evaluating this openness with the family is part of the therapeutic alliance and needs careful handling.

The fact that psychodrama is largely done in groups to maximize effectiveness does not mean that we eliminate individual intervention when indicated. We resorted twice to leaving out some members, once having the parents by themselves and once the younger generation. We sensed there was a need for separating them and the resulting interactions were very fruitful. Would they have been the same with all persons present? Of course not. Every participant makes for different interactions. Would these have been more productive? We do not know. We only know that some barriers seemed to be lifted.

What are the differences between the psychodramatic approach to families and other forms? Psychodrama actually fits very well into family therapy theories. What it offers is a set of instruments that are useful in deepening the learning process. One of the most intense is that of role reversal. But the way we deal with time and space in our format is another contribution. Family therapists describe themselves as action oriented. Psychodramatists go further, in that interactions are explored not as reported, but as re-enacted, embodied in time and space, in the spaces in which the events took place. Within a play context the drama soon becomes deadly earnest as the warming-up process proceeds.

A rather good plea for psychodrama may be extracted out of the following statement:

> When there is conflict within the family, family members try to figure out who is right and who is wrong. The harder they try to prove rightness and wrongness, the more the conflict accelerates. Very few people have been trained to become aware of this process. One way to understand the use of conflict or the attempt to prove right and wrong is to see it as a way of defining process and how people position themselves in relation to the other. One of the most helpful procedures for working with families in therapy is to stay tuned in to the process and not get caught up in the content that people present.
>
> (Howells 1979: 12)

Article 33

The Many Faces of Drama

Moreno, Z.T. (1997) Keynote Presentation to the National Association of Drama Therapists, New York University, New York, November 15, 1997

Zerka's comments

I was questioned about my statement in this speech that humans are not mere animals. I say here that drama comes out of our expanded capacity as human animals to form relationships through communication in sequential language that includes access to past, present and future associations, as well as emotions such as anger, fear and hurt.

A teacher of mine from earlier days taught me that a postprandial speech should be like a bikini in that it should be brief, should cover the essential points, and still leave room for further exploration. So it is my sincere hope that this speech will live up to these specifications.

In view of the fact that we are meeting here today to celebrate our involvement in various forms of drama as a healing category, it is a special pleasure to have this happen at New York University because it was in this very place that J.L. Moreno taught psychodrama, group dynamics and sociometry at the Graduate School of Arts and Sciences as adjunct professor from 1949 until 1966, when he was considered superannuated and retired. As he was then 77 years old it was probably just about the right time to end that part of his career. He had been appointed by Dr. Wellman Warner, head of the aforementioned department and his time here was very productive. One of his more celebrated students was Lewis Yablonsky, who also was the person who introduced Dr. Landy to psychodrama at the University of California at Northridge. So in a small way, Dr. Landy, this is a homecoming for me. I especially recall with a good deal of pleasure that J.L. asked me to take over two of the opening sessions of the 1958 semester as he was at that time lecturing and demonstrating around the Mediterranean, having begun his six-week tour in Spain, then going to Italy, Yugoslavia, Greece, Turkey and Israel. One of the outstanding students of that class was Robert Siroka.

One of the questions frequently asked of psychodramatists is "What is the relationship of psychodrama to the legitimate drama and to drama therapy? How do they resemble one another and how do they differ? Are these differences fundamental or only based on a difference of perspective?"

Let me state that I see a red thread running through all of them and that thread relates them. Ancient Greece was the citadel of western civilization, which also brought us the drama. Curiously, not everyone was enthusiastic about the drama.

Plato, for one, declared his outright opposition by explaining in the *Ion* that poets are "transported" while writing their plays and therefore temporarily insane, thus not totally responsible for what they create. He feared that these plays would incite the citizens to be disorderly and disruptive to the State. Perhaps Plato also feared the idea of the Dionysian festivals and the wild involvement of the citizenry in these doings. At the other end of the spectrum we learn from Aristotle that the citizens watching the tragedies are particularly affected by two emotions, pity and fear or even terror on behalf of the protagonist and are thereby cleansed or, as he put it, experience a catharsis of these emotions. In the *Poetics* he also claims that both comedy and tragedy first arose out of improvisation.

That classical tragedy was an outgrowth of the Dionysian festivals is witnessed by the fact that tragedy means "goat song" and Dionysius is most often depicted as being half-goat, half-man, representing both fertility and death. While Plato and Aristotle differed in their points of view, obviously that of Aristotle prevailed and gave drama a respectable basis.

We here today are the heirs of this tradition. But drama did not emerge readily out of the festivals. "The first Dionysian festivals," according to Daniel Boorstin in *The Creators, A History of Heroes of the Imagination*, "were a general community activity that moved about and required no permanent building . . . In the beginning, it seems, all present participated in that festival. Since there was no raised platform for the chorus, all stood on the same level" (Boorstin 1992: 207).

By the way, Boorstin points out that the chorus was circular, certainly a shape that influenced Moreno in the design of his theatre. Near the orchestra, which was a central dancing place, stood the temple of the god so he could witness the celebration:

> Except for the god there were no "spectators."
>
> In festive song and dance, any separation of citizens was invidious. Since the whole community reaped the benefits of the spring-insuring rituals, all should join. But when ritual became drama, a new separation marked the community as a new dimension was added to experience. Now some "acted" while others watched. Citizens became witnesses, with a new set of sentiments.
>
> (Boorstin 1992: 207–208)

Whatever contribution other dramaturges of all stripes have made to drama, it was especially Moreno's task to return the drama to the citizens.

Their creativity and spontaneity having been cut off in the classic form of drama, he now restored the role of the actor to the place of origin, that is within the actor himself. He discarded the script altogether and allowed the spontaneity and creativity of the actor to be the central motivating factor. It was a revolution in the drama.

To return now to the red thread referred to before, all aspects of our work are bound together by the fact that we are heirs of that form of drama, in one way or another. But there is something else that strikes me as significant and that is that they all share what may be called a non-linear philosophy. Let me explain that. It has recently come to my attention, upon becoming slightly familiar with the newer physics, that all forms of drama deviate from Freud in that respect. According to this insight, Freud is in the school of Newton, the old form of physics. He is deterministic, assuming that given certain facts which are the same for two or more individuals, the treatment can proceed along the same lines and the undertaking, if copied correctly, can be repeated by others with the same or at least very similar outcome. As far as I understand Moreno, for instance, he is in the category of the new physics, quantum mechanics, in that the only thing we can be sure of are probabilities and possibilities, but not certainties.

If we agree that all forms of drama therapies deal with spontaneity and creativity, then we are non-linear and not deterministic and we belong to the category of quantum mechanics. A quantum leap, for instance, is a jump of great magnitude on a subatomic scale and a metaphoric jump from what is to what could be without going in between. That is a representation of our practice in the world of therapy. Moreno described spontaneity as a form of energy that is non-conservable and which must be spent as it emerges; its outcome is often unpredictable and when linked to creativity it is most valuable, producing something not pre-existing, something that was not there before and at times totally unrelated to earlier events.

Contrast this with Descartes, who was especially pleased with mathematics because of the certainty and self-evidence of its proofs (Descartes 1960: 7). One can see that he would not be at home in this domain, nor, oddly enough, would Einstein, even though he was largely responsible for the advent of the new physics. He is often quoted as saying, "God does not play dice with the universe." Quantum physicists have found that when particles are propelled at what they know to be an impenetrable barrier, certain particles get through while others do not and they are unable to predict just which will be which. They find that they are dealing with the probability that a number of particles will and some will not proceed through the barrier.

I find it disheartening to read research reports in social sciences that are based on the old mathematical model and the principle of predictability because the fact is that these researchers use a wrong model. Humans are not stars, stones, plants, liquids or animals. Many medical researchers are disappointed with some of their outcomes in applying some substances to animals with positive results only to find that they fail as treatment in humans. They rest their ideas upon John Stuart Mill's notion that "There are such things in nature as parallel cases, that what happens once, will, under a sufficient degree of similarity of circumstances, happen again" (Mill 1843).

One difficulty, it seems to me, lies in determining "the degree of similarity" and how parallel the cases are. This model makes it very difficult for psychodramatists especially, but perhaps also for all those who practice the expressive arts therapies, to point to levels of improvement which can be generally agreed upon. One of Moreno's ideas was that the researcher is part of the research itself and should make the so-called subjects co-researchers, partners in the research and evaluation process. He presented that model in sociometry but it has yet to be used by therapists, as it is difficult to apply.

It was for me delightful, therefore, to read in a recent issue of MIT's *Technology Review* an article called "Subsumed by Science," by Samuel C. Florman which stated: "Even today, engineers agree that intuition, practical experience, and artistic sensibility are at least as important in their work as is the application of scientific theory" (Florman 1997: 39). Or, in an issue of *Parabola* dealing with the geometry of the labyrinth: "There is a definite path and a method that must be followed to the end, but sometimes to understand it fully or wholly, we must investigate the validity of a complementary path or of the same path presented differently" (Conty 1992: 14).

We are dealing with the relationship between two observables, not merely the individual. In quantum mechanics, for instance, "An elementary particle is not an independently existing, unanalyzable entity. It is, in essence, a set of relationships that reach outward to other things" (Conty 1992: 94). Or, quoting a friend of Jung's, the Nobel Prize-winning physicist, Wolfgang Pauli, "From an inner center the psyche seems to move outward, in the sense of an extraversion, into the physical world" (Zukav 1979: 31).

Is all this beginning to sound as if physics and psychology are finding a meeting place, and if so, how?

In an article written in 1943 by J.L. Moreno, entitled "Sociometry and the Cultural Order", he postulates the concept of the psyche being not inside the human body, but outside of it, the body being enveloped by the psyche. It is this psyche-outside-the-body concept that makes our "meeting of minds" possible, and that is where the human encounter takes place.

Now what meaning do these preliminaries have for the relationship, if any, between all the forms of drama therapy, including psychodrama? I admit that when I looked over the great variety of fascinating presentations in the program of this conference, I was somewhat at a loss to come up with a clear idea of what separates us or where we overlap. So I prefer to sum up our commonalities.

First, I assume we can agree that we all represent a nonlinear set of ideas and that we work in some ways that compare with quantum physics in that we take leaps of the imagination.

Second, a central notion we all cherish is that we are role players and we submit ourselves to what I think of as the discipline of the role. The role and role interaction encompass contact with each other's bodies as well as our minds, on a number of levels and that role interaction makes certain demands on us.

Third, we think of ourselves as heirs of classical drama who have gone beyond that realm and adapted it to the needs of our public.

Fourth, we work as a rule in groups, large or small, and our concern is as much with those who act as with those who do not.

Fifth, we aspire to produce some aspect of relief from pressures and difficulties brought about by life itself and from which we need surcease.

Sixth, in entering the realm of meeting of minds, we interact.

Seventh, we think of ourselves as a combination of artist and scientist and that combination creates subtle and at times difficult challenges for our skills.

Eighth, if we can begin to think of the mind as not being imprisoned in the body, but extending outwards from it, we can understand how we make contact with others on the nonverbal level and in a manner that influences our interaction, positively or negatively. We can then accept that there is between us a new form of energy which partakes of that of all the interactors and produces something new which we could not produce by ourselves, and represents more than the sum of its parts. We are, so to speak, in the flow. That flow is something special to which we all contribute and that Moreno referred to as the effect of tele, which in turn establishes co-conscious and co-unconscious states.

Ninth, we must all touch the autonomous healing center of our clients no matter which particular approach we use.

Because I represent psychodrama, it is not clear to me how much the other drama therapies rely on what I think of as the motor that drives psychodrama, namely role reversal, or how much the discipline of the role is understood. The role enables channels of expression, but what is too often overlooked is that it also creates its own restraints. It is somewhat unfortunate that the idea of catharsis as related to psychodrama has become a leftover from the past because in fact, we have moved beyond that and have begun to be much more supportive of the process of integration, intrapersonally as well as interpersonally or sociometrically. Thinking in terms of the protagonist's social atom, which is frequently revealed only piecemeal in the course of the drama, helps to bring about, on the part of the director, an integration that is more fundamental than an abreactive catharsis. The abreactive catharsis was to a degree inherited from psychoanalysis and it became a stumbling block until the catharsis of integration was highlighted as bringing more complete learning.

Let me explain that by describing a leap of the imagination that brought about healing for a recent protagonist. The protagonist, whom I will call Paul, a 58-year-old male schoolteacher of learning disabled students, sets up a scene from his own high school days in which he, as a single child in a fatherless family, his father having fallen as a soldier in the Second World War, senses his great inferiority. He comes from a poor family. His mother lives with him and his maternal grandparents. The grandfather is the only other male and though he is a good male role model, it is not his very own father. He is silently watching a group of four classmates who have good clothes, have an air of sophistication, talk about their sports-filled weekend at the country club. One of them has a car. In general, he feels like a worm when facing this group of schoolmates, totally deprived. As he sits on the floor, his head bowed while the others stand about looking self-possessed and nonchalant, he soliloquizes about his desolate state.

The director is aware that these others represent a world apart from Paul not merely because of their higher socioeconomic status, but because they have protection, they have fathers. When Paul stops speaking, the director says to him, "They have fathers." "That's right" is his immediate response. This is the sociometric leap on the part of the director. Paul is immediately role reversed into his deceased father and chooses an auxiliary ego to represent him. The auxiliary now kneels in a low-man-on-the-totem-pole position represented by Paul, while Paul in his father's role stands up on a chair which represents heaven and watches himself in his misery.

The father descends, picks Paul up from the floor, embraces and holds him and assures him that he is a fine young man and does not have any basis for feeling below anyone else in this world, no matter how well endowed they may be with worldly goods. Father knows he will develop into a guide for other deprived young people and be a wise mentor to them. The two weep together and at a certain moment the director tells them to reverse roles and now Paul hears his father's supportive declaration. Is this abreactive catharsis? By no means; it is an integrative one. Paul is strengthened by the presence of his father in a body, not only in his imagination, or as a shadowy figure from the past.

This also can be described as the psyche of the protagonist thrust outwards, meeting the psyche of the director so that the two connect, unspoken at first, and the need is brought to light.

The drama within is brought out into the open. That is what we all try, in our own fashion and with our own skills, to achieve.

Let me end with a declaration of what humanity means as expressed by a well-known therapist, Virginia Satir. The message was printed on a greeting card sent to me by a friend.

I want to love
You
Without clutching,
Appreciate you without
Judging
Join you without invading,
Invite you without demanding,
Leave you without
Guilt,
Criticize you
Without blaming,
And help you without insulting.
If I can have the same
From you
Then we can truly meet and
Enrich each other.

That is the red thread that ties all of us together. Thank you.

Chapter 5

The New Millenium and Beyond

2000–present

What is maturity?
Wisdom garnered
at the edges of life?
Insights gained
in dark corners
of the mind?
Happiness and
contentment with
small things?
The ability
to walk
at measured pace
where once
one flew,
no space
too great
or dangerously beckoning?
The strength
to look
at others
without fear
or rancor
acerbity or hate?
Palpable awareness
of their pain?

Compassion
at their anguish,
joy
at their joy?
Peace in the knowledge
of one's own
limitations?
Or,
Is it merely
laughter
in the gut?

From *Love Songs to Life*
Zerka T. Moreno

Article 34

In the Spirit of Two Thousand

Moreno, Z.T. (2000) Plenary Session Address to the American Society of Group Psychotherapy and Psychodrama, New York, March 21, 2000

Zerka's comments

I took this opportunity, on the occasion of the dawn of a new millenium, to let fly my thoughts, concerns, dreams and wishes to my psychodrama family.

Dear Friends and Colleagues:

It is indeed an honor to be asked to open this particular meeting of our Society, marking as it does the first year of the Millenium. I might say, along with Mark Twain, "If I had known I would live this long, I'd have taken better care of myself," but then it seems that nature was rather kind to me and either forgave my trespasses or they were offset by some fairly good genes. Something to be grateful for because at my age, there are many good friends who are no longer among us.

It is an opportunity for me to cover some ground of the past, before looking at what my dreams of the future are. My reason for doing that is that as Moreno's companion for 33 years, there were many gems of wisdom he produced but either never wrote down or created them at a moment's notice without taking them further into his theoretical framework.

So it occurred to me to point to an aspect of our work that is rather frequently ignored or overlooked. I refer to Moreno's idea of the warming up process. I note that Bill Wysong did a pre-conference workshop on this topic, and that is commendable. But too often we do not recognize the weight of this process in everyday life or in our work with groups of individuals. For instance, how often do we take the time to inquire from ourselves or our protagonists, "What was your warm-up to this session today? What are you carrying with you that needs some attention? How is your warm-up going to affect the process we are dealing with? And how can we change it if it is not a salutary or productive one?"

What I have gleaned from the warming up process over the years is best considered as follows: an overheated warm-up may lead to inappropriate interaction. An under-heated warm-up leaves us without spontaneity or creativity. And by the way, this applies equally to us in the role of therapist. The warming-up process is a complex phenomenon. Moreno sometimes referred to a number of starters; for example, coffee, alcohol, drugs and cigarettes are chemical starters. Some people need them to be available for social contact with others and depend on them. Physical starters are stretching, jumping on the spot, breathing deeply before a challenging entry, slapping one's body to get warmer, or running to an appointment. Mental starters are imaging and meditation.

Not so well known is Moreno's idea of the three dimensions of the personality, namely the Director, the Actor and the Observer. The Director issues orders to the organism, the Actor carries them out and the Observer watches, makes notes and comments on the Actor's performance. That Observer, a little Jiminy Cricket, may be sitting on one's shoulder, sometimes whispering in one's ear. How often do we hear that little voice that might say: "You're bungling this, you know." Or perhaps less often it might give one a positive stroke: "Good work, well done."

Seen from this perspective, it is clear that both intrapersonal and interpersonal conflict may result in discomfort at the least, in anxiety at its worst, when there is improper interplay between the three functions. Let us take a look at what sort of conditions such improper balance may produce.

Let us deal with the lack of the Observer in familiar situations. Having studied how people go through daily routines, such as their warm-up to getting up in the morning or preparing to go to bed at night, I was struck by how little attention we pay to what and how we are doing. We seem to have, over time, produced a deep track, going over the territory in the same way, as if we are in a groove that carries us along. These morning and night rituals may be so routinized that we no longer have to expend any energy or to think about them. One just goes through the motions. The Director is in charge first, the Actor carries out the demands and pursues the task, the Observer seems to be either absent or asleep. An example most of us can identify with is driving over a familiar route. Suddenly we find ourselves in part of the route without remembering how we got there, and yet maybe ten minutes have gone by. Where were we? Were we on automatic pilot and, if so, how does that happen? What does this absence of the Observer mean? Can it be dangerous if the groove we have carved carries us along without our active presence?

Now let us look at the converse, that of too overgrown an Observer. Because the Observer is not always supportive, it can produce anxiety. Possibly persons suffering from anxiety attacks exhibit this kind of imbalance in that the Observer is not merely overgrown but also too critical. Recalling that anxiety and spontaneity are functions of one another, when anxiety rises, spontaneity goes down; when spontaneity rises, anxiety goes down. Imbuing every day with spontaneity and creativity is the real task, the way to make life more meaningful. Thus spontaneity training, which superficially seems like a contradiction if not an oxymoron, is often the way for treatment to be taken.

Another problem with the track or groove that has been worn deeply is that it does not allow easily for interruption or a change of direction. When the Actor is in that groove which has its own dynamics, any intervening barrier makes a heavy demand on spontaneity. Deviating from the track means creating a new track, which means focusing on the here and now and finding a different route. I recall times when Merlyn, my companion for 21 years, and I sometimes had a cranky warm-up in the morning. When we met there was not much heat between us. We decided to scrap that warm-up, return to our previous spaces, come out and meet again, as if we saw each other for the first time, then we made our good morning greeting over again in a pleasant manner. We had to overcome the intervening barrier first before we could change the groove.

The depth of the track one has worn for oneself, if allowed to be deepened over time, may make deviation impossible. This may account for the rigidity of behavior and attitude observed in some elderly folk. Being able to maintain a modicum of freshness of experience can offset this effect. That is what spontaneity and creativity are about. The wrong warm-up routine in the morning may, in fact, ruin the rest of the day, while a false warm-up routine in the evening can, and often does, ruin one's night's sleep or make dream life unpleasant. Here meditation or relaxation techniques can be helpful by changing the warm-up track.

I will always be grateful for my training with psychotic patients because it taught me so much. A common finding in working with them was that when they came out of their most active phase and were brought into the theater to review their status and focus on their current needs for therapy, we often learned that they could not account for their actions. They were unable to recall how they had behaved. When we reconstructed some of their interactions with us by way of the mirror technique, while they watched us, they claimed they had never done such and so. At this stage they were not yet entirely safe to be discharged but not too fragile for this work to be undertaken. When they were faced with the truth by those with whom they had good sociometric contact, a sufficiently positive tele interaction, they could begin to look at what they had produced during their recent past. Was this a strong form of resistance? We decided this was far too simplistic an explanation. After all, they trusted us enough to allow us to plunge them back into some of the most feared aspects of their experience. There had to be another answer.

This same finding is described in psychiatric texts today, this phenomenon of the excited manic phase especially in bi-polar illness, namely that such patients cannot recall their very own behavior. They tend to fiercely deny it and it is generally accepted that they truly have no memory of it. We asked ourselves how this was possible. Our understanding of the warming up process in the three functions of the personality pointed the way to an explanation. When the protagonist is in the white heat of the act hunger syndrome, in the function of the Actor, the other two functions, those of the Director and Observer, have been burned away. The overheated Actorial function has completely taken over. It is, therefore, not correct to assume that patients are denying or resisting or repressing, because one can only repress that which has been observed and recorded. In this state of white heat there can be no recording and thus no recalling. The Observer function has been obliterated. Thus, no observing and no recording mean no remembering. It is not denial, repressing, lying or malingering. It is a blank.

Moreno decided that this was a dangerous situation for an adult, simply to lose months of living as if in a void. We made it part of the treatment program to reconstruct those months with auxiliary egos, in the mirror function, playing out the behavior of the patient who was watching. From time to time a small memory occurred, in a flash, but it was rarely a total Gestalt. More often there simply was no memory. When the mirroring was completed, the patient was allowed to be in his or her own role and encouraged to restore the situation as they saw fit. It was a very basic part of the treatment not to leave the patient in a no-man's land. It was also a corrective experience, an opportunity for acting-in.

The psychotic patient shows us the extreme aspect of the act-hunger syndrome. But we ourselves are often involved in situations in which we do not see ourselves. The idea in the olden days, as pronounced in classical psychoanalysis, that we must make the unconscious conscious is a chimera, a mythological fire-breathing monster. We just are not able to be that conscious, even if we are not psychotic. Besides, memory is so fallible. The most fascinating and confusing scenes in which psychodrama directors are involved are those dealing with families in which every person in the interaction has a completely different memory of what happened. Perhaps being 100% conscious is only possible if we lose the Director and Actor and just let the Observer take over, which would mean, of course, that we are totally inactive. But are even contemplatives completely conscious or merely observing the inner world?

So the warming up process involves us in these three functions with other persons, whose Director, Actor and Observer are also in action. This particular way of looking at interaction has not been sufficiently dealt with in either practice or literature. It is the balance between these three functions, in interaction with these same functions in the inter-actor, or actors, that makes our life so challenging. Research in this area should prove productive and fascinating. The problem is how to construct such research without upsetting the Actor.

So much for the warming up process.

There is another idea that has barely been touched upon in the past, and that is the phenomenon of the "psychodramatic baby" or "fantasy child."

In the course of working with married couples, we came across this phenomenon in their role as parents. Men as well as women may carry in their fantasy the image of their perfect child. It is not simply their ego ideal of a better version of themselves, it is a projection of "what their child must be like," a form of transference to an unborn ideal offspring. In families where this phenomenon takes over, one hears complaints from parents which sound like: "I don't understand you," "Why can't you be like so-and so?," "You are not listening to me," or some such remark. What is actually happening is that the parents in question place a mask over the face of the real child, the mask being that of the preferred kind of child, or fantasy child. In fact, it is the parent who is not seeing, hearing or listening to the child s/he is facing, but relating to some not-quite-here reality. This kind of interaction inevitably leads to greater distancing and difficulties between the partners and makes for distraught family members. Regrettably, it is found fairly frequently.

Our dealing with this type of intra-personal disturbance which manifests itself interpersonally, has been to treat the parent without the child present, allowing the parent to give birth, emotionally, to the ideal child. It may be necessary for the parent to live out this relationship through several sequential, developmental stages of what would be the child's normal development, at crucial stages of the life span. Once the parent has had satisfaction this way, the result is often that s/he can begin to see the real child more clearly, sometimes even finding some correspondences between that child and the fantasy one, and thus may be enabled to be more readily available for interaction with the real one. It follows an adage pronounced by George Bernard Shaw: "There is only one greater tragedy than not getting what you want, and that is getting what you want." Could it be that you no longer want it so much once you have it? Could that also be one of the problems we have with monogamy?

That brings me to another favorite topic that greatly preoccupies me and my thinking. Some of you have already heard me say this, but allow me to enlarge upon it here. Noting the number of divorces, single parents, neglected children both in and out of families, I have arrived at the conclusion that monogamy is not for the masses but for a small aristocracy. Those partners who can remain wed over many years and maintain a loving relationship we should honor and give medals for their achievement. The masses, on the other hand, suffer from what I call a sociometrically contraindicated condition known among us as monogamy. Why do I dare to make that diagnosis? Look around you. How many friends or relatives do you have who are either unhappily married, or have been divorced, some more than once, and how many are separated as compared to those who you can see are still happy to be together? How many of you here have been divorced? How many live separately from former mates? How many are single parents or have been single parents in the past? Is this what we are supposed to be ready to deal with when we get married? Are not the statistics of divorce exceeding those of marriage?

I realize that many people live and procreate together who are not legally married but as far as I am concerned, they are well and truly wed anyway. What we have is sequential or serial monogamy, that is, of course, not what is implied in the word monogamy, which the dictionary states to be the practice of being married once in a lifetime, or having only one mate. Even many who appear to be monogamous have extramarital relationships. I have had several female friends of my own who have told me that their extramarital relationship made their marriage possible. I have heard a French woman say, "I am always happier when my husband has a loving mistress because then he is so much more loving to me." Is that what monogamy is supposed to stand for? Or is it more a sort of social disease one just puts up with?

Why do we see these things occurring so generally? Maybe looking at this from the role repertoire system can throw some light upon it. We have observed that potentially we have a far larger role repertoire than life may call upon to be fulfilled. Roles develop and change and die out and project themselves into our lives without us always having control over that process. Assuming that we actualize only 10% of our role potential, it can well be imagined that we are neglecting the other 90%.

What happens when a new role suddenly thrusts itself into our awareness? Roles need interactors. Look at a couple's set of actualized roles and study how well they relate to those of their mate. But look also at their Directorial and Observer functions and see how well they mesh, intra-personally as well as inter-personally. What if one partner has a central role, one that is very important to that person, for instance the role of the parent, and the mate absolutely rejects that role, both for himself or herself and the mate? I know of a number of people whose marriages broke up over those decisions. Or, take another view, namely that both do want to be parents but each partner has a very different perception of how each of the partners should play that role. Is this a situation that demands intervention or are we just going to allow the offspring to become the battlefield? In other words, even if the partner has the role, the way in which it wants to manifest may be totally objectionable to the mate. Or imagine, as is often the case, that no new roles have come into their interaction and one or both partners experience role fatigue and boredom. Isn't this where the sexual arena is fraught with danger? Or, let us look at the fact that a role that was mutually productive for the partners dies out in one of them, or an entirely new role arises out of that formerly quiescent role repertoire pool, and the partner has no counter-role for it.

Can you all see the precipices these partners are teetering on? A classical example of a new role thrusting itself upon a family is that described in fictional form by Somerset Maugham of Gauguin in *The Moon and*

Sixpence. Gauguin was a highly respected member of the Paris Stock Exchange when, seemingly out of nowhere, arose the role of the creative artist. Surely the people of Tahiti had no sense of what it meant, that role, but at least they allowed him to be, which was more than could be said of the Paris of his former life. This "white heat of intensity" of the creative artist role burned all that away. Now imagine what happened back home. His wife lost her upper middle class status, her husband, the supporter of her and the two children, her erstwhile lover, the father of her children, and her physical and emotional partner, to mention but a few role interactions. It is likely that she and his former social atom thought him to have gone mad, and in fact, we see this type of changing of the personality in the psychotic. Being left without her protector and that of the children, she was forced to return with them to her own country, Sweden, there to be taken care of by her own family.

Artists often do not require a partner in marriage, they require inspiration and support for their ideas. Look at Picasso: he was brutal to his women even as they flocked to him. There is rather little reciprocity in that role structure. So much for a glimpse of the nature of role interaction in marriage. Our families need help. I will return to this later on in this presentation.

Then there is the mysterious aspect of human interrelations known as tele. Tele has been defined in a number of ways, as the glue that makes human contact possible and meaningful, the cement that ties people together. It is the projection of a unit of feeling into space, upon one or more others, enabling the viewer to see and appreciate the reality of that other and to have that view confirmed, as well as having the partner view the first person in a similar manner.

Recently I returned to a significant contribution of Moreno's, one among many, entitled "Sociometry and the Cultural Order," in which the following can be found:

> The biological picture of an individual places the psyche *within* the body (as an epiphenomenon). In the sociometric picture of the individual (person) the psyche appears as outside the body, the body is surrounded by the psyche and the psyche surrounded by and interwoven into the social and cultural atom.
>
> (Moreno, J.L. 1943: 319)

Another, still earlier version of a description of tele can be found in *The Theatre of Spontaneity*, written in German and published in 1924. Here is that quote as it appears in the English version:

> Medial understanding. On the legitimate stage our five senses seem to suffice; in spontaneous interplay a sixth sense is developed more and more for the partner's feelings. There are players who are connected

> with one another by an invisible correspondence of feelings, who have a sort of heightened sensitivity for their mutual inner processes. One gesture is sufficient and often they do not have to look at one another, they are telepathic for one another. They communicate through a new sense, as if by a "medial understanding." The more this sense is developed the greater is the talent for spontaneity, all other conditions being equal.
>
> (Moreno, J.L. 1947: 68)

The existence of tele has been experimentally validated. I am not aware that the same can be said of transference, which remains in the subjective and observational realm of the therapist. In *Who Shall Survive?* there is a chapter entitled "Sociometric Measurement of Social Configurations Based on Deviations from Chance," and I quote: "The chief hypothesis to be tested is the existence of and the degree to which a hypothetical factor, 'tele' operates in the formation of groupings." Without going into all the details of this study of twenty-six girls residing together in a single cottage at the Training School for Girls in Hudson, NY, the study proved quite conclusively that over and beyond chance based upon pulling three names out of a hat, and on chi-square test, the actual sociometric mutual choices were way beyond the chance projections. The factor responsible for this was declared to be tele.

Consider now, how far tele can stretch. It is my opinion that many wise men of India must have an enormous tele field. Here is such an example: I had a student in Finland who had gone to India to meet Shri Baba after several of his friends had gone to meet this man and had returned home full of the magnificence of their experience. As he was a therapist he could not get away at once and it took him six months before he was able to make the journey himself. Upon arriving at the ashram and being invited in to meet Shri Baba this enlightened man said to him: "Where have you been? I have been waiting for you for six months." Where is his tele? Another person, from another country, who is a disciple of this same guru, and who has been to India a number of times to bask in this man's presence informed me that when he walked outside the village at night, went up on a little hill and turned around to look at the village, he was astounded to see an enormous white halo surrounding this man's village. Apparently his energy, his telic talent, transforms the physical space around him and imbues it with this light.

A question that preoccupies me of late, and which is true for ourselves as therapists as much as for our protagonists and group members is, "Where *is* your tele, how is it affecting you and those in your social or cultural atom?" We must work on our tele connections and clean them of transference because our tele is out there somewhere, creating effects of all sorts, impacting on those it reaches.

An ongoing concern of mine is the problem of subjective perception. How can we be sure, either as protagonist or as therapist, that the presented perception is correct? The answer is, of course, that one can never be certain. I recall, for instance, doing a psychodrama about my relationship with my mother, early in my training. While I was in the mode of the actor, my inner observer spoke up for an instant and said to me: "Is this really the way she is? You make her appear to be almost monstrous." My actorial dimension replied, "But in this situation that is the way I experienced her." It must be reported that all this work I did on the relationship profoundly altered it for the better. But it took a lot of hard work.

When I raised this issue of the so-called correct perception with Moreno, his answer was: "But that is all you have. You can only present what is true for you. And that is how I approach the psychotic patient," he went on. "When a patient presents me with his or her perception of life, that is where we start, no matter how bizarre or distorted that perception may be. By accepting it and working it through, perhaps that is where the change can be facilitated and correction can enter into the picture." What he was teaching me was that perception is subject to change. Facts may not change but the way we perceive and deal with them can change. That gives us hope.

In the course of the years, I teach students over and over: "No human being has total perception of another. It is simply not given to us. We perceive parts, but not that other being's totality." At best, we may have partial perception, but too often it is distorted, or weak or disturbed and in need of clarification.

A remarkable event takes place in our life when someone we think we know well reveals himself or herself to us in a totally new way. We are then seeing aspects of that person which were invisible to us. That does not mean they were not there, it means we were blind to them. How many of you have had such an experience yourselves? It also means, inevitably, that it changes our relationship to that person as well, or at least it should, provided we have the spontaneity to meet that new perception.

There is the classic story of the prodigal son who returns home after seven years and is amazed how much his father has learned in those years. Or, as each of us may have experienced, we leave our familial and familiar home to go to camp or to school and upon returning, find the house has shrunk. The respect with which Moreno approached psychotic patients was due to the fact that he could accept their subjective perceptions, however skewed at that moment. It is probable that this is an area within which mediation works. Psychodrama often reveals aspects of the protagonists which were simply not visible before. While these may not always be appealing in themselves, we still need to deal with them. Of the appealing ones Moreno said that psychodrama is a "cosmetic for the psyche."

Appreciation for our subjective perceptions is a starting point for our change; having them accepted, no matter how absurd or inane, is a way of being able to release them. Role reversal with the significant other is obviously another way to open up our possibility for perceptual change.

Now I'd like to take a look at what has happened to the problem of catharsis. My sense is that something rather unfortunate has come to pass in that area, because of the frequent reference to psychodrama being designated as a way to achieve relief of various emotional tensions. The concern I have about it is that framing the process this way limits the idea of catharsis to what we must define as a "catharsis of abreaction," whereas in my experience that type of catharsis is not really the goal of our work. The catharsis of integration, intra-personally and interpersonally, while much less overt, is the real end we need to reach. It gets short shrift from those who strive for an immediate and obvious effect, such as crying, screaming, throwing things, etc., which, while they may be called for at times, are not the be-all and end-all of our quest.

It is my opinion, perhaps faulty, that much of this confusion came about because Moreno was very much a dramatist, a showman. His isolated position seemed to impel him to try to prove effectiveness to the psychiatric fraternity. These were not trained to see immediate change in a patient and when it happened so dramatically in Moreno's demonstrations, tended to put it down to his particular personality, that no one else could produce these effects, much to the chagrin of Moreno who, of course, set out to prove that this was a method that could be passed on to others and not subject to the power of magic of a single individual, namely himself.

But somehow, that idea stuck. It is time to disenchant the newcomers, to warn them that the real route to spontaneity and creativity is a rather different one. My injunction to students has therefore been for many moons: "Your protagonist does not owe you a catharsis. The process works in its own way and in its own time." It works because the human mind is basically psychodramatic. Psychodrama can well be considered a homeopathic remedy.

Our work is not linear. That is somewhat disconcerting to a lot of therapists who have been trained in a different philosophy. Like the quantum physicists, psychodramatists and sociometrists deal with uncertainties and possibilities. If you can use your creativity to take yourself, your protagonists and auxiliary egos into surplus reality, the reality beyond reality and even imagination, you will not be uncomfortable in this realm.

Today, therapists are asking themselves why, with all this therapy going on, the collective level of living is so unsettled, to say the least. If we question why upheavals on the macro-sociological level happen in spite of greater psychological insights and decades of psychotherapy perhaps an explanation can be found in the field of physics. Physicists, for instance, have found that rules which govern the macro-physical world, such as the magnetic field, do not apply on the micro-physical, subatomic level. Bacteria and viruses invisibly invade humans on the macro-sociological level in the form of pestilences and epidemics. Is, therefore, Moreno's hypothesis not possible, namely that these macro-sociological upheavals are, in fact, evidence of the micro-sociological problems or interpersonal ones? If so, we may have a link between the two areas and that means we are very much needed as future world workers. It also means we have to work on our own tele, not just that of our clients. Not much pursued is the idea of one's "autotele," the tele of one's self. That has to be in balance in terms of the Director, the Actor and the Observer.

Psychodrama is not just for recreating a disturbing experience. It is meant to do, undo, redo and reintegrate, producing closure. Subjective perceptions may be distorted in ways only others can reveal to us, therefore in that corrective interaction we can accept and integrate the correction. We are continuously processing our lives; we need to actively correct the past in ourselves and to help others to do so. Role reversal is a profound corrective and, if used with positive tele, a true reorientation.

When people ask me what changes I have made in the method, changes from what I was taught, I think these have been especially in four areas. The first is in the psychological history of the protagonist. Perhaps because Moreno wanted to distinguish himself clearly from Freud, he often started the protagonist with the present and moved that person into the future. My own experience was that protagonists bring their past with them, if not always as a striking trauma as Freud stipulated, but certainly with a good deal of ballast. That same ballast made moving into even the present difficult to overcome, so I began to try to help protagonists to clean up the past; that made moving into the living present and the future to come easier.

The other is in the way I use doubles. Because Moreno worked with very disturbed patients whose ideation was often extremely bizarre, he used doubles to enable him to understand the patient but also because the doubles were able to interpret the patient to him. The training I received was based on the premise that the patient cannot explain what is going on, often does not speak, therefore the double must speak and help to clarify the inner contents. Then, when we began to train others in this work, it struck me that it is really the work of the protagonist to enter into the deeper layers, that too often relying on the double to do this work made this an intellectual rather than an emotional exercise. It was actually a young male protagonist who, in a scene with his lady love, was so angered by her that he jumped up and said, "And now I must be my own double because nobody here can imagine how enraged and disappointed I am." He stood behind his chair, as his very own double, and let her have it. I made this the way to go henceforth. So now my instructions to the double are: "The protagonist really knows how s/he feels, so s/he will be her or his own double. You represent the outside." I am always grateful to learn from the process itself that there are new ways to do things.

The third area is probably in my use of role reversal, and keeping the protagonist in the role of the significant other for a long time. Indeed, I have run an entire session, except for the final scene, with a protagonist who knew that this was her task. She played several scenes in her father's role first, facing herself. She never fell out of it nor corrected the auxiliary in her role, but indicated when asked that the interaction was correct in its essentials. Another way I use role reversal is to have the protagonist in the reverse role position and interview that person, explaining the position of the protagonist and often challenging the protagonist in that role reversed position. Perhaps the protagonist has to be rather well integrated for this to work. And often they enjoy the ethical anger I express on their behalf. This challenging stand has to be carefully handled in order not to confuse the protagonist.

The fourth area is in the use of sharing. When sharing was first introduced by Moreno, he was concerned about the protagonist having denuded himself or herself through the drama; he declared this to be a form of love and categorically stated that love can only be repaid with love. Indeed, he disliked the term feedback, which, he reminded us, arises out of two electrical appliances being in discord with one another and creating nasty noises. He thought we should call it "love back." Sharing was regarded as the way to reintegrate the protagonist back into the group, but also as a form of group psychotherapy for the persons present. He declared it to be the group psychotherapy aspect of the psychodrama, but sharing is more focused than in the verbal form, because we have had a common experience which has touched us in a unique way.

The change I introduced was to have the auxiliary egos, who have been so profoundly involved in the drama, to share first, and from two aspects: from the role they portrayed and in what way the drama reflected their very own history. The depth with which auxiliaries are able to interpret the role of the absentee, often so dead right that the protagonist is hardly able to believe that they are strangers, is a repeatedly astounding experience. It brings the group members together into greater cohesiveness and facilitates their sharing. Another profit from this sharing by the auxiliary egos is that it enables them to clear out the role; it helps de-role them. When that process of de-roling is complete, the protagonist is asked to look at the auxiliary egos and to confirm that they no longer represent the absent other or others; this is especially important if any absent other represents a threatening or oppressive figure to the protagonist. Upon completion of this process the rest of the group members are invited to share.

That idea of de-roling arose during the training sessions, and not when Moreno was still with us. I cannot remember during my training ever having been asked if I needed to clean out a role; it was simply assumed that you would do this spontaneously and by yourself; aware that this role was imposed upon you by another, perhaps not even part of your role repertoire. To the extent that it is, however, a remnant of one's own role or a rejected one, it may continue to cling beyond its usefulness. In the case of working with the psychotic or severely disturbed patients, we were expected to jump in and out of roles while remaining aware that this was the patient's reality, not one's own. It may well be that my training was helpful in distancing me from the protagonist after the work, and in keeping my own status intact. Clearly, when working with peers, that creates a rather different type of contact, one in which meetings outside the theater take place. Thus de-roling and re-identifying oneself becomes more urgent.

So much for the past; it is time to turn to what I hope the future of this amazing method might be. Perhaps some of you will be inspired to pursue some of these ideas in practice. I certainly hope so, but I also think that they may be economically productive. Here is what I see as necessary to be established in the future.

1 Twenty-four-hour emergency psychodrama clinics in every community where people can come to work out their difficulties before violence or suicide ensues. These should be everywhere people live.
2 A pre-marital role testing and counseling center, where young and old can come to try out in action their present role structure and their future expectations, in terms of their own roles and those of their partners. A role testing prediction center for marriage or for living together means enabling them to test themselves and their partners to be, both alone and with one another.
3 Considering the problems we see in our families, some fine prophylactic and preventive work can be done. Some of the time this may mean breaking up couples before they make that final commitment, when it becomes clear that the relationship is not a viable one for the future. My sense is that this might well be a money making proposition for those who run such a clinic.
4 A school for would-be parents *before* the couple decides to have children; a place where they can first of all cleanse themselves of their own dysfunctional family background, so they do not duplicate the path of their parents. How often have we sworn to ourselves when young not to commit the missteps of our parents, only to find ourselves, to our horror, speaking to our child in such a way as to realize: "Oh, my god, I sound just like my mother or father." Let's give the protagonists a chance to toss their ballast overboard. Maybe, just maybe, we may reduce unhappiness and the rush to the divorce court. Having thus been prepared, they can undertake role tests for themselves and their partners, to check out how ready they are to become parents and how well they are able to fit each other as parents, partners in this most sensitive and trying role interaction.
5 It follows out of this that there should be a school for those who are already parents and who are having problems with that partnership as

well as with the children. It may be that they will require a similar training period as for the would-be parents. One of the essential aspects of both these sets of persons is learning to double and role reverse with their parents and their children.

6 A psychodramatist in every school system, one also skilled in sociometric intervention; that person might be able to spot the isolated and disenchanted ones, the potential trouble makers and violent actor-outers; they need a place to get action counseling but also intervention in the school setting itself. Right now we have parents who are afraid to send their children to school; is this a community we want to perpetuate?

7 A psychodramatist in every physical hospital, to help doctors and nurses and administrators to role reverse with some of their patients. I could tell you some horror stories of my own about the emotional abuse and emotional neglect of patients, and you probably have some of your own. We may be able not only to humanize the hospital but also to accelerate the rate of recovery.

8 How about one of us in Congress? I do not foresee that as a reality in my lifetime, but such a person might bring to the so-called representatives of the people some sense of the real concerns of their constituents. Such a task might seem almost superhuman, but treating psychotics was at one time considered impossible as well and there are times when we must ask ourselves if Congress is not a madhouse.

9 What would it be like to have one of us in the White House? Could we help those Presidents who are sexomanic or egomanic or even criminal? It's never been tried, but it's certainly worth considering.

Winston Churchill said: "The empires of the future are the empires of the mind." Let's see how you can exercise that kind of empire.

To end, let me restate for you those topics I have touched upon:

1 the warming up process, how you use it in life and work
2 the meaning of tele and how you find it operates, in all interactions
3 the three dimensions of personality – the Director, the Actor, the Observer – and how you deal with them and what effect your way has on others
4 the psychodramatic baby or child, your own or how you meet it in your protagonist and others in your life
5 the role structure in marriage, its import and effect; new roles that arise and disturb the marriage; old roles that refuse to die out
6 the problem of subjective perception and how you deal with it
7 the future of our work, in the clinics and other areas of life.

Article 35

The Function of "Tele" in Human Relations*

Moreno, Z.T. (2000) In J. Zeig (ed.), *The Evolution of Psychotherapy: A Meeting of the Minds*, Phoenix, AZ: Erickson Foundation Press

Zerka's comments

I decided to present on this topic because I didn't think many of the participants ever knew about tele. I wanted to show how Moreno went beyond the concepts of transference and counter-transference.

Many years ago I found in a New-Age journal a poem written by Theodore Roszak. It struck me once more that poets are able to convey in a few words what others state in a far less cogent way, and in a manner which opens us to new perceptions. It runs as follows, and not only sums up for me the very essence of the therapeutic relationship, but also represents an ideal model for all human interactions:

> You and I . . .
> We meet as strangers, each carrying a mystery within us.
> I cannot say who you are: I may never know you completely.
> But I trust that you are a person in your own right, possessed of a beauty and value that are the earth's richest treasures.
> So I make this promise to you:
> I will impose no identities upon you, and invite you to become yourself without shame or fear.
> I will hold open a space for you in the world and defend your right to fill it with an authentic vocation.
> For as long as your search takes, you have my loyalty.

You may ask what this has to do with the topic of "tele." Is this an example of the meaning of that term? What is meant by the word "tele"? How does it differ from empathy or transference? What exactly does it represent? Why is it necessary to introduce such a concept and term? How and what does it add to our understanding of human relations?

Maybe these questions will be elucidated herein. The term itself was introduced by J.L. Moreno in 1934 in his book *Who Shall Survive?* (Moreno, J.L. 1934: 158) in which he reports on his work with people in their living settings, not in the clinic. He first refers to Thales of Miletus who attributed to the magnetic power of ferrous material a "soul." As soon as the physical basis of this phenomenon was recognized, Thales' interpretation was discarded. More than two thousand years later Mesmer postulated an attractive power coming from "animal" bodies. He thought that during hypnosis a magnetic fluid is stored up and that through this medium one individual can act upon another. Since this could not be proven, it was assumed that the phenomena emerging in the process are subjective in origin. Later empathy and transference were described as feelings observed coming from one person to another under certain conditions. Moreno's position was that empathy and transference are both one-way processes and that therefore they cannot build mutuality, since they are projectional, not necessarily based upon the reality of the other. From that perspective transference especially is the dissociative factor. His concern was with what ties persons together, mutually, either positively or negatively, and how that process can be demonstrated in interaction and, above all, in reality.

During his experiments with improvisational theater in Vienna, Moreno reported on some of his findings in the book *Das Stegreiftheater* (Moreno, J.L. 1924: 57): "we could observe that some individuals have for each other a certain sensitivity as if they were chained together by a common soul. When they warm up to a state, they 'click.' It often was not the language symbol which stimulated them." In the English translation, *The Theatre of Spontaneity*, we find the following: "There are players who are connected with one another by an invisible correspondence of feelings, who have a sort of heightened sensitivity for their mutual inner processes . . . They communicate through a new sense, as if by a 'medial' understanding" (Moreno, J.L. 1947: 68).

In his magnum opus *Who Shall Survive?* the term "tele" appears for the first time with this description:

> a feeling complex does not run wildly into space but goes to a certain other person and that other person does not accept this passively like a robot but responds actively with another feeling complex in return. One tele may become inter-locked with another tele, a pair of relations being formed. Tele has no social existence by itself . . . But it is possible to classify it according to the equation of its social expansion, its "social effect."
>
> (Moreno, J.L. 1934: 163)

In the 1953 edition of *Who Shall Survive?* Moreno wrote: "I defined tele as the factor responsible for the increased rate of interaction between members of a group, 'for the increased mutuality of choices surpassing chance possibility'" (Moreno, J.L. 1953: 311–312). And on p. 314: "to express *the simplest unit of feeling transmitted from one individual towards another* we use the term tele, 'distant.'" On p. 53: "Tele is two-way empathy: like a telephone it has two ends."

Another investigator, Paul Deutschberger, stated: "Tele does not operate equally throughout the totality of an individual's social atom, but consists of an horizon in which awareness is great, level of choice expenditure high, and perception of inter-relationships accurate, and an unstructured region, marked by tentative and token choices to which reciprocation is hit-or-miss. This is the area between the chance level and the tele level wherein drives for acceptance and misperceptions about the role of the recipient may cover a range of pathological interpersonal relationships" (Deutschberger 1947: 249).

What distinguishes tele from either one-way empathy or transference is the emphasis on the two-way flow of feelings. Tele must always be considered in terms of mutuality between two or more persons. Both the original idea of empathy (Lipps 1907: 694) and Freud's concept of transference (Freud 1926) do not deal with the response of the "other" involved. From this point of view, the factor of counter-transference is a misnomer and unscientific. "Counter" is defined, among others, as "in the wrong way, contrary to the right course, or to encounter in opposition or combat, or in the reverse direction." Encounter, on the other hand, is defined as "to meet with, especially unexpectedly." Since transference is one-way as well as projectional, it is more precise to say that there are two processes going on, one from the client to the therapist, the other from the therapist to the client.

Whereas the client–therapist side of the transference may be dealt with in the course of therapy, the so-called counter-transference is never permitted to be a part of the therapeutic process; it remains in the dark. It is a parallelogram developing. We have been taught that the sides of a parallelogram meet in infinity. According to Freud, the transference neurosis must be resolved before treatment can be considered completed. But we have found that it may take an infinity for it to be resolved, and it is often the reason why some clients leave psychotherapy or seek help elsewhere.

Another strong distinction among tele, empathy, and transference is that tele is based upon the existential reality of the "other." It involves a mutual recognition of that reality. The major difficulty with transference lies in the impenetrability of the analyst, as deemed absolutely essential to the treatment process. There is no possibility for the client to assess "the reality" of the therapist. That is what the treatment enforces. Moreover, transference was discovered in an artificial setting, not in the stream of life outside. We consider transference the dissociative element, while tele is the cement that bonds people together. Therefore, if a relationship lasts throughout the buffeting of life's events with all its ups and downs, we claim it is based on tele.

To explain the term "social atom," another term coined by Moreno, it is described as "the smallest social unit, not the individual" (Moreno, J.L. 1947: 80). It is constructed by the relationships that revolve around an individual and form the connections with others. There are normally three types of social atoms: the private or personal, the vocational or work, and the socio-cultural. They may change from time to time in their membership but show a certain consistency. It is tele that makes these structures possible and creates the anchorage for them. It is a form of "social intelligence."

There are many forms of tele. It is based on the ability to assess and appreciate the reality of the other and must always be considered from the viewpoint of all the persons involved in the relationships, like sticks with two ends. Any interpersonal relationship encompasses three entities: the two persons plus the specific relationship between them. It is evaluated as the mutually positive, mutually negative, or incongruous, that is, one person choosing another and being either rejected in turn or feeling neutral or indifferent. From this perspective it is responsible for the cohesion or disintegration of a relationship. Mutually positive tele is the glue. Groups formed on the basis of transference are bound to fall apart. It is my belief that this is at least one of the reasons why so many marriages fail. It is particularly in the smallest unit of social interaction, the dyad, that the importance of tele becomes evident.

As with many elements found in nature, tele rarely exists in pure form. It requires cleansing of transference overlay. That is what is meant by working on a relationship. Tele is further complicated by interaction in a variety of roles in life.

Tele in the form of attraction or rejection can occur even between strangers. We have demonstrated over and over that a group of strangers meeting for the very first time already forms invisible bonds. To arrive at tele such a meeting must be cleansed of the transference aspect, with both or all partners willing to peel off the one-way projectional layers they bring into the relationship.

Unfortunately, negative tele expresses itself often more rapidly and clearly, and it too must be cleansed of transference properties to enable a real understanding of the other. It is particularly the reality of the other with which tele must connect. The reality may not always be attractive but at least it is based on a true essence, not a fantasy. Nevertheless, when in psychodrama two such contending individuals are able to role reverse honestly with one another, that negative aspect may become smaller, less significant, and sometimes may even disappear. It is often seen to happen when a rejected person in a group becomes the protagonist and reveals his or her anguish, that the perception of that person changes for members of the group.

If tele is the bond based on mutual recognition of the other, it follows that it is responsible for cohesion or lack of cohesion in a group. To establish the validity of this concept, its existence as well as how it operates, a study was proposed. *"The chief hypothesis to be tested is the existence of and the degree to which a hypothetical factor, 'tele,' operates in the formation of groupings"* (Moreno, J.L. 1953: 623).

A study of a residential training school for girls who inhabited one of the cottages under a housemother was undertaken to determine whether the choices for sitting together at a four-person table at three mealtimes daily would demonstrate that the number of mutual choices, that is, persons choosing one another mutually, would be greater than by chance. The research proceeded on four levels of intervention. The first was to allow the girls to seat themselves a moment after the dining room door was opened, the idea being that they could demonstrate their choices in action and the process could be observed. The result was utter chaos, with some girls sitting by themselves at different tables, not choosing, six other girls fighting over four seats at one table, five at another, one table having only two girls, another being completely empty, and a few girls standing about, looking defeated because their situation was unclear to them. No one was pleased with that opportunity since it did not come about as desired. In fact, it turned into anarchy which in turn became autocracy, the housemother having to intervene; she ordered the girls to sit according to her design, thus overthrowing the notion that laissez-faire is an acceptable solution.

The second approach was constructed mathematically, on the basis of chi-square, to determine what the number of mutual choices thus predicted would be according to chance.

Number three was done by drawing a name out of a box; putting that aside and drawing three names for that first person randomly as seatmates. This process was conducted for all the girls and the results recorded.

Finally, the fourth approach was to ask the girls themselves to write down three persons whom they wanted as tablemates. They were also requested to state their reasons for choosing each one. Obviously, none of the earlier three approaches could cover this aspect of the choice process, and yet the reasons for choice are what highlights the effect of tele. Tele not only relates to mutuality of choice, it also points the way to reciprocity via the reasons for choice. Frequently these duplicate the words used by the partners or are very similar.

The results of the last investigation, the sociometric form, left absolutely no doubt. The number of choices revealed through the sociometric test was far greater than was possible on the basis of chance or shown in the drawing of names. Here are the figures: "The probability of mutual structures is 213% greater in the actual (choice) configuration than in the chance and the number of unreciprocated structures is 35.8% greater by chance than actually" (Moreno, J.L. 1953: 633). So one can truly say: QED the hypothesis that a factor, assumed to be "tele," was responsible for tying people together by mutual choice (Lipps 1907: 694).

A number of later studies have also revealed some surprising and unprecedented effects of the impact of mutual tele and allowing groups to be reconstructed on the basis of choices made by the individuals concerned. One example deals with the reordering of seatmates at long tables in an institution for cerebral palsy children at mealtimes, again three times daily. The seating order was set by the staff. The administration was concerned to reduce problems arising regularly at mealtimes, such as squabbles or fights, breakage of dishes, and especially noise, none of which were controllable or contributed to the children's well-being. The request was for some investigators to come and study the situation and help deal with these concerns in a new fashion. At first the staff balked at any intervention, claiming, as many parents will, that they had made the best possible choices for their charges. We handled that by assuring them that if that were so, any intervention on our part would bear that out.

The children were asked at a group gathering to look around and write down the names of three seatmates. Those who had difficulties with writing were aided by staff as some were rather severely handicapped and could only point a finger or even a toe momentarily. When the records were completed we decided to take the role of the students and seated ourselves at the tables when no one was around. Taking the role of a profoundly spastic child, we came to the simple discovery that we want our seatmates sitting across from us, not next to us since the latter position made eye contact difficult and our uncontrollable movements would interfere with the space of the seatmates. That this had indeed been one of the bases for temper tantrums and fights was clearly highlighted by our role reversal. Armed with this information one of us moved to the other side of the table and sat across from the other. That was found to be far better suited to our needs and became the pattern for the reseating after the test results came in. We became acutely aware that tele involves two dynamic categories for living: namely time and space. With whom we share our time and our space is of critical importance to our welfare.

The seating order was made according to the choices indicated and keeping in mind the "optimal satisfaction," that is, to match the children to ensure that at least one child of their choice sat across the table. We had gained the insight of how determining a factor of physical proximity is in the building of tele.

The results were observed and recorded by staff: accidents, spillages, breakages, temper tantrums and squabbles, as well as noise, were dramatically reduced. However, one month after this sociometrically fertilized emotional soil the most startling finding was reported by medical staff: a general, overall improvement in the physical condition of the entire school population showed up on the health charts, an improvement several times larger than the previous curve for this item, including weight and height. We did not inquire at the time how the learning improved but it may well be assumed that this, too, was positively affected in those children whose physical balance is so precarious (Moreno, Z.T. 1966b: 231–232).

In this case we saw the relationship between observables. We are not linear thinkers. Like quantum physicists, we deal with uncertainties and probabilities; like them we do not assume an objective reality apart from our experience. We cannot observe something without changing it; we merely try to correlate experience correctly. What we learn from these examples is how significant human relations are, how central to our welfare, not only for the psyche but also for the body.

There are other findings that reflect the effect of tele on human relations. Sociometric investigators have reported that rejected, unchosen, isolated individuals within a work setting are the ones who are most frequently absent, ill or worse; they create accidents which are severe, repeated, and involve some of their co-workers as well. Studies of children on the school playgrounds have uncovered similar events among children, those who, for whatever reason, remain outsiders. They equally produce repeat accidents which can be severe and drag other children into their "vortex of misery." It may be evidence for the popular statement that "misery loves company." On the other hand, whenever a high-status child has an accident, it is usually a one-time event, not serious, and does not involve other playmates (Northway 1944). How can we account for these phenomena except by assuming that a lack of tele between people disturbs the possibility of their being rooted in the community? They are unable to partake of the normal give-and-take that happens around them.

School authorities throughout this land should take note and have some sociometric review of the social status of their students if we wish to avoid the kind of aggression of especially young males in our schools that we have witnessed recently. Individual counseling may not be sufficient; it is necessary to study the total school population to uncover these unfortunate beings and integrate them into their group in a more positive manner. It is also necessary to sensitize students to the fact that their negative stand towards some of their fellows and unpleasant behavior may well be a reflection of what they and their peers have produced. Tele awareness is needed to shed some light on their interactions (Hollander & Hollander 2000).

In "Sociometry and the Cultural Order," Moreno wrote in 1943 that perhaps we are mistaken in placing the psyche inside the body, as a biological concept. He suggested that the psyche may well be outside the body, the body being enveloped by the psyche. That would place the psyche "out there." To quote from that paper, the

> resistance against any attempt to break the sacred unity of the individual has one of its roots in the idea that feelings, emotions, ideas,

> must reside in some structure within which it can emerge, and within which it can function or disappear . . . These feelings, emotions and ideas "leave" the organism; where then can they reside? Group research shows that they find their expression between people, in interpersonal and intergroup relations, traveling throughout the network, sometimes visibly, sometimes not, but often without predictable effects. The energy involved in these streams of feelings and moods which feeds them we assume to be "tele."
>
> (Moreno, J.L. 1943: 320)

If these ideas sound far-fetched, let me quote a friend of Jung's, the Nobel Prize winning physicist, Wolfgang Pauli: "From an inner center the psyche seems to move outward, in the sense of an extraversion, into the physical world" (Zukav 1979: 56). Is all this sounding as if physics and psychology are finding a meeting place, and if so, how? Is it not conceivable that this psyche outside the body is making it possible also for our minds to meet and influence one another? That is how and where the human encounter takes place and it requires a two-way corridor to an open field along which to travel.

The expression of tele in sociometric investigation reveals also negative structures and relationships. In our culture positive feelings are valued, admitted, and considered desirable; negative ones are a serious concern. Not being chosen in return, overlooked, neglected or worse, rejected, can be devastating at worst, wounding at best. We identify it with being unloved and therefore unlovable; we become anxious, depressed, and generally feel unworthy. Nevertheless it is a part of reality that not everyone can love us, and actually there is no reason why they should. Sociometric research of children as young as in kindergarten shows quite clearly that even these beings are aware of positive and negative feelings to and from their peers. The sense for tele develops with age but it is already in the young that its effects are felt, even though the sense for mutuality comes gradually. This is clearly seen in the sociograms of childhood in *Who Shall Survive?* (Moreno 1934, 1953: 150–153) and in research by Mary L. Northway (Northway 1960: 455).

The essential reason for doing sociometric investigations is not just to make relationships visible and available for interpretation, but to reconstruct groups to maximize sociostasis and find some resolution to the problem of the unchosen and rejected. These measures are guides towards change in action in life itself. Group members become co-researchers with the investigator for their own groups, not merely verbally but in interaction. It is meant to activate the tele existing in the group and stabilize the relationships.

It is beyond the scope of this paper to go into more detailed reports about the various groups which have been researched, as a great deal of work has already been done and written about. The main problem is first of all that the researcher has the authority not only to investigate but to reorganize the group. Because of that, many of the first investigations were done in closed settings, schools, prisons, the military, but later found applications in industry, clinics and mental hospitals. When the group members realize that the investigation is meant to improve their relationship and interaction with others and find their choices respected and acted upon, the level of the group's morale is greatly enhanced, cooperation insured, and cohesion improved.

To illustrate the great difficulties in obtaining authority to carry out this work, which is probably the major reason why there are now so few who practice it: in all groups studied, groups of a large variety, approximately 15% of persons are found to suffer from some form of isolation. Just imagine what this means in terms of human misery. Project that figure onto the world's population even without considering wars, revolutions, and starvation, and one has some idea of the size of the problem. The studies referred to earlier represent what is called "objective sociometry," in that everyone in the study was involved. True sociometry is done with a view to change the group, not merely as a form of academic exercise (Northway 1960; Northway and Detweiler 1956).

Because of some of the difficulties already mentioned, another form of measuring tele emerged, called "perceptual or subjective sociometry." As the term indicates, it is based on the subjective perception of every individual in a group and of the relationships based between them; this goes for choices and rejections for everyone. When the individuals and their connections are drawn, a perceptual map of the structure of the group emerges. The usual symbol for the male is a triangle, for the female it is a circle. The perceived choices and rejections are drawn between the symbols. Usually the color red is used for attraction, black for rejection, but if colors are not available densities of line can be employed.

Choices are made on action criteria such as: "With whom do you want to work on this committee?" or "With whom do you want to be in this discussion group?" There are circumstances where the negative choices may not be suitable for inclusion and the group should have the right to make that decision, though where groups are in trouble and an investigator is called in, these must be included even if results are not disclosed, as in the case of children and young adults. Reorganization of the group uncovers the choices and rejections to some degree but no specific point is made of it. Group members should be reminded to give reasons for choices and rejections. Choices should not be made on the basis of acquaintance or friendship, as these involve multiple criteria in themselves. They should always be based on a common interaction relevant to the group.

The criterion is the handle around which choices are made. Just as we are multiple role players in life, we are also multiple criteria carriers. No one should be evaluated on the basis of a single criterion. Choice patterns vary from one criterion to another. Perceptual sociograms, feeling ourselves into others, sharpen our sense for tele. It is even recommended that everyone makes up a perceptual sociogram at regular intervals, to assess the state of one's situation on three levels: private, work, and community. All the relevant criteria of a person's world are part of that profile. Our interactions rest upon multiple criteria which are often the source of differences between us, and these may have to be negotiated under given circumstances.

Certain individuals are shown to receive larger numbers of choices or rejections than others; these are called stars of attraction or rejection, but this can only be so determined on a number of criteria; one may be a star in one group and not in another. The criteria determine that.

It is not my purpose here to go into the kinds of structures which are usually found in the sociograms since this information is readily available in a number of books, but it should be pointed out that those who are overchosen often have clear tele contact with others as revealed through their mutual choices, and in the reasons for choice which very frequently are quite similar. Stars often choose one another, which obviously greatly influences and enhances their position in the group. We have found triangles and quadrangles of mutuality in some groups.

There are, on the other end of the scale, others who use their choices only to reject others. These may, in addition, form pairs of rejection, mutually negative tele, and they may also be stars of rejection. Out of this sector come many of the violent actor-outers who may get together in gangs where rage and anger is brought to bear on the bitterly rejected outsiders. The English adage, "thick as thieves," comes to mind. Needless to say, these are the individuals that would require our special attention. We see evidence of their existence almost daily as they deliver death and disaster upon others. Our history, recent as well as past, is replete with examples.

We have observed that tele may die out between people even though they are still alive; on the other hand, it may continue beyond a beloved person's life such as with the dead with whom unfinished business continues to haunt some individuals. In psychodramatic work these ongoing tele-connections are brought to life by auxiliary egos, therapeutic actors who take the role of these beings after the protagonist has shown in role reversal how they are and what they mean to the protagonist. Exploring the sociogram of life and death, we work this way with suicidal patients, many of whom have suffered recent loss or losses. If the sociogram of life is greatly impoverished, the pull from the sociogram of death threatens to pull protagonists over to the other side. Impoverishment of tele connections in life throws the intensity of the tele of the dead into bright relief, making the latter more alluring. Working with this type of client and having the protagonist role-reverse in the drama with the lost beloved while the auxiliary ego portrays the client, I have never yet found that the beloved other gives the protagonist permission to join him or her. On one occasion when the protagonist in his deceased alcoholic father's role wanted to draw him over, the protagonist immediately reversed back into his own role, facing the auxiliary ego father, and very firmly informed him that he knew his father wanted to have him join him, but he was not going to follow his negative example: he chose to live. The ongoing power of tele is clearly demonstrated, whether positive or negative, even when the recipient is absent. When an important relationship is lost, we actually lose two entities; the person plus the specific relationship, both of which are carriers of tele.

Quoting Immanuel Kant: "Sensibility and understanding must be brought into connection with each other by means . . . of imagination, because otherwise the former, though indeed yielding appearances, would supply no objects of empirical knowledge, hence no experience" (Arendt 1982: 81). Perhaps tele can be understood as combining sensibility and understanding. My own interpretation of the essence of tele is "liking, loving and respecting in one." Too often tele is split and clients say, "I like you but I don't love you," or the converse, "I love you but I don't like you."

Another aspect of the function of tele is to set up islands of security between humans. In a world plagued by uncertainties, this is essential. Psychodrama deals with uncertainties and unpredictabilities and tries, in action, to make sense of them. The genuinely interactive purpose of tele makes the process relevant and admissible. For those who do not partake of this security, the rejected or unchosen life is a morass of unlived possibilities. In her book *The Human Condition* Hannah Arendt said, "The remedy for unpredictability, for the chaotic uncertainty of the future, is contained in the faculty to make and keep promises" (Arendt 1958: 237). In Robert Frost's words: "For I have promises to keep and miles to go before I sleep." Sensing that the other will keep promises is a core experience in the exchange of tele.

Action therapies lead the protagonist into interaction with others in a safe setting, thus planting the seeds for tele connections otherwise not available. Hannah Arendt reflected upon the meaning of action:

> Action, as distinguished from fabrication, is never possible in isolation; to be isolated is to be deprived of the capacity to act . . . Action, moreover, no matter what its specific content, always establishes relationships and therefore has an inherent tendency to force open all limitations and cut across all boundaries.
>
> (Arendt 1958: 188, 190)

In psychodrama, tele operates among director, protagonist, and group members. A common finding in our work is that a group member, strange to the protagonist, is chosen for a role in the drama. In the subsequent sharing by that auxiliary ego upon completion of the interaction, we hear the auxiliary say, "It is amazing you picked me because . . ." and out will come a parallel experience. Although this is almost becoming an expectation, it still has power to surprise us. It happens so frequently that it is clear that tele reaches outward into space and is a "knowing beyond knowing."

Tele is responsible for another phenomenon in psychodrama. Protagonists start the drama in a state of "as if" but as the involvement develops, the "if" falls away and becomes "as." When that occurs, the protagonist may "see" and "hear" the auxiliary ego as the person being portrayed, the tele taking over the process.

I experienced such an occurrence the first time I worked in Finland. The translator was fluent in English and understood, or as we say, doubled, my role so well that she was able to copy my movements as well as my intonation even though she did that in Finnish. The result was that after the end of the session the protagonist walked up to me and said in his language, "But you spoke in Finnish!" Nothing could have been further from the truth, but he experienced the two of us as one. This facilitated the work among the translator, the protagonist, and me.

In recent years I have come to see my role as not that of a psychotherapist because I cannot be sure I heal any psyches; instead, I see it as being that of a relationship therapist. It is through the relationship as carried by tele that healing may be facilitated. A golden rule in psychodrama, however, for both director and auxiliary ego is not to abuse tele; therefore we warn our students in training: "Be sure you are not doing *your* psychodrama on your protagonist."

In *Psychodrama Volume II* there is discussion of tele by, among others, Gordon W. Allport: "Dr. Moreno defines tele as 'insight into,' 'appreciation of,' and 'feeling for' the 'actual makeup' of the other person. Thus defined it is indeed the foundation of all sound therapy, as it is of all wholesome human relationships" (Moreno, J.L. & Moreno, Z.T. 1975: 15).

That it has in fact a respectable basis is shown in the work of Bessel van der Kolk:

> Prone to action, and deficient in words, these patients can often express their internal states more articulately in physical movements or in pictures than in words. Utilizing drawings and psychodrama may help them develop a language that is essential for effective communication and for the symbolic transformation that can occur in psychotherapy.
> (van der Kolk *et al.* 1996: 195)

Dr. van der Kolk has further indicated that these methods induce changes in the brain cells of traumatized clients, as shown in before and after treatment by MRI and other forms of diagnosis; these clearly reveal that brain cells which had shown destruction were restored to balance.

That psychodrama has made comparatively few inroads into psychiatric or psychotherapeutic practice in this country is somewhat hard to understand because it is now quite respectable and paid for by various health insurances abroad. There seems to be some fear of this way of dealing with clients, as if one were, like the sorcerer's apprentice, in front of an unknown and unpredictable quantity. Possibly understanding the function of tele will bring a greater sense of security into this realm.

Article 36

Suicide Prevention by the Use of Perceptual Sociometric Intervention

Moreno, Z.T. (2004) Unpublished paper

Zerka's comments

The issue of suicide is always touchy and difficult to approach. One day it struck me once again: we cannot do a decent diagnosis without knowing the sociometric environment of our clients. Without it, how can they feel understood and how can we treat them properly? I wrote this to speak to that point.

Suicide is defined by the dictionary as: "The intention of taking one's own life." It also gives another definition: "The destruction of one's own interests." What these two definitions have in common is that the status quo ceases to exist. In sociometric terms we can also say that the tele, which connects the individual with others, has been eliminated. Tele is a concept introduced by J.L. Moreno. It transcends the ideas of empathy and transference in that it encompasses both and adds another dimension, which involves mutuality. Tele always deals with the connection between at least two persons. It entails the capacity to "walk in the other's shoes," to represent the other's perspectives and includes these perspectives towards oneself. To a small degree it reminds one of the Socratic "dialogue with oneself." Role reversal is a concept created within the psychodramatic frame and relates to the capacity for tele.

Exploring the social atom of the suicidal patient whose interactions show the cut off of tele highlights these ideas. A social atom is the picture of the patient's meaningful relationships, always considered in terms of mutuality. This mutuality can be of positive, neutral or negative dimensions. A balanced social atom describes an emotionally healthy individual. An imbalanced one indicates the opposite. Restoring balance is one purpose of the psychodramatic and sociometric treatment. The following psychotherapy sessions describe the use of sociometric investigation and psychodramatic action, specifically role reversal.

In the course of working with post-suicidal and potentially suicidal protagonists I found that such protagonists carry within them two different sociograms, properly titled "The sociogram of life" and "The sociogram of death." By first exploring these two sociograms in psychodramatic action, resolutions offered themselves, as indicated by the sociogram of life. My theory was that the sociogram of death must be strongly opposed by making the life sociogram more meaningful than the pull being brought to bear upon the client by the sociogram of death.

Here are a few illustrations.

An 18-year-old girl, Penny, just released from a state institution comes for a psychodrama session. The first thing I do is to reverse her into the role of the psychiatrist who discharged her. With Penny in his role I ask: "Is she still depressed?" "Yes she is." "Why did you discharge her?" In the shocked back of my mind I recall Carol Burnett's famous statement: "My father, a doctor, operated on the principle that dead men tell no tales." Apparently he wanted nothing further to do with her. I have the good sense not to go into the meaning of this response, merely stating: "I see." At this point I tell Penny to change back into her own role and ask: "Why did you want to end your life?" "How would you feel if six of your best friends all died in one year?" she asks rather defiantly. "Suicidal," is my reply. Penny appears to relax a bit. I ask her to take six chairs and set them up in a circle on the stage, indicating which person belongs in which chair by putting paper with each one's name on it so as not to burden both our memories.

As Penny proceeds to role reverse with each one, it becomes evident that she is an unusually bright girl, a top student. Her friends died of a variety of illnesses, accidents, overdosing – and so on. Remarkably, in role reversal, without exception, not one of them gives her permission to join them. Instead they plead with her to stay alive, go to college, make her life a productive one, to offset their own failures. No matter how hard the auxiliary ego taking her role pleads with them, she is not to be moved.

When all six have been presented, I ask her about her parents, since they did not appear in this gallery of support. "My mother has been schizophrenic all our life and my father is busy keeping her out of the mental hospital." The irony of this state of affairs is hard to escape. Clearly there is a tremendous gap between the older generation and the younger, which includes an older brother who, according to Penny, is the only one in her family who cares about her. In fact, the two of them form as solid a pair as the elders do and they have kept each other safe. What I now discover is that there has been another profound loss in Penny's world, one which tilted her in the direction of eliminating herself, namely, that this beloved older brother has recently married and moved to another state, thereby leaving Penny totally adrift in the world. She does not mention this loss until we start to look at the family sociogram, as perceived by the protagonist.

That family sociogram shows a fairly complete separation between the parents and the children. The only link charged with some tele is between the father and his offspring, but when I ask her to indicate which of the lines should be thicker, those between the parents and those between the children are the heaviest, with the lines from and to the father much lighter. There is no connection with the mother from either child.

With the advent of her brother's marriage and his focus upon his new wife, Penny was cut off from whatever ties held her to her family.

I decide to get into action once more and ask her to take the role of her brother, now living in a state far west. I ask Penny in Bob's role: "Did you know your sister has been suicidally depressed?" Bob's (Penny's) eyes grew alarmed. "No, I didn't." "You mean to say she did not inform you?" "No, she didn't, I guess she did not want to burden me since I just got married." "Yes, I understand that. But tell me Bob, just how would you feel if you knew that she had been successful?" At this point Bob's (Penny's) eyes fill with tears and we can barely hear him say: "My God, dreadful." "Under these circumstances would you have wanted to be of help if you could, if Penny had turned to you, let you in on her secret? I imagine you'd have felt pretty guilty if you could have had the opportunity to help her." "Yes, of course." "You realize Penny does not want to interfere with your marriage? That's why she has not taken the chance for you to help her. Would that have affected your marriage as well? Your feeling guilty?" "Yes, I think so." "Well, there is still time to do something about it. I will talk to Penny. Thank you for coming."

At this point I role reverse Penny back into her own role. "It seems to me you should write to your brother. Would you do that now?" Penny agrees. Paper, pen, envelope were soon supplied. We send the letter off.

The answer from her brother, indicating that she should come and live with him and his wife while attending college, made it possible for Penny to continue her life productively.

The second protagonist, Anne, whose sociogram displays this introjection of the sociogram of death into her life, is a second year medical student who has twice attempted suicide and in her last attempt broke her ankle. She is in a neuropsychiatric hospital as a patient, and volunteers for the psychodrama I am conducting there for the staff.

Exploring her family structure she enacts her mother as a depressed woman, recently widowed, her second husband having been killed in a car accident; she is totally overwhelmed and does not understand her daughter. There is a younger half-sister of this second marriage who lives with their mother.

In the course of the psychodrama it becomes clear that the protagonist's real attachment is to her stepfather. She has never known her biological father and the stepfather was the anchor of her life. It was after his death that she first made her suicide attempts.

The scene facing her mother yields no suitable material for further investigation. I decide to make her reverse roles with the absent, beloved stepfather, while I take her role. As I make her get out of her wheelchair to sit in a seat set up for him, the nurses rush in to stop me, but in turn I stop them, assuring them she is safe with me. While I understood their anxiety over her physical welfare, there was irony in the fact that they were unable to grasp her tenuous hold on life.

I had observed how the protagonist made the wheels of her chair twist when facing the empty chair of her stepfather, so I commence to make the same twirling motions in her wheelchair, while asking him: "Why did you die? You know you were the person I love the most. I want to join you, to be with you." The protagonist shoots up straight sharply and reproaches me: "No, no, you mustn't do that. I depend upon you to take care of your sister. She needs you. You know yourself your mother is incapable of handling her right. I've shown you how to take care of a young child. I love you and would not have left you if it could have been prevented, but now you must not join me, that would only make me feel worse. I'm so sorry I let you down. Now let's not let your sister down. You get well, go home, continue your studies and take care of your sister. I count on you to do that for me." At that point we reverse roles and she hears the message. She promises me, as her father, that she will listen to him.

The next day, I received a report from two residents who had been present and were in charge of her, that "her face lost that mask and she looks completely different." She was subsequently discharged from the hospital. It was not clear at the time if she resumed her medical studies.

To summarize, I theorized that the sociogram of life versus that of death could be revealed in action, that this exploration could reveal the pull from one or another sociogram in terms of depth of attachment for the protagonist. This attachment from the death sociogram may be just as strong as, or even stronger than, that which points to life. In that event the death sociogram has to be revealed and countermanded, and the life sociogram re-weighted with meaningful contacts for the protagonist not to be pulled over to the other side.[1]

Notes

CHAPTER 1: BEGINNINGS

1. Role Analysis and Audience Structure

1 An observation that supports this contention can be found in the foreword to volume eight of *Sociometry, A Journal of Interpersonal Relations* (also called *Group Psychotherapy: A Symposium*). Dr. Winfred Overholser, superintendent at Saint Elizabeths Hospital, Washington, DC, professor of psychiatry at George Washington University School of Medicine and then president-elect of the American Psychiatric Association, wrote:

> Two trends of thought, converging now and here, make most logical an intensified interest in the application of psychotherapeutic methods to and within the group – one is the recognition . . . that behavior is the result of the response of the organism-as-a-whole to environmental influences among which people are the most important; the other is the fact, demonstrated all too painfully during the recent war, that the supply of psychiatrists is far below the demand. Thus, whether we view the needs of the situation theoretically . . . or practically . . ., we are inescapably forced to recognize the need and value of group psychotherapy.

2 In this, Zerka's very first article, the reader will get a flavor of the way the early open psychodrama sessions were conducted – the protagonist (sometimes called the subject) would briefly prepare auxiliaries backstage by telling them about the qualities of the "character" they were about to portray. In most psychodrama sessions today, the group is in on this transmission of information, obtained when the director puts the protagonist in role reversal.

3 In the original article, a footnote indicated by an asterisk here reads "The psychiatric analysis of the director is omitted here because of space limitations."

4 This section to the end of the article has been edited and rewritten for clarity.

5 A bibliography at the end of this article includes the following authors (please see the bibliography at the end of this book for full citations): Burgess 1941; Cottrell and Gallagher 1941; Hendry 1944; Meyer 1941; Moreno, J.L. 1939a, 1941a, 1947; Moreno, J.L. and Dunkin 1931, 1941; Moreno, J.L. and Jennings 1936; Moreno, J.L. and Toeman 1942; Sarbin 1943; Solby 1941; Umansky 1944; Wilder 1942; Zander and Lippitt 1944.

3. A Sociodramatic Audience Test

1 Table 3.1 has been modified to include results for Audience IX that originally appeared separately.

4. Audience Reactions to Therapeutic Films

1 There is an asterisk at this point in the text of the original article; the note reads: "Therapeutic film, a term coined and defined by Moreno as 'a type of motion picture whose main object is the treatment of audience'" (Moreno, J.L. 1945c: 11).

7. The "Double Situation" in Psychodrama

1 In the original article, a footnote at the bottom of the page reads: "Both sessions were directed by J.L. Moreno."

2 A footnote to this statement reads: "Subjects often express resentment at the double situation. This resentment is greater the closer the auxiliary ego comes to crossing this threshold, reaching a full duplication of many of the subject's carefully concealed experiences. It is like an unexpected intrusion. The subject is frequently determined to keep the truth to herself alone. 'The truth hurts.'"

3 A wire recorder, precursor to the magnetic tape machine, was used.

CHAPTER 2: EARLY PIONEERS

8. History of the Sociodramatic Movement in Headlines

1 Chronologies for subsequent years can be found in Jonathan Fox's compendium of Moreno's writings *The Essential Moreno* (1987), and René Marineau's biography *Jacob Levy Moreno 1889–1974: Father of Psychodrama, Sociometry, and Group Psychotherapy* (1989).

9. Psychodrama in a Well-Baby Clinic

1 A list of references at the end of this chapter includes the following authors (please see the bibliography at the end of this book for full citations): Moreno, J.L. 1944d; Moreno, J.L. and Moreno, F.B. 1944; Toeman 1946, 1948.

10. Psychodrama in the Crib

1 A footnote at this point in the original text reads: "The literal definition of 'auxiliary ego' is – to be auxiliary, an aide, to another individual, here a mother or mother-surrogate to an infant. The customary definition of auxiliary ego in psychodrama is to represent to the protagonist an 'absentee' (a father, a wife, etc.)."

2 A footnote in the original text reads, "Read in conjunction with this article: J.L. Moreno, "Psychodramatic Treatment of Psychosis," *Sociometry*, Vol. III, 2: 115–132, No. 1, 1941 (see for definitions of double, mirror and role reversal techniques); Zerka Toeman (Moreno), "Clinical Psychodrama, Auxiliary Ego, Double

and Mirror Techniques," *Sociometry*, Vol. 9, Nos 2–3, 1946; "The 'Double Situation' in Psychodrama," *Sociatry*, Vol. 1, No. 4, 1948; "Psychodrama in a Well-Baby Clinic," *Group Psychotherapy*, Vol. 4, Nos 1–2, 1952.

11. Note on Spontaneous Learning "*In Situ*" versus Learning the Academic Way

1 A note at this point in the original text reads: "Helen Keller, *The Story of My Life*, published by Doubleday & Co."

2 At the end of this article is a list of readings as follows. For complete citation please see the bibliography at the back of this book: Lippitt 1948; Moreno, J.L. 1944c, 1949; Moreno, J.L. and Moreno, F.B. 1944; Moreno, J.L., Moreno, Z.T., and Moreno, J.D. 1955; Moreno, Z.T. 1954.

13. A Survey of Psychodramatic Techniques

1 A number of techniques were presented in both this article and Article 14. Due to space considerations we have pooled the descriptions, and divided them up as follows: soliloquy, hallucinatory psychodrama, multiple double, role reversal, dream presentation, and therapeutic community are covered in this article, along with non-duplicate descriptions. Therapeutic soliloquy, self-presentation, double, mirror, and future projection are described in Article 14.

14. Psychodramatic Rules, Techniques and Adjunctive Methods

1 A number of techniques were presented in both this article and Article 13. Due to space considerations we have pooled the descriptions, and divided them up as follows: therapeutic soliloquy, self-presentation, double, mirror, and future projection are described in this article. Soliloquy, hallucinatory psychodrama, multiple double, role reversal, dream presentation, and therapeutic community are covered in Article 13.

15. The Saga of Sociometry

1 Editors' note: Since the publication of this article, *McCall's* Magazine no longer exists. Permission for the reproduction of this questionnaire has been granted by Gruner & Jahr, USA.

CHAPTER 3: TRANSITIONS

16. Sociogenesis of Individuals and Groups

1 To avoid duplication and conserve space, a section of text has been omitted here that refers to the description of a study of children with cerebral palsy in an institutional setting, involving the children's sociometric choices of dining mates. The reader is advised that the original source (*International Handbook of Group*

Therapy, pp. 231–242) contains this text. For a description of the study within the current volume, please see Article 35, "The Function of 'Tele' in Human Relations."

17. Evolution and Dynamics of the Group Psychotherapy Movement

1 It should be noted that the Society of Group Analysis was also forming at this time.
2 This report was also contained in *The First Book on Group Psychotherapy*, published in 1957 to mark a quarter century of group psychotherapy.

18. The Seminal Mind of J.L. Moreno and His Influence upon the Present Generation

1 A footnote in the original article reads: "A quarterly magazine, of which J.L. Moreno was editor-in-chief, published by Anzengruber Verlag, Vienna, 1918."
2 Editors' note: Moreno got his wish. Zerka saw to it that the tombstone on his honorary grave in City Center, Vienna, has this inscription.

20. Moreneans, the Heretics of Yesterday are the Orthodoxy of Today

1 A footnote in the original article reads: "Moreneans, practitioners following Moreno's principles. Morenism, related to J.L. Moreno's work and related developments."
2 Years after Moreno's death we were gratified to learn that a street in Mittendorf have been named "Dr. Moreno Strasse."

CHAPTER 4: ON HER OWN

25. The Significance of Doubling and Role Reversal for Cosmic Man

1 A bibliography at the end of this article lists the following sources. Please see the bibliography at the back of this book for full citations: Moreno, J.L. 1946c, 1953; Moreno, J.L. and Moreno, Z.T. 1959.

26. The Function of the Auxiliary Ego in Psychodrama with Special Reference to Psychotic Patients

1 The following is a list of references that appear at the end of the original article. For full citations, please see the bibliography at the back of this book: Moreno, J.L. 1946a, 1946c, 1973; Moreno, J.L. and Moreno, Z.T. 1959, 1969.

28. Psychodrama

1 Due to space considerations, the section "Rules and techniques" is not reproduced here, because the same material may be found in Chapter 2, Articles 13 and 14, "A Survey of Psychodramatic Techniques" and "Psychodramatic Rules, Techniques, and Adjunctive Methods."

2 The following references appear at the end of the original article. For full citations, please see the bibliography at the back of this book: Allport 1954; Bischof 1970; Dreikurs and Corsini 1954; Ezriel 1950; Fromm-Reichmann and Moreno, J.L. 1956; Moreno, J.L. 1937, 1939e, 1941a, 1946c, 1947, 1957b, 1966; Moreno, J.L. and Dunkin 1941; Moreno, J.L. and Fischel 1942; Moreno, J.L. and Moreno, Z.T. 1959; Sacks 1960.

30. Psychodrama, Role Theory and the Concept of the Social Atom

1 For all references noted below, please see the bibliography at the back of this book for full citations: Blatner 1985; Buchanan and Enneis 1980, 1984; Compernolle 1981; Diener 1971; Erickson 1958; Goldman and Morrison 1984; Hollander and Hollander 1978; Lieberman 1985; Longinus 1952; Moreno, J.L. 1924, 1932, 1934, 1937, 1938, 1939c, 1945a, 1946c, 1947, 1973; Moreno, J.L. and Jennings 1937; Moreno, J.L. and Moreno, Z.T. 1969; Moreno, J.L., Moreno, Z.T. and Moreno, J.D. 1955; Moreno, Z.T. 1952, 1954, 1958b, 1959, 1965a, 1967, 1969a, 1969b, 1971, 1972, 1974, 1978, 1983, 1987; Rank 1968; Starr 1977; Toeman 1944, 1946, 1947b; Weiner and Sacks 1969; Yablonsky 1976.

CHAPTER 5: THE NEW MILLENIUM AND BEYOND

35. The Function of "Tele" in Human Relations

1 It should be noted that the article cited here, "Sociogenesis of Individuals and Groups," has been edited within this volume and therefore does not contain mention of the study involving children with cerebral palsy. The reader is directed to the original article for the full discussion.

36. Suicide Prevention by the Use of Perceptual Sociometric Intervention

1 References at the end of the original article are as follows. Full citations may be found in the bibliography at the end of this book: Moreno, J.L. 1953, 1957a, 1957c.

Bibliography

Alger, I. and Hogan, P. (1967) "The Use of Videotape Recordings in Conjoint Marital Therapy," *American Journal of Psychiatry*, 123: 1425–1430.

Allport, G.W. (1938) *Personality: A Psychological Interpretation*, New York: Holt.

—— (1954) "Comments on: J.L. Moreno, 'Transference, Countertransference, and Tele, Their Relation to Group Research and Group Psychotherapy,'" *Group Psychotherapy, A Quarterly Journal*, VII, 3–4: 307–308.

Ardrey, R. (1966) *The Territorial Imperative*, New York: Atheneum.

Arendt, H. (1958) *The Human Condition*, Chicago: The University of Chicago Press.

Arendt, H. (1982) *Lectures on Kant's Political Philosophy*, Chicago: The University of Chicago Press.

Aristotle (1974) *Nicomachean Ethics Book IV*, London: Longmans, Green.

Ben Ali, B. (1958) "An Experience with a Frustrated Group," *Group Psychotherapy*, XI, 2: 153–158.

Biddle, B.J. and Thomas, E.J. (1966) *Role Theory*, New York: Wiley.

Bischof, L.J. (1970) *Interpreting Personality Theories*, New York: Harper & Row.

Blatner, A. (1985) "The Dynamics of Catharsis," *Journal of Group Psychotherapy, Psychodrama and Sociometry*, XXXVII, 4: 157–166.

Boorstin, D. (1992) *The Creators: A History of Heroes of the Imagination*, New York: Random House.

Buchanan, D.R. (1984) "Moreno's Social Atom: A Diagnostic and Treatment Tool For Exploring Interpersonal Relationships," *The Arts in Psychotherapy*, XI: 155–164.

Buchanan, D.R. and Enneis, J.M. (1980) "The Central Concern Model: A Framework for Structuring Psychodramatic Production," *Journal of Group Psychotherapy, Psychodrama and Sociometry*, XXXIII: 47–62.

Burgess, E.W. (1941) "An Experiment in the Standardization of the Case-Study Method," *Sociometry, A Journal of Interpersonal Relations*, IV, 4: 329–348.

Bychowski, G. and Despert, J.L. (1952) *Specialized Techniques in Psychotherapy*, New York: Grove Press.

Compernolle, T. (1981) "J.L. Moreno, an Unrecognized Pioneer of Family Therapy," *Family Process*, 20: 331–335.

Conty, P (1992) "The Geometry of the Labyrinth," *Parabola: The Search for Meaning*, XVII, 2: 14.

Corsini, R.J. (1957) *Methods of Group Psychotherapy*, New York: McGraw-Hill.

Cottrell, L.S., Jr and Gallagher, R. (1941) "Developments in Social Psychology, 1930–1940," *Sociometry Monograph No. 1*, Beacon, NY: Beacon House.

Criswell, J.H. (1935) "Racial Cleavage in Negro–White Groups," *Sociometry, A Journal of Interpersonal Relations* I, 1–2: 81–89.

Descartes, R. (1960) *Disclosure on Method and Meditations*, New York: Liberal Arts Press.

Deutschberger, P. (1947) "The Tele-Factor: Horizon and Awareness," *Sociometry, A Journal of Inter-Personal Relations*, X, 3: 242–249.

Diener, G. (1971) "Relation of the Delusionary Process in Goethe's *Lila* to Analytic Psychology and to Psychodrama," *Group Psychotherapy and Psychodrama, A Quarterly Journal*, XXIV, 1–2: 5–13.

Dreikurs, R. and Corsini, R.J. (1954) "Twenty Years of Group Psychotherapy," *American Journal of Psychiatry*, 110: 567.

Erickson, E. (1958) *Young Man Luther*, New York: W.W. Norton.

Ezriel, H.A. (1950) "Psychoanalytic Approach to Group Treatment," *British Journal of Medical Psychology*, 23: 59.

Florman, S. (1997) "Subsumed by Science," *MIT Technology Review*: 39.

Freud, S. (1926) *Vorlesungen zur Einfuehrung in die Psychoanallyse*, Vienna: The International Psychoanalytical Press.

Fromm-Reichmann (1950) *Principles of Intensive Psychotherapy*, Chicago: University of Chicago Press.

Fromm-Reichmann, F. and Moreno, J.L. (eds) (1956) *Progress in Psychotherapy*, New York: Grune & Stratton.

Gaylin, W. (1984) *The Rage Within: Anger in Modern Life*, New York: Simon & Schuster.

Goldman, E. and Morrison, D. (1984) *Psychodrama: Experience and Process*, Dubuque, IA: Kendall Hunt.

Grinker, R. (1966) "Complementary Psychotherapy," *American Journal of Psychiatry*, 123: 633–638.

Harrow, G.S. (1951) "The Effects of Psychodrama Group Psychotherapy on Schizophrenic Patients," *Group Psychotherapy, Journal of Sociopsychopathology and Sociatry*, III, 4: 316–320.

Haskell, M.R. (1957) "Psychodramatic Role Training in Preparation for Release on Parole," *Group Psychotherapy, A Quarterly Journal*, X, 1: 51–59.

Hendry, C.E. (1944) "Role Practice Brings the Community into the Classroom," *Sociometry, A Journal of Inter-Personal Relations*, VII, 2: 196–204.

Hendry, C., Zander, A. and Lippitt, R. (1944) "Reality Practice as Educational Method," *Psychodrama Monograph No. 9*, Beacon, NY: Beacon House.

Hollander, C. and Hollander, S. (1978) *The Warm Up Box*, Denver, CO: Snow Lion Press.

—— (2000) "A Sociometric Autopsy of Violence: In Memory of Columbine High School," paper presented at American Society of Group Psychotherapy & Psychodrama conference, New York, March 2000.

Holmes, P. and Karp, M. (1991) *Psychodrama: Inspiration and Technique*, London: Routledge.

Homans, G. (1950) *The Human Group*, New York: Harcourt Brace.

Howells, J.G. (ed.) (1979) *Advances in Family Psychiatry*, Vol. 1, New York: International Universities Press.

Johnson, P.E. (1959) *Psychology of Religion*, Nashville, TN: Abingdon Press.

Karpel, M.A. and Strauss, E.S. (1983) *Family Evaluation*, New York: Gardner Press.

Keller, H. (1988) *The Story of My Life*, New York: Doubleday.

Lieberman, E.J. (1985) *Acts of Will: The Life and Work of Otto Rank*, New York: The Free Press.

Lippitt, R. (1948) "Psychodrama in the Home," *Sociatry, Journal of Group and Intergroup Therapy*, I, 2: 148–167.

Lipps, T. (1907) "Das Wissen von Fremden Ichen," *Psychologische Untersuchungen*, 1.

Longinus (1970) "On the Sublime," in W.J. Bate (ed.) *Criticism: The Major Texts*, New York: Harcourt Brace Jovanovich.

Loomis, C.P. and Pepinsky, H.B. (1948) "Sociometry, 1937–1947," *Sociometry, A Journal of Inter-Personal Relations*, XI, 3: 262–286.

Mann, J. (1965) "Evaluation of Group Psychotherapy," in J.L. Moreno (ed.), *International Handbook of Group Psychotherapy*, New York: Philosophical Library.

Marineau, R. (1989) *Jacob Levy Moreno 1889–1974: Father of Psychodrama, Sociometry, and Group Psychotherapy*, London: Routledge.

Masserman, J.H. (1955) *The Practice of Dynamic Psychiatry*, Los Angeles: W.B. Saunders.

Meyer, A. (1941) "Spontaneity," *Sociometry, A Journal of Inter-Personal Relations*, IV, 2: 150–167.

Mill, J.S. (1843) *A System of Logic*, Toronto: University of Toronto Press, 1973.

Minear, V. (1953) "An Initial Venture in the Use of Television as a Medium for Psychodrama," *Group Psychotherapy, A Journal of Sociopsychopathology and Sociatry*, VI, 1–2: 115–117.

Mittleman, B. (1948) "The Concurrent Analysis of Married Couples," *Psychoanalytic Quarterly*, 17: 182–197.

Moreno, J.L. (1920, 1922) *Das Testament des Vaters*, Berlin: Kiepenheuer Verlag; trans. (1941, 1974) *The Words of the Father*.

—— (1924) *Das Stegreiftheater*, Berlin: Kiepenheuer Verlag; trans. (1947) *The Theatre of Spontaneity*, Beacon, NY: Beacon House.

—— (1931) *Application of the Group Method to Classification*, New York: National Committee on Prisons and Prison Labor.

—— (1934, 1953) *Who Shall Survive?* Beacon, NY: Beacon House.

—— (1937) "Inter-Personal Therapy and the Psychopathology of Inter-Personal Relations," *Sociometry, A Journal of Inter-Personal Relations*, I, 1–2: 9–76.

—— (1938) "Psychodramatic Shock Therapy – A Sociometric Approach to the Problem of Mental Disorders," *Sociometry, A Journal of Inter-Personal Relations*, II, 1: 1–30.

—— (1939a) "Creativity and Cultural Conserves, with Special Reference to Musical Expression," *Sociometry, A Journal of Inter-Personal Relations*, II, 2: 1–36.

—— (1939b) "Psychodramatic Shock Therapy," *Psychodrama and Group Psychotherapy, Monograph No. 5*, Beacon, NY: Beacon House.

—— (1939c) "Psychodramatic Treatment of Marriage Problems," *Sociometry, A Journal of Inter-Personal Relations*, III: 1–23.

—— (1939d) "Psychodramatic Treatment of Psychoses," *Sociometry, A Journal of Inter-Personal Relations*, III, 2: 115–132.
—— (1939e) "Mental Catharsis and the Psychodrama," *Sociometry, A Journal of Inter-Personal Relations*, III: 209–244.
—— (1940) "A Frame of Reference for Testing the Social Investigator," *Sociometry*, III, 4: 317–327.
—— (1941a) "The Philosophy of the Moment and the Spontaneity Theatre," *Sociometry*, IV, 2: 205–226.
—— (1941b, 1974) *The Words of the Father*, Beacon, NY: Beacon House.
—— (1943) "Sociometry and the Cultural Order," *Sociometry, A Journal of Inter-Personal Relations*, VI, 3: 299–344.
—— (1944a) "A Case of Paranoia Treated Through Psychodrama," *Sociometry, A Journal of Inter-Personal Relations*, VII, 3: 312–327.
—— (1944b) "Sociodrama, a Method for the Analysis of Social Conflicts," *Psychodrama Monograph No. 1*, Beacon, NY: Beacon House.
—— (1944c) "Spontaneity Test and Spontaneity Training," *Psychodrama Monograph No. 4*, Beacon, NY: Beacon House.
—— (1944d) "Psychodrama and the Psychopathology of Interpersonal Relations," *Psychodrama Monograph No. 14*, Beacon, NY: Beacon House.
—— (1945a) *Group Psychotherapy: A Symposium*, Beacon, NY: Beacon House.
—— (1945b) *Psychodrama: Collected Papers*, Beacon, NY: Beacon House.
—— (1945c) "Psychodrama and Therapeutic Motion Pictures," *Psychodrama Monograph No. 11*, Beacon, NY: Beacon House.
—— (1946a) "Psychodrama and Group Psychotherapy," *Sociometry, A Journal of Inter-Personal Relations*, IX, 2–3: 249–253.
—— (1946b) "Psychodrama and the Psychopathology of Interpersonal Relations," *Psychodrama Monograph No. 16*, Beacon, NY: Beacon House.
—— (1946c) *Psychodrama, First Volume*, Beacon, NY: Beacon House.
—— (1947) *The Theatre of Spontaneity*, Beacon, NY: Beacon House.
—— (1948) *Psychodrama and Sociodrama in American Education*, Beacon, NY: Beacon House.
—— (1949) "The Spontaneity Theory of Learning," *Spontaneity and Sociodrama in American Education*, Beacon, NY: Beacon House.
—— (1951) *Sociometry, Experimental Method and the Science of Society*, Beacon, NY: Beacon House.
—— (1952) "Psychodramatic Production Techniques," *Group Psychotherapy, A Journal of Sociopsychopathology and Sociatry*, IV, 4: 243–273.
—— (1953) *Who Shall Survive? The Foundations of Sociometry, Group Psychotherapy and Psychodrama*, Beacon, NY: Beacon House.
—— (1954) "Transference, Countertransference and Tele: Their Relation to Group Research and Group Psychotherapy," *Group Psychotherapy, A Quarterly Journal*, VII, 2: 107–117.
—— (1955) *Prelude to My Autobiography*, Beacon, NY: Beacon House.
—— (1956a) *Sociometry and the Science of Man*, Beacon, NY: Beacon House.
—— (1956b) "Philosophy of the Third Psychiatric Revolution," *Progress in Psychotherapy*, I: 29.
—— (1957a) "The Social Atom and Death," *Sociometry, A Journal of Inter-Personal Relations*, X, 1: 80–84.

—— (1957b) *The First Book on Group Psychotherapy*, Beacon, NY: Beacon House.
—— (1957c) "Organization of the Social Atom," *Sociometry, A Journal of Inter-Personal Relations*, X, 3: 287–293.
—— (1958a) "Group Training vs. Group Therapy," in R. Blake (ed.), *Sociometry Monograph No. 35*, Beacon, NY: Beacon House.
—— (1958b) "The Sociometry of Subhuman Groups," *Sociometry Monograph No. 38*, Beacon, NY: Beacon House.
—— (1959) "Psychodrama," in *American Handbook of Psychiatry*, New York: Basic Books.
—— (1961a) "The Role Concept, a Bridge Between Psychiatry and Sociology," *American Journal of Psychiatry*, 118: 518–522.
—— (1961b) (ed.) *The Sociometry Reader*, New York: Free Press.
—— (1965) "Psychodrama in Action," *Group Psychotherapy, A Quarterly Journal*, XVIII, 1–2: 87–117.
—— (1966) "Psychodrama of a Marriage, Text of a Motion Picture, Including Psychodrama of a Dream," *Group Psychotherapy, A Quarterly Journal*, XIX, 1–2: 49–93.
—— (1973) "The Function of the Social Investigator in Experimental Psychodrama," *Group Psychotherapy and Psychodrama*, XXVI, 3–4: 7–30.
Moreno, J.L. (1987) *The Essential Moreno* (J. Fox, ed.), New York: Springer.
Moreno, J.L. and Dunkin, W.S. (1931) *Impromptu* Magazine, I and II.
—— (1941) "The Function of the Social Investigator in Experimental Psychodrama," *Sociometry, A Journal of Interpersonal Relations*, IV, 4: 392–417.
Moreno, J.L. and Fischel, J. (1942) "Spontaneity Procedures in Television Broadcasting with Special Emphasis on Inter-Personal Relation Systems," *Sociometry, A Journal of Inter-Personal Relations*, V, 1: 7–28.
Moreno, J.L. and Jennings, H.H. (1936) "Spontaneity Training," *Sociometric Review*, I: 17–25.
—— (1937) "Statistics of Social Configurations," *Sociometry, A Journal of Inter-Personal Relations*, I, 1–2: 342–374.
—— (1941) "The Advantages of the Sociometric Approach to Problems of National Defense," *Sociometry, A Journal of Inter-Personal Relations*, IV, 4: 384–391.
Moreno, J.L. and Moreno, F.B. (1944) "Spontaneity Theory of Child Development," *Psychodrama Monograph No. 8*, Beacon, NY: Beacon House.
—— (1945) "Role Tests and Role Diagrams of Children," *Sociometry, A Journal of Inter-Personal Relations*, VIII, 3–4: 426–441.
Moreno, J.L. and Moreno, Z.T. (1959; 2nd edn 1975) *Psychodrama, Second Volume*, Beacon, NY: Beacon House.
Moreno, J.L. and Moreno, Z.T. (1969) *Psychodrama, Third Volume*, Beacon, NY: Beacon House.
Moreno, J.L., Moreno, Z.T. and Moreno, J.D. (1955) "The Discovery of the Spontaneous Man," *Group Psychotherapy, A Quarterly Journal*, VIII, 2: 103–129.
Moreno, J.L. and Toeman, Z. (1942) "The Group Approach in Psychodrama," *Sociometry, A Journal of Inter-Personal Relations*, V, 2: 191–196.
Moreno, Z.T. (1952) "Psychodrama in a Well-Baby Clinic," *Group Psychotherapy, A Journal of Sociopsychopathology and Sociatry*, IV, 1–2: 100–106.
—— (1954) "Psychodrama in the Crib," *Group Psychotherapy, A Quarterly Journal*, VII, 3–4: 291–302.

—— (1958a) "Note on Spontaneous Learning 'In Situ' Versus Learning the Academic Way," *Group Psychotherapy, A Quarterly Journal*, XI, 1: 50–51.
—— (1958b) "The 'Reluctant Therapist' and the 'Reluctant Audience' Technique in Psychodrama," *Group Psychotherapy, A Quarterly Journal*, XI, 4: 278–282.
—— (1959) "A Survey of Psychodramatic Techniques," *Group Psychotherapy, A Quarterly Journal*, XII, 1: 5–14.
—— (1965a) "Psychodramatic Rules, Techniques and Adjunctive Methods," *Group Psychotherapy, A Quarterly Journal*, XVIII, 1–2: 73–86.
—— (1965b) "The Saga of Sociometry," *Group Psychotherapy, A Quarterly Journal*, XVIII, 4: 275–276.
—— (1966a) "Evolution and Dynamics of the Group Psychotherapy Movement," in J.L. Moreno (ed.), *International Handbook of Group Psychotherapy*, New York: Philosophical Library, pp. 27–35.
—— (1966b) "Sociogenesis of Individuals and Groups," in J.L. Moreno (ed.) *International Handbook of Group Psychotherapy*, New York: Philosophical Library, pp. 231–242.
—— (1967) "The Seminal Mind of J.L. Moreno and His Influence Upon the Present Generation," *International Journal of Sociometry and Sociatry, A Quarterly Journal*, V, 3–4: 145–156.
—— (1968) "Psychodrama on Closed and Open Circuit Television," *Group Psychotherapy, A Quarterly Journal*, XXI: 2–3: 106–109.
—— (1969a) "Moreneans, the Heretics of Yesterday are the Orthodoxy of Today," *Group Psychotherapy, A Quarterly Journal*, XXII, 1–2: 1–6.
—— (1969b) "Practical Aspects of Psychodrama," *Group Psychotherapy, A Quarterly Journal*, XXII, 3–4: 213–219.
—— (1971) "Beyond Aristotle, Breuer and Freud: Moreno's Contribution to the Concept of Catharsis," *Group Psychotherapy and Psychodrama, A Quarterly Journal*, XXIV, 1–2: 34–43.
—— (1972) "Note on Psychodrama, Sociometry, Individual Psychotherapy and the Quest for 'Unconditional Love,'" *Group Psychotherapy and Psychodrama, A Quarterly Journal*, XXV, 4: 155–157.
—— (1974) "Psychodrama of Young Mothers," *Group Psychotherapy and Psychodrama, A Quarterly Journal*, XXVII, 1–4: 191–203.
—— (1975) "The Significance of Doubling and Role Reversal for Cosmic Man," *Group Psychotherapy and Psychodrama, A Quarterly Journal*, XXVIII: 55–59.
—— (1978) "The Function of the Auxiliary Ego in Psychodrama with Special Reference to Psychotic Patients," *Group Psychotherapy, Psychodrama and Sociometry*, XXXI: 163–166.
—— (1980) "The Eight Stages of Cosmic Beings in Terms of Capacity and Need to Double and Role Reverse," unpublished paper.
—— (1983) "Psychodrama," in H. Kaplan and B. Sadock (eds) *Comprehensive Group Psychotherapy*, 2nd edn, Philadelphia: Lippincott, Williams & Wilkins, pp. 158–166.
—— (1986) "J.L. Moreno's Concept of Ethical Anger," *Journal of Group Psychotherapy, Psychodrama and Sociometry*, XXXVIII, 4: 145–153.
—— (1987) "Psychodrama, Role Theory and the Concept of the Social Atom," in J. Zeig (ed.) *The Evolution of Psychotherapy*, New York: Brunner/Mazel.

—— (1990) "Note on Some Forms of Resistance to Psychodrama," *Journal of Group Psychotherapy, Psychodrama and Sociometry*, LXIII, 1: 43–44.
—— (1991) "Time, Space, Reality, and the Family: Psychodrama with a Blended (Reconstituted) Family," in M. Karp and P. Holmes (eds) *Psychodrama: Inspiration and Technique*, London: Routledge.
—— (1997) "The Many Faces of Drama," Keynote presentation to the National Association of Drama Therapists, New York University, November.
—— (2000a) "In the Spirit of Two Thousand," Plenary session Address to the American Society of Group Psychotherapy and Psychodrama, New York, March 21.
—— (2000b) "The Function of 'Tele' in Human Relations," in J. Zeig (ed.) *The Evolution of Psychotherapy: A Meeting of the Minds*. Phoenix, AZ: Erickson Foundation Press.
—— (2004) "Suicide Prevention by the Use of Perceptual Sociometric Intervention," unpublished paper.
Murray, H. (1947) *Assessment of Men*, New York: Rinehart.
Myrdal, G. (1944) *An American Dilemma: The Negro Problem and Modern Democracy*, New York: Harper & Row.
Northway, M.L. (1944) "Outsiders: A Study of the Personality Patterns of Children Least Acceptable to their Age Mates," *Sociometry, A Journal of Inter-Personal Relations*, VII, 1: 10–25.
—— (1946a) "Sociometric Studies at the University of Toronto," *Sociometry, A Journal of Inter-Personal Relations*, IX, 2–3: 151–153.
—— (1946b) "Sociometry and Some Challenging Problems of Social Relationships," *Sociometry, A Journal of Inter-Personal Relations*, IX, 2–3: 187–198.
—— (1946c) "Personality and Sociometry Status," *Sociometry, A Journal of Inter-Personal Relations*, IX, 2–3: 233–241.
—— (1954) "A Plan for Sociometric Studies in a Longitudinal Programme of Research in Child Development," *Sociometry, A Journal of Inter-Personal Relations and Experimental Design* XVII, 3: 272–281.
—— (1960) "A Plan for Sociometric Studies in a Longitudinal Programme of Research in Child Development," *The Sociometry Reader*, Glencoe, IL: The Free Press.
—— (1968) "What is Sociometry?" *Group Psychotherapy, A Quarterly Journal*, XXI, 2–3: 110–112.
Northway, M.L. and Detweiler, J. (1956) "Children's Perception of Friends and Non-Friends," *Sociometry and the Science of Man*, Beacon, NY: Beacon House.
Northway, M.L. and Quarrington, B. (1946) "Depicting Inter-cultural Relations," *Sociometry, A Journal of Inter-Personal Relations*, IX, 4: 334–339.
Overholser, W. and Enneis, J.M. "Twenty Years of Psychodrama at St Elizabeths Hospital," *Psychodrama Monograph No. 36*, Beacon, NY: Beacon House.
Peirce, C.S. (1931) *Collected Papers*, Cambridge, MA: Harvard University Press.
Rank, O. (1968) *Art and Artist*, New York: A.A. Knopf.
Richardson, R.F. (1918) *The Psychology of Pedagogy and Anger*, Baltimore: Warwick & York.
Sacks, J. (1960) "Psychodrama and Psychoanalysis," *Group Psychotherapy, A Quarterly Journal*, XIII, 3–4: 199.

Sarbin, T.R. (1943) "The Concept of Role-Taking," *Sociometry, A Journal of Inter-Personal Relations*, VI, 3: 273–285.

Satir, V.M. (1966) "Family Therapy: An Approach to the Treatment of Mental and Emotional Disorder," in J.L. Moreno (ed.) *The International Handbook of Group Psychotherapy*, New York: Philosophical Library.

Schutz, W. (1967) *Joy: Expanding Human Awareness*, New York: Grove Press.

Solby, B. (1941) "The Psychodramatic Treatment of Marriage Problems," *American Sociological Review*, VI, 4: 523–530.

Sorokin, P. (1966) *Sociological Theories of Today*, New York: Harper & Row.

Speroff, B.J. (1964) "The Identification of Hidden Sociometric Leaders," *Group Psychotherapy, A Quarterly Journal*, XVII, 2–3: 96–103.

Speroff, B.J. and Simon, D. (1963) "Problems and Approaches in Child Group Psychotherapy in a Public School Milieu," *Group Psychotherapy* XVI, 1–2: 39–45.

Spiegel, J. and Bell, N. (1959) "The Family of the Psychiatric Patient," in S. Arieti (ed.) *American Handbook of Psychiatry*, Vol. 1, New York: Basic Books.

Starr, A. (1977) *Psychodrama: Rehearsal for Living*, Chicago: Nelson Hall.

Strokvis, B. (ed.) (1959) *Proceedings of the Second International Congress of Group Psychotherapy*, Basel: Karger.

Sutherland, J.D. and Fitzpatrick, G.A. (1945) "Some Approaches to Group Problems in the British Army," *Sociometry, A Journal of Inter-Personal Relations*, VIII, 3–4: 443–455.

Tagiuri, R., Kogan, N. and Bruner, J. (1960) "The Transparency of Interpersonal Choice," *The Sociometry Reader*, Glencoe, IL: The Free Press.

Toeman, Z. (1944) "Role Analysis and Audience Structure," *Sociometry, A Journal of Inter-Personal Relations*, VII, 2: 205–221. Also *Psychodrama Monograph No. 12*, Beacon, NY: Beacon House.

—— (1945a) "Psychodramatic Research of Pre-Marital Couples," *Sociometry, A Journal of Inter-Personal Relations*, VIII, 1: 89.

—— (1945b) "A Sociodramatic Audience Test," *Sociometry, A Journal of Inter-Personal Relations*, VIII, 3–4: 399–409.

—— (1945c) "Audience Reactions to Therapeutic Films," *Sociometry, A Journal of Inter-Personal Relations*, VIII, 3–4: 493–497.

—— (1946) "Clinical Psychodrama: Auxiliary Ego, Double, and Mirror Techniques," *Sociometry, A Journal of Inter-Personal Relations*, IX, 2–3: 178–183.

—— (1947) "Psychodrama: Its Relation to Stage, Radio and Motion Pictures," *Sociatry, Journal of Group and Intergroup Therapy*, I, 1: 119–126.

—— (1948) "The Double Situation in Psychodrama," *Sociatry, Journal of Group and Intergroup Therapy*, I, 4: 436–446.

—— (1949) "History of the Sociometric Movement in Headlines," *Sociometry, A Journal of Inter-Personal Relations*, XII, 1–3: 255–259.

Umansky, A.L. (1944) "Psychodrama and the Audience," *Sociometry, A Journal of Inter-Personal Relations*, VII, 2: 179–189.

van der Kolk, B., McFarlane, A.C., and Weisaeth, L. (eds) (1996) *Traumatic Stress: The Effects of Overwhelming Experience on Mind, Body and Society*, New York: Guilford.

Watzlawick, P. (1987) "If You Desire to See, Learn How to Act," in J. Zeig (ed.) *The Evolution of Psychotherapy*, New York: Brunner/Mazel, pp. 91–100.

Weiner, H.B. and Sacks, J. (1969) "Warm-up and Sum-up," *Group Psychotherapy, A Quarterly Journal*, XXII, 1–2: 85–102.
Wilder, J. (1942) "The Psychodrama as Compared with Other Methods of Psychotherapy," *Sociometry, A Journal of Inter-Personal Relations*, V, 2: 185–190.
Yablonsky, L. (1976) *Psychodrama: Resolving Emotional Problems Through Role-Playing*, New York: Basic Books.
Zander, A. and Lippitt, R. (1944) "Reality Practice as Educational Method," *Sociometry, A Journal of Inter-Personal Relations*, VII, 2: 129–151.
Zukav, G. (1979) *The Dancing Wu Li Masters*, San Francisco: Fontana/Collins.

Index

For Product Safety Concerns and Information please contact our EU representative GPSR@taylorandfrancis.com Taylor & Francis Verlag GmbH, Kaufingerstraße 24, 80331 München, Germany